ORIGEN

ORIGEN

by
JEAN DANIÉLOU

Translated by
WALTER MITCHELL

SHEED AND WARD
NEW YORK

COPYRIGHT, 1955
BY SHEED AND WARD INC.
LIBRARY OF CONGRESS CATALOG CARD NUMBER 55-7487

Nihil Obstat: Carolus Davis, S.T.L.
CENSOR DEPUTATUS
Imprimatur: E. Morrogh Bernard
VIC. GEN.
Westmonasterii, Die 17a Januarii, 1955

This book is a translation of *Origène*, published by
La Table Ronde, Paris

MANUFACTURED IN THE UNITED STATES OF AMERICA

CONTENTS

PAGE

INTRODUCTION vii

PART I

ORIGEN AND HIS TIMES

CHAPTER
I. THE LIFE OF ORIGEN 3
II. ORIGEN AND THE CHRISTIAN BACKGROUND . 27
   1. Christian Worship 28
   2. The Christian Community . . . 40
III. ORIGEN'S THEOLOGY OF THE SACRAMENTS . 52
   1. Baptism 52
   2. The Eucharist 61
   3. Penance 68
IV. ORIGEN AND THE PHILOSOPHICAL BACKGROUND 73
V. ORIGEN AS AN APOLOGIST 99

PART II

ORIGEN AND THE BIBLE

I. ORIGEN AND BIBLICAL CRITICISM . . . 133
II. THE TYPOLOGICAL INTERPRETATION OF THE
   BIBLE 139
III. THE NON-CHRISTIAN TRADITIONS OF EXEGESIS 174
   1. The Rabbis 174
   2. Philo 178
   3. The Gnostics 191

PART III

ORIGEN'S SYSTEM

CHAPTER   PAGE
   I.   COSMOLOGY   209

  II.   ANGELOLOGY   220

        1. The Angels of the Nations   .   .   .   224

        2. The Angels and Christ   238

 III.   THE FORERUNNER   246

  IV.   CHRISTOLOGY   251

        1. The Father, the Logos, the *Logikoi*   .   .   251

        2. The Incarnation   262

        3. The Redemption   269

   V.   ESCHATOLOGY   276

PART IV

ORIGEN'S THEOLOGY OF THE SPIRITUAL LIFE

        CONCLUSION   310

        NOTES   315

        APPENDIX   339

        INDEX   341

INTRODUCTION

ORIGEN and St. Augustine were the two greatest geniuses of the early Church. Origen's writings can be said to mark a decisive period in all fields of Christian thought. His researches into the history of the different versions of the Scriptures and his commentaries on the literal and spiritual senses of the Old and New Testaments make him the founder of the scientific study of the Bible. He worked out the first of the great theological syntheses and was the first to try and give a methodical explanation of the mysteries of Christianity. He was the first, too, to describe the route followed by the soul on her way back to God. He is thus the founder of the theology of the spiritual life, and it may be questioned whether he is not to some extent the ancestor of the great monastic movement of the fourth century.

His influence on other writers has been unlimited. In the third and fourth centuries he had disciples everywhere; only the greatest can be mentioned here. The first ecclesiastical historian, Eusebius, who succeeded him at the school at Caesarea, inherited his ideas and defended him with the utmost conviction. At Alexandria, his work in the fields of exegesis and mystical theology was continued by Didymus. The great Cappadocians inherited his teaching, which was transmitted to them by his pupil, Gregory the Wonderworker, the apostle of Cappadocia. Basil and Gregory of Nazianzos collected extracts from his works in the *Philocalia*, which we still possess. Gregory of Nyssa rejected his excesses but entered fully and with great understanding into the spirit of his theology of man and his teaching about the spiritual life. Evagrius Ponticus, one of the greatest of writers on the spiritual life, depends closely on him and was responsible for the spread of his teaching among the monks of Egypt. Through Evagrius, it was handed on to Cassian and, as Dom Marsili has pointed out, through Cassian it reached the monks of the West.[1] The great doctor of the mystical life, Maximus the Confessor, was completely under his influence for a time, as Fr. von Balthasar has shown. [2] In the West, his work was made known by Rufinus of Aquileia. Hilary of Poitiers and Ambrose of Milan owed much to his exegesis.

At the same time, his teaching gave rise to the most violent opposition. As early as the end of the third century, Methodius of Olympus attacked his ideas about the previous existence of the soul and the nature of the risen body. [3] At the end of the fourth century, Epiphanius accused him in his *Panarion* of subordinating the Son to the Father and of thus being a forerunner of Arius. [4] St. Jerome was at first a great admirer of his and in matters of exegesis remained his disciple to the end, but he attacked his errors in the *Contra Joannem Hierosolymitanum*, which he wrote under the influence of Epiphanius. In the year 400, a council met at Alexandria, at the instigation of Theophilus, and solemnly condemned his errors. The question came up again in the sixth century in connection with opinions maintained by certain monks in Palestine who claimed his authority for their views. The Emperor Justinian himself intervened in the dispute and in 543 Origen was condemned at the Oecumenical Council of Constantinople.

What, then, is the verdict to be? Origen was the first to try and carry intellectual activity as far as it would go in searching into the mysteries of the faith. He sometimes went too far, but it was perhaps necessary that he should if the limits were ever to be fixed exactly. At a time when they had not yet been determined, he tried to see just how far the mind could go. That is what gives his undertaking its extraordinary nobility. He always acted, too, in a spirit of obedience to the rule of faith. If some of his ideas were afterwards condemned, he himself was never formally a heretic, because his erroneous opinions always bore on points not yet settled by the Church.

In his own time, feeling ran high about him. It still does today. There is still nothing like universal agreement about the essential nature of his writings. Some scholars, like De Faye and Hal Koch, hold that he was essentially a philosopher—a Platonist or neo-Platonist—and that his ideas had nothing to do with Christianity. Others, like Bardy and Prat, see him as a theologian and exegete—a position which Huet (the one to

whom La Fontaine dedicated his famous *Epitre*) had taken up
long before them. Völker would have it that he was first and
foremost a master of the spiritual life. But Fr. Lieske has shown
that his teaching about the spiritual life is based on his theology
of the Logos. In reality, he was all these things at once. All
scholars who have studied him up to the present have made
the same mistake about him: they have all tried to reduce his
personality to one or another of its aspects; whereas the characteristic thing about Origen was that he combined several
different kinds of activity and thus, more than any other
Christian thinker before St. Thomas, came to see the world as
a single whole.

The plan followed in the present work will, I hope, make this
clear. From a study of Origen's life, we shall first see that he
was a loyal member of the Church and that he is one of the
chief authorities for the faith and life of the Christian community of his time. We will then try to discover how far he was
influenced by philosophy. This is one of the points where
research has made some headway in the last few years, though
it has not yet reached anything like finality. When we come to
deal with the question, we shall have to give an outline of the
trends in philosophical opinion current in Origen's day, if we
are to determine with any degree of precision how he stands
with respect to the intellectual life of his time.

We will then tackle the question of his attitude to the exegesis
of the Bible, a matter in connection with which students of
Origen usually confine themselves to making general observations on his use of allegory. We will attempt to define his
position with regard to his predecessors. We shall see how the
wish to simplify his views must be resisted and that as a matter
of fact more than one type of exegesis is to be found in his
works. This last point ought to be one of the things that stand
out most plainly when the enquiry is finished.

We will then examine his theological system and study some
of the essential features of it. We shall not spend much time on
his theology of the Trinity, because a masterly study has
recently been made of it by H. C. Puech at the Ecole des
Hautes Etudes and also because it is not the essential part of
the system, as De Faye clearly shows. His doctrine of the Fall,
his theology of the Redemption, his angelology, his teaching

about the Resurrection and his ideas on the future life are just as important. Here we shall have to see exactly what his attitude was, show where his teaching was ultimately rejected by the Church and also decide how much of it is worth keeping.

We will conclude with a study of his theology of the spiritual life, which is perhaps the most noteworthy part of his achievement. Origen was a great master of the spiritual life. He provides a link between the eschatological standpoint of men like Ignatius of Antioch and Tertullian, who saw the spiritual life in function of martyrdom, and what came in the fourth century to be the standpoint of the monks, who centred their spiritual teaching round contemplation. By his teaching on the place of the Logos in the spiritual life, he is the distant ancestor of the entire devotional tradition centring on the humanity of Jesus and expressed in the works of such writers as St. Bernard and St. Bonaventure. In that respect, he is nearer to medieval western ideas on the spiritual life than the spiritual teaching of Evagrius Ponticus, Gregory of Nyssa or the Pseudo-Dionysius.

With regard to method, our aim will be in the main to make a detailed study of the sources. In Origen's case, these are considerable in bulk, for he was one of the two most prolific writers in the ancient world, whether pagan or Christian, St. Augustine being the other. "What point would there be," Eusebius asks, "in giving a full list of his writings here? . . . I compiled one for the Life I wrote of Pamphilus, the holy man who was martyred not so very long ago. To show what pains he took about the things of God, I put into the Life the catalogue of the library he had collected of books by Origen and other ecclesiastical writers."[5] Unfortunately, this Life of Pamphilus is now lost. But the list of Origen's works was copied by St. Jerome and may be found in his Letter XXXIII to Paula. Eusebius, too, mentions a considerable number of his master's books elsewhere than in the Life of Pamphilus. From the list thus obtained, it can be seen that some of Origen's works are now missing.

There is also a further difficulty, the crucial one in any study of Origen, and that is that a large proportion of his works, and not the least important, have been preserved not in the Greek text but in fourth-century Latin translations. This is the case with many of the homilies, several of the commentaries and, most serious of all, with the *De Principiis*. The translations are the work chiefly of Rufinus of Aquileia and St. Jerome. The history of the disputes which set the two of them against each other may be read in F. Cavallera's *Saint Jérôme* (Louvain, 1922), or in F. X. Murphy's *Rufinus of Aquileia* (Washington, 1945), the latest books to go into the question.

We know for certain that the translations, especially those made by Rufinus, are not accurate. There are two reasons for this. The first, the more general one, is that Rufinus wanted to adapt his author to the Latin-speaking public and therefore did not hesitate to abridge passages that seemed to him to be too long or to add explanations when he thought it advisable. He explains his practice clearly enough. "I certainly had no lack of work," he says, "over the things you pressed me to translate into Latin. . . . Origen had delivered them extempore in church, in the assembly, more with the idea of saying something edifying than of explaining the texts, and I wanted to fill out what he had said. This I did when I was dealing with the homilies or talks on Genesis and Exodus and particularly when I came to his lectures on the Book of Leviticus: he had delivered them in the oratorical style but I translated them as if they had been straightforward commentaries. I undertook this laborious task of supplying missing threads because I was afraid that readers of the Latin version would not stomach his habit of raising questions and leaving them in the air, as he often did when he was preaching. On the other hand, I translated the sermons on Josue, the Book of Judges and the Thirty-Sixth, Thirty-Seventh and Thirty-Eighth Psalms simply as I found them and without much effort. It was laborious enough for me to put in what he had left out of the works I mentioned just now, but the labour required of me over the present work, the Epistle to the Romans, was *immensus . . . et inextricabilis . . .*"[6]

This very valuable passage shows exactly what Rufinus did when he translated the homilies. His translations of the homilies on Judges and Josue can be relied upon, but in the other cases he filled out Origen's text, perhaps with the help of commentaries now lost. He also added such explanations as would be needed by the Latin-speaking public the translations were made for. These additions are easily brought to light. When we read, for instance, that "in Greek this is called ἐγκρυφίας [hidden], which means that the bread is hidden or concealed ",[7] we know that the remark can come only from Rufinus. Jerome's translations of the homilies on Isaias, Ezechiel and Jeremias are more faithful. As the Greek text of the homilies on Jeremias has been preserved, his versions can be compared with it and shown to be substantially accurate.

But another question arises, a more serious one. It particularly affects one of Origen's most important works, the *De Principiis*, the book that contains his boldest theories. The book was translated by Rufinus in 398. Rufinus says himself in his introduction that he followed the example set by Jerome in his translation of the homilies. "Here and there," he says, "things are found in the Greek that might give offence. Jerome whittled all that down when he made his translation and expurgated the text so that no one reading the Latin would find anything in it at variance with our faith."[8] He was all the more convinced of his right to do this in that he thought that Origen's books had been altered by heretics, as he explains in his *De Adulteratione Librorum Origenis*. Jerome produced a more faithful translation of the book to take the field against Rufinus's, but it is now lost. Rufinus's translation therefore has to be used, but with caution. Dr. Koetschau's edition supplements the Latin text with the Greek fragments that have come down to us through the *Philocalia*, Justinian's *Florilegium* and writers like Gregory of Nyssa, in whom we may expect to find traces of Origen's teaching, as they were influenced by him. Besides Koetschau's edition, M. Bardy's *Recherches sur l'histoire du texte du De Principiis* deals with the point, and so does De Faye's book on Origen's philosophy, which discusses points of detail in Rufinus's text.

Origen's chief works are his books on Scripture. These form the main bulk of his output. The Hexapla, which were composed between 240 and 245, are a collection of all the available texts of the Bible, both Greek and Hebrew. The exegetical works can be divided into three classes. First come the commentaries, which reflect the teaching he gave in the *didaskaleion*. The *Commentary on Genesis*, though still extant in the time of St. Ambrose, who had it before him when he wrote the *De Paradiso* and the *Hexaemeron*, is now lost, and all that remains of the forty-six books of the *Commentary on the Psalms* is the series of fragments

preserved in the catenas. Eusebius of Caesarea also drew on it
extensively for his commentary on the same book. On the other
hand, we still have part of the *Commentary on the Song of Songs*
(which dates from 240–1) in Rufinus's translation; Books X to
XVII of the *Commentary on St. Matthew* in Greek and the rest in
a Latin translation (*Commentariorum Series*); the *Commentary on
St. John*, eight books of which are extant in Greek, the first part
being prior to Origen's departure from Alexandria and the
second dating from the end of his life; and a translation by
Rufinus of the *Commentary on the Epistle to the Romans*, in ten books,
which he appears to have recast from the original material.
Fragments of the Greek text recently found in Egypt will make
it possible to estimate the value of Rufinus's work in this last
instance.

Next come the homilies, which are an echo of the sermons
Origen preached at Caesarea towards the end of his life. We
have sixteen homilies on Genesis, thirteen on Exodus, sixteen
on Leviticus and twenty-eight on Numbers, all in Rufinus's
translation. We also have twenty-eight homilies on Josue, nine
on Judges and nine on the Psalms, again in Rufinus's translation. We have St. Jerome's translation of twenty-five homilies
on Isaias and fourteen on Ezechiel. Twenty homilies on Jeremias are extant in Greek and two in Latin, in St. Jerome's translation. We also have St. Jerome's translation of thirty-nine
homilies on Luke.

The last class are the scholia or σημειώσεις, which are
short notes on difficult passages. No collection of these has
survived. There must be plenty of them in the catenas, but
it is very difficult to tell which are fragments of the lost
commentaries.

Origen's great theological work, the *De Principiis*, may be
taken next. It was finished before 230 and is one of the earliest
things he wrote. It consists of four books, dealing respectively
with God and celestial beings, the material world and man,
freewill, and Scripture. All that we now have of it is Rufinus's
Latin translation. In addition, we have the great apologetic
work, the *Contra Celsum*, which is a reply to the "True Discourse" of the philosopher, Celsus. We have the full text in
Greek. The work belongs to the later part of Origen's life and
was written after 248. The ten books of the *Stromata* have not

survived. But we still have two ascetical treatises, the *Exhortatio ad Martyrium*, written for Ambrose at the time of the persecution of Maximinus (235) and the *De Oratione*, which belongs to the category of instructions for catechumens on the mysteries of Christianity. In this work Origen first explains prayer in general and then comments on the Our Father. This sort of commentary was a regular part of the preparation for Baptism. A similar plan is found in Tertullian's *De Oratione*, Gregory of Nyssa's *De Oratione* and Ambrose's *De Sacramentis*. Of his endless correspondence only two letters have been preserved. One deals with exegesis and was written to Julius Africanus about the canonicity of the story of Susanna; the other, on the relationship between profane learning and Christianity, was written to St. Gregory the Wonderworker.

In addition, the catenas of exegetical passages from the Fathers have recently been critically examined and have already yielded a considerable number of fragments of lost works. René Cadiou has also edited some unpublished fragments by Origen on the Psalms.[9] There is an article by Mgr. Devreese in the supplement to the *Dictionnaire de la Bible*[10] on the whole question of the catenas. It is sometimes difficult to establish the authenticity of the fragments. Fr. von Balthasar has shown in an important article that fragments on the Psalms attributed to Origen in the *Patrologia Graeca* are in reality by Evagrius.[11] M. Cadiou, again, has proved that the fragments in the catenas are often mere summaries of the original material. Consequently, there can be no absolute certainty that what they say is what Origen really thought.

On the other hand, the corpus of works acknowledged as his has received some important additions in consequence of discoveries recently made in Egypt. The results of these discoveries were set out by M. Guéraud, who teaches at the Lycée Français at Cairo, in an article in the *Revue d'Histoire des Religions*.[12] The bundle of papyri discovered contains two particularly important documents. The first is a set of two Easter homilies. Apart from what it may reveal about Origen's opinions, the interest of this discovery is that it may shed light on another problem at present under discussion, the question of the origin of a group of Easter homilies included in the spurious works of Chrysostom. Fr. Charles Martin thought that the homilies could be attributed to Hippolytus of Rome, but his opinion has been vigorously challenged by Dom Connolly.[13] Two recently-discovered documents will enable the discussion to be carried further. One is the Easter homily by Melito of Sardis (end of the second century) edited by Campbell Bonner, the other the manuscript of these two homilies of Origen's. In addition, the bundle of papyri discovered in Egypt contains an account of a minor council at which Origen enquired into the orthodoxy of a Bishop Heracleidas. It was known before this that Origen had several times been called upon to conduct such enquiries, especially in Arabia, but the newly discovered passage cannot be taken to refer to any of those episodes. Yet the passage is of the greatest interest as affording a sight of Origen in the exercise of his official functions in the Church and particularly as showing his orthodoxy on Trinitarian questions.[14]

With regard to books and articles about him, at this stage I will mention only a few general works to which I shall often have occasion to allude. The bibliography for the specific points studied in the book I will give as we come to them. The manuals of patrology (Cayré, Rauschen-Altaner, Steidle), the histories of ancient Christian literature (Bardenhewer, Puech, Tixeront), and the histories of dogma (Harnack, Seeberg, Tixeront) I need say nothing about. Among the chief works on Origen, the most important seventeenth-century one is Huet's *Origeniana*.[15] Of all existing accounts of his theological opinions this is still the most accurate and discerning, although, of course, it is out of date on textual and historical questions. The most important nineteenth-century work is Redepenning's *Origenes, eine Darstellung seines Lebens und seiner Lehre*, published at Bonn, 1841–8. In French, besides Mgr. Freppel, there was M. J. Denis, who in 1844 produced *De la philosophie d'Origène* (Paris). He gave a general outline of the system under the headings of theology, anthropology and eschatology, but he treated the sources uncritically. In English, the book to read is Bigg's *Christian Platonists of Alexandria* (Oxford, 1886), the second part of which is devoted to Origen. It makes some interesting suggestions about Origen's relationship to his Alexandrian background and also about his exegesis. Fr. Prat's little book, *Origène, le théologien et l'exégète* (Paris, 1907) is a collection of extracts. The introduction is important on account of the author's very favourable attitude to Origen and because of what he says about his exegesis.

We now come to the more recent books, the chief of which were responsible for the present controversy about Origen. The one that started the dispute was Eugène de Faye's *Origène, sa vie, son oeuvre, sa pensée* (Paris, 1923-8). The book is of outstanding merit, but De Faye takes up an extreme position in it on two points: he severely criticizes the sources and is cautious about using the Latin translations; he also holds that Origen's system is esssentially philosophical and non-Christian. The first volume deals with the life and works, the second with the philosophical background and the third with the system. Bardy's article, "Origène", in the *Dictionnaire de théologie catholique*, xi, cols. 1489-1565, is a reply to De Faye; it defends the biblical character of Origen's teaching, while his *Etudes sur le texte du De Principiis* react against De Faye's ruthless treatment of the Latin translations.

On the other hand, Hal Koch's book, *Pronoia und Paideusis, Studien über Origenes und sein Verhältniss zum Platonismus* (Leipzig, 1932), aims at working out De Faye's thesis in greater detail by taking certain specific points and showing how Origen's treatment of them compares with the treatment given them by some of the philosophers of his time. M. René Cadiou's fine book, *La jeunesse d'Origène; Histoire de l'école d'Alexandrie au début du IIIe siècle* (Paris, 1935), proceeds along similar lines but is much more moderate. It shows how Origen's ideas were built on a Christian foundation but were also influenced by current philosophical trends. The same writer's *Introduction au système d'Origène* (Paris, 1932) forms a complement to this book. While all these writers are primarily concerned with the sources of Origen's ideas, Fr. von Balthasar's essay, "Le mysterion d'Origène",[16] tries to see from the inside the way Origen looked at the world. His deep insight makes this article the best introduction for anyone who wishes to gain some understanding of Origen.

A further problem was raised by another book of first-rate importance, Walther Völker's *Das Volkommenheitsideal des Origenes* (Tübingen, 1931), a study of Origen's teaching about the spiritual life. The book drew a reply from Fr. Aloysius

Lieske—*Die Theologie der Logosmystik bei Origenes* (Münster, 1938)—which proved that Origen's theories on the spiritual life depend on his theology of the Logos and his teaching about the union of the soul with the Logos. This aspect of the case has not been examined by Völker (not that the omission detracts from the importance of his work). Attention has been called to another facet of Origen's spiritual teaching by Dom Etienne Tavares Bettencourt in his book, *Doctrina Ascetica Origenis, Seu Quid Docuerit De Ratione Animae Humanae Cum Daemonibus* (Rome, 1945). The point in question is the part played by the good angels and the bad in the spiritual life. It will be seen that the conclusions I come to are almost the same as Dom Bettencourt's, although I had not seen his book when I wrote this one. I am also greatly indebted to M. H. C. Puech's lectures at the Ecole des Hautes Etudes and to advice given me by Fr. Lebreton.

PART I

ORIGEN AND HIS TIMES

I

THE LIFE OF ORIGEN

WE KNOW more about Origen than about the majority
of the great figures of the early Church. We possess,
in fact, several valuable sources of information about
him. The first is Book VI of the *Ecclesiastical History* of Eusebius
of Caesarea. Eusebius lived in circles where Origen's memory
was still very much alive, as Origen had spent the last twenty
years of his life at Caesarea, from 230 onwards. Eusebius, who
was living there by about 300, knew men who had been
Origen's companions. He says himself: "The little I have to say
about him I will put together from letters and from information supplied by those of his friends who are still alive." [1]
Further on he adds: "A great deal of information about
Origen has been supplied from memory by presbyters still
living." [2]

Moreover, a predecessor of Eusebius at Caesarea had started
to collect material relating to Origen and at the same time to
put his library in order. This was Pamphilus. "The essential
facts about Origen," Eusebius says, "can be read in the
Apologia which I wrote in his defence with Pamphilus, the
holy man who was martyred not so very long ago. We worked
together when we composed it, because the people it was meant
for were so censorious, and we took great pains with it." [3] It
is not known whether Pamphilus had known Origen personally, but he was living at Caesarea shortly after Origen's death.
He was the one who introduced Eusebius to Origen's library.
And together they composed their Apologia for the master.
Unfortunately, all that remains of this Apologia is the first
book, in Rufinus's translation. It is concerned only with the
theological problems.

A third source is the farewell speech made by Gregory of
Neo-Caesarea out of compliment to Origen, whose pupil he

had been at Caesarea, before he left him and went back to Pontus, where he came from.[4] The speech contains few biographical details but it provides a good deal of important material bearing on Origen's personality and activities. Gregory of Neo-Caesarea was the great apostle of Cappadocia. He was a saint, and a saint's testimony to Origen's worth is a thing well worth having. Moreover, in Gregory we have the link between Origen and the Cappadocians. It was Gregory who converted Macrina, the grandmother of Gregory of Nyssa and Basil. The faith was not his only gift to her; he gave her, too, his own admiration for the master who had made him see how splendid the faith was.

Our plan will be to follow Eusebius's narrative, supplement it from other documentary sources and fill it out with such information as Origen's own works provide us with. René Cadiou's *La jeunesse d'Origène* and the first volume of De Faye's *Origène, sa vie, son oeuvre, sa pensée* deal with the biographical question, but they are both concerned more with the history of Origen's intellectual life than with his relationship to the Christian community, which is the point I want to stress here —we shall see that his life yields information not only about his own personality but about the life of the Church in his day as well. A. von Harnack's *Die Kirchengeschichtliche Ertrag der exegetischen Arbeiten des Origenes,*[5] a book of outstanding value, which brings together everything in Origen's exegetical works that bears on the life of the Church, will be of great use in this connection. People need reminding that Origen was first and foremost a loyal member of the Church, *vir ecclesiasticus,* as he calls himself in his sixteenth homily on St. Luke,[6] because the fact is often forgotten.

Eusebius begins with an account of the martyrdom of Origen's father, Leonides, which took place at Alexandria during the persecution of Severus. That in itself is information of considerable value. Origen was born in Egypt, perhaps at Alexandria. He was born into a Christian family—an important point, for in him we see the kind of fruit that Christianity was beginning to produce now that it had been in existence for several generations. There is an important passage in Eusebius about the education Origen received from his father. Speaking of Origen's earliest years, Eusebius says: "In addition to

putting him through the usual educational curriculum his father
was very anxious that he should learn about the Bible. . . .
Every day he would set him to learn passages by heart and then
give an account of what he had learned. The child complied
without the slightest reluctance; in fact, he even went about it
too enthusiastically. He was not content with the straightforward, obvious meaning of the Scriptures; he wanted something more, and even at that time would go in pursuit of
the underlying sense. He even embarrassed his father by
the questions he asked. . . . When he was there, Leonides
would pretend to rebuke him and advise him not to aim at
what was beyond him at that age . . . but he was really very
glad about it." [7]

In reading these lines, allowances must be made for the
element of exaggeration that went with the hagiographical
style in early times, as it still does sometimes today. Eusebius
saw the six-year-old Origen as he was in his maturity, applying
himself to the $\theta\varepsilon\omega\varrho\iota\alpha$ $Ba\theta\upsilon\tau\acute{\varepsilon}\varrho a$, i.e., to the pursuit of the
spiritual sense of Scripture. Shortly before this he says: "In
my opinion, everything about Origen, even the things he did,
so to speak, in the cradle, deserves to be remembered." [8] The
words are just a little disturbing. But all the same, what he
tells us is substantially true and of value. We are shown, first
of all, a Christian child receiving instruction from the *gram-
maticus* at the pagan school on the one hand, and on the other,
being made by his father to learn part of the Bible every day.
St. Basil's sister, Macrina, was made to do that too. Again,
there is one expression that fits Origen with his Coptic temperament too well to be an exaggeration—the one about the
excessive enthusiasm, the passionate eagerness with which he
applied himself to Scripture from the very beginning. A little
further on, Eusebius speaks of the special fondness that he had
for the word of God even at that age. Origen may be said to
have given his heart to the $\theta\varepsilon\iota o\varsigma$ $\lambda\acute{o}\gamma o\varsigma$ when he was a child.
As a child, he deliberately made choice of the Word, and
knowledge and love of the Word were always what counted
most for him, whether $\lambda\acute{o}\gamma o\varsigma$ stood for God's subsistent Word
or for his word in Scripture.

Before we take our leave of Leonides, we must look at an
incident that shows his faith and his love for his son in a striking

light. "It is said that often when the boy was asleep, he would go up to him and uncover his chest and reverently kiss it, because the Holy Spirit had made his sanctuary within it, and that he thought himself singularly blessed in being the father of such a child."[9] Among the early Christians, the kiss was a ritual gesture denoting veneration. That is why the priest kisses the altar and the Gospel book. And that was why Leonides kissed his son's body, the temple of the Holy Spirit.

Besides being fed on Scripture, the young Origen was exposed to another influence characteristic of the Christianity of the time; the influence of martyrdom. He was a child when the persecutions were at their height. By telling us which one Leonides died in, Eusebius provides us with a means of determining the chronology of Origen's life. "Severus too started a persecution against the Churches."[10] The Severus in question was Septimius Severus, the founder of the dynasty of the Severi then ruling in succession to the Antonines. Septimius Severus adopted a more severe policy towards the Christians: the initiative in proceeding against them was now taken by the State. Edicts of this kind alternated with periods of calm unti the end of the third century. And yet the Emperor had at first seemed well-disposed towards the Christians. It was to him that Tertullian had written his Apology in 198. But that did not stop him from promulgating a harsh edict in 202, the year in which Leonides was martyred.

The feelings aroused by these persecutions in the eager young Origen, who was now growing up, are vividly described by Eusebius. "Severus was in the tenth year of his reign," he says (Severus had succeeded Pertinax in 193), "Laetus was governing Alexandria and the rest of Egypt and Demetrius had only just taken over the government of the Churches there from Julian. The fires of persecution rose to a great height and thousands of Christians received crowns of martyrdom." It was during this persecution that Perpetua and Felicity were martyred in Africa. "Such a desire for martyrdom took hold of Origen, mere boy though he still was, that he would gladly have gone out to meet danger and rushed off with all speed to the contest." His mother "begged him to have some consideration for her maternal feelings, but when he heard that his father had been put in prison, he was more intent on martyrdom than ever and did nothing but think about it. Seeing how it was with him, his mother hid all his clothes and so forced him to stay indoors. But he . . . was not one to remain inactive; he sent his father a pressing letter urging him not to shirk his martyrdom. . . . 'Do not dream of changing your mind,' he wrote, 'on our account.'"[11]

Here again we see the beginnings of something that was to be a permanent feature in Origen's life. All through his life, his thoughts ran on martyrdom. In that respect, he is one of the best embodiments of the Christianity of his time. During the persecution of Maximinus, he wrote the *Exhortation to Martyrdom*, which is the child's letter to his father over again, with the amplifications that seemed necessary to the mature man. Origen stands with Ignatius of Antioch by reason of his desire for martyrdom, with Tertullian because he exalted martyrdom as a victory over the devil, with Clement of Alexandria because he taught that martyrdom was the perfection of love. He was tortured himself under Decius. "For many days he had his feet in the stocks at the fourth hole and was threatened with fire."[12]

We will return later to the question of the prime importance of martyrdom in Origen's theological system. Here we need only observe that he regarded it as one of the proofs of the truth of Christianity, not merely because it showed that Christians were capable of dying for their faith—other people die too, for their country or their ideas—but because in the Christian martyrs contempt for death was a sign that they had already defeated the powers of evil that use death as their instrument of torture (1 Cor. xv. 55). Martyrdom brought the Resurrection, in a way, into the present as a living reality; the martyrs' charismata, impassibility in particular, were a sort of foretaste of the Resurrection. Martyrdom was thus a continuation of the work of redemption.[13]

But to come back to Origen's life. On his father's death, he found himself at the age of seventeen in charge of the family. This piece of information enables us to fix the year of his birth: he must have been born in 185, as his father died in 202. "After his father's martyrdom," Eusebius says, "he was left with his mother and six younger brothers. His father's property was confiscated for the royal treasury and he and his family were reduced to want . . ."[14] But he had the good fortune to be able to continue his studies, thanks to the help he received from a "very rich and . . . remarkable woman".[15] Eusebius does not say who she was. Origen was already well up in his work and after his father's death he applied himself even more intently than before. He was thus soon in a position to teach grammar and so provide for the needs of his family.[16]

One thing Eusebius says about the benefactress is worth noting in passing, as it brings out another feature in Origen's character. "She showed great kindness and respect," he says, "to a man from Antioch who was well-known in heretical circles at Alexandria. . . . The heretics used to flock to this Paul, as he was called, and so did our brethren, because he seemed to be a learned man; but Origen would never consent to stand with him in prayer. Thus, he kept the rule laid down by the Church right from his youth. As he says somewhere himself in so many words, heretical teaching made him feel sick."[17] The point is an important one. Eusebius may be stressing it for apologetic purposes, but it is characteristic of Origen all the same. Origen never departed from the rule of faith which he gave at the beginning of the Περὶ 'Αρχῶν and never aimed at anything but defending the faith against heretics.[18] His writings were to a large extent directed against the heresies of the time, particularly against the teaching of Marcion and Heracleon. Some of his opinions were afterwards rejected by the teaching authority, but he had always acknowledged the Church's right to condemn them and had brought them forward only as tentative suggestions.

The noticeable thing about him in this connection is his deep feeling for the Church and its unity. This feeling for the Church grew stronger as his life went on. His finest treatment of the theme and his theology of the Mystical Body are to be found in one of his latest works, the homilies on Josue. This one extract will serve as a specimen of the best things in the book: "I bear the title of priest and, as you see, I preach the word of God. But if I do anything contrary to the discipline of the Church or the rule laid down in the Gospels—if I give offence to you and to the Church—then I hope the whole Church will unite with one consent and cast me off."[19] This feeling, then, for the Church and its unity, which recalls the teaching of

Origen's great contemporary, Cyprian, dates from his youth and remained a feature of his life to the end.

Origen was a teacher of grammar when the decisive event recorded by Eusebius in Chapter III occurred. "When he was teaching at Alexandria, as he says himself in one of his books, there was no one to do the catechizing: persecution had been threatened and all the catechists had left the town. Some of the pagans, who wanted to hear God's word, therefore came to him. . . . He was eighteen when he was made head of the catechetical school. . . . He saw that more and more people were coming to him for instruction and as he was the only one commissioned by Demetrius, the head of the Church, to do the catechizing, he concluded that teaching grammar was now incompatible with his work of giving religious instruction. He at once stopped teaching grammar, as it seemed useless and a hindrance to his religious studies. . . . He got rid of all his editions of the classics, beautiful copies though they were."[20]

The implications of this passage are of the greatest importance for their bearing on one of the main topics in the religious history of the time, the question of the school of Alexandria. The phrase, "school of Alexandria", gives the impression of a permanent institution providing advanced teaching in theology and having Clement and Origen as its principal lecturers. With this idea as a starting-point, the passage has been taken as a record of Origen's appointment to this high teaching post in succession to Clement, and Clement in turn is regarded as the successor of Pantaenus. Such in particular is the view held by De Faye.[21] M. Cadiou was the first to protest against that interpretation.[22] The question was taken up once more by M. Bardy in a masterly article[23] which, to my mind, settles the dispute. It is clear from M. Bardy's essay that a distinction must be made between three different kinds of school. In the first place, the pagan philosophers of the time had their own schools—i.e., their pupils formed groups round them—and the same was true of Christian philosophers like Justin and Clement. But these were not permanent institutions. At one point in his life, Origen too set up a sort of school for advanced studies and in it taught the liberal arts, philosophy and Scripture. But that is not what is referred to in the passage we are concerned with.

Secondly, the expression "school of Alexandria" may denote a group of thinkers holding similar opinions but not belonging to any common institution. That is the proper meaning of the term. But again, it is not what is involved here. In the third place, the end of the second century and the beginning of the third saw a new development in the organization of catechetical instruction. Hitherto, preparation for Baptism had to some extent depended on chance contacts, but by this time some degree of organization was being introduced into it. Bishops were entrusting the task to well-informed laymen—giving them the book but not laying hands on them: they remained laymen. This can be gathered from one of the books dating from this time, Hippolytus of Rome's *Apostolic Tradition*.[24] The Order of Lector arose out of the practice.

This is evidently the kind of school the passage in question is referring to. "Eusebius makes it quite clear what it was that Demetrius appointed Origen to do. His job was to catechize. It had nothing to do with advanced teaching; it was limited to elementary instruction. The aim was not to produce learned theologians or give Christians who had already received Baptism an introduction to the gnosis, but to prepare pagans for receiving Baptism."[25] Origen himself describes the catechist's functions in more than one of his books. He had both to teach doctrine[26] and to give instruction on the Christian life. "If you want to receive Baptism," he said later in one of his homilies, "you must first learn about God's word, cut away the roots of your vices, correct your barbarous wild lives and practise meekness and humility. Then you will be fit to receive the grace of the Holy Spirit."[27]

We can now see, then, exactly what Eusebius was referring to. It was in the middle of a period of persecution and there was nobody to see to the instruction of candidates for Baptism. The fact that Origen was approached, in spite of his youth, shows how much attention his attainments had attracted even then. He took everything seriously. M. Bardy is right in saying that he "took his new functions seriously, even tragically".[28] He stopped teaching grammar and even sold his beloved books, which Eusebius says were such "beautiful copies". He meant to give his new duties his undivided attention.

Henceforward, his life was to be devoted exclusively to the

study of Scripture and the instruction of catechumens. Thus, after a preliminary period in which he acquired a knowledge of literature and some practice in the art, at this point in his life he devoted himself exclusively to Scripture. Eusebius says so more than once. "He would spend the greater part of the night," he says, "in studying Holy Scripture."[29] "At Alexandria he laboured incessantly, night and day, giving religious instruction to all who applied to him. He unhesitatingly sacrificed his leisure to his religious studies and his pupils."[30] This was the first stage in his work on the Bible. He must have gained a deep knowledge of Scripture at this time, but he acquired it solely in view of the instruction he had to give his catechumens.

The instruction was given, too, in particularly moving circumstances. The people who came to Origen to be catechized knew that they were thereby running the risk of martyrdom. Thus, in his view, teaching them the faith and preparing them for martyrdom were one and the same thing. That explains why he was so absorbed by his task. Teaching them what to believe was not the only thing he did for them; he gave them a moral impetus as well by the example he set them. Eusebius describes the part he played at the time. "He had a great name with all the faithful," he says, "for the way he always welcomed the holy martyrs and was so attentive to them, whether he knew them or not. He would go to them in prison and stay by them when they were tried and even when they were brought out to die. . . . Often, when he went up to the martyrs unconcernedly and kissed them, regardless of the consequences, the crowd standing by—being pagan—flew into a passion and very nearly made an end of him. He was persecuted day after day, until the . . . city . . . became too small to hold him. He went from house to house, changing his lodgings all the time and being turned out of every place he went to because such crowds came to him to learn about the things of God . . . What made so many people want to imitate him was, first and foremost, the divine power that governed his actions."[31]

The passage shows to the full what life was like in the Christian community at that time, while the persecution was going on. To attend on the martyrs was one of the most sacred

Christian duties. Tertullian several times speaks of it, particularly in his treatise *Ad Uxorem*. Thus, in addition to his duties as a catechist, Origen undertook to visit and console the martyrs. But in his view, the two things were one. His teaching was so inspiring, Eusebius says, that some of the people he instructed distinguished themselves publicly and were afterwards martyred.[32] He includes a Plutarch, a Serenus and a Heraclides among Origen's "disciples" and mentions two women, Herais, who was martyred while still a catechumen, and Potamiaena.

If Origen abandoned his professional activities as a teacher of grammar, it was in order to devote himself exclusively to his duties as catechist; but the change also marked the beginning of a new life for him, a life of perfection according to the Gospel. It meant what Eusebius calls embarking on the "philosophers' way of life."[33] At that time, philosophers were not so much teachers of theory as masters of practical wisdom. Philosophy meant ceasing to bother overmuch about temporal affairs, such as politics and professional matters, and putting the things of the soul first. The philosopher's ideal was the quest for the perfect life, unlike the rhetorician's, whose object was the glory this world bestows. Conversion, in the ancient world, meant conversion to philosophy.[34] The same idea was found in Christian circles: there were Christians too who forsook the ordinary ways of living and tried to live a kind of life which had a greater perfection. That was the beginning of the movement that was to issue a century later in monasticism.

Origen's move thus affords a glimpse of what at that time was a new aspect of Christian life. It is worth noting, too, that in his case this new thing makes its appearance in connection with the outlook that regarded martyrdom as the goal of the spiritual life. If in the third and fourth centuries Christian ascetic theory was often stated in terms used of the philosophical life, that in no way detracts from its specifically Christian character. It was essentially eschatological, i.e., it was not based on purification of the mind and contempt for the body, as pagan asceticism was; it rested on desire for the ultimate meeting with Christ and on the provisional character of the present world. Its spirit was the one St. Paul showed when he said: "The time is drawing to an end; nothing remains but for

those who have wives to behave as though they had none"
(1 Cor. vii. 29).

Eusebius shows what the "philosophical" life amounted to
in Origen's case. "He forced himself," he says, "to live as
austerely as possible, now fasting, now allowing only the
scantiest measure of time for sleep, which he tried not to take in
bed as a general rule: he preferred to snatch what rest he could
on the floor. He thought that people ought to take more notice
of what our Saviour says in the Gospels about not having two
garments or using sandals or wearing oneself out with worry
about the future. . . . In ways like that, his existence was a
model of what the philosopher's life ought to be."[35] It is well-
known that in his excessive enthusiasm for conformity to the
letter of the Gospels, he took literally the words "Some have
made themselves eunuchs for love of the kingdom of heaven"
(Matt. xix. 12). He afterwards admitted that he had been
wrong on that point. But the essential thing to note at the
moment is that he chose to base his life on the Gospel counsels,
and that before teaching others to be perfect and becoming a
great authority on the spiritual life, he began by practising the
counsels himself. As Gregory the Wonderworker says, he
"strove to be like his own description of the man leading the
good life; he provided a model, I mean, for those in search of
wisdom".[36]

Up to this point, we have seen Origen as a devoted catechist
enthusiastically instructing converts in the Christian faith and
life. But as he pondered on the Scriptures, he came to realize
that much remained to be done in the way of arranging for the
more advanced study of the Bible. It was a turning-point in his
life. Eusebius says that he "saw he could no longer manage to
study theology adequately or work at Scripture and expound it
if he went on teaching the people who came to him for catechetical instruction, as they left him no time even to breathe. . . .
He therefore divided his crowd of disciples into two classes and
chose Heraclas to help him with the catechetical work. . . .
Heraclas was devoted to the things of God; he was an excellent
speaker, too, and had some knowledge of philosophy. Origen
appointed him to give the beginners their first introduction to
Christian doctrine and kept the more advanced teaching for
himself."[37]

M. Bardy is right in saying that it "would be impossible to exaggerate the importance of the change thus effected".[38] What had happened was not that the catechetical school had split in two; the school continued its existence as before, except that it was now under Heraclas. What Origen had done was to found a new institution. Through talking to cultivated pagans, Jews and philosophers, he had come to realize that biblical studies were apt to raise difficult problems. What was wanted was the establishment of a centre for the scientific study of the Bible. Origen explains his ideas on the subject in one of his letters, which Eusebius has preserved. "After I had begun to deal with Scripture exclusively," he says, "I was sometimes approached by heretics and people educated after the Greek model, particularly in philosophy. I therefore thought it advisable to make a thorough study both of heretical doctrine and of the philosophers' views about the truth. In this I was imitating Pantaenus, who before my time had acquired no small store of such knowledge and had benefited many people by it."[39] The reference to Pantaenus makes it clear what Origen was about. Pantaenus is an elusive character: he left nothing behind him in writing and little is known about him except that he had taught Clement of Alexandria. Origen had been acquainted with him. Pantaenus had opened a school of philosophy also and Clement had afterwards taught in it. What Origen proposed to do was to work along the same lines as Pantaenus had done. There was no question at all of his foundation's being a catechetical school—which was an institution maintained by the Church; his school was a private *didaskaleion* like the one kept by Justin at Rome.

This implied a radical change of attitude towards secular learning—which is why it was so important for his work. It will be remembered that when he decided to devote himself entirely to catechizing, he sold his non-religious books. He now realized that there was scientific work to be done on the Bible and that for that purpose secular learning was indispensable. The school he was going to found would thus have to be one in which secular studies could be pursued as a preparation for the scientific study of the Bible, the crown of the whole structure. It became in fact a university, offering an introduction to the whole field of learning. Origen himself taught the various subjects. Another side of his life is discernible here.

Eusebius tells us what Origen's school was like, who attended it and what was taught in it. "Many well-read people," he says, ". . . went to see what his attainments were like. . . . Thousands of heretics and many of the most eminent philosophers eagerly flocked to hear him and were not ashamed even to pick up points about secular philosophy from him as well as to hear about Christian doctrine. If he saw that a pupil of his had talent, he would set him to study philosophy, geometry, arithmetic and the other elementary subjects; after which he would explore with him the tenets of the various schools of philosophy, examining, explaining and commenting on their writings one by one. The Greeks themselves admitted that he was a great philosopher."[40]

Two things may be pointed out in connection with this. The first is that the school was open to all who cared to attend. Origen was no longer offering preparation for Baptism; his object now was to distribute scientific knowledge. And if he sometimes had the pleasure of seeing a pupil's conversion to Christianity, as in the case of Ambrose, who became his patron as well, there were others, as he says in the *Contra Celsum*, who simply showed some improvement in their moral conduct. The question of the curriculum is more interesting. The expression Origen used for the curriculum is ἐνκύκλια γράμματα. What he meant by it was the whole cycle of studies as it existed in the ancient world from the classical period until the collapse of classical civilization. It is found in Philo, who sings its praises, and in Clement of Alexandria. M. Marrou has studied the use St. Augustine made of it.[41] It comprised seven essential branches—grammar, dialectics, rhetoric, music, astronomy, arithmetic and physics. Philosophy came in at the end to crown the structure.

It is of great interest to see what Origen's attitude towards pagan learning was, for it is the one found everywhere among the Fathers after him. On the one hand, he condemns pagan learning in so far as it represents a view of the world opposed to the Christian one. "There are many different kinds of literary study in this world," he says. "You find people beginning with grammar, in the course of which they study the works of the

poets and the plays of the comic writers. . . . They then pass on
to rhetoric, where they try to acquire all the tricks of fine
writing and speaking. After that, they come to philosophy, go
through dialectics, see how syllogisms are fitted together,
experiment with measurements in geometry and enquire into the
orbits of the stars and the laws that govern the heavenly bodies.
They take in music as well. They become accomplished through
studying all these widely differing subjects but they learn nothing from them about the will of God. They accumulate . . .
wealth but they take it from the stores of sinners."[42]

But, on the other hand, pagan learning is not entirely bad so
far as its foundations are concerned. All knowledge comes from
God—"All wisdom is from the Lord"[43]—whether it be knowledge of geometry, of music or of medicine. Hence it may
legitimately be made use of, within certain limits. The first
thing to do is to acquire a good grounding in the faith.[44] Pagan
learning must be purged of its errors.[45] Students must not
forget that it is useful for expounding the Gospel to others but
not for actually acquiring knowledge of divine things.[46] And
finally, it is to be used to obtain a better understanding of
Scripture. "If in addition to what we are taught by the Law
. . . we meet with things in secular culture . . . like the study of
literature or 'grammar', geometrical theory, the law of numbers or the subject of dialectics, we lay it all . . . under contribution for our own education."[47] This is one of the passages
that show Origen's dependence on Philo; there can be no
doubt that he is here continuing the same tradition. He states
his ideal in a letter to his former pupil, Gregory the Wonderworker. "I should like to see you use all the resources of your
mind," he says, "on Christianity and make that your ultimate
object. I hope that to that end you will take from Greek
philosophy everything capable of serving as an introduction to
Christianity and from geometry and astronomy all ideas useful
in expounding the Holy Scriptures; so that what . . . philosophers say of geometry, music, grammar, rhetoric and
astronomy—that they assist philosophy—we too may be able
to say of philosophy itself in relation to Christianity."[48]

We know from Gregory the Wonderworker's farewell discourse what this discovery of all the branches of intellectual
enquiry could be like for a young man when made under the

guidance of a master like Origen, and what enthusiasm it could arouse. Gregory had been Origen's pupil at Caesarea, not at Alexandria, but the master's method was still the same. He shows us Origen winning him over by a mixture of persuasive charm and forcefulness to the love of philosophy, so that his "heart was set ablaze with love for the beloved Word and for the man who was his friend and interpreter".[49] Origen first taught him rhetoric: "The part of the mind that judges of words [i.e., grammar] and speech [i.e., rhetoric] was educated."[50] Then he opened up before him the different branches of scientific knowledge, which moved him to wonder at the variety and wisdom discernible in the structure of the world— he taught him physics, which explain the elements of things and the changes occurring in them, "holy mathematics, incontrovertible geometry, astronomy that sets a ladder to the things of heaven".[51] It is worthy of note that this admiration for the visible creation, this scientific, cosmic spirit, is a thing that was known to the ancient world, particularly to the Stoics, but is not found in Origen himself, although the elementary teaching he gave in his school was the means of transmitting it to Gregory the Wonderworker. From Gregory it passed to the Cappadocians, who had an extensive scientific equipment, Gregory of Nyssa in particular.

But this was only a preparation. It was followed by the study of philosophy. Gregory the Wonderworker has some very interesting things to say in this connection about the method Origen used in teaching philosophy to Christians. Origen's principle was that a hearing should be given to all systems. "He told us to approach philosophy by collecting all the extant writings of the ancient philosophers and poets . . . and not to reject anything . . . except the works of the atheists [i.e., the Epicureans] . . . who deny the existence of a Providence. He wanted us to read . . . all the others without preferring one system . . . or rejecting another: . . . we were to hear them all."[52] The reason was that the minds of the learners were not yet ripe for judging, and that the worst risk they could run, as far as Origen could see, was that they might become attached to the first system that came along and so be captivated by an opinion for the sole reason that it was the first to present itself. To Origen's mind, that was at the root of disputes among philosophers. "They never listen to people who think differently from themselves. That is why no old man ever succeeded in persuading any of the young . . . to embrace his system of philosophy."[53] Thus, paradoxical though it might seem, it was blind chance and not reason that led philosophers to adopt one system rather than another.

Origen's point of view was the direct opposite of that. In his opinion, we should make trial of all systems, take what we find good in them and become adherents of none, for we owe allegiance to God alone and His prophets. Gregory the Wonderworker gives an enthusiastic account of what this sifting of philosophical systems was like under the guidance of such a master. "Not wishing us to be in the same position as the majority of men," he says, "Origen took care not to introduce us to one philosophical system only or to allow us to settle down in any single one of them. He took us through them all and would not have us ignorant of any. He himself was our guide . . . on this journey . . . He was a past master of the art of philosophy, which he had frequented for so long that it had no secrets from him. . . . In every philosophy he picked out what was true and useful and set it before us, while what was erroneous he rejected. . . .[54] He advised us not to give our allegiance to any one philosopher, even though he should be universally acclaimed as perfect in wisdom, but to cleave to God alone and His prophets."[55]

It is easy enough to see from Origen's own writings that Gregory is interpreting his method correctly in this passage. Origen several times mentions the same principles himself. Thus, in his eleventh homily on Exodus he says, "If we too ever find evidence of wisdom in a pagan writer, we should not automatically reject his ideas just because of his name. The fact that the law we follow was given us by God does not entitle us to swell with pride and refuse to listen to the wise. No; as the Apostle says [1 Thess. v. 21], we should 'scrutinize it all carefully, retaining only what is good.'"[56] The rule is quite clear: there is to be neither contempt *a priori* nor unreflecting infatuation, but each case is to be examined separately. The reason is that in fact there is only one master, the word of God. If education in literature and science is a preparation for philosophy, philosophy in turn is only a preparation for the

supreme science, the science of the word of God, the scientific
study of Scripture. After Origen the teacher of rhetoric and
Origen the philosopher, Gregory shows us Origen the exegete.
The catechist of Alexandria has given place to the scholarly
interpreter of the Bible. Origen had been making a close study
of the texts and in order to fit himself for the task, Eusebius says,
had learned Hebrew. He had also made a collection of current
versions of the Scriptures, those by Aquila, Symmachus and
Theodotion. He was soon to compose his Hexapla.

But to his mind, this textual work was only the first of the
exegete's tasks; his chief business was to explain the meaning of
God's word as it was contained in the Holy Scriptures. Gregory
shows us how Origen fulfilled this function. "He used to
explain the obscurities in Scripture," he says "and he could
shed light on them because he was such a wonderfully understanding hearer of God's word—or he would expound parts
that were clear in themselves or at any rate were so to him. Of
all men now living, I have never known or heard of one who
had pondered as he had on the pure and luminous words and
had become so expert at fathoming their meaning and teaching
·them to others. The Spirit who inspires the prophets and all
divine and mystic discourse honoured him as a friend and had
appointed him His interpreter. . . . The same grace is needed
for understanding the prophecies as for making them."[56] We
will discuss Origen's achievement as an exegete at length later
on. For the moment, it will be enough to point out that
Gregory considered Origen's powers of interpreting Scripture
in accordance with the tradition of the Church to be a charisma.
He often comes back to the point. In the present instance, he
says that Origen possessed the "sovereign gift of being the
interpreter of God's words to men. He had the power to listen
to God and understand what He said and then to explain it to
men that they too might understand".[57]

That explains why Gregory retained such wonderful
memories of his student days. "Nothing was kept from us," he
says, "nothing concealed or made inaccessible. We could learn
about any theory, barbarian or Greek, mystical or moral . . .
go into them all . . . and enjoy the good things of the mind.
Everything true in the teaching of the ancients provided us
with a wonderful store of material for thought of the most

delightful kind. . . . To our minds, it was really . . . an image
of paradise."[58]

That is not the only piece of evidence. Eusebius says that the
"Greek philosophers themselves testified to Origen's success".[59]
And certainly, Porphyry does pay tribute to the quality of his
teaching, in spite of attacking him for his Christianity.

Between the years 215 and 230 or thereabouts, Origen was
fully occupied in teaching in the school he had founded, but it
is evident from Eusebius that he was carrying on two other
activities as well. In the first place, his reputation was spreading
widely and people were asking for him on all sides. He had
first had occasion to travel when he was still a catechist: he
went to Rome, Eusebius says, during the reign of Pope Zephy-
rinus. But he had made the journey because he wanted to see
Rome and not because he had been summoned or asked to go.
He no doubt studied for a time under Hippolytus while he was
there. At any rate, Jerome says that Hippolytus recognized
him at one of his lectures and spoke to him. Hippolytus,
being the first Christian writer to produce continuous commentaries on Scripture, in that respect provided a model for
Origen.

But at the time we are concerned with, it was quite another
thing: requests for Origen's services were coming in from all
quarters. Eusebius says that one day "when he was teaching at
Alexandria, a soldier came with a letter from the Governor of
Arabia to the bishop of the city, Demetrius, and the Eparch of
Egypt, asking them to send Origen as soon as possible to tell
him about his ideas".[60] Origen duly accomplished this mission.
Then, when the peace was disturbed at Alexandria in consequence of Caracalla's proscriptions, he went to Palestine and
taught at Caesarea. He had not received the priesthood, but the
bishops asked him to lecture and expound the Scriptures in the
Church assemblies all the same. The practice was traditional,
he tells us, in Palestine. The interesting thing is that for the
first time we here see him engaged in preaching, an activity
that was to occupy a prominent position in the latter part of his
life and constitute an important part of the literary legacy he
left behind him.

One of his journeys is of particular interest for the history of
the times. "The Emperor's mother, Mamaea," Eusebius

writes, "was a religious woman if ever there was one. . . . Since Origen was talked about everywhere . . . she determined to see him and find out what his grasp of theology was like, as everyone said it was so wonderful. When she was staying at Antioch, she sent an escort of soldiers to summon him to her presence. He stayed with her for some time and told her a great deal about the glory of the Lord and the virtue of His divine teaching."[61]

To understand the bearing of this passage on contemporary history, we must remember what the religious life of the pagan world was like at the time. M. Cumont has shown that it was characterized by two things: the inroads made by eastern cults and the appearance of syncretism. The first of these had begun with the spread of Egyptian cults under the Antonines. The period was the one in which Plutarch wrote the *De Iside et Osiride* and Apuleius gave his account of initiation into the mysteries of Isis in the *Golden Ass*. The movement reached its peak with the spread of Syrian cults under the Severi. The head of the dynasty, Septimius Severus, had married the daughter of a Syrian high priest and his wife, Julia Domna, introduced Syrian cults at court, especially the cult of the sun. "The influence exerted by these cults," Cumont says,[62] "became more or less the dominant one when the accession of the Severi brought them the support of a half-Syrian court." The third successor of Septimius Severus was a young priest from Emesa, Heliogabalus, who regarded himself as the priest of the sun-god. In these circles there was intense curiosity about anything to do with religion. It was for Julia Domna that about this time Philostratus wrote the *Life of Apollonius of Tyana*. The characteristic thing about it is its syncretism, which combines all the different cults. Similarly, Alexander Severus, the successor of Heliogabalus, used to pray every morning before images of Orpheus, Apollonius of Tyana and Jesus.

The Julia Mamaea described as being such a religious woman and as asking Origen to come and tell her about the Saviour's glory was the mother of Alexander Severus and the aunt of Heliogabalus. She exerted a far-reaching influence on the whole of the period. Origen thus found himself among the chief devotees of the syncretist movement. The syncretistic tone of the circle also provides an excellent explanation of the reason for the queen's invitation. The object, as far as she was concerned, was only to secure initiation into a fresh form of religion; she had no thought of actually becoming a Christian. She was simply following the custom of the time, according to which devout pagans would have themselves initiated into the mysteries of Eleusis, Mithra and Isis all alike. We find few allusions, however, in Origen's writings to these devotional trends in paganism. It is thus all the more interesting to see that he had some experience of them all the same.

In addition to these commissions abroad, another characteristic of his activities at this time was that he ceased to limit himself to oral teaching and began to write and publish his commentaries and other works. "At this time," Eusebius says, "Origen too [i.e., like Hippolytus] began his commentaries on the Holy Scriptures."[63] The first five books of the *Commentary on St. John*, the first eight books (now lost) of the *Commentary on Genesis*, the commentaries (now extant only in fragments) on the first twenty-five Psalms, and the *Περὶ 'Αρχῶν* all date from this period. Origen says himself at the beginning of the *Commentary on St. John* that he was induced to undertake the work by the entreaties of his friend, Ambrose. Eusebius says that besides encouraging him, Ambrose also provided him with the material means of carrying on his work. "Seven or more shorthand-writers worked in relays and took down what he dictated," he says, "and there were as many copyists and girls trained in calligraphy. Ambrose provided amply for their subsistence."[64] The passage is of the greatest interest for the light it sheds on the history of literary composition in the ancient world.

Origen's teaching activity at Alexandria came to an end in 230. The incident which terminated it is one of the obscure points in his history, but it was evidently caused by the hostility of his bishop, Demetrius. Demetrius was the man who had appointed him head of the catechetical school. But various occurrences show that a change had gradually come about in their relationship. When Origen was in Palestine, his bishop had suddenly ordered him to return immediately and had reproached him for preaching in church in spite of not being a priest. What was the cause of this tension? It seems that Demetrius was not satisfied with the direction Origen's activities

had taken and that he was growing uneasy at the extent of his
influence. Perhaps he distrusted his ideas as well. The distinction between the teaching conveyed through hierarchical
channels and the teaching given by the *didaskaloi*, a distinction
found as early as the second century, came in again here, too.
The relationship between the two was not yet clearly defined in
the Church.

Whatever the explanation may be, the event that took place
in the year 230 was decisive in the relationship between the
two men. While on a visit to Palestine, Origen was ordained
priest by the local bishops. As M. Cadiou observes, the ordination was "irregular on two grounds. Origen had received
the priesthood without leave from his own bishop and in spite
of the mutilation he had deliberately undergone".[65] The
synod convened by Demetrius in consequence did not go so far
as to declare the ordination invalid, but it did pronounce
Origen unfit for catechizing and expel him from the Church of
Alexandria. He therefore went to Caesarea, where he was
gladly welcomed by the Palestinian bishops. "Alexander, the
head of the Church of Jerusalem and Theoctistus, the Bishop
of Caesarea, never left his side . . ." Eusebius says. "They
regarded him as the one and only master and authorized him
to set up as a scriptural exegete and to expound the rest of the
Church's teaching too."[66]

The latter and longer part, then, of Origen's life, occupying
as it did more than sixty years, had the Christian community
at Caesarea for its setting. He went on at Caesarea with what
he had been doing at Alexandria. He founded another
didaskaleion and continued with his teaching. It was in this
school that he taught Gregory the Wonderworker.[67] He went
on writing, too: it was at this time that he finished his commentaries and wrote the *Contra Celsum*. During the persecution
of Maximinus he wrote the *Exhortatio ad Martyrium*, which he
dedicated to Ambrose. He was still consulted on all sides. He
was asked to go to Arabia and dispute with Beryllus of Bostra
whose opinions were suspect. He took part in other "councils"
of the kind as well. In consequence of a discovery recently made
in Egypt, we are now in possession of an account of one of
these διάλεκτοι and we shall soon have an edition of it from
M. J. Schérer.[68] Origen was also in correspondence with all

the great men of the day, throughout the world—men like the
Emperor Philip the Arabian, Julius Africanus and Pope Fabian.

But the new feature introduced into his activities at this time
was preaching. At the bishop's request, he expounded the
Scriptures nearly every day from the pulpit in the church at
Caesarea. The majority of these sermons were never written
down. However, tradition had it, so Eusebius says, that
"when Origen was over sixty and through long practice had
attained a high degree of accomplishment, he had the talks he
gave in church taken down by fast writers, a thing he had never
allowed before".[69]

A considerable number of his homilies have been preserved
in this way; they constitute the oldest corpus of Christian
sermons. They show us a final facet of Origen's activities and
let us see what he was like as a preacher. The subject is dealt
with in two articles by M. Bardy[70] and in Fr. de Lubac's
introduction to the homilies on Genesis.[71]

Origen looked on his task as a preacher in the same light as
he had formerly regarded his work as a catechist. To his mind,
preaching meant explaining the word of God and nothing
more. What were the circumstances in which preaching was
done at Caesarea at this time? Very little information is available on the subject. Some of the extant homilies preached there
were delivered on Sundays or at Easter. But Origen used to
preach nearly every day. Pamphilus says so in his *Apologia*
when he speaks of the *tractatus* he held "nearly every day in the
church".[72] And Origen himself reproaches his hearers for
coming only on Sundays, as if the other days were not feast-
days as well.[73] His explanations followed the text. We sometimes find him stopping his commentary at a particular point
and returning to it the next time he preached.

From our present point of view it is more important to see
what sort of ideas he had about preaching. There is a great
deal of work to be done on the question. What had to be
explained in preaching was the word of God. The only person
who could inspire the interpreter of the Scriptures was the One
who had inspired the sacred writers themselves: that, as we
have seen, was Origen's principle in exegesis. Consequently,
the preacher had to be first and foremost a man of prayer.
When faced with a specially difficult passage, Origen would

often stop and ask his hearers to pray with him for a better understanding of the text.[74] He was appalled by the task confronting him, for what he had to do was not just to state the truth but to state it in such a way that his hearers could grasp it. "I often think of the maxim: 'It is dangerous to talk about God, even if what you say about him is true.' The man who wrote that must, I am sure, have been a shrewd and dependable character. There is danger, you see, not only in saying what is untrue about God but even in telling the truth about him if you do it at the wrong time."[75]

Origen here seems to be alluding to his theory that there are certain higher truths which are to be communicated only to those who have made some progress in Christianity. The quotation needs balancing with this other statement: "It may be that I shall offend some people if I discuss this question, but even if I do, I must obey the Lord's command rather than seek the favour of men."[76]

The sense of responsibility is evident, too, in passages like this. "All sinners in the Church . . . deserve punishment, but their punishment will depend on the rank they occupy . . . A catechumen deserves more mercy than one of the faithful. . . . A deacon has a better right to pardon than a priest. What follows from that you do not need me to tell you. . . . I fear God's judgment and I keep before my imagination a picture of what will happen at it. . . . I bear in mind the saying: 'If a weight is too heavy for you, do not lift it.' What good is it to me to be enthroned at the master's desk in the place of honour . . . if I cannot do the work my position demands? The torments I shall be punished with will be all the more painful because everyone treats me with respect, as though I were good, whereas in fact I am a sinner."[77] But although the preacher's functions were so awe-inspiring and could be carried out only with fear and trembling, Origen did nevertheless exercise them to the utmost of his ability, because in him zeal was stronger than fear and he thirsted to impart the word of God.

His life ended, as it had begun, in a period of persecution. The death of Alexander Severus in 235 brought the dynasty of the Severi to an end and was followed by a period of confusion comprising the reigns of Maximinus, the Gordians and Philip

the Arabian. In 247, Caius Messius Decius, an Illyrian, became
Emperor under the name of Decius. As he wanted to arrest
the progress of Christianity, which had made considerable
strides, he started the persecutions again and they became more
violent than ever. All the inhabitants of the Empire had to do
sacrifice on pain of death and obtain certificates (*libelli*) to prove
that they had done so. Fabian, the Bishop of Rome, met his
death in this persecution. St. Cyprian went into exile then.
The martyrdom of St. Denis at Paris is said to date from the
same period.

Origen did not escape persecution, even if he did not lose his
life through it. "The sufferings he underwent because Christ
had commanded it were many and intense. He was put in
chains, his body was tortured, he was tormented with the iron
collar and kept in the innermost dungeons in the prison. For
several days he was set in the stocks with his feet in the fourth
hole and threatened with burning. His enemies inflicted many
other sufferings on him too and he bore them all bravely. A
clear and exact account of it all and of the outcome—for the
judge did all he could to spare him—will be found in his many
letters."[78] These letters are not extant, but Eusebius had
handled them and we can trust what he says about them. If
Origen did not die of these persecutions, he at least died shortly
afterwards and perhaps in consequence of them. In any case,
his desire to suffer for Christ had been fulfilled. And to his
mind, the title of martyr was worth much more than the title of
doctor. That is why we have had to see what his life stood for
before we could begin to look at his teaching.

II

ORIGEN AND THE CHRISTIAN BACKGROUND

Origen was first and foremost a faithful son of the Church. Before we look at his personal view of things and even before we see him against the intellectual background of his time, we must first place him in his proper setting, the Christian community. We have seen from his life that he had been catechist, lector, priest, doctor and martyr by turns: the whole of his life was spent in the discharge of ecclesiastical functions. In that respect, his works are deeply rooted in the Christianity of the time. It will be interesting to consider them first of all from this point of view and see what they can show us about the life of Christians—their usages, beliefs and manners—at that time. In so doing, we shall also see what Origen himself thought about all these things. The majority of books about him do not go into this question at all. They give the impression that the atmosphere he lived in was philosophical rather than Christian—which is not the case.

In this chapter we will touch first on the Christian community and its hierarchical structure, then on Christian traditions in liturgical matters and finally on the sacramental life. With reference to each of these points we shall have to consider on the one hand the evidence Origen provides about the concrete facts as they were in his time, and on the other his own personal view of the hierarchy, Christian worship and the sacraments. As a matter of fact, it is impossible to separate the one from the other. In dealing with these questions, which have received very little attention up to the present, we shall be using chiefly the following two works: for the material facts, Harnack's *Der Kirchengeschichtliche Ertrag der exegetischen Arbeiten des Origenes*[1] and for the theology of the mysteries, Fr. von Balthasar's "Mysterion d'Origène".

1. CHRISTIAN WORSHIP

Origen had no special concern with liturgical functions. In the first place, his own work was the ministry of the word. In the second, the cast of his mind inclined him to regard the sensible signs as mere shadows of the spiritual things behind them and prevented him from becoming attached to them. It will therefore be all the more worthwhile to pick out the passages in which he describes the customs of the Church in his time and explains their significance. We may take as our starting-point in this enquiry a passage from one of the homilies on Numbers in which he alludes to various Christian customs. "There are things," he says, "among the Church's observances, which everyone is obliged to do, and yet not everyone understands the reason for them; e.g., . . . the fact that we kneel to pray, and that of all the quarters of the heavens, the east is the one we turn to when we pray. . . . And can you readily explain the reason for the way we receive the Eucharist, for the rites it is celebrated with or for the words, gestures, commands, questions and answers made in Baptism?"[2]

He comes back to the question of turning to the east for prayer in the *De Oratione*. "I must also say a word or two about the part of the world we ought to look to when we pray. . . . You will all immediately point to . . . the east as the direction we should turn in, for reasons of symbolism, when we say our prayers, since the soul ought to keep its eyes steadily turned towards the rising of the true light. Suppose a man has a house . . . facing another way and prefers to turn that way when he says his prayers, on the ground that where the doors and windows do not face east, the sight of the sky is more conducive to recollection in the soul than the sight of a wall. He should be told that . . . his house faces this quarter of the globe or that because men have decided that it should, whereas the superiority of the east to the other parts of the world comes from nature. What is of natural law must be considered superior to what is laid down by positive law."[3]

I have written elsewhere of the importance of prayer towards the east in the early Church. [4] We find it attested by Tertullian —"The figure of the Holy Ghost loves the east, which is a figure of Christ"[5]—and by Clement of Alexandria[6] about the same time as Origen and by Justin a little later.[7] Origen returns to the point elsewhere.[8] But the interesting thing about the passage quoted is that it shows that the tradition concerned not only public prayer but private prayer as well, and thus gives us a glimpse of the private religious practice of the early Christians, a sphere we have very little information about. The custom may not be observed in private devotion today but it was in the earliest times, and it provides the real explanation of the practice still in force of setting crucifixes in private houses for people to turn to when they pray, as has been shown in an important article dealing not with Baptism or the Christian assembly but precisely with this question of prayer in private houses. The article in question, Erik Peterson's "La croce e la preghiera verso l'oriente", is to be found in the *Ephemerides Liturgicae*, Rome, 1945, 59, pp. 52 et seq.

Peterson quotes a passage from the *Acts of Hipparchus and Philotheus*: "In Hipparchus's house there was a specially decorated room and a cross was painted on the east wall of it. There, before the image of the cross, they used to pray seven times a day . . . with their faces turned to the east."[9] It is easy to see the importance of this passage when you compare it with what Origen says. The custom of turning towards the rising sun when praying had been replaced by the habit of turning towards the east wall. This we find in Origen. From the other passage we see that a cross had been painted on the wall to show which was the east. Hence the origin of the practice of hanging crucifixes on the walls of the private rooms in Christian houses. We know too that signs were put up in the Jewish synagogues to show the direction of Jerusalem, because the Jews turned that way when they said their prayers. The question of the proper way to face for prayer has always been of great importance in the East. It is worth remembering that Mohammedans pray with their faces turned towards Mecca and that one reason for the condemnation of Al Hallaj, the Mohammedan martyr, was that he refused to conform to this practice.

As for the symbolical significance of the custom, Origen says that it was observed because Christ is the Sun of the new universe, the Church. Peterson has another theory about the

symbolism and connects the eastward position for prayer with
the adoration of the cross. What was behind the practice in the
early Church was a belief of an eschatological nature, a waiting
for the return of Christ, "who mounteth . . . to the east"
(Ps. lxvii. 34) and would come back, the angel of the Ascension
had said, in the same way as they had seen him going up to
heaven (Acts i. 11). When Christ returned to earth, he would
be preceded by a shining cross. This shining cross was what
Hipparchus had painted on the east wall of his cell. The
development which has taken place since in Christian asceticism
and teaching on the spiritual life has transformed it into the
cross of the Passion.

Another tradition the significance of which was often not
realized in Origen's time was that of kneeling for prayer. Here
again the *De Oratione* sheds light on the meaning of the posture.
The normal position for prayer was the standing one. Here is
Origen's description of it. "There is no limit," he says, "to the
number of postures the body can take up, but the position to be
preferred is unquestionably the one we adopt when we stretch
out our hands and lift up our eyes, as it is the best bodily
expression of the soul's attitude in prayer." He also says that
we ought, so to speak, to stretch out our souls before we
stretch out our hands and raise our minds to God before we
raise our eyes to him. Before we stand up, we should free our
minds from all preoccupation with the earthly and so stand
them before the God of the universe. We should put aside any
resentment we may feel at wrongs done to us if we want God to
forgive us for the wrong we have done ourselves.[10] The passage
is interesting by reason of the comparison it suggests with the
posture of the *orantes* shown in paintings in the catacombs, and
also because of the symbolism involved.

But if the standing position was the usual one, people might
be forced by circumstances to pray in some other position, as
Origen with great commonsense reminds them. "I say that
this should be observed when there are no obstacles. But
circumstances may sometimes lead you to pray sitting down,
e.g., if you have . . . bad feet; and if you have a temperature,
you may even have to lie down. . . . For the same reason, if you
are on board ship, for instance, or if your business makes it
impossible for you to go to some quiet place to discharge your

debt of prayer, you will not be able to insist on standing when you pray. As for prayer in a kneeling position, what you must realize is that it is necessary when we confess our sins to God and beg him to forgive them and restore us to health. It is a symbol of that prostration and submission that Paul speaks of when he says: 'I fall on my knees to the Father of our Lord Jesus Christ, that Father from whom all fatherhood in heaven and on earth takes its title' [Eph. iii. 14]. This spiritual bending of the knee, so called because all creatures worship God and humble themselves before him, when they hear the name of Jesus, is, to my mind, what the Apostle is thinking of when he says: 'Everything in heaven and on earth and under the earth must bend the knee before the name of Jesus' [Phil. ii. 10]." He goes on to say that in any case the text cannot be taken literally.[11]

The passage is important as showing how ancient the practice of γονυκλισία by Christians is. It could be compared with what Tertullian says in the chapter he devotes to the question in the *De Oratione*. He begins by reminding his readers that Christians refrain from kneeling only *die dominico Resurrectionis*, i.e., on Sundays, and *spatio Pentecostes*, i.e., in Paschaltide. Then he goes on: "But we would none of us dream of not prostrating ourselves before God at least for the first prayer, the one we begin the day with. And on fast-days and station-days, all prayers . . . are said kneeling."[12] The two factors mentioned by Origen—penance and adoration—are thus present here too. It is quite likely that Origen's *De Oratione* depends on Tertullian's at this point—Tertullian had published a Greek edition of some of his works.[13] Or there may be a common source in a traditional catechesis on prayer with each of its points fixed.

One would be led to think that this was so by the fact that in both writers the next point dealt with is the question of the place of prayer. Here again Origen has some valuable information to give. "As far as place is concerned," he says, ". . . any place will become suitable for prayer if you pray well in it. . . . However, if you want to say your prayers in greater quiet and without so much distraction, you may choose a special place in your own house, if you can, a consecrated place, so to speak, and pray there. . . . Special grace and benefit are to be had

from the place of prayer, the place, I mean, where the faithful
assemble; for it is reasonable to suppose that the angelic
powers are present when the faithful meet together; the influence [δύνκμις] of our Lord and Saviour must be there too and so
must the spirits of the saints—the spirits, to my way of thinking,
of the dead who have gone before us and obviously, too, the
spirits of those saints who are still alive, though how, it is
difficult to say."[14]

Here again there are many interesting features. The passage
is evidence of the existence of oratories in private houses. This
links up with what we have just said about the cross painted on
the wall. Prayer is possible anywhere, but still, the place of
prayer is holy, and Origen raises the question as to whether
married people can use their bedroom to pray in. But a more
interesting idea is the one about the invisible presence of
Christ, the angels and the saints at the assembly of the faithful.
It is worth seeing how Origen works it out in detail with regard
to the angels. "What must be said about the angels is this. If
the angel of the Lord encamps beside those who fear the Lord
and brings them deliverance [Ps. xxxiii. 8] . . . it would seem
that when a number of people duly meet together for the glory
of Christ, they will each have their own angel encamped beside
them, since they all fear the Lord. Each angel will be with the
man he has been commissioned to guard and direct. Thus,
when the saints are assembled, there will be two Churches, one
of men and one of angels."[15] We shall have to return to the
theology of the angels later, but it is important that we should
note this point now if we are to understand the "mystery" of
the liturgy.

The idea recurs in other passages, too, in connection with
various aspects of divine worship. The angels are present at
Baptism. "As soon as a man believes in Jesus Christ, the
Gospel Law is written in his heart, while Israel's sons look on.
Yes, the powers of heaven were present when the sacrament of
faith was given you; the hierarchies of angels, the Church of
the firstborn, were there [cf. Heb. xii. 23]. If we realize that
'Israel' means 'seeing God mentally', we shall see that the
name is even more appropriate when used of the angels who
minister to us; for, as the Lord said when speaking of the
children—and you were a child yourself when you were

baptized—their angels always see the heavenly Father's face
[Matt. xviii. 10]. . . . Such were those sons of Israel who were
present, gazing on God's face, when the sacraments of faith
were given you . . ."[16] One of Origen's disciples, Didymus the
Blind, says that Baptism consists of being plunged into the
Holy Ghost in the presence of the angels.

Again, when he speaks to the Christian assembly, Origen
does not forget that in addition to the faithful themselves he
also has their angels before him. "I have no hesitation in saying
that the angels are present in our assembly too, and present
not merely as a body, as they are in every Church, but in an
individual capacity. The Lord was speaking of these angels
when he said: 'They have angels of their own . . . that behold
the face of my heavenly Father continually' [Matt. xviii. 10].
There are two Churches, a Church of men and a Church of
angels. Whenever we say anything in conformity with the real
drift and meaning of the Scriptures, the angels rejoice at it and
pray with us. And because the angels are present in the Church
—at any rate, in any Church that deserves to be called Christ's
—St. Paul orders that when women go there to pray, they
should have their heads veiled, for the angels' sake [1 Cor. xi.
10]. These are evidently the angels that stand by the saints
and rejoice over the Church. We cannot see them, because our
eyes are darkened by the filth of sin, but the Disciples saw them
—Jesus said to them: 'Believe me when I tell you this; you will
see heaven opening, and the angels of God going up and coming
down upon the Son of Man' [John i. 51]."[17]

To a much greater extent than the angels, the Lord of the
angels is present among the faithful through his δύναμις
when they are gathered together in his name. "You may look
at the Saviour now, if you will, with your own eyes, in this
assembly and in this church; for when you set the most spiritual
part of your soul to contemplate God's Wisdom, his Truth, his
only Son, your eyes do look on Jesus. Blessed was that community whose members, Scripture tells us, all had their eyes
fixed on him [Matt. xiii. 16]. If only this assembly too could
deserve the same testimonial and all of you, catechumens and
baptized Christians, men, women and children, could look at
Jesus, not with your bodily eyes but with the eyes of the soul!
When you look at him, through his grace and his gift of

contemplation, your faces shine with a clearer light and you can say: 'The light of thy countenance, O Lord, is signed upon us' [Ps. iv. 7]."[18] Harnack points out that the passage also contains interesting evidence of the presence of children at the Christian assembly.

Then there is the question of the times of prayer. First comes the daily cycle. Origen deals with it in the *De Oratione*. He thinks that a "saint's whole life . . . ought to be one long continual prayer. What is commonly called prayer is only part of this, the part that has to be offered at not less than three specific times during the day".[19] He mentions the usual texts in support of these three times for praying and then goes on to say: "If we omit this prayer, we are not using the night properly, for David says: 'I rose at midnight to give praise to thee' [Ps. cxviii. 62]."[20] This piece of evidence should be compared with that provided by the *Apostolic Tradition*, ch. 35. The distinction between actual prayer and virtual prayer should also be noted.

When we look at what Origen says about the liturgical year, we find that he regards that too from a similar point of view. The details he gives us about it are valuable for the history of its formation; they also show in what light it was regarded at the time. One of the key passages comes from the *Contra Celsum*, where he is defending the Christians against the accusation of impiety brought against them by Celsus on the ground that they would have nothing to do with the cults prescribed by the State. Why, Celsus asked, have you neither altars nor statues nor temples? What is there to prevent you from attending the public celebrations? Celsus's accusation bore on two points. It turned first of all on the fact that Christians did not take part in the worship of idols. That was one of the chief things they were blamed for. But from a more general standpoint it turned on the fact that they had neither βωμοί nor ἀγάλματα nor νεῴ. That, too, is certainly the way Origen takes it in his reply. The accusation is thus a valuable piece of evidence for the state of Christian worship at that time.

Here is Origen's reply. Celsus "does not see," he says, "that the soul of every just man among us is an altar and that sweet-smelling offerings, i.e., the prayers put forth by a good conscience, are offered on it in spirit and in truth [cf. John iv. 23].

As the Apocalypse says [v. 8] . . . the incense is the prayers of the saints. The right sort of statues and offerings to give to God are not the kind made by craftsmen. No, they are carved in our souls and given shape by the divine Logos: they are the virtues, likenesses of the Firstborn of every creature [Col. i. 15], who has patterns of all the virtues in himself—patterns of justice, prudence, fortitude, wisdom and all the others. . . . Those who are quit of the old self . . . and clothed in the new self, that is being refitted all the time for closer knowledge, so that the image of the God who created it is its pattern [Col. iii. 9–10]—those who succeed in becoming images of their Creator —carve in their own souls the sort of statue the God who reigns over all things wants to see. . . . Thus, in every just man, who strives to become as much like the Saviour as he can . . . there is a statue which is an image of God. The man carves it himself, keeping his eyes fixed on God, keeping his heart pure and trying to become like God. All Christians, in short, strive to build altars and statues like these—things not devoid of life and feeling but capable of receiving God's spirit. . . . Compare the kind of altar I mean with the kind Celsus is talking about or the sort of statue the devout erect to God in their souls with the sort produced by Phidias and Polycletes. . . . Anyone who cares to do that will see that the one kind are corruptible and in time will perish, while the others, being in immortal souls, will last." [21]

The passage is full of interest. External worship is sharply contrasted in it with worship in spirit and in truth. This is a question of capital importance in the history of Christian worship. The Jewish rites prefigured a reality beyond themselves, and Christ abolished them when he brought that reality about. As soon as the real Temple—the whole Christ—was there, there was no reason why the Temple made of stone should continue to exist. This Origen explains when he says: "We have not the slightest objection to building temples in keeping with the sort of statues and altars I have been talking about; we merely refuse to build lifeless, inanimate temples to him who is the Author of all life. If I cannot prove this to Celsus's followers except by comparing their temples with ours, I will tell them (if they will listen) how we have been taught that our bodies are temples of God. If by impurity and sin we

destroy these temples, we shall be destroyed ourselves, because
we shall really be guilty of impiety towards the true Temple.
There is a Temple superior to all else that bears the name and
different from them all—the pure and holy body of our Saviour
Jesus Christ."[22]

The idea that emerges from this passage is of first-rate importance for the theology of the presence of God. Under the old
covenant, the presence of God was restricted to the material
temple at Jerusalem, but from the time of the Incarnation ("The
power of the Most High shall overshadow thee") it has dwelt
in the human nature of Jesus and his members. The presence
of God is to be found in the Christian community, not in the
stone-built church; the successor of the Temple is the community. It may be noted, too, that when Origen comes to
speak of this increase in the spiritual character of worship,
he uses the same terms as Plotinus. He speaks of Christian
worship not as πνευματικόν but as νοητόν. In particular, the
image of the statue carved in the soul is typical of Plotinus,
who says: "If you can see no beauty in yourself, do what men
do when they are carving what they want to be a beautiful
statue. They remove bits here and there, they scrape, they
polish. . . . Be like them; carve away at the statue you are
making out of yourself, until the brilliance of the divine . . .
stands revealed and you see temperance seated on her holy
seat."[23] We are here dealing with a process characteristic of
Origen, the transcription of biblical ideas into the language of
Hellenistic philosophy—a process which is not a deviation but
a refraction.

And yet this increase in the spiritual character of worship
might seem to present a problem. Was there not a danger that
it would undermine the visible side of Christian worship?
Origen considers the question—as it happens, in connection
with the subject before us at the moment, the liturgical year.
He begins by reaffirming the old idea that the life of the
Christian is a continual prayer and a continual feast. "The
man who does his duty, prays without ceasing and continually
offers unbloody victims to God in his prayers, celebrates the
feast as it should be kept."[24] He quotes St. Paul's words: "You
have begun to observe special days and months, special seasons
and years. I am anxious over you; has all the labour I have

spent on you been useless [Gal. iv. 10–11]?" "But," he goes on, "suppose someone brings up against us our own observance of Sundays, the days of preparation or the paschal feast or what we do at the season of Pentecost?"[25] The passage is of great value, chiefly because it shows what the essential parts of the liturgical cycle were in Origen's day. They amounted to four: Sundays, Fridays, the Pasch, i.e., Good Friday, and the great fifty days. We see from this that in the primitive Church there was only one feast, Easter and the Easter season. Dom Casel has written a notable article on the subject.[26] There is no trace of the Epiphany or the Ascension or any other solemnity at this date.

But Origen's reply to the objection is more interesting still. "We must answer," he says, "that if a man is perfect, he is always busy in thought, word and deed with the Word of God, who is Lord by nature, and therefore it is always the Lord's day for him; he regards every day as a Sunday. The man who is all the time preparing for the true life, abstaining from the earthly pleasures that lead most people astray and refusing to harbour fleshly thoughts . . . never stops celebrating the day of preparation. Those who reflect that Christ, our Paschal Victim, has been sacrificed for us [1 Cor. v. 7] and that the feast is to be celebrated by the eating of his flesh, the flesh of the Word, are celebrating a perpetual Pasch. 'Pasch' means 'passing over', and these people are always passing over in thought, word and deed from the things of earth to God and hastening on towards the City of God. Those who can honestly say: 'We are risen with Christ' [Col. iii. 1] and: 'He has raised us up too, enthroned us too above the heavens, in Christ Jesus' [Eph. ii. 6], live in the season of Pentecost always, especially when they go into the upper room like the Apostles . . . and give themselves to prayer, asking to be made worthy of the strong wind [Acts ii. 2] that comes from heaven and destroys sin in men and all connected with sin, worthy too of some share in the tongue of fire that comes from God."[27]

The passage is of value as showing the significance ascribed to the various liturgical solemnities at this date. In particular we see from it that Easter is the feast of the passing from death to life, the mystery of the death and resurrection of Christ; while Pentecost, on the other hand, is the feast of the mystery

of Christ as seen at once in the Resurrection, the Ascension and
the coming of the Holy Ghost—a single feast of a single mystery
and not yet divided into a multiplicity of solemnities, as it was
to be in the fourth century. The other important point is that
the mysteries of Christ's life are relived, inwardly, by the
spiritually minded; their lives are a participation in these
mysteries—that is the main thing. The central idea is always
the same, viz., that the Christian's whole life is a feast. And
this is not the only place where Origen writes in the same
strain. Thus, in the homilies on Genesis he says, "You come to
church only on feast-days; but tell me, are not the other days
feast-days too? Are they not the Lord's days? The Jews had
days fixed at long intervals for the celebration of their solemnities and the Lord said to them: 'I cannot bear your new moons,
your sabbaths and your great day' [LXX, Isa. i. 13]. So, then,
God detests those who think that there is only one day set
apart for the Lord as a feast-day. Christians eat the flesh of the
lamb every day, i.e., they receive the flesh of the divine word
every day, for Christ, our Paschal Victim, has been sacrificed
for us [1 Cor. v. 7]. The laws governing the celebration of the
paschal feast prescribe that the paschal meal should be eaten in
the evening. Hence the Lord suffered in the evening of the
world to enable . . . you, who until the morning comes will
always be living in the evening, to eat the flesh of the word for
ever."[28]

The fact that this passage comes from a homily shows that
Origen did not regard the teaching in it as something to be kept
for the perfect alone. Not the perfect only but all Christians
without exception should make God's word their staple food,
for we are all living in the evening of the world and should all
keep vigil while we wait for the eternal day to dawn. Something of the eschatological expectancy of the first generations of
Christians is discernible in this. But it is also a transposition
of an old theme in philosophy which Origen had revived—the
idea of life as a continual feast is found in Aristotle, and Philo
of Alexandria had taken it from him.[29] The words in which
Origen explains the daily eating of the lamb as the eating of
the word also call for notice. They certainly do not imply a
denial of the Real Presence in the Eucharist. But Origen was
speaking to the catechumens as well as to the faithful. His own

ministry, too, was the ministry of the word, which, to his mind, was also a sacrament: a divine food was hidden away in it beneath the rind of the Scriptures. He was forbidden, in any case, by the *disciplina arcani*, to reveal the mysteries of the sacraments.

Yet this does not at all mean that he rejected outward worship and in particular the observance of liturgical feasts. He explains his position in these terms: "The mass of the faithful, who have not reached this state [the state of the perfect], either will not or cannot live in this way all the time and so need models perceptible to the senses, by way of reminder, if they are not to forget altogether. This, I think, was what Paul had in mind when he called a feast fixed for a particular day to the exclusion of any other a 'part of a feast' [Col. ii. 16]. He used that expression because he wanted to show that if you always live as God's Word would have you live, you are not just sharing in part of a feast but feasting all day and every day. Consider, again . . . whether our feasts . . . are not holier than the pagans' . . . It would take too long to explain why God's Law ordains that the bread of affliction [Deut. xvi. 3] and unleavened bread and wild lettuce [Exod. xii. 18] . . . should be eaten on feast-days. . . . Composed as he is of two parts . . . man cannot possibly celebrate the feast with the whole of himself."[30]

This shows what Origen's idea of the liturgical year was. The liturgical feast was a ὑπόμνημα, necessary as a reminder but directed to an interior, spiritual end. In another passage he explains that the perfect too ought to observe these external forms of worship. "It is reasonable enough to suppose," he says, "that the true worshipper is required to observe certain figurative practices even though he worships in spirit and in truth, to the end that by such condescension he should bring deliverance to those enslaved by the figure and lead them on to the truth the figure signifies. . . . The point to note is that not only will true worshippers worship in spirit and in truth in the future but that they are already doing so now."[31]

The memorable points in this theology of worship and the sacraments are three in number. The first is the all-important assertion that the external, figurative worship of the Old Testament has come to an end and has been replaced by

worship in spirit and in truth. The second is the no less definite
assertion that this worship in spirit and in truth, the worship
of the New Testament, has a visible side to it. The third is the
explanation given of this visible worship. On this point Origen
was still feeling his way. He did not see clearly enough that a
sacramental economy was involved, one governing the whole of
Christianity. His spiritualizing tendencies would lead him to
underestimate the importance of the visible side. But he did at
least see that this side of the matter is bound up with the fact
that man is by nature a creature with a body and a creature
meant for society—and that was the line of thought followed
by later theologians when, in their instructions on the sacraments, they set out to show that external worship satisfies the
requirements of human nature.

2. THE CHRISTIAN COMMUNITY

Origen gives us, first of all, a certain amount of general
information about the state of the Church in his time. In the
Contra Celsum, which is a piece of apologetics, he paints an
idealized picture of the Christian community and represents
Christians as living in detachment from the things of this
world.[32] In one curious passage, he compares the Christian
communities to cities. "To take an example," he says, "at
Athens the Church of God is a tractable, dependable body . . .
but the secular assembly is riddled with intrigue . . . And if you
compare the senate of God's Church with the senate of any
town, you will see that in God's Church there are senators
worthy of their position . . . whereas in the cities, the senators
show no sign at all of being superior to the other citizens. . . .
It is the same, too, if you compare the governors of the Churches
with the governors of the towns."[33]

But when he is talking to the Christian community, both in
the commentaries and in the homilies, he changes his tone and
does not hesitate to reproach the people for their faults with the
freedom of one speaking in God's name and the humility of one
who knows that he is himself the first to incur the condemnation
he is pronouncing.[34] Admittedly, there were still miracles in the
Church as in the early days. "Traces of that Holy Spirit who
appeared in the form of a dove are still to be found among

Christians. There are Christians who drive out devils, cure many diseases and see a certain amount of the future, because the Word wants them to.... Many people have been converted to Christianity almost against their wills: a . . . spirit came to them when they were dreaming, or in their waking hours, and converted them from hatred of the Logos to the desire to die for him. I could tell you of many such cases."[35] In another passage he speaks of cures made by reading the Gospel or repeating the name of Jesus.[36] But these charismata were becoming rarer and were found only among those whose "souls had been purified by the Word".[37]

And not only was this true of the extraordinary manifestations of the spirit, but faith and holiness as well were on the decline. In the homilies he composed at Caesarea just before the persecution of Decius, at a time when the Christian body was increasing in number, Origen wistfully harked back to the days of the martyrs, when Christians were more numerous and more fervent. "Actually," he says, "if we judge things as they really are and not by numbers, if we judge by people's attitude of mind and not by the crowds we see assembled, we shall see that nowadays we are not real believers at all. The days of real faith were the days when there were many martyrs, the days when we used to take the martyrs' bodies to the cemetery and come straight back and hold our assembly. They were the days when the whole Church was in mourning and the instructions the catechumens received were meant to prepare them for martyrdom and help them to acknowledge their faith right up to the moment of their death, without wavering or faltering in their belief in the living God. Christians saw amazing signs and wonders then, we know. There were few believers then but they were real ones; they followed the narrow road that leads on to life [Matt. vii. 14]. Now there are more of us who believe, but as not many can be chosen [Matt. xx. 16; xxii. 14] . . . few get as far as election and beatitude."[38]

Origen portrays the various members of the community in greater detail. First he reproaches the mass of the faithful with want of assiduity in hearing the word of God. "The Church sighs and grieves," he says; "when you do not come to the assembly to hear God's word. You go to church hardly ever on feast-days, and even then not so much out of desire to hear

the word as because you want to take part in a solemn function.
. . . The Lord has entrusted me with the task of giving his
household their allowance of food . . . [i.e., with the ministry of
the word] at the appointed time [Luke xii. 42] . . . But how can
I? Where and when can I find a time when you will listen to
me? The greater part of your time, nearly all of it in fact, you
spend on mundane things, in the market-place or the shops;
some of you are busy in the country, others wrapped up in
litigation. Nobody, or hardly anybody, bothers about God's
word. . . . But why complain about those who are not
here? Even those who are, those of you who have come
to church, are paying no attention. You can take an interest
in tales that have become worn out through repetition, but
you turn your backs on God's word and the reading of Holy
Scripture."[39]

He makes similar criticisms elsewhere, thereby giving a
picturesque sketch of the sort of assembly that might be found
at the time. "There are some of you who leave as soon as you
have heard the lessons read," (i.e., before the homily), he says,
"without making any effort to get at the meaning . . . or
comparing one text with another. . . . Others have not even the
patience to wait until the reading of the lessons is over. . . .
Others do not even know that the lessons are being read, but
stand in the most distant corners of the Lord's house and talk
about secular things."[40] "How many of us are present in mind
as well as in body when God's word is being explained? Some
take to heart what is read, but others . . . have their hearts and
minds set on business matters, on what is going on in the world
or on financial calculations. Women . . . think about their
children, their needlework or their household affairs."[41] Elsewhere again he complains of the failure of his efforts to interest
the young men in Scripture study. "I often urge the young
men to apply themselves to the study of Scripture. But as far as
I can see, the only result is that I have wasted my time. I have
never succeeded in inducing any of them to study the Bible."[42]
In particular, he attacks those Christians who believe the true
faith but live in sin. "There are people in the Church who
certainly have faith in God and accept all his commandments;
they are even respectful and considerate to God's servants . . .
and always ready to decorate the church and give service. But

in their actions and way of living they are sunk in vice and are not at all quit of the old self [Eph. iv. 22]."[43]

In another interesting passage he shows how the old Christian families despised the converts, although they were themselves inferior to the converts. "The fact that they have only recently been converted or that their parents are unsatisfactory," he says, "need not stop them from quickly rising higher than many of those who have grown old, so to say, in the faith, if they are generous in the combat and observe the commandments. Those who boast that they were brought up as Christians by their parents have a combat to face, too, if they are to destroy their pride, especially where they boast of having parents or ancestors who were considered worth putting in the bishop's seat or promoting to the dignity of the priesthood or the diaconate for the service of God's people. . . . Do you realize that there is no ground . . . either for boasting of being 'first' [Matt. xx. 16] or for behaving as though you were less than the 'first' simply because you came to Christianity after they did?"[44] This gives us a glimpse of the sort of opposition there was to the newly-acquired elements in the community on the part of the old Christian families.

These divisions in the community arose not merely from differences of a religious kind but from social distinctions as well. There were people who were snobbish about their ancestry. "Some people set themselves up above the rest because they are the children of leading citizens and belong to families which have produced men who are considered great because they have held public office. Such people are proud of a thing indifferent in itself and independent of the will; they have no justification for their pride. Others think highly of themselves because they have power over human lives and have attained the eminence, as they call it, of having the right to cut off men's heads. . . . Others pride themselves on their wealth, though it is not real wealth but is good only for this world. Others again . . . are proud of having a fine house or vast estates."[45] To complete the list of the commonest vices, we should have to add to coteries in the community and neglect of religion, drunkenness,[46] the frequenting of immoral shows,[47] anger with servants, and immorality.[48]

A certain number of groups stood out from the community

and constituted the hierarchy. Origen enables us to see something of the way in which the Church was organized in his
day. The various categories found in the second century—
bishops, priests and deacons, doctors, virgins, monks and lay-
people—are again met with in his writings. But in the meantime, the organization of the Church had assumed a more
definite form. Some groups—the prophets and the widows—
he scarcely mentions. The clerical hierarchy was tending to
absorb the functions of the doctors and prophets. Origen shows
great severity towards it. He attacks the clergy for their
ambition. "Even in Christ's Church," he says, "men are
found who accept banquets . . . and like to occupy the highest
places at them. Some intrigue to be made deacons . . . then
aspire to the priest's . . . office, and some, not content with that,
intrigue to obtain bishop's rank."[49]

He reproaches the clergy, too, for their pride. "Sometimes
we have more pride than the gentile princes, wicked as they
are, and we all but give ourselves bodyguards, like kings. We
terrify people and make ourselves inaccessible, especially if
they are poor. If anyone comes and asks us to do something for
him, we are more insolent to him than the cruellest tyrants and
princes would be to their petitioners. You can see this happen
in many a well-known Church, particularly in the big cities."[50]
Other clerics, he tells us, both bishops and priests, tried to
feather the nests of members of their own families instead of
filling high ecclesiastical positions with men fit to occupy them.

We may also note the passages in which he alludes to the
injustice some of the faithful fell victims to when they were
excluded from the community *non recto judicio.* "It sometimes
happens that a man who has been turned out is really still
inside, and one who seems to be inside may really be outside."[51] This may be an allusion to his own expulsion from
Alexandria. In another place he reminds the bishops that one
of their responsibilities is to keep the faithful alive to the duty
of charity towards the poor.[52] It would be easy to produce
other passages containing general criticisms of the clergy.[53]
He also gives a reminder that heads of Churches are not allowed
to make a second marriage.[54]

But this external criticism of the lives of the clergy hides a more
fundamental attitude, which involves a certain depreciation

of the whole clerical hierarchy. "Anyone can celebrate solemn liturgical functions before the people, but there are not many men who lead holy lives and know a great deal about Christian doctrine, men of proved wisdom and undoubted capacity for teaching others the truth about things."[55] Origen contrasts the external hierarchy with the spiritual one, the hierarchy dependent on holiness. This latter hierarchy, with its three grades—beginners, those busy acquiring perfection, and the perfect—was the one men ought to want to belong to. In saying this, he did not mean to deny the existence of the visible hierarchy. "I admit that it is one thing to discharge the functions of the priesthood and quite another to be learned and perfect in every way." All the same, he did belittle the external hierarchy to some extent, because his sacramental view of things led him to make it a mere figure of the inner hierarchy. "Bishop, priest and deacon symbolize what they contain."[56]

His ideal was the "doctor", who was at once a man of deep spiritual life, a speculative thinker and an exegete. It can be seen emerging in the second century from the raw material provided by the lives of the gnostic *didaskaloi* and it attained its ideal realization in Origen himself. It had originally constituted a specific office in the community, distinct from the priesthood. Origen's own history shows that the period was one in which the organization of the Church was becoming more uniform. Lay doctors still had the right to speak to the Church in Palestine but they had not in Alexandria. That was why Origen had himself ordained. The teaching office, then, was being incorporated into the priesthood and becoming simply one aspect of the priesthood. Such was the state of affairs even in Origen's time.[57] Nevertheless, of the two functions of the priesthood, the one that occupied the more prominent position in his estimation was the ministry of the word. All his works converge more on the sacrament of Scripture than on the sacrament of worship. The principle involved was linked to one of the most notable phenomena in the life of the Church during the second century. On the one hand, there were two streams of activity in the community, one coming from the doctors and one from the *episcopi*; while side by side with that, each community tended to have a group of spiritually minded men, possessing the rudiments of a more advanced type of knowledge and inclining to consider themselves superior to the general run of the faithful. The book to refer to on the point is Damian van den Eynde's masterly work *Les normes de l'enseignement chrétien dans la littérature patristique des trois premiers siècles* (1933). Fr. Lebreton has also dealt with the question in an important article in the *Revue d'histoire Ecclésiastique* (1924, pp. 481 et seq.) entitled "Le désaccord de la foi populaire et de la théologie savante dans l'Eglise chrétienne au IIIe siècle".

A magnificent passage from the homilies on Leviticus will serve as an introduction to the subject.

> The priest who takes away the skin of the victim offered in holocaust . . . is the man who removes the veil of the letter from God's word and reveals the members—the spiritual meaning—behind. These members, this inner meaning of the word, he puts down not just anywhere but on the altar; the place he puts them in is raised above the ground and holy. In other words, the men he reveals God's mysteries to are not the undeserving, whose lives are base and earthy, but those who are God's altars, those in whom the divine fire, continually consuming the flesh of the victim, never ceases to burn. It is on men like that that the victim of the holocaust is placed and divided limb from limb. The man who divides the victim limb from limb is the one who can systematically explain and show with the proper distinctions what degree of spiritual progress is involved in touching the fringe of Christ's garment and what in washing his feet with one's tears and wiping them with the hair of one's head. He can show, too, how anointing Christ's head with scented ointment implies more than that and how resting on his bosom indicates a still more advanced state.
>
> To explain the reasons for all that and set some before beginners, others before people who have already acquired some knowledge of Christ's faith and others again before the perfect in charity . . . is to divide the victim limb from limb. And suppose a man can show that the Law was only a beginning, that the prophets were a great advance on the Law and that the fulness of perfection is found in the Gospel. Or again, suppose he can tell you how the word should be given like milk to those who are little children in Christ,

how it should be used like vegetables to restore strength to those whose faith is weak and how it can provide solid, nourishing food for building up Christ's athletes. Anyone who can reason about that spiritually and see the distinctions involved—any *didaskalos* of that kind—may be considered to be the priest who divides the victim limb from limb and puts it on the altar. [58]

The same outlook is discernible here as in Origen's theology of worship. The visible, figurative priesthood of the Old Testament has been succeeded by a spiritual priesthood in the New. The Christian community consists of a hierarchy in which every Christian has a place corresponding to the degree of spiritual perfection he has attained, and the business of the *didaskalos* is to give each class of soul the food it needs. The different aspects of himself that Jesus manifests in the Gospel (to the woman with the issue of blood he shows himself a Healer, to the sinful woman a Redeemer, to Mary of Magdala and John the beloved disciple a Master) symbolize the different ways in which he should be presented to different classes of people. And we are to notice that the woman with the issue of blood touches the fringe of his garment, the sinful woman his feet, the Magdalen his head and John his heart. This passage is absolutely typical of Origen; the same ideas often occur elsewhere in his works. It will be seen how he has transposed the levitical priesthood: the altar is now any saintly soul and in particular any woman consecrated to God. He uses the image elsewhere, too.

The priest is the doctor, for since the New Law has altars of living souls in place of stone-built altars, its priests must be those who offer these souls the Victim, must be, that is, the men who give them Christ in the likeness of the Word, the living Logos who is the food of living souls. The Logos is present in the Scriptures but hidden under the husk of the letter. The priest's business is to analyse the letter and bring out the various facets of the Logos hidden beneath it—the various members of the Logos—and to put before every soul the facet it needs, according to the degree of spiritual progress it has attained. Thus, the levitical priesthood is brought to its fullness in the ministry of the word. The one was a figure, the

other is the reality. But the perennial difficulty recurs once
more; it is not quite clear from the passage what position is
occupied in the New Testament by the visible priesthood, any
more than by visible worship. As Origen sees it, the Church is
the hierarchy of the faithful in their various degrees of holiness,
grouped round the spiritual master, rather than the ecclesiastical
community grouped round its bishop. [59]

Another passage from the homilies on Josue presents a similar
picture. "When Jesus said, 'Listen, you that have ears to hear
with' [Matt. xiii. 9, etc.], it was because he knew that his
words were meant for the inward ear, were for the mind to
ponder on. (Hearing him speak is of no use, is it, unless you let
his words sink into your mind and stay there?) I say the same
thing now, on scriptural authority, about the reading and
explanation of the Bible to the people in church. Never let it
be said that though Jesus has been reading to you—for when
people have ears to hear him with, he does read them the Law
—he might as well not have spoken at all, as far as the majority
of you are concerned. Jesus has extended the Lord's Church to
include women, children and proselytes. . . . If we analyse
those three categories and remember that they are a sort of
extension of the Church, we shall say that the men are those
who are given solid food . . . and that by those called women,
children and proselytes we must understand the people who
still need milk . . . or vegetables. Covering the whole field of
the Church, then, we shall take . . . men to be . . . the perfect
and women those who cannot yet satisfy their needs from their
own resources and have to imitate the men and follow their
example. . . . The children will be those who came to the faith
only a short while ago and are still being fed on the milk of the
Gospel; and it will be seen that the catechumens are those who
want to join the faithful. . . . When Jesus proclaims the Law to
you and gives your minds a grasp of its spiritual meaning, do
not stay for long as proselytes, i.e., as catechumens, but go on
as soon as you can to receive God's grace. . . . If you are
children, do not be content to think childish thoughts but keep
the innocence of children [1 Cor. xiv. 20] . . . If you are
women, do all you can to become perfect like strong men." [60]

From these various passages, it can be seen that Origen
recognizes different degrees in the Christian mysteries. The

didaskalos is one who by his spiritual knowledge has succeeded in fathoming the secrets of the mysteries.[61] "The things belonging to the mysteries are hidden away in the sanctuary and only priests are allowed to approach them. Access to them is denied to all men leading animal lives and even to those who apparently have a certain amount of learning and accomplishment, if their merits and their lives have not yet raised them to the grace of the priesthood."[62] Only such *didaskaloi* as are perfect and proficient in the mystic words have access to these mysteries. And they ought not to make them public. "A priest is one who has the sacred vessels, i.e., the secrets of the mysteries of wisdom, entrusted to him. He ought to take a lesson from them and realize that he should keep them behind the veil of his conscience and not be too ready to show them in public. If circumstances require him to transmit them to the uninstructed, he should not present them without some concealment, or he will be committing homicide and destroying the people."[63] The idea recurs elsewhere. The *didaskaloi* are "those who dispense God's word in the Church. They should therefore listen, to make sure that they will not be entrusting God's words to the polluted; . . . in simple faith, they should choose souls that are pure and virgin . . . and confide to them the secret mysteries, the word of God and the hidden truths of the faith . . . that so Christ may be formed in them by faith".[64]

It should, however, be noted that the *didaskalos* is not just a man who has reached perfection and received special light through the gnosis; he has an official position in the Church as well. Thus, a man may occupy the pulpit as *didaskalos* without being worthy of it, and there may be unworthy presbyters, too. Origen says so himself. "It often happens," he says, "that men with a low, mean outlook and a relish for the things of earth belong to the upper ranks of the priesthood or occupy the pulpit as doctors. Others may be spiritual in their outlook and not at all earthbound in their lives—so much so that they can judge everything without being judged by anything themselves—and yet they will belong to one of the lower orders of the ministry or even still be among the common herd. . . . There are priests who glory in their rank as presbyters. Is that acting as their position requires, do you think? Is that doing what their office

demands? And do you consider that the way deacons behave
is in keeping with their place in the ministry? Why is it that
one so often hears people speaking ill of a bishop, a priest or a
deacon and saying: 'Look at *him*'? . . . And then there are the
virgins and monks and the people who profess to be religious."[65]

It will thus be seen that Origen was faced with two problems,
both of them created by the circumstances of the time. The
first one turned on the relationship between the visible hierarchy
of presbyters and the visible hierarchy of doctors. There were
two distinct types of authority in the early Church. Both could
be traced back to the charismata of the early days, but they
were each derived from different ones. The two hierarchies
took up different attitudes on certain points. The presbyters
turned more towards the worship of God, the *didaskaloi* rather
to the ministry of the word and to Scripture. The presbyters
regarded martyrdom as a redemptive sacrifice, the *didaskaloi*
saw it as the perfection of the gnosis. Clearly, Origen represents
the viewpoint of the *didaskaloi*. But his writings belong to a
period when the two hierarchies were showing signs of
coalescing. The teaching office was in process of becoming a
function of the priestly hierarchy. However, in Origen a certain
dualism is still perceptible. As Van der Eynde says,[66] he regards the office of doctor as belonging to the bishops and
priests; but all the same, he considers that "theoretically the
various degrees of the gnosis coincide with the degrees of the
hierarchy".

Nevertheless, he does not at all deny that ordination to the
priesthood confers special powers on the visible hierarchy. He
alludes to the ordination of priests.[67] He declares that the
"form of the Churches is given to priests".[68] Only, his idea of
Old Testament typology inclines him to think that the levitical
priesthood is brought to its perfection in the spiritual hierarchy,
the hierarchy depending on the charismata. Fr. von Balthasar
puts the matter very clearly when he says[69] that Origen hardly
states the relationship between the levitical priesthood and the
ecclesiastical hierarchy in explicit terms at all but rather takes
it as known, just as he supposes the letter of the Scriptures to be
known. As soon as he possibly can, he begins to explore the
relationship between the levitical priesthood and the priesthood
of the Mystical Body. And he never becomes reconciled to the

idea of dissociating the powers of the priesthood from the holiness of the priest.

The distinction between power and holiness was cleared up once and for all by Augustine in the Donatist controversy and it later gave rise to the doctrine of sacramental character. But we may agree with Fr. von Balthasar, all the same,[70] that the Church cannot regard the identification of the two hierarchies as a vain chimera; it is a strictly necessary requirement. Augustine's resignation to the actual state of affairs is part of the truth, but Origen's refusal to admit that unworthy clerics can communicate grace nevertheless expresses a demand for holiness which is also part of the truth. It shows not that he looked down on the priesthood but that he had a great regard for it, because he would have had every priest a saint. In other words, what Origen gives us here, as elsewhere, is evidence of the existence of a visible priesthood and some idea of the significance of that priesthood. But he does not dwell on that side of it, because, to his mind, what matters is not the institution but holiness, the spiritual reality behind it. The point of view is very like the one we saw him taking over the theology of the worship of God.

III

ORIGEN'S THEOLOGY OF THE SACRAMENTS

I N THE passage in the homilies on Numbers where he
enumerates some of the rites forming part of the unwritten
παράδοσις, after mentioning prayer towards the east and
prayer in a kneeling position, Origen speaks of the "words,
gestures, rites and questions occurring in Baptism, and the
eucharistic rites ".[1] His theories about the sacraments form one
of the most difficult and controversial elements in his teaching,
particularly where Penance and the Eucharist are concerned.
The only general study of the question is Fr. von Balthasar's
essay, "Le mysterion d'Origène". Harnack's book mentioned
above also provides a collection of essential passages. I will say
a word or two about each of the three sacraments mentioned
above and in each case set out the evidence provided by Origen
about the sacramental practice of his time and also show what
views he held himself, as I did in the case of Christian worship
and the hierarchy.

1. BAPTISM

Origen's teaching on Baptism occupies a place apart in his
theology of the sacraments.[2] His ideas on the question are just
as much an expression of the Church's tradition as his conception of the worship of God is a consequence of his personal
standpoint as a *didaskalos*. His teaching on Baptism and what
he says about redemption and martyrdom form a single block
uninfluenced by the speculations we find him making elsewhere. This must be attributed to the fact that there was a
definite tradition in the community about those doctrines even
at that period. Also, in the case of Baptism, Origen had soaked
himself in the common tradition when he was a catechist.

With regard first of all to the discipline observed in connection with Baptism in Origen's day, we must note that a

beginning had been made at organizing the catechumenate. In the early Church, when a pagan wanted to become a Christian, he would go to a relation or friend and get him to instruct him and present him to the head of the community. We have a picturesque echo, a caricature rather, of this clandestine Christian propaganda in Celsus's *True Discourse*, which Origen quotes in his refutation. By way of attack on the Christians for their proselytising, Celsus had written: "Woolworkers, shoe-makers, fullers and men without any sort of education or culture can be seen in people's houses. As long as the masters, men of mature age and sound judgement, are there, they dare not say a word; but if they manage to draw aside a few children or women, as wanting in commonsense as they are themselves, they at once begin to talk of wonders."[3] This caricature shows what the situation was like at the time when Celsus was writing, i.e., at the end of the second century.

In his reply, however, Origen describes the situation obtaining in his own day. He protests against the assertion that the catechists were like the itinerant philosophers of the time. Those philosophers "speak in public," he says, "and do not choose their hearers; people stop and listen as they please. Christians begin, as far as possible, by testing the dispositions of those who want to hear them. They instruct them in private and then, when their pupils . . . have shown that they are keeping their resolution to lead good lives, they admit them to the community. Newcomers who have not yet received the sacrament of purification are put into a special group and another group is formed of those who seem to have given proof of a firm intention not to do anything unbefitting a Christian. . . . People are appointed to make enquiries about the lives and conduct of new members."[4] This amounted to an organized catechumenate. It was the germ of the catechumenate as we know it in the fourth century, by which time it had reached its final stage of development. It now consisted, in the first place, of an indeterminate period during which the candidate was in sympathetic contact with Christianity and was instructed by private persons; after which came the time of the catechumenate, the time of instruction, properly so-called, during which instruction and training were given by people appointed for the purpose.

The question has been dealt with by Dom B. Capelle in his article on the introduction of the catechumenate at Rome[5] and by Fr. Lebreton in his essay on the development of ecclesiastical institutions at the end of the second century.[6]

As he had been a catechist himself, Origen's testimony to the content of the ordinary pre-baptismal catechesis is of great value. The preparation given in the catechesis was to some extent a moral one; hence he has much to say about the dispositions necessary for Baptism. The point was one on which the early writers dwelt at length, for the simple reason that initiation into the pagan mysteries did not require any moral transformation at all: it was not conversion. Nock brings this out in his excellent book, *Conversion*.[7] It was essential, then, to stress the fact that Christianity did imply a moral transformation. "If a man wishes to be baptized, let him go forth. For if a man remains in the state he was in before and does not abandon his former habits and conduct, he certainly cannot present himself for Baptism in the proper frame of mind. Hence, all that [John the Baptist] said to them [i.e., to those who came to him to be baptized] he says to you as well, catechumens, since you too are preparing for Baptism."[8] And again: "Go and repent, catechumens, if you want to receive Baptism for the remission of your sins. . . . No one who is in a state of sin when he comes for Baptism can obtain the remission of his sins. Therefore, I beg you, show the utmost care and circumspection before you come to be baptized; show the acceptable fruit of repentance [Matt. iii. 8]. Live pure lives for a time . . . and then you will obtain the remission of your sins."[9]

Origen often addresses the catechumens in his homilies, as they formed part of his audience. He lays great stress on the necessity of moral conversion before Baptism. "If you want to receive Holy Baptism . . . you must first learn about God's word, cut away the roots of your vices, correct your barbarous wild lives and practice meekness and humility. Then you will be fit to receive the grace of the Holy Spirit."[10] And again he says: "Go and repent, catechumens, if you want to receive Baptism for the forgiveness of your sins."[11] He always stresses the importance of receiving the sacraments in the right frame of mind. He even goes so far as to say that no one who comes for Baptism *peccans* can obtain the remission of his sins.[12] And with reference to the symbolism of Baptism, he writes: "You must first die to sin if you would be buried with Christ."[13]

But while stressing the importance of the right dispositions for receiving the sacrament, he also teaches that the sacrament produces its effect by its own inherent virtue. In a passage well worth noting, he compares it with the miraculous cures performed by Christ. "The amazing δυνάμεις," he says, "in the cures the Saviour wrought, were symbols of the healing the Logos has always bestowed—healing of sickness and infirmity of every kind. But even as physical cures, they were effective in bringing such people to the faith as had received the necessary grace. In the same way, when a man offers himself to God, the bath of water, which is a thing for cleansing, symbolizes the cleansing of his soul from all stain and malice; but it is also a principle or source of divine grace, just as much as the virtue in prayer to the adorable Trinity."[14] The parallel here drawn between Christ's humanity and the visible rite as instruments of grace deserves the closest attention. It puts the sacramental question in exactly the right perspective.

But the catechist's business is not simply to prepare the heart; he has to instruct the mind as well. Hence Origen defines the nature of the baptismal "grace": it is a mystery that involves dying with Christ and rising with him. "To be baptized is to be baptized in Christ's death; through Baptism we are buried with him in death."[15] He sees this mystery in the exodus. "We will make a three days' journey into the desert and offer sacrifice to the Lord our God. These are the three days that Moses was eager for, the days that Pharaoh set his face against [Exod. v. 3]. . . . He would not allow the children of Israel to reach the place where miracles were to be wrought; he would not let them go far enough to enjoy the mysteries of the third day. The prophet says, remember, that on the third day the Lord 'will raise us up again, to live in his presence anew' [Osee vi. 3]. For us, the first of these days is the day the Lord suffered, the second the one on which he went down to hell, the third the day of the Resurrection. Thus it was that on the third day God went before them, 'by day in a pillar of cloud, by night in a pillar of fire' [Exod. xiii. 21]. If the Apostle is right, as we said above that he was, in telling us that these words refer to the sacrament of Baptism, it follows that those who have

been taken up into Christ by Baptism have been taken up into
his death and buried with him, and with him they will rise from
the dead on the third day [Rom. vi. 3]; for as the Apostle says,
God has 'raised us up too, enthroned us too above the heavens,
in Christ Jesus' [Eph. ii. 6]. When, therefore, you receive the
mystery of the third day, the Lord himself will begin to guide
you and show you the way of salvation."[16] Two of St. Paul's
explanations of Baptism have been merged together in this
passage: there is an allusion on the one hand to 1 Cor. x. 2—
Baptism in the cloud and in the sea—and on the other to Rom.
vi. 3—Baptism as dying with Christ and rising again with him.

Another thing about Baptism that appealed immensely to
the early Christians was its efficacy as a means of deliverance
from the devil's power. This too is found in Origen. Here
again, the topic that leads him on to the subject is the exodus
from Egypt. He mentions the exodus in connection with St.
Paul's interpretation of it—"Nobis . . . qualem tradiderit de his
Paulus Apostolus intelligentiae regulam videamus"[17]—and
then goes on to say: "You see what a difference there is between
the literal sense and what Paul tells us. What the Jews thought
was a mere crossing of the sea, Paul calls Baptism; what they
believed to be a cloud, Paul declares was the Holy Spirit." The
only use he makes of this interpretation is in connection with
the point we are concerned with at the moment—a point of
great importance for the light it sheds on the significance the
early Christians attached to Baptism. "If [Paul] calls this
[crossing] Baptism, conferred . . . in the cloud and in the sea,
it is that you, who have been taken up into Christ by Baptism
in water and the Holy Spirit, may know that the Egyptians are
in pursuit of you too and want to get you back into their service.
By Egyptians I mean 'those who have the mastery of the world'
and the 'malign influences' you used to serve [Eph. vi. 12].
They make every effort to pursue you but you go down into the
water, where you are safe and sound. Cleansed from your sins,
you come up a new man, ready to sing the new song."[18] This
brings out one of the essential things about Baptism—its
implication that the devil's sway is renounced and Christ's
kingship accepted. It is to this side of Baptism that the catechumen's renunciation of Satan and his confession of faith in
Christ belong. The connecting-link between Baptism and the

theory that the redemption was a victory over Satan is also furnished by it. And martyrdom is a continuation of it, for martyrdom too can be regarded as victory over Satan. All this represents the side of Origen's teaching where he faithfully echoes the belief of the whole Church, because he is delving deep down into his own experience of Christianity, the experience he acquired as a catechist and as a martyr.

As Origen sees it, then, Baptism is a mystery involving death and resurrection, rejection of the devil's rule and entry into Christ's kingdom; but it is much else besides. It is a new birth, and a sharing in God's nature through charity;[19] it means being added to the body of the Church;[20] it is a return to paradise[21] and an anointing of priests.[22] To take only one of his descriptions, the one referring to Baptism as a mystical union between Christ and the soul, we find him saying: "Everywhere, you see, the mysteries correspond; the figures of the Old Testament and the figures of the New are in harmony. In the Old Testament, Jacob goes to the wells and their water to find his wives; the Church's union with Christ is celebrated in the water-bath."[23]

We have seen that Origen generally expounds the theology of Baptism with the aid of figures taken from the Old Testament. In that too, he depended on the existing methods of catechetical instruction. As a trace of his dependence on the traditional typology in exegesis, it is all the more interesting in that habitually his mind worked on quite different lines. The crossing of the Red Sea was one of the things traditionally taken as figures of Baptism, the Jordan was another. "In support of the idea that the Jordan is of sovereign virtue and very good to drink, I may with advantage mention Naaman the Syrian and the healing of his leprosy. . . . Just as no man is good save God the Father [Matt. xix. 17], so no river is good save the Jordan. No other river can rid a man of leprosy, but this one can if the man has faith and washes his soul in Jesus."[24] A further episode is the crossing of the Jordan by Elias and Eliseus. "It should be noted, too, that before Elias was carried off by the whirlwind 'as it were to heaven', he took his mantle and folded it together and struck the water with it. The water divided in two and both Eliseus and he crossed over [4 Kings ii. 8]. Through being thus baptized in the Jordan—for Paul, as I have said, calls this miraculous crossing of the water Baptism—Elias was made

fitter to be carried up on high."[25] The passage throws light
on those mysterious lines in Clement of Alexandria's *Eclogæ
Propheticæ* which run: "Does not Baptism itself, the sign of
regeneration, mean escaping from matter through the great,
impetuous flood of the Saviour's teaching? . . . The river of
matter was divided, was torn asunder by two prophets, wielding
the power of the Lord."[26]

However, although he uses a traditional theme in his treatment of the question, Origen gives it a form of his own. Two
figures of Baptism—the crossing of the Red Sea and the crossing
of the Jordan—were known to Tradition. They were used
indifferently. Origen combined them both and looked on them
as two separate stages in the process of initiation into Christianity. "You have only just forsaken the darkness of idolatry,"
he says, "and now you want to come and hear the word of
God. You are beginning, then, by forsaking Egypt. When you
have joined the catechumens and begun to obey the commandments of the Church, you will have crossed the Red Sea. . . .
You may then come to the sacramental fount of Baptism and in
the presence of the priests and levites receive initiation into the
mysteries, those venerable, majestic mysteries which no one
may be taught unless it is right and proper that he should be.
You will thus with the priests' help have crossed the Jordan
and you will enter the Promised Land."[27] Here the entire
journey, from the departure from Egypt to the arrival in the
Promised Land, prefigures the various stages in the process of
initiation into Christianity. It is a typical instance of Origen's
manner. He alludes to the common interpretation but he
develops it on lines of his own.

So far, we have seen what Origen's ideas were on preparation
for Baptism and on Baptism itself. But a further point still
remains—Baptism gives the soul the principle of spiritual life
but it is only the first stage in that life. This is made quite plain
in the moral sphere by Origen's reproaches to the faithful who
formed his audience in the church at Caesarea. He reproaches
them with being unfaithful to the grace they received at their
Baptism. "Not all who are sprung from Israel are truly
Israelites [Rom. ix. 6]," he says, "and not all who have been
washed in the water have therefore been washed by the Holy
Spirit. . . . There were catechumens in the Bible, I see, who

were found worthy to have the grace of the Holy Spirit after Baptism, while others were not. . . . You may be sure that there are still men like Cornelius among the catechumens and men like Simon among the faithful."[28] The whole of the spiritual life ought to develop, as Fr. Hugo Rahner so clearly shows, from the grace given at Baptism.

A further question concerns the relationship between baptism with water and the baptism that will take place at the end of time. As Origen sees it, there are three kinds of baptism—the purely figurative baptism of the Old Testament and John the Baptist; Christian baptism, which is at once the reality signified by the Old Testament figures and a figure of the reality to come; and lastly, baptism with fire, which will be conferred on Christians before they enter into glory. This is very well brought out by Fr. von Balthasar,[29] when he says that the "sacrament is at once a figure and the thing the figure represents. It removes all stains by the virtue inherent in it and by the same virtue takes the place of the consuming fire of the spirit. But this supposes that the recipient's dispositions are as perfect as the Apostles'. . . . Thus, far from conceiving τύπος and ἀλήθεια as irreconcilable opposites, Origen regards them both as parts of a single, many-sided analogy which has no clear-cut separation between its degrees."

The remarkable vista thus opened up enables us to establish a relationship between the various degrees of purification— Baptism, purgatory and the different kinds of purification achieved in the mystical life correspond to three aspects of one and the same truth, viz., that any creature seeking union with a God who is holiness itself must first be cleansed from all impurity and become holy in its turn. It also gives Baptism a prophetic and eschatological character, a thing well in keeping with the economy of the sacraments, although the fact is often not appreciated. Fr. de Montcheuil's article on the eschatological significance of the eucharistic meal[30] is illuminating in that respect. What is true of the Eucharist is true of Baptism as well: it takes in the whole of time. "Recolitur memoria, mens impletur gratia, futurae gloriae pignus datur." It commemorates the Passion and Resurrection, communicates grace now and is a figure of the soul's ultimate transfiguration.

The first passage in which Origen deals with the question is to be found in his *Commentary on St. Matthew.* "Those who have followed the Saviour," he says, "will sit on twelve thrones and be judges over the twelve tribes of Israel [Matt. xix. 28]. They will receive this power when the dead rise again. It will be a rebirth, a new birth. They will be made new creatures. A new earth and a new heaven [Isa. lxv. 17] will be created for them; there will be a new covenant given and a new cup. The prelude to this rebirth is what Paul calls [Tit. iii. 5] the regenerating bath which, with the newness resulting from it, renews the spirit. It may be true that no one who has had a merely natural birth is free from sin, even if he lives no longer than a day [cf. Job xiv. 4–5]. The mystery of human birth is such that every child begotten can say of himself, as David did: 'For indeed I was born in sin' [Ps. l. 7]. But it is otherwise with rebirth through the bath. All who are begotten from on high through water and the Spirit will be free from sin. Admittedly, their freedom will be, so to speak, like 'a confused reflection in a mirror' [1 Cor. xiii. 12]; but when the Son of Man comes in glory and takes his seat on his throne, there will be a further rebirth: all who then are reborn in Christ will be quite free from sin—their freedom this time will be 'face to face'. And the reason why they have obtained this rebirth will be that they were previously reborn in the bath. . . . When we are reborn of water, we are buried with Christ. When we are reborn . . . of fire and the Spirit, we shall become like Christ's body . . . on its throne in glory, and we shall sit on the twelve thrones ourselves—at least, we shall if we have forsaken everything, through Baptism especially, and followed him."[31]

This admirable passage applies to the sacramental order St. Paul's teaching about the contrast between the *speculum* and seeing face to face. Baptism is a rebirth *in speculo*, i.e., it is a real rebirth but it is only a shadow of the final, complete purification; the two rebirths are one a continuation of the other. A whole theology of the sacraments could be built on that foundation. Yet Origen does not determine the nature of the second rebirth, the one preceding the soul's entry into glory. He does, however, treat the question in greater detail in the twenty-fourth homily on St. Luke, where he asks: "When does Jesus baptize with the Holy Spirit and when does he baptize with fire? Does he do both at the same time or each at a different time? . . . 'There is a Baptism with the Holy Spirit,' he said, 'which you are to receive, not many days from this' [Acts i. 5]. The Apostles were baptized with the Holy Spirit after his ascension into heaven [Acts ii. 4], but Scripture does not say that they were baptized with fire. Just as John was waiting to baptize some of the people who came to the banks of the Jordan, while others he turned away, so will the Lord Jesus stand in the river of fire with the sword of fire, and every man who wants to go to paradise when he departs this life and needs to be purified he will baptize in that river and bring to his desired goal, but he will refuse to baptize in the river of fire those who do not bear the marks of the first baptism. The reason is that a man must first be baptized with water and the Spirit, so that when he comes to the river of fire he can show that he has kept the purity conferred by the water and the Spirit and deserves to be baptized by Jesus Christ with fire."

These lines have been studied at length by C. E. Edsman.[32] We have no need to examine the eschatological ideas they presuppose or the origin of those ideas; it will be sufficient to observe that Origen brings two themes together, the theme of the sword of fire guarding paradise and the theme of an eschatological river of fire. The important thing for us to note is that this eschatological theme is built round Baptism. It occurs elsewhere, too, in Origen's works. In the homilies on Exodus (6, 3), it is correlated with the theme of the Red Sea, which destroys sinners and allows the just to pass through without taking hurt. It takes his theology of Baptism into the field of eschatology and is the final touch which makes it a perfect expression of the common faith of the Church.

2. THE EUCHARIST

With the Eucharist, on the other hand, we come back to Origen's personal views. His eucharistic teaching never aroused controversy in the early Church, yet it is one of the points which have attracted most attention from modern theologians. Protestants have appealed to him in support of their symbolical theory of the Eucharist and their denial of the Real Presence. Catholics have had no difficulty in showing that certain passages

clearly state that Christ is really present in the Eucharist, but
the obviously symbolical passages they generally reject as having
no connection with it.[33] Separating the two classes of passages
like that, however, means doing violence to Origen's ideas and
arises, as Fr. von Balthasar has shown,[34] from a failure to
understand the peculiar point of view from which he looked at
things. Here as always, to understand what he thought about
the sacraments it is essential to bear three things in mind. The
first is his idea of typology: the institutions of the Old Testament prefigured the invisible things of the New—they did not
refer to the visible Church. In the second place, as a *didaskalos*,
he stressed the sacrament of preaching much more than the
sacrament of the liturgy. In the third place—and here his
Platonist turn of mind becomes evident—he was interested in
the visible signs of worship only in so far as they were signs of
spiritual things. Making allowances for this, we can see that
he by no means denied the reality of the Eucharist but that for
these three reasons he would be led to minimize it. His testimony to it will therefore be all the more valuable.

We have seen that in the passage from the homily on Numbers which we began with, Origen talks about explaining the
way in which the Eucharist was received and the rites it was
celebrated with.[35] No plainer allusion to the sacrament of the
Eucharist could be desired. The *Contra Celsum* contains another
interesting passage: "We give thanks to the Creator of the
universe and eat bread which has been offered with thanksgiving [εὐχαριστία] and prayer . . . It has become in some sense
a body consecrated by prayer and, for those who use it in the
proper frame of mind, a source of sanctification."[36] Here we
have a definite allusion to the prayer for consecrating the bread
—the prayer called the Eucharist—the effect produced by the
consecration, the sanctifying effects of Communion and the
dispositions required for Communion. The passage could not
be clearer. Further on we read: "We have a sacrament, with
which we give thanks to God—the Bread called the Eucharist."[37] Far from weakening the force of the previous quotation,
as has been maintained, these lines really confirm it. And there
are two other distinct allusions to rites accompanying the
Eucharist. The first concerns the kiss of peace: "In consequence
of this text [Rom. xvi. 16] and others like it, the custom grew

up and is still observed that after prayers in church the brethren
should kiss one another. The Apostle calls this kissing holy.
He thereby shows us that the kisses given in church are not
impure and, secondly, that they ought not to be hypocritical.
. . . The kisses the faithful give one another . . . should be the
fruit of peace and sincerity and unfeigned charity."[38] Another
passage alludes to the practice of receiving the consecrated
Bread in the right hand. "Those of you who often come to the
celebration of the divine mysteries know how, when you receive
the Lord's body, you hold it with great care and reverence, for
fear that a particle should fall and something of the gift you are
holding should be lost."[39]

Thus, Origen does say something about the eucharistic
ceremonies, but, as in the case of Baptism, the point he stresses
most is that special dispositions are necessary for the worthy
reception of the sacrament. There was nothing he found more
uncongenial than the sort of theory that dwells exclusively on
the efficacy of the sacrament as such and minimizes the spiritual
side. The following passage, being clear and fairly general in
scope, will serve for our first quotation: "You make light of
God's judgments [on the negligent] and the Church's warn-
ings," he says. "You are not afraid to come to the Eucharist
and receive Christ's body in Communion, as though you were
pure and innocent and not in the least undeserving, and you
think that God will not judge you for it. You never think of the
text: 'Many of your number want strength and health'
[1 Cor. xi. 30]. Why do many want strength? Because they
do not see what they are, or examine themselves, or realize
what it means to communicate in church and come to such
great, such exalted sacraments."[40] Here we have as it were an
echo of the protestations of humility later found in the prayers
that came to precede the eucharistic liturgy.

But we must face the fact that in other passages Origen
stresses the dispositions of the recipient to such an extent that
he seems to leave no room for the action of the sacrament as
such. That is the case in the following important though
difficult passage: "With regard to the Lord's body, its virtue is
communicated to all who partake of it, provided that they
receive this bread with a clean mind and an innocent conscience.
Thus, if we do not eat this bread that has been sanctified by the

word of God and prayer [1 Tim. iv. 5], we do not by the mere
fact of not eating it lose any benefit, nor, if we do eat it, do we
[by the mere fact of eating it] gain any benefit. Loss is caused
by malice and sin, and the cause of gain is right living and
virtuous conduct. As Paul says: 'We gain nothing by eating,
we lose nothing by abstaining' [1 Cor. viii. 8]."[41] The passage
is of interest, first of all because of the distinct allusion in it to
the consecration, but still more for the strong emphasis it lays
on the necessity of being in the right frame of mind if the grace
given through Communion is to be received with profit.
Origen might even seem to be denying any efficacy to the
sacrament as such. But we have seen that that was certainly
not what he intended. What he means is simply that the
material eating as such, apart from the spiritual dispositions of
the recipient, is of no use to the soul. He had, moreover, already
explained that the bread "sanctified by the word of the Lord
and prayer does not necessarily sanctify all who partake of it.
If it did, it would also sanctify those who eat the Lord's bread
unworthily".

The explanation he gives after this is not clear. He dis-
tinguishes between two different elements in the "food sanctified by the word of God and prayer". "As matter, it goes into
the belly and is evacuated; as something that has been prayed
over, it benefits the recipient in proportion to his faith [Rom.
xii. 6] and enables the mind to see where benefit lies. The
material bread is of no benefit to those who eat it, even if the
way they eat it is not unworthy of the Lord. What is of benefit
to them is the word spoken over the bread." That is clumsily
put, but the thought behind it is clear. Origen is saying that
what sanctifies is the sacrament, yet not the bread as such
but the bread plus the prayer said over it. It remains true,
however, that he seems to envisage the bread from two points
of view. Thomist theologians make a distinction between the
substantia and the *species*. Origen, being more of a Platonist,
seems to recognize two zones of existence, the corruptible
matter apparent to the senses and the incorruptible reality of
Christ's body.

It is thus beyond question that his theology of the Eucharist
is orthodox, even if he is sometimes not too sure of the best way
to formulate it. But it is true all the same—and this fits in with

his general theories about worship—that he somewhat under-
rates the Eucharist as compared with the spiritual eating of the
Word in Scripture. "This is said," he continues, "of the typical
and symbolical body. The same could be said of the Word
himself, who became flesh and a real food." Here again we see
the contrast coming out between the two kinds of eating, the
eating of the Sacramental Body and the eating of the Word
himself in his word. And we find the same contrast elsewhere
too. It is one of the constants in Origen's theology of the
Eucharist. Thus, he writes in the homilies on Numbers, "we
are said to drink Christ's blood not only in the sacramental rites
but when we receive his words". [42] Here the contrast between
the two sacraments, the sacrament of the rite and the sacrament
of the word, is very clear. And of these two ways of receiving
the Word, Origen seems to prefer the second. Thus in the commentary on John he says: "It is enough if the bread and the cup
are understood by the simple as being the Eucharist, as the
common interpretation has it; but those capable of going deeper
should take it of the Word of Truth, who is divinely promised
us as our food." [43] Similarly, in a passage we have already
quoted in part, the one where he reminds his hearers what care
Christians ought to take not to drop crumbs from the Eucharistic
Bread when It is laid on their right hands, he says: "If you take
such care to keep his body safe, and rightly so, how can you
think it less sinful to neglect God's word than to neglect his
body?" [44]

Faced with these passages, the reader will inevitably think of
what Origen says when, with reference to Easter, he contrasts
the masses who need sensible signs with the spiritually-minded
who need no more than a spiritual Easter. Visible worship and
the sacraments seem necessary for the simple only. Spiritual
eating is plainly asserted to be superior to material. In this
connection, it should be noted that as Origen sees it, bread is a
symbol of the Logos in the Old Testament as well as in the
New. It is a figure not of the Eucharist but of the Word himself. The difficulty about determining the position occupied by
the sacramental world in his scheme of things is always the
same. In the present instance, passages giving this interpretation of texts from both the Old Testament and the New
can be found in plenty. In the homilies on Leviticus he writes:

"Our Lord and Saviour says: 'You can have no life in your-selves, unless you eat my flesh and drink my blood' [John vi. 54]. Because Jesus is absolutely and entirely pure, every bit of his flesh is food and every bit of his blood is drink, for all that he does is holy and all that he says is true. That is why his flesh is real food and his blood real drink. With the flesh and blood of his word he restores the strength of the entire human race and gives it drink."[45]

A few sentences occurring a little further on clearly show in what light these words should be understood. "Those who do not want to hear this may distort it or turn a deaf ear, like the people who said: 'How can this man give us his flesh to eat? Who can be expected to listen to him?' and walked no more in his company [John vi. 53, 61, 67]. But you, if you are children of the Church and have been taught the spiritual meaning of the Gospel, must recognize that what I say comes from the Lord. . . . You must realize that what is written in the Bible is figurative, you must study and interpret it like spiritually-minded men, not like the fleshly-minded. If you take it as the fleshly-minded do, it will do you harm instead of nourishing you. Even in the Gospel there is a letter that kills [2 Cor. iii. 6]." This shows how the various planes interacted in Origen's mind. As he sees it, the contrast here is between the material worship of the Jews, which he condemns with good reason, and Christian worship, a purely spiritual thing. As always, the significance of the visible side of Christian worship is passed over.

But it would be a mistake to suppose that he fails to recognize its importance. That he does not so fail is evident from another passage. "'[This people] will never rest till it has . . . drunk the blood of slaughtered men' [Num. xxiiii. 24]. If they deserved so much . . . how came they to drink the blood of slaughtered men, when feeding on blood was forbidden by God in such stringent terms? . . . I would like to know who this people is that is in the habit of drinking blood. When the Jews in the Gospel heard about it, they found it a stumbling-block. . . . But Christians listen and accept it and follow him who said: 'You can have no life . . . unless you . . . drink my blood' [John vi. 54]. We are said to drink Christ's blood not only in the sacramental rites but when we receive his words, for there is life in his words."[46] Here Origen is setting over against the crude, literal construction put on Christ's words by the Jews not only the eating of the word but the eating of the sacrament, which is thus brought under the heading of spiritual worship.

Only, the Eucharist represents a lower degree of spiritual worship and mystical drunkenness the heights. "This bread which God the Word declares is his body is the word that feeds men's souls, the word that comes from God the Word, bread from the Bread of Heaven. . . . And this drink which God the Word declares to be his blood is the word which is pre-eminently the heart's drink, the word that more than any other makes the drinkers of it drunk in their hearts. . . . What God the Word called his body was not the visible bread he was holding in his hands but the word in sign or sacrament of which this bread was to be broken. . . . Can the body and blood of God the Word be anything but the word that gives nourishment, the word that makes men exult?"[47] The wine that makes men drunk is the final touch. It is an allusion to the liturgical use of Psalm xxxii, which was sung during the Easter vigil and formed a kind of symbol of the sacraments. The eucharistic liturgy, then, is unquestionably the underlying subject of the passage. But the immediate subject is the ecstasy conferred on the soul by the Word—the spiritual side again, the strictly mystical side this time.

This brings us to a final consequence: with Origen a feature appeared that was henceforth to be a permanent characteristic of the theology of the sacraments in the Eastern Church, viz., the establishment of a parallel between the sacraments and the theology of the spiritual life. This characteristic makes its appearance with Origen; it was developed by Gregory of Nyssa and it received its ultimate and perfect expression from Nicholas Cabasilas. The essential article on the question is Mme Lot-Borodine's "La grâce déifiante des sacrements d'après Nicolas Cabasilas".[48] We are told that Baptism is the sacrament of initiation, Anointing the sacrament of progress and the Eucharist the sacrament of union. Each of these three degrees has one of Solomon's books corresponding to it: Proverbs corresponds to conversion, Ecclesiastes to illumination, the Song of Songs to union. "The theology of the sacraments, to which we were first introduced by the theory of rebirth through

Baptism, links up with the theology of the different stages of
the mystical life and throws open to Christians the way to union
with God, ἕνωσις—θέωσις."[49]

3. PENANCE

In Origen's teaching on Penance we shall find the same outlook as we did in the case of the other sacraments. Fr. von
Balthasar is wrong in thinking that Penance is an exception in
that respect. In this instance, as in the others, Origen lays great
stress on the recipient's dispositions. So much so that in Hal
Koch's opinion,[50] his view is that "as committing sin is not
incurring a debt but turning the will from the good, the essential thing is the return to willing the good and not the appeasing
of God's anger". In other words, Penance is simply conversion. Koch bases his theory partly on the theses put forward
by Poschmann,[51] and maintains that in the early Church,
sinners showed they were worthy of pardon merely by accepting
punishment, and that reconciliation with the Church affected
the external sphere alone and was not absolution in the dogmatic sense of the term. Koch also appeals to Origen's idea
that punishment in general is essentially directed to bringing
about the conversion of the free. The idea rests, he thinks, on a
concept of Penance as a merely external penalty meant to
promote the sinner's amendment.

Actually, Origen's views were not at all like that. Far from
supplying arguments in support of Hal Koch's thesis, his
teaching about Penance is in fact the most explicit of any in the
early Church about the part played by the priest's absolution
in the remission of sins. Here again, and here more than anywhere else, Origen provides important evidence of what the
Church believed.[52] It is true, of course, that here, as everywhere, he lays great stress on individual dispositions and on the
virtue of Penance. His idea of punishment in general as being
medicinal and educative enables him to give a positive significance to the penalties imposed by the Church and so bring
them within the general framework of his thinking. It does not
at all prevent him from holding that sins are remitted by the
Church. Here again, the most that could be said is that he
does not lay much stress on the ritual side of the sacrament,

because his mind at once goes out to the cure wrought in the sacrament by the Word.

The position is clearly stated in the second homily on Leviticus, where he writes:

When people hear what the Church's teaching is, they will perhaps say: "The ancients [i.e., the Jews] were treated better than we, since in their day, sinners could obtain pardon through sacrifices offered according to one or other of a number of rites, whereas in our case there is only one pardon for sins, the one given at the outset through the grace of Baptism. The sinner is shown no mercy and given no pardon after that." Certainly, it is fitting that the Christian should be under stricter discipline, since Christ died for him. Oxen . . . and sheep were slain for them; God's Son was put to death for you, and still you take pleasure in sin. But perhaps these thoughts may not so much stimulate you to practise virtue as make you fall into despair. Therefore, as you have heard how many sacrifices there were for sin under the Law, I want you to hear now how many ways there are in which sins can be remitted under the Gospel.

The first way is by being baptized "for the remission of sins" [Luke iii. 3]. The second is by suffering martyrdom. The third is by almsgiving, for the Lord says: "You should give alms out of the store you have, and at once all that is yours becomes clean" [Luke xi. 41]. The fourth is by bringing back a sinner from the wrong path, for Scripture says: "To bring back erring feet into the right path means saving a soul from death, means throwing a veil over a multitude of sins" [Jas. v. 20]. The sixth is by abundance of charity: the Lord himself said . . . that the woman's sins were forgiven her because she had loved greatly [Luke vii. 47]. There is also a seventh way, a hard and painful one, and that is by penance, when the sinner drenches his pillow with his tears [Ps. vi. 7] . . . and is not ashamed to confess his sin to one of the Lord's priests and ask him for a remedy. [53]

Things belonging to various categories are brought together in this passage, but the reference to sacramental confession is quite plain. How was the ministry of Penance carried out in Origen's time? He gives us valuable information on the subject himself, particularly in the passage of the *De Oratione* where he says: "There are men who have been filled by Jesus with the Spirit, like the Apostles. It can be seen from their fruits that they have received the Holy Spirit and become spiritual through being led by the Spirit, as the Son of God was, and so behaving reasonably in all respects. Such men forgive what God forgives and when sins are incurable, they retain them [John xx. 23].[54] . . . Some people arrogate to themselves a greater power than priests possess, and though they may lack the knowledge priests should have, boast that they can remit sins of idolatry, adultery and fornication . . . as if the prayers they say for people who have dared to commit these crimes wiped out even mortal sins."[55]

There are several things to note in this difficult but important passage. The first is the allusion to a prayer said for sinners by the priest, who has the power to remit at any rate some sins. Fr. Galtier considers that this is the oldest and clearest allusion to sacramental absolution that we have. The second point is the reference to sins that cannot be remitted. Origen does not mean that these sins are incapable of remission from God's side or even from the Church's; he is referring to the fact that immediate absolution is impossible. They have to be "retained"; i.e., the sinner has first to submit to penance as a preliminary to being absolved. The same interpretation is suggested by the other relevant passages. Thus, in the homilies on Leviticus, Origen reminds his hearers that under the Old Covenant adultery, which was one of the incurable sins, was punished with death, "but now", he goes on to say, "no corporal penalty is imposed, and men are cleansed from sin not by bodily suffering but by penance".[56] This penance took the form of exclusion from the community for a definite length of time and the performance of certain good works by way of expiation. Thirdly, by the very fact of distinguishing between the two classes of sin, the text does not show that in addition to public penance, which had to do with incurable sins, there was sacramental absolution, corresponding to our private penance, for the others. The final point is the degree of spiritual perfection required of the priest giving the absolution.

The most important of these points and the one concerning

which Origen's witness is of exceptional value is the distinction
between the two kinds of penance and hence the assertion that
private penance was absent at that time. He twice mentions
two classes of sins, one involving exclusion from the community and the other not. Thus, speaking of the duty incum-
bent on the Church's pastors to shut out black sheep, he says:
"When I say this, I do not mean that people should be shut out
if they commit only trifling sins."[57] Speaking of the same kind
of sins in another work, he says: "Sins like that can be atoned
for at any time; you are never forbidden to do penance for such
sins. Where graver sins are concerned, penance is allowed only
once. But these common sins, which we fall into often . . . can
be pardoned over and over again without limit."[58]

Penance for these graver sins involved the intervention of a
priest. "The layman cannot get rid of his sins on his own. . . .
He must have a priest or even someone of higher rank than
that; he needs the High Priest, the Pontiff, if he is to have his
sins remitted."[59] And again: "I will go so far as to say that
unless a man is anxious to be holy he will never think of doing
penance for the sins he commits; he cannot seek the remedy.
It is the saints who do penance for their sins. They it is who
feel their wounds, seek out a priest and ask for healing and
cleansing from the Pontiff."[60] It would be impossible to state
more clearly than this that sins of weightier moment were
remitted by absolution from a priest.

In all this, Origen is in harmony with the ancient tradition.
His personal ideas, however, come out on one point, viz., in the
connection he posits between holiness and the power to remit
sins. If he fully admits that this power is restricted to the priesthood, he nevertheless will not allow that it is exercised validly
when the priest is unworthy. "Those who claim bishop's rank,"
he says, ". . . assert that what they bind . . . on earth is bound
in heaven and what they remit on earth is remitted in heaven.
It must be admitted that what they say is sound, provided that
they are doing the work Christ had in mind when he said to
Peter: 'Thou art Peter, [and it is upon this rock that I will
build my Church]' [Matt. xvi. 18]. The gates of hell will not
prevail against the bishop when he binds and looses. But if he
is himself caught in the toils of his own wrong-doing [Prov. v.
22], he binds and looses in vain."[61] Thus, in Origen, the power

of the keys stands at the point, so to say, where the two hierarchies meet. This way of representing the question is evidence
of a time when all powers, whatever their nature might be,
were concentrated in the clerical hierarchy. But as some of
those powers seemed to Origen to require perfection for their
exercise, he wanted priests to be perfect. If he went too far in
the direction of making the power of the keys depend on
holiness, he nevertheless was right in looking on the priesthood
as a state requiring holiness the moment it takes up functions
that need holy men to discharge them. For the Church, as Fr.
von Balthasar says, [62] the identity of the two hierarchies is not
a vain chimera but a strictly necessary requirement. Origen's
attitude to the question is evidence not of disdain but of the
high estimate he had of the priesthood.

IV

ORIGEN AND THE PHILOSOPHICAL BACKGROUND

W E HAVE seen from the foregoing chapters that Origen's life and thinking were deeply rooted in the Christian community and its faith, sacraments and ideals of holiness. But his ideas also took shape through his contacts with the Greek philosophy of the time. We have seen what the circumstances were that led him to study philosophy. Unlike Justin or Clement, he was not a philosopher who had been converted to Christianity and kept his philosophical outlook. He was an apostle, a missionary, who saw that if he was to expound Christianity to the leading minds of his day, he must know the philosophy by which they lived, for only so would he be in a position to answer their difficulties and stress the factors in Christianity likely to appeal to them most.

This helps us to understand his attitude to philosophy. On the one hand, he looked down on it in so far as it was of this world, whereas faith was a participation in the real world; he attacked it in so far as it was a coherent view of the world opposed to the Christian view. "Do not covet the deceptive food philosophy provides; it may turn you away from the truth."[1] The reader will remember the passage in which Gregory the Wonderworker tells how Origen took his disciples through all the different systems of Greek philosophy, omitting nothing and advising them not to devote themselves exclusively to any master, even if they found one universally regarded as perfect in wisdom, but to "cleave to God alone and his prophets".[2] In that respect, he was far from sharing the optimism of Clement of Alexandria, who compared philosophers to the prophets and considered that they were inspired by the Logos.[3]

But on the other hand, he realized that although Christian dogma is of itself absolutely independent of philosophical

73

systems and their topical value, it nevertheless needs to be expounded with reference to the problems that are to the fore in current philosophical discussion. Hence, in his case, there can be no question of literal dependence on pagan philosophers, as there is, for example, in Clement's. Origen was a theologian and he thought for himself. Very few quotations from philosophers or definite references to them can be found in his works, except in the *Contra Celsum*. But for all that, his theology took the form it did because of his awareness of the questions forming the chief subject of discussion among philosophers at the time. The characteristic thing about philosophical speculation in the second century was that it was all directed to the problem of the relationship between God and man, i.e., to the problem of Providence. Philosophers were divided into two groups: the atheists—Epicureans and Aristotelians—denied Providence or limited its scope; the others—Stoics, Platonists and Pythagoreans—defended it, each in a slightly different way. Freewill and fate, the manifestation of God by oracles and the part played in the world by demons were the sort of questions round which controversy was apt to centre. They occur in Lucian of Samosata and Apuleius of Madaura, in Ælius Aristides and Maximus of Tyre, in Albinus and in Celsus. [4]

Origen was deeply concerned with all these problems. In her curious book, *Celsus und Origenes, die Gemeinsame ihrer Weltanschauung* (Giessen, 1926), Frau Miura Stange shows how in spite of being opponents, Celsus and Origen both had the same outlook, the ordinary outlook of their day. Does it, then, follow that Origen's philosophy was Hellenistic, a link in the Platonic chain? De Faye, and Koch [5] particularly, maintain that it does. Koch presses the theory with some vigour. The idea of *pronoia*, he says, is at the core of Origen's system. But the idea of Providence was the central problem in the philosophy of the time. Therefore, Origen's idea of Providence was derived from the philosophy of the time. Put in that form, the thesis is entirely untrue. The truth, as we shall see, is this: The problem of Providence was the one philosophers were most interested in in the second and third centuries. That was why Origen stressed such features in Christianity as were relevant to it. He represented Christianity as history, as the working-out of a divine plan meant to bring human creatures little by little to acknowledge God's excellence, of their own freewill. The theme had already been dealt with by Irenaeus and is in fact specifically Christian.

The precise task before us is thus to place Origen in the philosophical context of his day and, first, to describe the intellectual movements of the time. This is one of the points on which research has made most headway in the last twenty years; a greater number of new factors can be brought to bear on this question than on the others. Secondly, we shall have to search Origen's works for the most evident traces we can find of the influence of the contemporary philosophical outlook. This will show itself chiefly in the way the problems are put, but sometimes there will be evidence of dependence properly so-called. Lastly, we shall have to examine a particular case, that of the *Contra Celsum*, where we shall see a philosopher's reaction to Christianity and follow the defence Origen puts up against him. This study of Origen as an apologist will show how he presented the Christian message to a cultivated pagan of the time—will show, that is, how he accomplished the aim which had led him to devote himself to philosophy in the first place.

What was the philosophy with which Origen was most familiar? It is universally agreed that it was some form of Platonism. But which form precisely? The question is patient of three answers, each of which corresponds to one side of the problem. The first is to say that he was familiar with Plato's works themselves. There is some truth in that thesis. It is certain that Origen read Plato in the original text; we have Porphyry's formal testimony on the point—"He was always reading Plato".[6] A glance at Koetschau's index to the *Contra Celsum*, moreover, is enough to show how many references there are to Plato in that work alone. Origen was conversant with Aristotle and Chrysippus as well: as we saw from Gregory the Wonderworker's panegyric, he was eclectic. But even so, it still is true that of all the ancient philosophers, Plato was far and away the one to whom he was most in debt. The great Platonic themes—a God distinct from creation, the immortality and pre-existence of the soul, the power of contemplation to make the soul like God—all occur in his writings. Yet one is at once struck by a number of points. Certain aspects of Platonism, such as the dialectical side and the theory of ideas, are no more

to be found. Origen's Platonism is the Platonism of a few
dialogues, the *Timaeus*, the *Phaedrus*, the *Laws* and the *Letters*.
And many non-Platonist elements, such as a Stoic vocabulary
in psychology and an Aristotelian standpoint in dialectics, are
discernible. We thus reach the conclusion that although Origen
had personal knowledge of Plato's works, his Platonism was
not the pure doctrine of the master. Further research is evidently called for.

A second hypothesis sees Origen as a neo-Platonist. This
view is based on the passage in Porphyry where he is represented as a disciple of Ammonius Saccas. "Some people,"
Porphyry writes, "are bent on finding a means of avoiding the
limitations imposed by the Jewish Scriptures, and yet they do
not want to break with them altogether. They therefore use
commentaries that do not hang together and have no bearing
on the text. . . . This absurdity originated with a man I knew
when I was young—Origen. He is still very well known because
of his books, and he has a great reputation among the people
who teach these theories. He used to go to the lectures of
Ammonius, the philosopher whose success has been so notable
of late. He learned much from him that helped him to attain
proficiency in rhetoric, but as far as sane conduct of life was
concerned, he went in the opposite direction to his master."[7]
The passage is of the highest interest, since Ammonius Saccas
was the founder of neo-Platonism and the master of Plotinus.
It is thus certain that Origen had been in touch with the circles
where neo-Platonism came to birth.[8] But can we draw from
that conclusions definite enough to determine the interpretation
of his writings?

M. Cadiou thinks that we can; that is the main contention of
his book on Origen's early life, *La Jeunesse d'Origène*. The third
part deals with the beginnings of neo-Platonism in Alexandria
and has sections on the influence of Ammonius Saccas on
Origen and on the school-traditions common to Origen and
Plotinus. But for several reasons, the assumption that Origen
was under neo-Platonist influence does not seem to be very
well-founded. The first is that it rests on an historical hypothesis which is far from certain—it is based not merely on the
passage just quoted, which does beyond question refer to
Origen, but on other passages from Porphyry's *Life of Plotinus*

where a man called Origen is mentioned. The chief of these passages is the one reading: "Herennius, Origen and Plotinus had agreed together to keep secret the theories their master, Ammonius, had explained to them in full detail in his lectures. Plotinus . . . kept his promise. Herennius was the first to break the agreement and Origen followed his example. He wrote no more than a treatise on demons and, during the reign of Gallienus, a treatise on the theme that kings alone are poets."[9] This is very interesting as an introduction to Ammonius's school of philosophy; but it is very difficult to see how the author mentioned in the passage can be the Origen we are concerned with. No trace of the two treatises mentioned by Porphyry can be found among Origen's works. The subjects they deal with, too, seem quite foreign to the habitual direction of his thoughts. Moreover, Gallienus began to reign in 253, and we have reason to believe that Origen was no longer alive at that date.

To this historical difficulty concerning Origen's connection with Ammonius may be added the further fact that we know hardly anything about what Ammonius taught. Like all the ancient philosophers, and like Plotinus himself, he wrote nothing. In the case of Plotinus, the only echo of his teaching that we have comes from the notes his hearers took. But in Ammonius's case, even that is missing. All we have is a summary by Photius[10] of a work by Hierocles, a fifth-century neo-Platonist, in which Ammonius's name is associated with certain theories on Providence, the soul and the cosmos. The theories are very like Origen's, so much so that Hal Koch regards them as an echo of his teaching and a trace of his influence on Hierocles. Again, in his treatise on the nature of man, universally attributed during the Middle Ages to Gregory of Nyssa, Nemesius, the fifth-century Bishop of Emesa, twice summarizes some of Ammonius's theories.[11] But they are mixed up with ideas of Numenius's and are hard to separate. It is thus difficult to agree with M. Cadiou that "these two documents are enough to restore the founder of neo-Platonism to his rightful place".[12]

Failing the influence of Ammonius, which is hard to prove, can we find any evidence that Origen was influenced by Plotinus? The question is important. Origen and Plotinus were the two outstanding figures of the late Hellenistic world.

They belonged to the same intellectual circle. It is certain that they were both pupils of Ammonius. But did they ever meet? Here again Porphyry's *Life of Plotinus* contains a passage of the greatest interest. At Plotinus's lectures, he says, they first read commentaries by "Severus, Cronius, Numenius, Gaius and Atticus, and of the peripatetics those of Aspasius, Alexander, Adrastes and any others they chanced upon. But they never merely read a passage and left it at that. Plotinus always added original speculations of his own and explanations after the style of Ammonius. . . . One day Origen came to his lecture. Plotinus blushed and tried to stand up. When Origen begged him to speak, he said you had no desire to when you were talking to people who, you were sure, knew what you were going to say. He continued the conversation for a while and got up to go ".[13]

But here again the Origen in question is certainly not the one we are concerned with, whatever M. Cadiou may say. The incident took place when Plotinus was teaching at Rome, which he began to do about the year 245. But there is no trace of any journey made by Origen to Rome at so late a date. Moreover, Plotinus was twenty years younger than Origen: he was born in 205 and Origen was born in 185. It cannot readily be supposed that Origen would be influenced by one so much his junior. And how could he have become acquainted with Plotinus's philosophy, when Plotinus wrote nothing and taught at Rome? It is impossible to see how he could ever have come into contact with him. Nevertheless, M. Cadiou points out analogies between the teaching of the two thinkers,[14] and in the same way Fr. Arnou notes that the theme of creative contemplation is common to them both.[15] But once again, this was due to the existence of a common set of problems, with reference to which both Plotinus and Origen worked out their ideas on parallel lines. It was not due to the influence of one thinker on the other.

Hence, if we set aside the influence of Ammonius Saccas as not susceptible of proof and the influence of Plotinus as improbable, we cannot call Origen a neo-Platonist. In that case, how can we account for his teaching and the affinities it has with Plotinus? Only by supposing common influences to which neo-Platonism on the one hand and Origen's theories on the other are both responses. And that is just what the sources clearly show. With this we come to the heart of the problem. If we look once more at the extract from Porphyry about Origen we shall find this: "He was always reading Plato. The works of Numenius, Cronius, Apollophanes, Longinus, Moderatus, Nicostratus and experts in the Pythagorean philosophy were his mainstay. He also used the books of Chairemon the Stoic and Cornutus."[16] We have no need to look elsewhere for the sources of his philosophy. In addition to Plato's works, he was familiar with the writings of the Pythagoreans, Platonists and Stoics of the second century. And when we look at Porphyry's *Life of Plotinus*, we see that at Plotinus's lectures "commentaries by Severus, Cronius, Numenius, Gaius and Atticus" were read. We thus find the same names in both cases. We now have all the factors we need for determining the nature of Origen's philosophical training. On the one hand there was his personal knowledge of some of Plato's works, and at the opposite end of the scale came the oral teaching of Ammonius Saccas, the scope of which it is difficult to determine. But the essential factor seems to lie between these two and to consist of Origen's contacts with the philosophers and commentators of the previous generation. It is there that the real nursery in which his philosophy matured is to be found.

De Faye brings this out very clearly in the second volume of his *Origène*. He gives a sketch of the philosophical movement of the first and second centuries and examines the teaching of Plutarch, Maximus of Tyre, Lucian, Celsus, Numenius and Apollonius of Tyana. But his essay is written on very general lines and does not show in detail how one thinker was influenced by another. Hal Koch tackles the problem at closer range in his *Pronoia und Paideusis* and shows that the philosophical background to Origen's ideas was provided by the second-century school of Platonists with which Gaius, Albinus, Atticus, Maximus of Tyre, Celsus and Numenius were connected—the school, that is, known as Middle Platonism. Some attention has been devoted to this hitherto neglected school since Koch worked on it. H. C. Puech's *Numenius et les théologies orientales au second siècle*[17] and Guy Soury's *Aperçus sur la philosophie religieuse de Maxime de Tyr* (1942) show some of the factors involved. But the most important work on the question is R. E. Witt's *Albinus*

and the History of Middle Platonism,[18] which was followed by the
publication of Albinus's *Epitome,* edited by P. Louis.[19]

We must not forget that among the authors used by Origen
Porphyry mentions the Stoics, Cornutus and Chairemon.
Neither must we forget the principle Origen taught his pupils—
that they should try out all systems but give their allegiance to
none, and should pick out of each whatever seemed worth
taking. What we need, then, if we are to understand the background of Origen's writings, is a general picture of philosophy as
it was at the end of the second century, provided we realize
that the systems called atheistic, especially the Epicurean, are
rejected *a priori* and that the influence of the Platonists is predominant. The materials for such a picture may be found in
the histories of philosophy, in De Faye's book and, in a very
readable form, in Marcel Caster's *Lucien et la pensée religieuse de
son temps,* a book which states the problems very well. Lucian
of Samosata lived at the end of the second century. His works
are a picture-gallery containing sketches of all the philosophers
of his time and enabling us, if we can see through his caricatures,
to form a general idea of them all.

Aristotelianism could number no eminent philosophers among
its adherents in the second century. Porphyry mentions the
Aristotelian Adrastus among the philosophers commented on
by Plotinus. The best-known Aristotelian was Alexander of
Aphrodisia. As Caster so aptly remarks, the "peripatetic
school had for several hundreds of years been specializing in
work requiring positive observation. Their habit of systematically examining nature according to an objective method and
noting and classifying the facts protected them against the
temptation to confuse the natural sciences with magic".[20]
Unlike the Stoics, who aimed at the acquisition of wisdom, the
Aristotelians were all for objective scientific research. They
were somewhat positivist and they denied Providence and the
immortality of the soul. Hence Christians generally regarded
them with suspicion. Origen reproaches them with denying
the efficacy of prayer[21] and not believing in dreams, visions and
miracles.[22] M. Bardy has written on the question.[23] They
were the opposite of the pious Stoics without, however, being
disrespectful like the Cynics or ferociously irreligious like
the Epicureans. But their turn of mind was positive and

antimystical. Some of the technical points in their dialectics and psychology had been incorporated into the philosophy then current and can be found in Origen's writings. The chief thing Lucian says about them is that they were not disinterested. The same feature is brought out by Justin.[24] It was not out of place in men for whom philosophy was not wisdom but technique.

The Sceptics had something in common with the Aristotelians, inasmuch as they too were chiefly interested in problems concerning method. "While the other sects were principally in quest of wisdom, with the sceptics dialectics mainly took a methodological turn."[25] As Robin says, second-century scepticism was dominated by the scientific spirit. Thus it by no means represented a failure of self-confidence on the part of the reason, with a consequent leaning towards mysticism; it was simply one form, a classical form, of Greek rationalism, and it had made its appearance as early as Socrates. Lucian represents the sceptic as proving that the diversity of opinions about the world and the nature of the gods shows that no knowledge is possible on those points (*Icaromenippus*), and again that oracles are impossible or that belief in them rests on a fatalism that makes them useless (*Zeus Cross-Examined*). Their master in the second century was Sextus Empiricus. They come under the heading of atheists, whose books Origen forbade his pupils to read, "for fear their souls should become sullied through hearing things which, far from inclining them to piety, were incompatible with the worship of God".[26]

Such, too, were the Cynics. They were like the Stoics in so far as they looked on philosophy chiefly as a kind of wisdom and an art of living, but unlike them in their hatred of dogmatism. Castor defines the essentials of their attitude very well when he says that they were "obsessed with the idea of freedom. To be free, a man must be able to satisfy all his requirements himself. Consequently, he must not encumber himself with anything superfluous, whether it be material possessions or complicated theories". This detachment was not accompanied by hope in another life; the Cynics had no interest in anything like that. In their view, the sole reason for human existence was that men should live as free beings, despising all social and family conventions. They considered that all men were equal. Their mission was to use their freedom of speech to shock and to encourage. In his *Demonax* Lucian depicts a fine type of Cynic, a man at once charitable, moderate and cultivated.

Thus, although Cynicism was indifferent to religion, its asceticism, the renunciation it required and its universalism made it in some sense akin to religious systems of morality. Second-century Epicureanism, on the other hand, was always in rebellion against the religious feeling of the time—which, incidentally, is why, in an age so steeped in religious feeling, it had so small a following. The Epicureans made open profession of atheism. In consequence, of course, they denied the existence of any sort of Providence. They were the people Origen was chiefly thinking of when he talked about "atheists" and forbade his disciples to read their books. He was further away from Epicureanism than from any of the other schools of philosophy. The repudiation of Epicureanism he shared with all forms of philosophy, whether Stoic or Platonist, which affirmed the existence of a Providence. We have thus no need to consider the Epicurean tenets at length. The system was a commonsense thing, somewhat limited, hostile to complication and directed towards the attainment of wisdom in practical matters. Lucian's ideal was Epicurean, except that he was an artist, whereas they disdained παιδεία.

We need not spend much time over these various schools of thought, because in the first place they were not much in favour in Origen's day, and in the second they were so foreign to his temperament. We may note, too, that Porphyry does not mention any of the members of these schools among the writers familiar to Origen. It was otherwise with the schools we shall have to consider next: we shall find in them the environment in which Origen learned to use his mind.

We come first to the Stoics. Lucian paints a highly disrespectful picture of them, but the essential points in their conception of life are recognizable in it, all the same. Lucian's Stoic is a man of great dignity and gravity, with a shaven head and a long beard. His chief characteristics are over-development of logical reasoning and a passion for pedantic discussions. He is deeply convinced of the value of men of wisdom and very full of his own importance. In theology he is an ardent defender of Providence, a fact which leads him to take a keen interest in oracles, miraculous cures and visions. This portrait should not be allowed to obscure the fact that the second-century Stoics had some great men like Marcus Aurelius and Epictetus among them. But they acted on their times more by their example than by their teaching. Origen's reference to Epictetus in the *Contra Celsum*[27] is made in this latter connection.

Apart from a whole vocabulary of stoic terms—ἡγεμονικόν, κατάληψις, ἀπάθεια, τὸ ἐφ᾽ ἡμῖν, etc.—which had become part of the common tradition and been adopted by the neo-Platonists, the only point with regard to which Origen seems to depend on them is, as Porphyry points out, their allegorical interpretation of the Homeric poems. The Stoics were the first of the Greeks to interpret the myths as symbols. The chief Stoic mentioned by Porphyry as being used by Origen is Cornutus, a first-century writer who had taught the poet Persius at Rome. We have a *Theologia Graeca* by him (published in the Teubner series) in which he extracts Stoic theology from the text of Homer: Zeus is the soul of the world, Hermes the Logos, and so forth. As for Chairemon, he was a strange figure, an Egyptian, who had been a copyist of sacred books and afterwards became tutor to Nero. He too saw the Stoic theories in a non-Stoic source, which in his case was not Homer but the traditions handed down by the priests of his own country. He was also an astrologer and he wrote about comets.[28]

Moderatus and Nicomachus come next on Porphyry's list. The Moderatus in question was Moderatus of Gades, a second-century Pythagorean, the Nicomachus Nicomachus of Gerasa, who wrote a treatise on arithmetical theology. Pythagoreanism was not properly speaking a philosophy at all; it was a school of thought about religious matters, the essence of it being belief in the immortality of the soul and acceptance of a pure and meditative life as the ideal way of living. It had some influence on Plato and was very much alive round about the beginning of the Christian era, particularly at Rome. The subject is dealt with in Carcopino's book, *La basilique pythagoricienne de la Porte Majeure*. In the second century it produced those two extraordinary figures, Apollonius of Tyana and Alexander of Abonuteichos.

We are well-informed about Apollonius because we have his Life, written at the beginning of the third century by Philostrates, himself a Pythagorean and the confidant of the Empress

Julia Domna, who often had him at her house. The book describes Apollonius's childhood, his attraction to philosophy and his travels, particularly in the Indies and Egypt. In the Indies, Philostrates makes him visit the kings and the Brahmans. He becomes a pupil of the Brahmans and their chief, Sarchas. He learns astrology, divination and medicine. Afterwards he goes to see the gymnosophists in Egypt; then he returns to Italy. There he comes up against the Emperor Domitian, who wants to put an end to his activities, and he mysteriously disappears. It is difficult to know how far the book is historical. But in any case, it shows us what the ideal Pythogorean was like: he was a philosopher but he was a wonderworker as well—"magus and philosopher", Origen calls him.[29] He knew how to interpret dreams. Above all, he was deeply religious and worshipped the sun every day. "These pious men, with their linen clothes and their long hair, lived pure and thoughtful lives remote from the world and won men's respect and sympathy."[30] Their teaching about the transmigration of souls and the symbolism of numbers may have had some influence on Origen.

When we come to the Pythagoreans, we are not far from the Platonists, the school which from every point of view is the most important for our present purpose. Second-century Platonism was steeped in Pythagorean piety, to such an extent that we can perfectly well speak of the Platonism of men like Apollonius and, conversely, regard people like Numenius as Pythagoreans. The links between Platonism and Pythagoreanism go back as far as Plato himself and are evident in the neo-Platonism of Porphyry and Iamblicus. Nevertheless, it will be well to keep the name "Pythagorean" for those philosophers who continued the tradition of symbolism and mysticism proper to Pythagoreanism, and to class as Platonists those whose ideas link them to the master of the Academy, even if they were influenced by Pythagoras.

We thus come to the Platonist school. The history of this school between Plato, who represents early Platonism, and Plotinus, who represents neo-Platonism, has yet to be written. The treatment accorded it in books like M. Bréhier's history of philosophy is not adequate. When he reviewed Witt's book on Albinus in the *Chronique annuelle de l'Institut international de collaboration philosophique* in 1939, M. Bréhier himself said that "very little was known about Middle Platonism, the period in the history of Platonism stretching from the fourth century before the Christian era to the Platonic revival at Alexandria at the end of the second century".[31] A general study of the school would be the most useful contribution to the study of ancient philosophy that could possibly be made at the present moment. While not, of course, claiming to be doing that here, I would like all the same to point out the chief landmarks in the history of neo-Platonism, as they cannot be found collected anywhere else. De Faye's book is totally inadequate in that respect. The only work that is of any use is the first part of Witt's *Albinus and the History of Middle Platonism* and Hal Koch's chapter "Origenes und die Griechische Philosophie" in his *Pronoia und Paideusis*, particularly pp. 225–304.

I will not dwell on the early development of the school, but a word must be said about it if we are to understand the situation obtaining in the second century of the Christian era. Xenocrates and Crates, the first leaders of the Academy after Plato's death, contented themselves with systematically expounding and commenting on the master's works. Another school of thought made its appearance with the new Academy of Arcesilas and Carneades, two important personalities (Carneades was ambassador to Rome), whose work we know to a great extent through Cicero's *New Academics*. Dom David Amand, of Maredsous, has recently produced a book on Carneades— *Fatalisme et liberté dans l'antiquité grecque: Recherches sur la survivance de l'argumentation anti-fataliste de Carnéade chez les philosophes grecs et les théologiens chrétiens des quatre premiers siècles* (Louvain, 1945). The book is six hundred pages long and it amounts to a real *summa* of the opinions held on the problem of freedom in the ancient world. Dom Amand says that with regard to the theory of knowledge, Carneades "asserts that theoretical knowledge or science is impossible, because there is no criterion of truth. . . . Yet he is not an out-and-out sceptic; he does admit that there is a standard to measure practical living by. As M. Robin puts it, he builds up a phenomenology of truth, which enables men to act, but he takes care not to touch the reality behind it, because that is unknowable."[32]

The point is important, because the form of Platonism we are concerned with came into existence by way of reaction against this sceptical attitude. The chief representative of the reaction was Antiochus of Ascalon, who lived at the beginning of the first century B.C. Our knowledge of him comes mainly from Cicero (*De Legibus, De Finibus* 2 and 3, *Tusculan Disputations* 3 and 4). Witt devotes two chapters (4 and 5) to him in his *Albinus*. Koch had previously given him a few pages. M. Bréhier's observation on Witt's book needs to be borne in mind. "Little is known of this Antiochus," he says, "and when Mr. Witt lists the passages in Cicero, Stobaeus, Sextus Empiricus and Clement of Alexandria from which he proposes to dig out the philosophy of Antiochus, he is aware that they have been variously interpreted, and he himself asserts more often than he proves."[33] But making allowances for this, we can say that the substance at any rate of Antiochus's philosophy is known to us. Clitomachus succeeded Carneades, Philo of Larissa succeeded Clitomachus and Antiochus was the successor of Philo. Cicero, who had been a pupil of Philo and Antiochus, tells us[34] of the breach that occurred between them. Antiochus held that the moral life rested on knowledge. In this dogmatic attitude he resembled the Stoics. Like them, too, he laid great stress on Providence. His tendency, in fact, was to unite all the providence-systems into one against the atheists. His system was basically Platonic (his teaching about the idea of God, his cosmology, which comes from the *Timaeus*, and his theories about the soul, are Platonic); but he took logical and psychological principles from Aristotle, moral ones from the Stoa and eschatological ones from Pythagoreanism. Above all, the aim of philosophy, as he saw it, was first and foremost to give life a meaning, and not to seek truth by speculation. He thereby broke with the speculative Platonism taught by Carneades and returned to a mystical variety of Platonism. Of the two elements in Plato's philosophy, the one that attracted him was the mystical one. The victory was a lasting one. In one form or another, Platonism remained a religious philosophy from this time until the end of the ancient world.

The influence of Antiochus of Ascalon thus appears as decisive. It was under him that Middle Platonism, the school that lasted until Plotinus and provided the environment in which Origen's mind was trained, took shape. Middle Platonism was fundamentally Platonist in inspiration, but what it kept of the Platonic system was the general outlook rather than the details. The theory of ideas played no part in it at all. And it included eclectic elements. This eclectic Platonism was followed by most philosophers from the first century to the third. Sometimes it was more eclectic, sometimes less. Albinus's reaction against Numenius, for instance, turned on that point. But the general tone of thought was common to all who are classed as belonging to the school. To the Fathers of the Church, that was the main thing. When they talked about Plato, the Platonism they were referring to was this eclectic, mystical kind. And when people talk about the Platonism of the Fathers, this is the Platonism they mean. The point concerns the narrower sphere of the history of ideas, but it is one of the chief gains resulting from the investigations at present being pursued into the history of early Christianity. Here again, a detailed study of Antiochus of Ascalon in our own language would be extremely useful at the present moment.

Now that we have seen what Middle Platonism was, we need do no more than look at a few particularly typical exponents of it. Antiochus belonged to the first century B.C. The following century introduces us first of all to Plutarch (A.D. 50–A.D. 125). His ideas on religion have been studied in two recent works, *Les idées religieuses de Plutarque* by B. Latzarus (1920), and *La démonologie de Plutarque* by Guy Soury (1942). For our present purpose, the best study of him is De Faye's.[35] M. de Faye was struck by analogies between Plutarch's ideas and Origen's. "As far as their main ideas are concerned," he says, "their views are amazingly alike. The one is a help to the understanding of the other."[36] It is a fact that Plutarch was one of the most typical philosophers of the eclectic religious school of Platonism descended from Antiochus of Ascalon. Origen was acquainted with his writings. He explicitly quotes him in the *Contra Celsum*[37] and several times refers to him as well in the same book.[38]

The same points are noticeable in Plutarch as in Antiochus. Like Antiochus, Plutarch abandons the Platonic dialectic and the theory of ideas. He also stresses the transcendence of God, as Antiochus does against Stoicism, but at the same time he dwells on God's activity in the world, his φιλανθρωπία and his providence. A typical dialogue in that respect is the one on the slow working of divine justice. Patrocleas and Olympicus have just heard an Epicurean railing against Providence. They are indignant, but all the same, they are disturbed at the slowness with which God's justice works. Plutarch replies by elaborating a medicinal theory of punishment. God's aim is not to punish but to cure. As he knows the culprit's soul, he knows what can be hoped of him. He gives him time for repentance. Exactly the same idea is found in Origen. It is one of the points where his Middle Platonism is most evident.

Another point characteristic of Plutarch is the importance he attributes to intermediaries between God and man. First of all there is his theology of the Logos, which has been compared with the views of his contemporary, Philo, on the same question, and appears to reveal Stoic influence.[39] Demonology, in particular, occupies a conspicuous place in his philosophy.[40] Its prominence is in keeping with popular interest in manifestations of the supernatural—oracles, miracles and visions— and with the religion of the people in general, which is here rehabilitated. A similar interest is found throughout neo-Platonism from Plutarch's time onwards. It is well-known what importance was attached to oracles by the neo-Platonist Porphyry. The oracles were attributed to δαίμονες. These demons were of a nature intermediate between the gods and men and they suffered the same passions as men. Plutarch recognizes good ones and evil ones. In particular, he thinks that every man has a good angel and an evil demon allotted to him.[41] Both interest in demons and angels and the idea that every man has a demon occupy a prominent place in Origen's writings too.

One other work by Plutarch is relevant to our present purpose—the De Iside et Osiride—because in it the allegorical method of the Stoics and Pythagoreans is applied to an Egyptian myth. It is evidence of Plutarch's syncretism and also a further link with Origen. It shows how common the allegorical temper was in Middle Platonism. Plutarch mentions Stoic allegories and Pythagorean ones, i.e., allegories founded on the symbolism of numbers, and he gives a Platonist one himself. He thinks that the Egyptians are justified in maintaining that the soul of Osiris is eternal and incorruptible, since being, which is also understanding and goodness, is above all corruption and change. From it flow all the images that are moulded in corporal, sensible matter. But these images do not last for ever. They are seized by the disorderly, rebellious principle that fights against Horus, the god engendered by Isis as a sensible image of the intelligible world. But with the help of Hermes, i.e., the reason, Horus eventually triumphs.

It will be remembered that Horus was an important figure in the Valentinian gnosis. The passage in Plutarch just referred to is of the highest importance, because it shows how Platonism and the theology of the Egyptian scribes came into contact with each other. The mingling of the two gave rise to a whole series of very important works in the second and third centuries: it was through contact with Platonism and Egyptian religion that the Valentinian gnosis and the Hermetic system grew up in Egypt. The Hermetic books in particular are very Platonist in tendency. Origen knew these forms of philosophy. He had, in fact, to assert the rights of Christianity against the gnosis. But the conflict could be regarded as one between two forms of the same Platonic view of things, the gnosis representing the distortion of this world-view by oriental dualism and Christianity its transposition into theological terms. We will not, however, devote any more time to the Hermetic system or the gnosis at the moment: they came into being in the same mental atmosphere as Middle Platonism, but they always remained parallel to it and were never an integral part of it.

Plutarch is not mentioned by Porphyry among the writers used by Origen, but Numenius, one of the most important figures in second-century Platonism, is included in the list. There is an excellent study of this mysterious character by H. C. Puech[42] and an article on him by Rudolf Beutler has since appeared in Pauly's *Realencyclopaedie*.[43] Numenius had more influence on neo-Platonism than any other philosopher. According to Nemesius,[44] Ammonius Saccas was influenced by him. In any case, Porphyry tells us that Plotinus used him in his lectures and that he was accused by some of merely plagiarising him. This leads Porphyry to defend Plotinus. "Far from copying Numenius and repeating what he had said, Plotinus aimed at following the Pythagorean theories," he says.[45] Puech points out that the Latin neo-Platonists (Arnobius,

Chalcidius, Macrobius) were steeped in his philosophy. Above all, he was one of the writers whose works had their place in Origen's library. We can thus be sure that he was one of the sources of Origen's philosophical opinions. Origen himself explicitly quotes him four times in the *Contra Celsum*. We shall have to come back to those very important passages later.

Numenius lived in the second half of the second century. He thus comes just before Origen. He lived at Apamea in Syria, which was also where Posidonius came from. Apamea is in the neighbourhood of Antioch, an important meeting-place of Greek and oriental ideas, Judaism and the new Christianity. Numenius himself may have been a Jew (the similarity between his name and the word νουμηνία has been remarked upon); he was in any case a Semite. His origin showed itself in one of the specific characteristics of his philosophy, the influence of oriental ideas and particularly of Judaism. He is the first Greek philosopher known to have been thoroughly conversant with Judaism. In one of the works referred to by Origen, he mentions the Jewish tradition about the two magicians, Jamnes and Mambres, who "showed themselves capable of warding off from Egypt the appalling calamities that Moses let loose on the country". More specifically still, he quotes Moses and the prophets,[46] and he is the author of the famous phrase quoted by Clement of Alexandria[47] to the effect that Plato was a "Greek Moses".

He is often classed as a Pythagorean. Even in the ancient world he was so considered by Proclus, and Origen himself speaks of "Numenius the Pythagorean".[48] But Beutler has no hesitation in assigning him to the Middle Platonists. What Numenius really did, as Puech shows, was to stress the Pythagorean element in Plato. But he is a typical second-century Platonist. His Platonism is steeped in Pythagoreanism and in religious doctrines borrowed from Judaism, as Plutarch's was in Egyptian religion, and it is essentially mystical; yet by its main tenets—the antithesis between being and becoming, the attribution of the title βασιλεύς to God,[49] the doctrine of the two souls[50] and the theory of the two opposing gods[51]—it remains Platonic. It will be noticed that all this belongs particularly to the Platonism of the Letters. However, it lays great stress on dualism, a fact which gives it an affinity with

Plutarch's theories and betrays an alien influence. Puech regards this as evidence of the distortion of Hellenism by the oriental gnosis.[52] It is at any rate certain that Plotinus reacted strongly against Plutarch on this point in the name of the traditional Hellenism.[53]

He will be relevant to our present purpose to see what points in the philosophy of Numenius were expressly remarked upon by Origen and were therefore familiar to him. In one passage, we are told that "Numenius the Pythagorean was much superior to Celsus and in many ways showed himself to be very discerning. He made a thorough study of many systems and what he took to be the truth he pieced together from many sources. In the first book of his treatise 'On the Good' he sets out the views of the pagan writers on the incorporeal nature of God, in so far as he was acquainted with them, and he also draws on the Jews. He did not scruple to lay the prophets under contribution for his book and to interpret them spiritually".[54] As we shall see, the question of the incorporeal nature of God was one of those most stressed by Origen in the *De Principiis*.

In another passage, where he asserts, against Celsus, that it was at least possible for Christ to work miracles, he says that some of the pagan philosophers believed in supernatural intervention in human affairs. "We read of such things in Chrysippus . . . and Pythagoras and also in more recent writers, like Plutarch of Cheroneus . . . and the Pythagorean Numenius . . . who were born only the other day. These men are not regarded as inventors of myths" but show themselves to be as genuine philosophers and lovers of truth as any.[55] The point is of interest for its bearing on the cast of mind of Numenius, Plutarch and Origen and the light it throws on their interest in supernatural phenomena, which, as we have said, was a feature of the age.[56]

The most important passage concerns the theory of the three gods. Numenius is not mentioned by name, but information given by Proclus[57] enables us to identify the theory as his. The passage runs: "[The Greeks] made no bones about teaching that the universe was divine. The Stoics thought it was the first god, some of the Platonists the second and others the third."[58] This is an echo of Numenius's theory of the three gods—the father, the creator and the cosmos, or the father, the son and the grandson. The theory had considerable influence because on the one hand it prepared the way for the neo-Platonist triad and on the other it was considered by Eusebius as a revelation of the Trinity. Its influence on the Christian theology of the Trinity was not without its dangers. It doubtless had something to do with the way Origen conceived the Logos. If he condemned the idea that the cosmos was the third god, he was influenced, all the same, by the concept of the second god. That this was the case becomes quite evident when we find Numenius, in a fragment preserved by Eusebius,[59] calling the first god αὐτοαγαθός and saying that the demiurge is good only in so far as he imitates the first god. He is not good of himself; his goodness is derived from the first god. The same statement is found textually in Origen as well.

The case of Maximus of Tyre is particularly interesting because it shows how Platonism was the most widely-accepted philosophy at that time. Maximus was a rhetorician, like Ælius Aristides, but he took philosophical subjects as themes for his speeches. The forty-one dissertations of his that we still possess show what subjects people were most keenly interested in at the time and reveal the kind of problem that was uppermost in their minds—which is what we are looking for at the moment. The subjects he deals with include such questions as the object of philosophy (Teubner edit., ch. 33), whether statues should be erected to the gods (ch. 2), whether bodily ills are worse than spiritual ones (ch. 7), Plato's idea of God (ch. 11), whether divination is contrary to belief in freewill (ch. 13), whether the active life is better than the contemplative (ch. 15), and the question of love (ch. 19).

Maximus is absolutely typical of the Platonists of the period. His God is Plato's god, a transcendant being incapable of suffering. Between God and the world are the demons, who form the connecting link between heaven and earth, as they are immortal like the gods but passible like men. They give healing and counsel, bring messages from the gods and accompany men throughout their lives. Every good man has his demon. Maximus attaches the highest importance to oracles and visions. He once saw the heavenly twins; another time it was Æsculapius. And he knows that Achilles appears to people at

Scyros. For man, the business of life consists of escaping from the world of appearance by means of ἔρως, which provides wings on which to fly up into the regions of calm and there attain the good. Those who are incapable of that can at least contemplate the heavenly bodies and the demons.

Very little has been done as yet by way of studying the resemblances between Origen and Maximus. Hal Koch devotes a disdainful note to the question;[60] De Faye notices only one point.[61] But anyone reading Maximus will constantly meet with the same problems that Origen discusses and, what is more, with the same answers. Is it right to erect statues? "If the spirit has strength enough to raise the soul directly to heaven and so come to the divine, there is no need of statues" (ch. 2). But there should be σημεῖα for the people. And a little further on, he says that as God, the Father and Creator of the world, is invisible and cannot be adequately discussed in words, we use images to help us to direct our thoughts to him. The argument is exactly the same as the one Origen uses in the *Contra Celsum* to justify the use of outward worship in Christianity. The question whether philosophy and poetry have the same object he answers in the affirmative. But, he says, in early times men were simple and needed μουσική, like children, who have to be told stories by their nurses before they will go to sleep; whereas, when the human race grew up, it could not bear αἰνίγματα any longer and took to using plain, open λόγοι instead. This is very like some of Origen's interpretations of Old Testament symbolism.[62]

There are still closer parallels between the two writers. In his eleventh discourse, Maximus deals with the question of prayer. He first rules out absurd prayers: "God will not grant a request for anything bad." But what about prayers of petition in general? Can they make God change his mind? They cannot make God give a man something he is not fit to receive or refuse a man something he deserves to have. That does not mean, however, that God will always give a favourable hearing to those who deserve to receive what they ask, because his providence watches over the whole and so must sometimes sacrifice the part. Moreover, if what you ask for is good, God will give it you even if you do not ask for it, and if it is bad he will not give you it even if you do. But if that is the case, what

is the use of praying at all? There must be some use in it,
because Pythagoras, Socrates and Plato used to pray. Only,
their prayers did not consist of requests for specific objects;
they were rather a conversation with the gods. And Maximus
concludes with the remark that although there is little good in
mankind, it is nevertheless that little which saves the whole.
Anyone looking at the *De Oratione* will see that at the beginning
of that work Origen deals with the same questions and gives
the same answers as Maximus. As for the last phrase, the idea
behind that occurs in the *Contra Celsum*[63] and had previously
been used by Philo.

We may take two more examples, bearing on specific doctrines. First a theory of truth and falsehood. "To my mind,"
Maximus says, "it is not advisable for a god, or for a good man
either, to speak the truth in any and every circumstance.
Speaking the truth has no value in itself, unless it makes for the
good of the person hearing it. Thus, a doctor will often lie to
his patients, a general to his men, a pilot to the crew of the
ship" (ch. 13). The same idea is found in Origen,[64] together
with the illustration about the doctor. It plays a considerable
part in his theology as an explanation of anthropomorphic
expressions in Scripture.[65] Then there is the question of the
origin of evil. The first solution Maximus offers ascribes evil to
the ἐξουσία ψυχῆς but he subsequently looks on it as an
inevitable consequence of the reception of good (ch. 41). The
same two theories will be found in Origen as well. His general
thesis is that evil takes its rise from freewill, but there is a
passage in the *Contra Celsum*[66] where he regards it as a non-
willed consequence of the good willed by God, like the shavings
that fly out from beneath the carpenter's plane.

The philosophers we have been talking about up to the
present all drew their inspiration from Platonism, although the
systems they subsequently evolved were each of them quite
individual. A further group remains to be considered, the
second-century commentators on Plato. Just as men like
Alexander of Aphrodisia commented on Aristotle, so others
commented on Plato. It is, in fact, among them that we find
the Platonic school-tradition in all its purity. The one we
know least about is Taurus. We know a little more about
Atticus, from fragments quoted by Eusebius.[67] Atticus is

interesting chiefly because he represents a reaction against the introduction of an Aristotelian element into Platonism. This return to a purer form of Platonism, in reaction against the syncretism of Alexander of Ascalon, is characteristic of the whole group. They are distinguished, too, not so much by a trend towards mysticism as by concern for philosophical technique. Thus, two tendencies can be seen taking shape in Middle Platonism—a mystical one in the case of Maximus of Tyre, Numenius and Cronius, an academic one in the case of Atticus, Taurus and Albinus.

Of these writers, the one we know most about is Albinus. Witt has written an important book about him (*Albinus and the History of Middle Platonism*) and we now have a translation of the *Didaskalikos*. The book has been known for a long time. A summary or epitome of Platonist theories is found at the beginning of some manuscripts of Plato, without any indication of the author's name. In collections of early writers, it was ascribed to Alkinoos. But Freudenthal has proved that there is a scribe's error involved: Alkinoos never existed; the person meant was Albinus. Thus, we are now sure that in the *Didaskalikos* we have an account of Platonism dating from the end of the second century—a very valuable thing.

Albinus is also known as one of the best commentators on Plato. He is known to have been the master of the Platonist physician, Galen. Tertullian discusses his ideas on the soul. [68] Proclus regards him as a leading Platonist. It is not impossible, either, that his name ought to be read in place of the rhetorician Longinus's in the list of writers mentioned by Porphyry. He was at one time a pupil of the Platonist Gaius at Athens. Striking resemblances have been noticed, too, between his *Didaskalikos* and other Platonist works of the time, particularly the *De Platone Eiusque Dogmate* of Apuleius and an anonymous commentary on the *Theaetetus*, a fact which leads Koch to put forward the hypothesis of a "Gaiosgruppe". Witt takes it rather as evidence of common subjection to the influence of Arius Didymus, a non-Platonist philosopher of the first century.

One or two features in the book are worth noting. Albinus divides philosophy into three parts—dialectics, "theory" and ethics. He deals first with dialectics, in which he depends closely on Aristotle. In Chapter VII he enters on a discussion of

theory, which he divides into theology, physics and mathematics. "The object of theology is the knowledge of first causes;
the aim of physics is to discover what is the nature of the
universe, what species of animal man is, what place he occupies
in the universe, whether God's providence extends to the whole
universe and whether other gods are subordinate to that providence."[69] This is much more to the point. It will be remembered that Origen's great "theoretic" work is called Περὶ
᾽Αρχῶν.[70] The book follows almost the same plan, too, as
the *Didaskalikos*—viz., God and divine things; the world, man,
the demons; then freewill, which corresponds to the study of
ethics, the last thing Albinus deals with.

What are the principles, the ἀρχαί? Albinus first deals
with matter, which he describes, in the same terms as the
Timaeus, as being shapeless, formless and without quality. The
constituents of the second principle are the ideas, which in
Albinus's system do not subsist outside God but are God's νόησις
and the model after which the world is made. This represents
a corruption of Plato by Aristotle and is typical of the abandonment of the theory of ideas by Middle Platonism in general.
The third principle Albinus considers is almost incapable of
formulation. It is the Good, because it spreads goodness everywhere to the extent of its power; it is the Father, because it is
the author of the universe.[71] That is Platonism. The principle
is incorporeal[72]—which is a hit against Stoicism. It can be
known in three ways—by abstraction, by analogy and by
consideration of the perfections of creatures, which it possesses
in an eminent degree.[73] As the cause of the universe, it has
made ordinances for the mind of the heavens and the soul of
the world. It keeps the mind of the heavens perpetually active.
It acts on this mind, though it is itself motionless. It called the
soul of the world from its sleep and turned it to itself, for it is
the principle from which mind came. And mind, once provided with its ordinances by the Father, in its turn makes
ordinances for everything else in this universe of ours.[74] There
is thus a δεύτερος θεός as well as the πρῶτος θεός. This second
god is the heavens, a living being with a mind and soul, a being
that makes ordinances for all the rest of nature below it.

The world is thus a god that has been begotten, endowed
with mind and soul and left to put order into nature on its own

and make a cosmos of it. This cosmos is described by physics.
The most perfect beings comprised in it are the heavenly bodies,
which are gods. Then come the demons. They too are gods
and have been begotten. There is one for each element, so that
no part of the world is without a soul. The demons have sway
over the sublunary world. They are responsible for oracles
(cf. Plutarch and Maximus of Tyre). All this was the Father's
doing. But there remained three other species, which were to
be mortal: winged creatures, creatures of the water and
creatures of earth. The creation of these was left by God to his
children, the gods. The human race was the object of special
solicitude on his part. He sent souls down to earth for them,
equal in number to the heavenly bodies, and set each soul in
the star allotted to it as in a chariot. He explained to them that
mortal passions would come to them from their bodies and that
souls which mastered those passions would return to the stars
to which they had been assigned, while the rest would pass into
other bodies.[75] Man's perfection on earth is to be found in the
contemplation of the first God, and to that end he must become
like God; but Albinus states that the God on whom man is to
model himself is the second one, the one who contemplates the
first.

All these questions were dealt with by Origen. Sometimes he
shared the views of Albinus, sometimes he contested them. The
concept of the "First God" seems to be pretty much the same
in both writers. Origen as well as Albinus thought that the first
God could not be adequately described in words; he was
ἄρρητος.[76] The Platonist terms in which he speaks of him
are similar to those used by Albinus. God could be known in
various ways, and these, for Origen as for Albinus, were the
way of abstraction and the way of analogy.[77] Below the first
God, Albinus recognized a second one, the soul of the world, a
god not created by the first but awakened by him from the
lethargic condition in which he was before, awakened by an act
which set his face towards the first. When Origen criticized the
deification of the world, he was aiming chiefly at Albinus.[78]
But he kept the idea that the second God—whom he identified
with the Logos—was begotten of the first by contemplation.
He admitted, too, that the world was made after an intelligible
model; but this model was the Logos and not the world of ideas

subsisting in the mind of God. It will thus be seen that Origen concentrated in the Logos attributes which Albinus had distributed between the two Gods. As for first matter, Origen, like Albinus, described it as "formless". He does not, however, seem to have regarded it as an eternal principle.

The similarities are just as striking where the idea of the cosmos is concerned. The Logos sets the world in order in Origen, just as the soul of the world does in Albinus; the Logos envelops and supports the world as the soul does the body.[79] Origen did not dwell on problems concerning the elements, any more than he stressed questions relating to the human body (unlike Gregory of Nyssa, who was keenly interested in such things); but his general views on those subjects were the same as Albinus's: he too considered that the heavenly bodies were living, intelligent beings. All he asked was that they should not be worshipped.[80] Similarly, with regard to demonology, he thought that each element had an angel of its own and that oracles were to be ascribed to δαίμονες.[81] With regard to the creation of man, we find him maintaining the idea of the pre-existence of the soul and its descent into the body, as well as the theory that the passions are bound up with the nature of the body and are superadded to it. There may be differences of detail, but the main point of view is nevertheless similar in both cases.

V

ORIGEN AS AN APOLOGIST

W^{E HAVE} seen what Middle Platonism was and what Origen took from it. There were certain problems which he shared in common with the philosophy of the time; we have noticed some of them in connection with the ideas of God, the world, demonology, the soul and allegory. But within the framework of this common set of problems, Origen's mind pursued a course diametrically opposed to the one taken by the pagan philosophers. They were alike in that they asked the same questions, but the answers they gave were fundamentally different. Now that we have seen what they had in common, it will be interesting to examine the conflict between these two contrasting views of the universe. Fortunately for us, it happened that Origen had to refute the writings of a representative of this very school, so we can see from his book how Christianity came to grips with Middle Platonism. We thus come to the question of the *Contra Celsum*.

But was Celsus really a Platonist? We find, it is true, in his one extant work, the *Logos Alethes*, the greater part of which has come down to us through Origen, a spirit very different from that of men like Plutarch and Maximus of Tyre.[1] Celsus had a very caustic, critical mind; he is in many respects reminiscent of his contemporary, Lucian. Origen himself was mistaken about him. He confused the author of the book he was refuting with the Epicurean of the same name to whom Lucian dedicated his *Alexander, or The False Prophet*, and consequently he took him for an Epicurean. Then, to his astonishment, he found Celsus making statements as unlike Epicureanism as anything could be. The reason was that his Celsus was not the man to whom Lucian had dedicated his book; he was a Platonist, though his turn of mind was rather different from anything we have seen as yet among philosophers of that school.

99

He lived at the end of the second century. His book dates
from somewhere in the neighbourhood of A.D. 180: the point is
important, as Origen's refutation came sixty years later. We
know nothing else about his life. His mind we know from his
writing, which shows him to have been a highly cultivated man,
possessing in particular an excellent knowledge of Plato. He
was interested in anything to do with religion, had visited many
shrines and oracles and contrasted Christian miracles un-
favourably with the marvels he had met with himself. Like
Numenius, he took a special interest in Judaism and Christianity.
He took over some of the Jewish arguments against Christianity,
though that did not prevent him from criticizing others.

His first charge against Christianity was that it was open to
everybody, good and bad, learned and ignorant alike. "Those
who recruit for the other mysteries say: 'If your hands are
clean and your words are wise' or: 'If you are free from stain
and have no evil on your conscience, come to us.' . . . They
promise that those who come to them shall be cleansed from
what sins they have. But what do the people who recruit for
the Christians say? Sinners, the unintelligent, the childish and,
not to mince matters, outcasts of all kinds, will obtain the
Kingdom of Heaven, according to them. If you wanted to
form a gang of thugs, who else would you ask to join you?"[2]
Celsus is here contrasting the Greek mysteries, which would
not accept people for initiation unless they had respectability or
education to recommend them, with Christianity, which
appeals to all men without exception.

He makes this criticism over and over again. Christians
appeal to people who make no demands on the intellect and
are willing to believe anything. They will not give reasons for
their beliefs; they simply say: "Do not ask questions" or:
"Faith will save you."[3] He ridicules the Apostles, whom he
calls "miserable publicans and sailors",[4] and pours scorn on
Mary Magdalen[5] and the people who went about with Christ.
"'We do not want the cultivated to come to us,' they say, 'or
the wise or the prudent,' for they consider all that undesirable.
'But the ignorant, the unintelligent and the mentally back-
ward may come with all confidence.' By admitting of their
own accord that these are the people who are fit for their God,
they show that they neither will nor can convert any but the

feeble-minded, people of no account, people without intelligence, like slaves, women and children."[6]

Celsus is evidently thinking of Christianity in this passage first as something that was developing in the lowest strata of the population, and secondly as a system exalting humility and the spirit of suffering. The problem arising in this connection is of considerable importance. People can still be found making the same criticism today and regarding the Church as a haven for the flotsam and jetsam of life, a refuge for the outcast. Origen's answer to the question is of great interest. On the one hand, he was himself a cultivated man; he had given thought to the great problems of life and he could not but share to some extent the disdain Celsus felt for the ἀπαίδευτοι. But on the other hand, he was too good a Christian not to realize that there was ambiguity in Celsus's attacks, since they identified a spiritual attitude—humility—with human imperfection, which is quite another thing. And thirdly, he saw quite plainly that this bore on one of the essential differences between Christianity and philosophy, viz., that Christianity is a gift offered to everybody, while philosophy is the wisdom of a few.

Therefore, in the first place, he reacted against the injustice of the accusation. "Because the simple and the ignorant always outnumber the cultivated, it is inevitable that in a mass of people like this there should be more of the simple and ignorant than of the cultivated. But Celsus himself must admit that some Christians are sensible, have all their wits about them and are capable of understanding the spiritual meaning of the letter."[7] There is an implied antithesis here between the simple, who can know the letter only, and the spiritual, who see the underlying meaning. Moreover, the fact that Christianity addresses its message to the uneducated does not mean that it exalts lack of education; quite the contrary. In the Christian view, education is always an asset, and the preaching of Christianity is in itself an attempt at education. "As Christian doctrine is an introduction to wisdom, Christians are to be blamed if they like being ignorant and say, not what Celsus attributes to them—they are not so shameless as that . . .—but things which, though of slight moment, are likely to turn people from the pursuit of . . . wisdom."[8] Thus, the "real *paideia* is not a bad thing; in fact, it is a help to virtue".[9]

But this side of the question, the one that shows the high esteem in which both Origen and Celsus held *paideia*, is the most external one. There is more in it than that. The essential point is that the real *paideia* is not the sort of education the world can give. "There is a kind of human wisdom which we call worldly, a thing which in God's eyes is folly [1 Cor. iii. 19]. There is also the wisdom of God. That is not like worldly wisdom . . . God gives it through his grace, and it comes to those who fit themselves to receive it. The people Celsus calls ignorant and enslaved . . . are those who . . . have not been taught the subjects the Greeks study, whereas *we* mean by 'ignorant' those who are not ashamed to worship non-rational idols."[10] It all depends what Celsus means when he blames Christians for seeking out sinners. If he means that Christianity acquiesces in sin, he is wrong and his accusation amounts to calumny. But if he means that Christians seek out sinners in the hope of converting them, then it is true that in that sense Christ does invite sinners to come to him. Moreover—and here Origen gets to the heart of the matter—you will never find anyone who has not sinned at some time in his life.[11]

The difference between the two kinds of wisdom is that the wisdom of the Greeks is the work of men, and hence on the one hand is incapable of giving complete salvation and on the other is accessible only to the few. In contrast to this—and here we come to the essence of Origen's argument—the motive-force of Christianity is the power of God. "To be quite frank," he says, "the highly wrought style of Plato and others who write in the same convention has benefited few, if any, of their readers, whereas authors who have written . . . more simply and practically, in a style the general public finds persuasive, have done good to a far greater number of people. As everyone knows, Plato is not read, except, apparently, by people who have a taste for literature and learning. . . . I do not say this in condemnation of Plato—he has given the world many a fine thing. My object is to point out the goal aimed at by those who say that their message does not depend on persuasive language devised by human wisdom, but rather on the proof it gives of spiritual power [1 Cor. ii. 4]. This text from Scripture shows that mere clarity in stating the truth will not suffice to move a human heart if the speaker does not receive power from God,

if his words are not beautified by grace. When words bear
fruit, it is because the speaker has received this grace, which
God alone can give. I am, of course, willing to admit that
there are some doctrines held in common by Greeks and
Christians alike, but these have not the same power as the
specifically Christian ones to win the heart and set it in order." [12]

This brings us to the core of the question. In Origen's view,
Christianity is not so much a set of doctrines as a divine force
changing men's hearts. It is worth noticing that although the
opponents in this dispute are two rival philosophers, the real
arguments on both sides are not philosophical. It is not really
surprising, however, since as philosophers the two are practically in agreement: the dispute bears on facts rather than on
theories. The question is: In which system will the principles
both are agreed on be found to be properly applied? Celsus
claimed that the true application of the principles was to be
found in the traditional pagan teaching and denied that there
was anything transcendent or novel in Christianity. Origen's
essential argument, on the other hand, rests on the efficacy of
Christianity in achieving human salvation. "A doctor—whose
business is with the body—may bring healing to many, and yet
he cannot do so unless God helps him. If a man makes the soul
his business and brings conversion to many—if he teaches
everyone to live as God wills and to shun everything that might
displease him—the same must be said of him, and with all the
more reason." [13] The way Christianity transforms conduct . . .
the way it spreads, [14] the fortitude of the martyrs [15] and the
faith of the Apostles [16] are all evidence that some divine force
is at work. [17]

That divine force is Christianity. "Celsus refers us to
Epictetus and admires the noble words with which he accepted
the fact that his leg was broken. But those words will not bear
comparison with the astounding words that Jesus spoke or with
his deeds, of no account though Celsus thinks them. The
words that Jesus spoke he spoke with a divine power, and that
power still produces conversions, sometimes among the simple
but often, too, among those whose reasoning powers are well
developed." [18] The efficacy of his influence for good was not
limited to the time when he was among men in the flesh; his
"power still brings conversion and progress to those who come

through him to belief in God. The proof of this leaps to the
eye, viz., the fact that although there are no labourers working
at the harvesting of souls, as Celsus says and experience proves,
so fruitful a harvest has nevertheless been gathered in and
stored in God's granaries and the Church's throughout the
world ".[19] Thus, miracles are wrought not by the persuasive
power of human words but by God's grace. Celsus himself
sees this but he misinterprets it. "The astounding thing about
them," he says, "is that they can give no sound reason why
their system should be accepted. Their reasons are revolution,
the advantages they think they can get from it, and fear of
outsiders ". To which we shall reply, says Origen in turn, that
"what we teach certainly is based on reason, or rather, not on
reason but on the working of God. Its principle is God teaching
men through the prophets to await the coming of Christ, who
will save them ".[20]

Thus, the point that ultimately emerges from behind this
charge of lack of discrimination in recruiting is the fundamental
cleavage between the God of the philosophers, who is accessible
only to the cultivated, and the Christian God of grace, who is
approached through humility. The question at issue is the
problem of the knowledge of God or rather, as its context in the
third century was mystical, the problem of the vision of God.
Origen and Celsus both agree that the vision of God is the term
of human life. Hence the precise point on which they disagree
—the specific nature of Christianity—stands out all the more.
Celsus thinks the vision of God accessible but difficult, Origen
holds that it is inaccessible and easy. This is the crucial point
in the controversy between the two thinkers; it is also the core
of one of the most keenly debated of all religious questions—the
problem of the relationship between natural and super-natural
mysticism, between Platonist ecstasy and Christian ecstasy.

For Celsus, God is entirely outside men's reach as long as
they remain tied to the senses; but if they free themselves from
the body, they will gradually come to the point where they can
attain to him through a sort of illumination. The idea crops up
several times. "How can I know God? How can I find a road
leading to him? How can you possibly show him to me?"[21]
"They will ask me again," he says in reply, "how they can
know God if they cannot know him through their senses . . .

they will say: 'Can anything at all be known except by the senses?' That is no way for a man to talk, a spiritual being; that is the language of the flesh. 'Listen,' I will answer—if so craven a race, enamoured of the things of the body, can listen to anything; 'You must put the life of the senses to sleep and lift up your minds, turn away from the flesh and open the eyes of your souls. By those means alone will you be able to see God.'"[22]

This theory of the knowledge of God through the awakening of the soul's inward powers of vision is an anticipation of neo-Platonism. Celsus bases it on a fine passage in Plato's seventh letter. "The idea of the first good simply cannot be expressed in words, but when a man has long been familiar with that good, a light suddenly appears and blazes out in his soul, as if it had flashed from a fire."[23] This is how he develops the theme: "Finding the creator and father of this universe is a very arduous business, and even if you do find him, you cannot possibly teach everybody else to find him. You know how seers have sought the way to truth and how Plato knew that it is not possible for everyone to walk in it. Thanks to him, a means has been found by which the cultivated may acquire a certain knowledge of the first being, even though he is beyond all words, and represent him through synthesis, negation or analogy. But what they try to say is incapable of being said, and I should be very much surprised if you could follow them, chained as you are to the flesh and thinking about nothing but the flesh."[24]

That is exactly what Albinus says, except that it strikes a more mystical note. The accent is decidedly on the transcendence of God, which, it will be noticed, is expressed by means of a special vocabulary (ἄρρητος, ἀκατονόμαστος). It will also be noticed that Celsus sees a certain connaturality between the human νοῦς and the divine νοῦς. Hence, in his view, there must be ways of attaining knowledge of the unknowable. These are essentially rooted in the process of becoming independent of the life of the senses. But they also involve an intellectual approach—which gives us the three operations found in Albinus: negation, analogy and consideration of the per-fections of creatures, possessed by God in an eminent degree. This knowledge or vision of God is nevertheless something of a rarity. On the one hand, few men ever attain to it, because the majority are sunk in the life of the flesh; on the other, even for those who do, it comes only as a sort of flash of light.

Let us look at one more passage in which Celsus again puts these theories forward. "Being, becoming, the intelligible and the visible. Truth goes with being, error with becoming. Knowledge is concerned with truth, opinion with error. The object of intellection is the intelligible, the object of sight the sensible. The mind knows the intelligible, the eye the visible. In the visible world, the sun is neither eye nor sight; it enables the eye to see . . . and the thing seen to be seen, it is responsible for the existence of all sensible things and for its own visibility. Similarly, in the intelligible world, one who is neither mind nor intellection nor knowledge enables the mind to know, makes thought exist through himself and knowledge known through himself and gives being to all intelligible things, to truth and to being itself. Being above all things, he is intelligible in virtue of a power which is beyond all words." [25]

That is pure Platonism. It is even possible to identify its source in Plato himself, viz., the sixth book of the *Republic*, which contains exactly the same expressions as those used by Celsus. I will quote only the final words. "What the sun is in the visible world to sight and visible things, the Good is in the intelligible world to the understanding and intelligible things. . . . The sun not only enables visible things to be seen but causes their existence, growth and subsistence. . . . Similarly, intelligible things not only owe to the Good their ability to be known; they receive existence and essence from it as well, although the Good is not essence but is beyond essence, which it surpasses in dignity and in power." [26]

As we have comments on these characteristic passages by Origen himself, we can tell beyond any possibility of doubt what he thought about Platonism, and this in the capital instance of the question of the knowledge of God. Origen adopts the theory of the contrasting worlds, intelligible and sensible, and the idea of a transcendent God who cannot be known except by a mind set free from the senses. "Since we say that the God of the universe is mind or something beyond mind and essence, and that he is simple, invisible and incorporeal, we must also say that he is unknowable except to those

created in the image of that mind."[27] He shows how Scripture,
as well as reason, teaches that the soul has eyes altogether unlike the eyes of the body: "The Bible says that they ate and
their eyes were opened [Gen. iii. 6–7]. The eyes that were then
opened were their senses, which they had been keeping shut,
and rightly so, for fear they should be distracted and so prevented from seeing with their spiritual eyes. These spiritual
eyes, which they had hitherto kept open, delighting in God and
his paradise, they shut, it seems to me, when they sinned. . . .
For this reason, all who are really Christian keep their spiritual
eyes open and their other eyes—their senses—shut. Only in so
far as his nobler eyes are open and his bodily eyes or senses shut
can a man know and contemplate the God who is above all
things, know and contemplate his Son, who is Logos and
Sophia, know and contemplate all else."[28]

Origen is here integrating one of the great Platonist themes
with Christian tradition. It is a theme which had already
appeared in Theophilus of Antioch and Clement of Alexandria;
it occurs later in Gregory of Nyssa and Diadochus Photicensis.
But it seems to raise a very important question. Seen in the
light of this theory, Christian mysticism might look remarkably
like Platonist mysticism. It all seems to amount to this, that a
man has simply to develop the part of himself that is akin to
the divine. And is there not a dangerously aristocratic basis in
Celsus, the knowledge of God being the exceptional privilege
of a few philosophers with ability enough to rise above the flesh
through contemplation, and remaining for ever out of reach of
humanity in general? That is undoubtedly what Celsus
thought. One of his most frequent charges against the Christians was that they appealed to all men indiscriminately and in
particular to the ignorant and the simple.

Origen replies to the question further on in his commentary
on Celsus. He alludes to the passage from the *Timaeus* quoted
by Celsus in illustration of the difficulty of finding the Father
of the world and the impossibility of making him universally
known when found. "I admit," he says, "that this observation
of Plato's is sublime and deserving of admiration. But the
word of God is kinder to men than Plato, for it reveals him who
was in the beginning with God, God the Word Made Flesh.
This it does in order to make the Word universally accessible,

whereas Plato says that no one who has found him can possibly
speak of him in a way that all men can understand. Plato may
say that it is difficult to find the Creator and Father of the
universe; he may declare that it is impossible for human nature
to attain to perfect knowledge of God and even that . . . it is
impossible for anyone to attain to much more than the knowledge the masses have of him. (If this were true and Plato or
any other Greek philosopher had really found God, they would
not have forsaken him and called something else God and
honoured and worshipped that, or put him on a level with
things that will not bear comparison with him.) We too hold
that human nature is radically unequal to the task of seeking
God and really finding him, but we say that the God it is in
search of will help it himself. God will be found by those who
do what they can to find him but acknowledge that they need
help from him, because he shows himself to those to whom he
thinks fit, in so far as it belongs to his nature to be known by
man and to the nature of the human soul while still in the body
to know God." [29]

Thus, although the problem is the same in both cases—the
difficulty created by the idea that to see God is to achieve human
perfection—Origen's solution is radically opposed to the one
Celsus had given. Celsus had agreed with Plato that the vision
of God is within men's reach but at the price of great effort, and
that it is the privilege of the few. Origen rejects both propositions. In his view, the vision of God is beyond the reach of
all men without exception when they are left to their natural
resources, while on the other hand it is given by God as a
favour to all who turn to him for it, whether they are philosophers or not. This is one of the chief points where his outlook
shows a radical divergence from Celsus's. What for Celsus
would never be more than the privilege of a favoured few becomes for Origen, through Christ, a thing within the reach of
all mankind. In this we have the ultimate answer to the
complaint so often made by Celsus that the message of Christianity is addressed to all men.

Origen returns to the argument and confirms it a few lines
further on. Celsus thought that God could be known by
negation, synthesis and the attribution to him in an eminent
degree of the perfections possessed by creatures. By these

means it was possible to reach the threshold of the Good. "But when the Son of God said: 'No one knows the Father truly except the Son, and those to whom it is the Son's good pleasure to reveal him' [Matt. xi. 27], he showed that the means by which God is known is a divine gift, bestowed on the soul by divine intervention in a kind of inspiration. It is only reasonable that the knowledge of God should be above the capacities of human nature (a fact which has given rise to many errors on men's part about God); reasonable, too, that God's goodness and his love for men should lead him to confer knowledge of himself, through a divine extraordinary grace, on those whose lives he has in his prescience foreseen will make them worthy of it. . . . It seems to me that because God saw how . . . those who boasted of knowing God and the things of God through philosophy nevertheless ran after idols and their temples . . . he chose the most uneducated of Christians to humble them with, men who . . . pray everywhere [1 Tim. ii. 8], keeping their bodily eyes, their senses, shut, and opening their spiritual eyes and so transcending the world. The vault of the heavens, even, is no bar to them: led by God's Spirit, they go up to the supercelestial regions and offer their prayer as it were outside this world."[30]

The expressions used in this passage show a characteristic change in content. All the terms Origen uses to describe Christian ecstasy—the soul's ascent, the vault of the heavens, the supercelestial regions, contemplation of divine things—are Platonist and come from the *Phaedrus*. But contemplation has now become something that is granted to Christians whose intellectual equipment is of the scantiest, whereas it eludes the philosophers. Origen is thus in entire agreement with Celsus as to the end but he differs from him over the means. The vision of God, the thing the Platonists lived for, cannot be had through philosophy. It is given by grace alone, and Jesus gives it to whom he will. In saying this, Origen safeguards the essentials of the Christian viewpoint—the gratuitousness of God's gift and its universality—while keeping the typical outlook of a contemporary of Numenius and Celsus.

This side, then, of the case made out by Celsus against Christianity shows how a common vocabulary was used to express two fundamentally different things, the Christian and the Platonist ideas of God. Another line of attack adopted by

him reveals the difference between the Christian and the
Platonist ideas of man. It has been pointed out that his position
with regard to Christianity was ambiguous. On many points
he had no objection at all to offer. It is noticeable that he made
no criticism of the Christian view of life (the duty of forgiveness,
for example),³¹ the supernatural element in Christianity
(miracles and prophecies)³² or the Christian view of the divine
nature and the salvation of the soul, because he was thoroughly
in agreement with them. Hence his method was not to deny
the facts or question the theories behind them but to insist that
there was nothing extraordinary in them: paganism contained
all that Christianity claimed as peculiar to itself. The great
weakness of Christians was their lack of modesty, their claim
that they were the recipients of a special message, whereas in
fact the same things could be found elsewhere and even found
in a form of greater perfection.

He gives numerous examples of resemblances between
Christianity and other religions. The account of the Flood is
taken from the story of Deucalion, the destruction of Sodom
and Gomorrah comes from the legend of Phaeton,³³ the tower
of Babel from the story of the sons of Aloeus. The same pro-
cedure is followed for the New Testament. The Virgin Birth
is compared with pagan legends like the story of Danaë; the
Resurrection recalls the story of Aristaeus, who was removed
from mortal eyes by death but afterwards appeared again in
several different places.³⁴ And many besides Christians have
used the marvellous to attract the credulous; Zamolxis, the
servant of Pythagoras, did so, and Pythagoras himself did in
Italy.³⁵ Similarly with Christian doctrines: humility and forgiveness are in Plato³⁶ and so is the Christian teaching about
the heavenly regions. Celsus is all the time using the com-
parative method to reduce the specific content of Christianity
to the stock common to all religions.

He goes further, even, and tries to prove that Christianity is
an inferior form of religion. Thus, when he deals with the
biblical account of creation, he begins by making fun of it.
"He holds it against us that we say that man was made by the
hand of God."³⁷ Then he contrasts the Christian account of
creation with Hesiod's. Similarly with original sin. "Celsus
laughs . . . at the part about the serpent, which he says is like

an old wives' tale."[38] Origen's reply to this is most interesting. He counters the attack with a reference to Plato's *Symposium*, to show that some stories are not meant to be taken literally; their value lies in the allegory of which they form the basis. Then he applies this principle to the book of Genesis. "No one is competent to discuss Adam unless he knows that in Hebrew 'Adam' means 'man'. When Moses talks about Adam, he is talking about human nature. As Scripture testifies [1 Cor. xv. 22], all men have died with Adam, and all will be judged as if they had committed Adam's sin. Thus, the divine Logos is here speaking not so much about one individual as about the whole human race."[39] Similarly with the New Testament, Celsus pokes fun at the Apostles for their mean origins and wandering life and for the inclusion of the traitor Judas in their number; to which Origen replies that Plato too was betrayed by Aristotle.[40] That the Greek stories have more beauty in them than the Christian ones but not more truth is a fair summary of his attitude.[41]

After this, the chief charge brought by Celsus against the Christians is that they are ridiculously self-important. Jews and Christians are "like a lot of bats coming out of their nests or ants issuing from their ant-hills, like frogs sitting in council in a bog or worms holding their assembly in the mud and saying to one another . . . 'It is to us that God reveals everything beforehand and predicts it before it happens. He does not bother about the universe or the movements of the heavenly bodies, he takes no thought for this vast earth; he rules for our benefit alone. We are the only ones he sends his envoys to communicate with; and he keeps on sending them, one after another, to find means of uniting us to him for ever. . . . There is a God, but we come immediately after him. God created us and he made us like himself in all respects. Earth, water, air, the stars—all are beneath us. Everything was made for our benefit.' . . . It would be easier to tolerate rubbish like this if it came from worms and frogs instead of from Jews and Christians."[42] It will be noticed that Celsus brings his criticism to bear directly on the transcendence of Christianity and not on its nature. Which is clever of him.

But, fundamentally, what he is criticizing here is the Christian conception of the human person and its value. "He holds

it against us," Origen says, "that we say that everything was
made for man's sake, and he would like to prove from the
history of the animals and the many traces of intelligence
noticeable in them that the universe was no more created for
man's sake exclusively than for theirs."[43] Celsus gives many
examples of wisdom in animals: birds converse with one
another, elephants keep their promises.[44] Why then should it
be supposed that men are dearer to the gods than animals are?
"If someone said to me: 'Man is the king of the beasts because
he . . . feeds on their flesh,' I would answer: 'Why not say that
we exist for the benefit of the beasts, since they feed on us?'"[45]
This attitude is a consequence of a view of the world in which
the universal is all-important and the individual does not matter
at all. "The rest of the universe was not made for man. Man
was so created that as a work of God he should be perfect in
whole and in part. Everything was created as it is with a view
to the perfection of the cosmos; the cosmos was not created as it is
with a view to man's perfection. God's care is for the whole."[46]

Origen was in a very strong position for answering this, for,
as he points out himself, when Celsus attacked the Christians
he hit the Stoics at the same time. "They too teach that man
is more important than the animals and that Providence made
everything for the benefit of the human race."[47] That this was
so can be seen from Cicero's *De Natura Deorum*, 133. And
Origen is right in saying that Celsus seemed to be talking like
an Epicurean.[48] These passages are important, because they
bring out the contradiction lying at the heart of Middle
Platonism. On the one hand, Middle Platonism conceived of
reality as constituted by a world existing from all eternity
alongside of God;[49] on the other it was mystical and, as we
have said, was eager for manifestations of divine Providence
and for salvation, which God would bring to those who were
intimate with him. Origen was well aware of the contradiction
and he shows it up in Celsus. Celsus must choose between
Providence and destiny. That was the essential point on which
Celsus and Origen disagreed. Celsus saw the world as change-
less, Origen believed in something that had happened. The
same idea comes up again in connection with the question of
the endless recurrence of events. In this case it was not Providence but freewill that Celsus seemed to be destroying, because

if his theory were true, the value of human acts would vanish. Celsus lived in a world of unchangeable essences; Origen's world was one of persons and of liberty. The question brings us to two of the essential categories of Christian theology—historicity and subjectivity.

With the question of historicity we come to the last of the fundamental objections made by Celsus to Christianity, viz., that Christianity was revolutionary. Christians claimed to be introducing a new religion and were hostile to the traditional cults. We have seen that several of the philosophers we have been talking about combined a relatively pure conception of God with superstitious devotion to demons. The principal criticism that in a later age men like St. Augustine were to make of the greatest of the pagans, philosophers like Plato and Cicero, was that in spite of knowing the true God they still went on with idolatrous cults. Celsus was an eminent representative of that attitude; he may even have been the first to try and justify it. In his opinion, devotion to a multitude of secondary deities did not in any way detract from the worship due to the supreme God; in fact, it was a sign of deep piety. Where men were concerned, honour paid to one might give offence to another, but it would be absurd to take up the same attitude where God was concerned, because there was no jealousy in God. Anyone who honoured several gods would even be doing something highly pleasing to the supreme God, because he would be honouring members of God's family.[50] This is typical of an age in which, as Nock points out, a man's piety was estimated by the number of mystery-cults into which he had secured initiation.

Celsus placed the heavenly bodies highest among the secondary deities; they were the holiest and most powerful parts of the heavens.[51] We may note that Origen did not altogether disapprove of the veneration of the stars and planets, which he considered were beings of a very high order. He even granted that the cult of the heavenly bodies was given by God to peoples as yet incapable of knowing the true God, the God who is a Spirit, so as to turn them from the worship of demons. But Celsus worshipped demons as well as God. In his opinion they were minor deities, "satraps and ministers, dwelling in the air and on earth".[52] Unlike Plutarch, he held that they were subject to birth and destruction. Things on earth were given into their keeping. "That this is so can be learned from the Egyptians, who say that there are thirty-six demons (or more, according to some) set in charge over various parts of the body." [53] The good things of nature came to men through them. Whenever men ate bread, drank wine or tasted fruit, they received all these things from one or other of the demons, who had been given special charge of them. [54]

Oracles, visions and manifestations of the supernatural were also to be ascribed to them. Though he did not hanker after that sort of thing to the same extent as men like Maximus of Tyre, Celsus nevertheless found a place for it. His writings are full of the marvellous. He thought that many of the Greeks and barbarians had their Æsculapius, who cured diseases for them, granted them favours and predicted the future. He believed that Aristaeus of Proconnesus had mysteriously disappeared and then, long afterwards, had been seen of men once more. [55] "Oracles have been delivered in inspired terms," he says, "by prophets, prophetesses and other men and women speaking under divine inspiration. Amazing things have been heard in these sanctuaries. The future has been made known through the inspection of sacrificial victims and by other miraculous signs. There is no need to give examples. Some people have undoubtedly seen apparitions. Life is full of these things. Oracles have so often been responsible for the foundation of towns, the relief of sickness and famine . . . the restoration of the maimed to the use of their limbs; over and over again they have inspired acts of atonement for want of respect to temples. . . . There are cases where people have been killed by a terrible voice proceeding from the depths of the earth." [56]

Hence, when Christians refused to pay honour to the demons, they were committing the sin of impiety. Not only that, but the worship of demons was the constitutive element of family religion and civic religion. It was thus the religious basis of the State. Anyone who rejected the demons *ipso facto* rejected the social institution erected on that basis and exiled himself from human society. That was the line Celsus took, as Tacitus had done before him when he called Christians at once "atheists" and "misanthropists". It was considered that if Christians would not pay honour to the tutelary deities, they ought to withdraw from the community. "Those who refuse to respect the sacrifices and the priests in charge of them should be regarded as incapable of acting as adults; they ought not to marry or have children or perform any other function at all. They should all go away and they should leave no descendants behind them; then there would be nothing left of the race on earth. . . . If they want to marry, have children and enjoy the fruits of the earth, they must honour those who make those good things available for them; they must give them proper worship . . . otherwise they cannot but appear ungrateful."[57]

Celsus is here diverting his attack from Christian doctrine to the Christian attitude to social and political matters. He charges Christians with taking no interest in the State. "If everybody did the same," he says, "the king would be left high and dry, everything would fall into the power of the . . . barbarians, and your own sect and true wisdom as well would disappear from men's midst."[58] There is something moving in this cry from the heart. It seemed to Celsus that the whole of the ancient world, the entire civilization of Greece and Rome, a thing at once religious, political and cultural, was in danger; and his grievance against the Christians was that they would not exert themselves in its service. To his mind, the Christians were a factious league, an illegal secret society. "They make secret compacts, contrary to law."[59] Origen adds: "He slanderously says that what Christians call *agape* constitutes a danger to society."[60] A fresh aspect of the conflict between Christianity and the ancient world emerges from this. Christianity is seen championing the right of a purely religious society to exist in defiance of the totalitarian pagan State with its all-embracing claims to allegiance both in politics and in religion. It thus introduces a real novelty—a religion existing independently of the State.

This gave rise to the most serious of all problems primitive Christianity had to face, the one that led to the persecutions. It was inevitable that in a state where religion and politics were the same thing, Christians should be regarded as revolutionaries. Still, there were two possible courses open to them. One was to take part in political life but refuse to commit acts of idolatry, i.e., to combine intransigence with co-operation. That was the course Tertullian recommended when, in reply to attacks on Christianity, he said that Christians were not

Brahmans or exiles from life. Origen's attitude was more
eschatological. When Celsus appealed to Christians to "support
the Emperor . . . with all their power, take up arms for him and,
if need be, fight under his orders", Origen answered that they
ought to refuse public appointments because they had higher
offices of their own.[61] But whichever of these two attitudes
Christians might adopt, the essential thing, both in Tertullian's view and in Origen's, was that they should assert the
existence of another visible community distinct from the State.
In every city there was another city, the Church of God.[62]

Here again, the attacks Celsus made forced Origen to define
the specific characteristics of Christianity. The point questioned
this time was not the concept of God or the idea of man but
Christianity as it appeared in its historical reality. Celsus
accused Christians of being revolutionaries because they did
not abide by customs of long standing in the State. "The laws
laid down by the community must be observed. Subverting
what has been law since the very beginning of the State is an
impious thing."[63] To this Origen replied first that the mere
fact that a law was made long ago was not enough to make it a
just law. If Celsus were right, any tradition could claim to be
observed, simply because it was a tradition. But, he says, it is
for Celsus to show how breaking long-established laws ordering
men to commit suicide by fire, marry their mothers, kill their
guests or sacrifice their children to Saturn can be called
impious.[64] Moreover, the philosophers themselves have set an
example in the matter of breaking immoral laws.[65] On this
point Origen had behind him the weight of a definite tradition
in Greek philosophy itself, the one defending δίϰη against
θέμις and showing with Sophocles and Cicero that natural law
had higher claims than traditional customs.[66]

But this was only a preliminary reply; the real question at
issue was not so near the surface. In Celsus's opinion, what
gave the laws proclaimed by the State their value was the fact
that they had been laid down at the beginning and hence
represented an immutable order imposed on things by the gods.
It was Platonism again in a new guise. Celsus saw the divine as
the eternal, unmoving world of ideas. The terrestrial world was
the created reflection of this intelligible world, but it shared in
the immobility of its archetype. "There were no more ills in

the world formerly and no fewer than there are now; there will be no more hereafter and no fewer. The universe is always essentially the same and evil always occurs in the same proportions."[67] Or again: "The course mortal things have to run is the same from beginning to end. Of necessity, their existence has always been regulated by some definite cycle, is now and always will be."[68] The laws established by the State were one element in this terrestrial world and they shared in its immobility. The idea that there could be any change in the eternal order seemed impious and contradictory. The very "novelty" of Christianity was enough to condemn it. This was the point where the fundamental objection came in, the one which more than all the rest expresses the refusal of Hellenism to accept Christianity, the objection based on the length of time that had elapsed before the Incarnation. "So after all that time God suddenly thought, did he, that he would make man good again? Did he never trouble about it before?"[69]

The problem thus put to Origen was none other than the problem of history and its significance for Christianity. How could God's unchangeableness be reconciled with the Incarnation, which was an event? It was another of those critical points at which Christianity came up against the demands of the Greek philosophers and made its own originality clear in consequence. Origen's reply was, first, that "Christ's coming into the world may have been a recent event, but Christ himself existed before anything else did."[70] In the second place, Christ had never been without interest in humanity. He had always been present to mankind: he had always been active in men's souls and he had raised up the prophets for the Chosen People. "God has always wanted to make men good again and has always taken the trouble to inspire them (since they are rational animals) to do good. In every generation God's Wisdom has come into the souls of the pious and made them his friends and prophets."[71]

But why did Christ not come sooner? That is the kernel of the problem. Origen's answer revives the arguments already elaborated by Irenaeus. Before Christ could come, the way needed to be prepared.[72] The necessary preparation was done in the Old Testament. In the *Commentary on St. John*, Origen uses the image of seedtime to describe it. Amalgamating two

texts—"One man sows, and another reaps" (John iv. 37), and
"Lift up your eyes and look at the fields, they are white with
the promise of harvest already" (John iv. 35)—he writes:
"Consider whether the sowers may not be Moses and the prophets, because they wrote to instruct us who come at the end
of time and announced the coming of Christ. And may not the
reapers be the Apostles, because they received the Lord and
saw his glory [John i. 14]—they understood the mystery hidden
from all ages and revealed in these the last times [Col. i. 26],
and so they reaped the crop produced from those spiritual
seeds, the prophecies about him. According to this interpretation, the fields the seed was sown in are the books containing the Law and the writings of the prophets. They were
not white, because the Lord had not yet come to them."[73]
The seed is the word of God sown in the Scriptures, which are
made comprehensible only by the coming of Christ: they were
obscure to the prophets and only the Apostles understood them.
Thus God's plan is conceived of as an affair of growth and
progress.

But why was this preparation necessary? In explaining the
point, Origen makes use of the great idea Irenaeus had put
forward about God's instruction of the Chosen People. God
had wanted men to know the mysteries from the beginning,
but in the actual communication of them he revealed only as
much as men could bear at the time. That is the significance
of the carnal economy of the Old Testament. "It was in God's
providence that the Holy Spirit should enlighten the ministers
of the truth—the prophets and the Apostles—by the Logos,
who abode, at the beginning of time, with God [John i. 2].
His aim was to reveal such mysteries as bore on human affairs,
with the intent that if men had the capacity to learn, they
should search into them and devote their efforts to acquiring
as deep an understanding of the text as possible. They would
thus come to know all that God had planned. . . . But for the
sake of those who could not stand the effort involved in this
pursuit, the Holy Spirit devised another plan. This was to hide
his teaching about the mysteries in various passages of Scripture. Some of these passages refer to temporal things . . . such
as the creation of man and the succession of events from the
time of the first human beings to the time of the untutored

masses in question. In others, the Holy Spirit tells of the deeds of the just and the sins they sometimes committed, as they were men, and also of the wickedness, pride and impurity of the unjust and the impious. What is more amazing, those capable of probing beneath the surface find that he reveals some of his secrets through accounts of wars, through tales of conquerors and conquered. And more amazing still, the written Law is a prophecy of the laws of the Truth; everything in it hangs together and is expressed with a forcefulness typical of God's wisdom. The first thing to be set before men was the garment in which the spiritual truths were clothed—the corporeal side of the Scriptures. It is of considerable value in many ways and can improve the mass of the people, the extent to which it does so depending on the degree to which they are acquainted with it."[74] Origen is not here speaking directly of the actual things mentioned in the Old Testament but of the scriptural accounts of them. The essential idea, however, is the same. The object of those things is to prepare the mass of men, who are not yet capable of searching into the mysteries, to come to the knowledge of them one day.[75]

In a more personal passage, Origen shows this preparation as arousing desire for Christ's coming through the knowledge it gave of him, so that when he did come he found men ready to receive him. "The Church wants to be united to Christ," he writes. "She is like a woman saying: 'I have everything. Presents were heaped on me for my dowry before I was married. When I was preparing for my marriage with the King's Son, the first-born of all creation [Col. i. 15], I had the holy angels to serve me, and they gave me the Law as a betrothal-gift.' (We are told that the terms of the Law were dictated by angels, acting through a spokesman [Gal. iii. 19].) 'I had the prophets, too, for my servants. They told me a great deal about the Son of God; they showed him to me, they pointed him out to me. They described his beauty, his splendour and his meekness, so as to set me ablaze with love for him. But the world is nearing its end now and I have still not been favoured with his presence.'"[76]

So much for the justification of history. It remains to be seen now what the idea of progress applies to. The New Testament was an advance on the Old. But was it an advance in the real order only (Christ being first promised and then given), or was there progress in the order of knowledge as well? Origen raises the question in connection with the text about seed-time and harvest just quoted. "Some people," he says, "will have no hesitation in agreeing that there were truths hidden from previous generations, even from Moses and the prophets, but revealed to the holy Apostles when Christ came and enlightened them and gave them knowledge of the whole of Scripture. But others will hesitate to admit that. They will not dare to say that the great Moses and the prophets failed during their life on earth to obtain knowledge of things known to the Apostles, for those things were like seeds sown in the Scriptures of which they were ministers themselves. The first group will support their position with the text: 'There have been many prophets and just men who have longed to see what you see, and never saw it' [Matt. xiii. 17], or by quoting: 'A greater than Solomon is here' [Matt. xii. 42]; and they will add what Daniel said after his vision: 'There was no interpreting it' [Dan. viii. 27]. But the other group will demolish all those arguments with the text: 'The wise man will understand what comes out of his mouth' [cf. Prov. xvi. 3], and say that Moses and the prophets understood what they were ministers of, yet did not transmit it to others or reveal the mystery of it."[77]

Origen seems to have thought at first that the great saints of the Old Testament had received a full revelation of the mystery. "Christ's coming in the body was not his first coming. There had been another before that, his spiritual coming to the perfect: in their case, the appointed time [Gal. iv. 4] had come already. This was so, for instance, for the patriarchs and for Moses and the prophets, who saw his glory."[78] Not only did they proclaim that Christ would come, but the *theologia*, i.e., the relationship between Son and Father and between Father and Son, could be learned from them just as much as from the Apostles. "They were witnesses to Christ."[79] In a longer passage, well worth quoting, he says that the Incarnation "was not the first time that the Word who abides in the Father's bosom [John i. 13] revealed the Father to men, as though previously there had been no one capable of receiving the revelation he made to the Apostles; for he existed before ever Abraham came to be [John viii. 58], and he tells us that

Abraham rejoiced to see his day and was glad of it. The words: 'Of his fulness we have all received, and grace for grace' [John i. 16] show still more clearly that the prophets were given the grace to know Christ in his fullness and that they received the second grace after the first—under the leading of the Spirit they were first introduced to the figures and afterwards got as far as sight of the truth."[80]

Origen is here echoing the Pseudo-Barnabas. The people in general stopped short at the figures, but the prophets knew the truth the figures signified. "'Have you never read . . . how God said . . . at the burning bush, I am the God of Abraham, the God of Isaac, and the God of Jacob? Yet it is of living men, not of dead men, that he is God' [Mark xii. 26]. These words prove that the saints had something more than most people and knew the mysteries of the Godhead even before Christ came in the body. They were taught by God's Word before he became flesh—for he had always been at work, like his Father, of whom he said: 'My Father has never ceased working' [John v. 17]. If these men were considered by God to be among the living, we must admit that, being alive, they had the knowledge the living have. And they had it because Christ gave it them before he became incarnate. He could well do so, for he was born before the day-star was created [Ps. cix. 3]. If they had life, it was because they shared his life who said: 'I am life' [John xi. 25] and as heirs of such promises [Eph. iii. 6] were visited by angels in visible form and had God manifested to them in Christ. As they probably knew the true likeness of the God we cannot see [Col. i. 15]—for whoever has seen the Son has seen the Father—Scripture says of them that they saw God and understood what they saw."

Origen gives various examples in illustration of this idea. "It is quite clear," he says, "that Moses saw in spirit the *reality* foreshadowed by the Law and the spiritual meaning of what he wrote. Josue knew about the *real* division of land that took place after the defeat of the twenty-nine kings; he could see better than we can what the things he had done were shadows of. It is clear, too, that Isaias understood the mystery of the One seated on the throne, and the significance of the two seraphim and their wings, the altar, the coal and the *velatio* of the seraphim's face and feet. I could take one example after

another to show that in the ages before the Apostles, the perfect
received a revelation from Christ just as they did; they knew
Christ because he revealed himself to them, just as he taught
the Apostles the mysteries of religion. But as I do not want to
labour the point, I will say just one word more and then I will
leave the reader to make up his own mind and come to what
decision he pleases. Paul says in the Epistle to the Romans:
'There is one who is able to set your feet firmly in the path of
that Gospel which I preach . . . a Gospel which reveals the
mystery, hidden from us for countless ages, but now made
plain through what the prophets have written and through the
coming of Jesus Christ' [Rom. xvi. 26]. It was the writings of
the prophets, then, that made plain to the Apostles the mystery
hidden from men through countless ages. If the prophets
understood what they were saying—and being wise men, they
would—they must have known what it was they were making
plain to the Apostles. Thus it cannot be said either that the
Apostles knew more than the prophets or that Moses and the
patriarchs were wiser or more blessed than the Apostles. The
same is true both of those in the Old Testament whose virtue
particularly entitled them to divine manifestations and shew-
ings and to revelations of the great mysteries, and also of those
who will be present at the *parousia*." [81]

Origen concludes by explaining that he has taken up this
position the better to withstand those who exalt the New
Testament at the expense of the Old, whether they do so as
gnostics or as orthodox Christians acting with perfectly good
intentions. "I have dwelt on this question at length," he says,
"because many people, wanting to show how important
Christ's coming was, say that the Apostles knew more than the
patriarchs or the prophets. Consequently, they either invent
another God, one greater than the God of the Old Testament
[this refers to the gnostics], or else, if they do not dare to do
that, they at least deprive the patriarchs and prophets of the
grace Christ gave them. (This at any rate seems to be their
position—it is difficult to tell exactly what they think.) But
everything was made by Christ. If so, then it is clear that the
holy and perfect things revealed to the patriarchs and prophets
were symbols of the holy mysteries of our religion." [82]

But the question then arises as to what difference there is

between the two Testaments. As Molland points out,[83] Origen's attitude "implies a concept of history difficult to reconcile with the significance attaching to the Incarnation as a unique event". The danger inherent in any marked reaction against gnosticism was that the oneness of the two Testaments would be stressed to such an extent that the differences between them would cease to be perceptible. Origen was well aware of the difficulty. He met it by making a remarkably interesting distinction. "Those who do not accept what we teach," he says (about the knowledge of the Christian mysteries by the patriarchs), "may object to the sense we give to the word 'revealed'. Would it not be possible to answer them by taking 'reveal' in two senses, so that in some cases it would mean 'understand' and in others 'fulfil a prophecy'? In the second sense, a thing would be revealed when the prophecy about it was fulfilled. The prophets knew that the nations were to be joint-heirs with the Jews, because it had been revealed to them. But as they only knew what had been revealed to them and did not yet see it happen, the things to come were not as clear to them as they were to those who saw them happen before their own eyes, as the Apostles did. In the first sense, the Apostles had no more knowledge of revealed things than the patriarchs and prophets. In the second, the text about the things not revealed to former ages applies to them, because in addition to knowing the mystery, they saw it in action when the thing revealed in prophecy actually took place."[84] This was also the position Irenaeus had taken up. He too admitted that the prophets had knowledge of Christ and that what was new in the Incarnation was the accomplishment of what it was already known would happen. But as the point he stressed was the divinization of man, the essential thing, in his view, was the fulfilment of the prophecy; whereas for Origen, who stressed the gnosis, the question was much more difficult. If the prophet had full knowledge of Christ, the value of the Incarnation was very much diminished.

It is worth noting that Origen's opinions on the point underwent development. He gradually came to admit that there was a difference between the two Testaments even in the purely cognitive order. Even at the time when he wrote the *Commentary on St. John*, he admitted that Christ's coming brought a fullness of knowledge or gnosis beyond what the saints of the Old Testament had known. "Moses and the prophets knew the spiritual meaning of what was in the Law and the prophecies but, as was only right, when they (so to speak) sowed the seeds of it, they wrote cautiously, in veiled terms. But it is clear that the Apostles, who possessed the seeds of the deep, secret truths known to Moses and the prophets, obtained a much fuller sight of the truth, because Jesus *lifted up* their eyes and gave light to their minds. This greater fullness is the harvest that was waiting to be gathered from the fields white with the ripe grain. It does not follow that Moses and the prophets were less than the Apostles and that they failed to see from the beginning all that the Apostles saw when Christ came. But they were still waiting for the appointed time, when the coming of Jesus Christ *par excellence* would make known more wonderful things than anything ever said or written in the world before."[85] It is evident from this how much Origen was hesitating before his exalted idea of the saints of the old Law with their knowledge of spiritual things on the one hand, and his desire to show on the other that the Incarnation had brought something new into the world. The word he uses is worth noting: the Incarnation is the principal coming of Christ (ἐξαίρετος), but it is only one of many. However, what he seems to be saying is that the difference between the Apostles and the prophets was that the Apostles had more light to see by, and not that there was any difference in the substance of the mystery seen by both alike.

He is more precise in the homilies on Josue. We have only Rufinus's Latin text of these homilies, but as Rufinus himself tells us that he did not take much trouble over the translation, we may assume that his rendering is faithful enough. "The men of old, who lived under the Law, had knowledge of the Trinity, but it was not perfect, integral knowledge; it was only partial. What was lacking to it was the knowledge of the Incarnation of God's only Son. They believed in his coming; in fact, they not only believed but they preached the rest of the economy of it; and yet they were unable to see and touch what they believed in. As Christ said: 'There have been many . . . who have longed to see what you see, and never saw it' [Matt. xiii. 17]. Their faith was not complete, because the economy of the Incarnation had not yet been made present in Christ. What we now believe in as something over and done with, they believed in as yet to come. Hence, these three 'tribes' were not given two shares, because the Fathers were not to be excluded from faith and salvation in the Trinity. And they were not given three whole, perfect shares, for fear it might seem that the mystery of the Trinity had been manifested to them fully. They were given a third number" (neither the one nor the other).[86]

Thus, the Trinity was known to the patriarchs, but the mystery of the Second Person was not fully revealed until the Incarnation. Origen goes on to propound a remarkable theory to show that in the same way the Third Person, though known to the Apostles, is fully revealed only in the Church. "At this point another idea comes into my mind. I wonder if perhaps our knowledge is imperfect and incomplete even yet, in spite of the coming of Jesus, in spite of the Incarnation. He was taken out and crucified, he accomplished all he had to do, he rose from the dead; but even so he will not disclose everything to us in its fullness himself. We need Another to reveal it to us and make it plain. You find the Lord himself saying in the Gospel: 'I have yet many things to say to you, but you cannot bear them now. The Spirit of truth, who proceedeth from the Father, will come. He shall receive of mine and shall shew it to you' [John xvi. 12–14; xv. 26]. So Moses, you see, was not the only one to be denied a complete shewing of the number three. . . . Again, Jesus said to his Disciples: 'No one can have understanding unless the Spirit comes to him,' because it is by the Spirit and in the Spirit that the perfection of the Trinity attains completeness. . . . Our Lord and Saviour preached penance and conversion from evil ways to good. And forgiveness of sins is granted to all believers. But even so, perfection, the sum of all the good qualities possible to a man, is more than all that: it means being worthy to receive the grace of the Holy Spirit. Nothing can be considered complete in one who is without the Holy Spirit, the Spirit who gives the mystery of the Blessed Trinity its completeness."[87]

The analogy enables us to see what Origen really meant by his idea of the gradual unfolding of the economy of revelation. In his view, the only thing that had ever conferred salvation,

right from the beginning, was faith in the Trinity. The patriarchs had had explicit knowledge of the Trinity. But revelation
was also a gradual process, because the Second Person was not
known fully until the Incarnation, which revealed the mystery
of his death and resurrection; and the Third Person was not
fully known until he came to dwell in men's souls through grace.
Revelation was thus at once a single entity and a gradual unfolding. It is important to realize that if, in Origen's view,
revelation implied an advance in knowledge, it also meant an
advance in the working-out of salvation. The concept he finally
arrived at is of the greatest interest. It is the same as the one
later used by Gregory Nazianzen, the theologian of the Trinity
par excellence, in the fifth of his Theological Orations. That
does not mean that the way Origen envisaged the relationships
between the divine Persons can in every instance be accepted
without question. But the point that does emerge here is that
in what he said of history as a gradual manifestation of the
Trinity, he was continuing the work of Irenaeus and foreshadowing Gregory Nazianzen. He thus stands out as a major
link in the chain of theological tradition.

The first point established, then, is that the Trinity, the object
of θεολογία, was known from the beginning but, for all that,
was revealed only gradually: the number three had been set
before men from the beginning, but not in all its fullness. However, the observation with which this statement must be quali-
fied introduces another side of the problem. In the Old Testament, knowledge of the Trinity was granted only to the perfect,
to the patriarchs, Moses and the prophets; but they wrote of
the mysteries cautiously and in veiled terms. We have come
across this question several times already. It is dealt with in
some detail in a noteworthy passage in the *Commentary on St.
John*, where Origen explains that it is possible to know God
without knowing the Father. Such was the case, he says, in the
Old Testament. "Although any number of prayers can be
found in the Psalms, the prophets and even the Law, I have
never found a single one in which God is called 'Father'.
When they prayed to God, the men of the Old Testament did
not say 'Father', doubtless because they did not know him as
Father. Before they could call him anything but 'God' or
'Lord', they had to wait until Christ had come, for it was

Christ who poured out the Spirit of adoption both on them and on those whom he led to believe in God after the Incarnation."[88] That might give the impression that there was no knowledge of God before the New Testament. But Origen goes on to say: "Except that they had always had the spiritual presence of Christ, and that as they were perfect, they had received the Spirit of adoption. But when they wrote and spoke about God the Father to ordinary people, they did so in veiled terms and not in words likely to be understood. They did not want to anticipate the knowledge that Jesus, who calls all men to adoption, was to give the entire world through grace."[89] The passage makes it clear that the patriarchs had knowledge of the Trinity but did not communicate it in plain terms to other people. Hence a further element in the Gospel message becomes apparent: Christianity extends to all men what was hitherto the privilege of a few. The idea is one of Origen's favourite ones: the universality of grace shows how utterly novel a thing the Incarnation is.

Thus we come back once more to the dominant feature in his defence of Christianity. It is worth noting that although he does not go into the theology of the Church—for, as we shall see, the Church occupies only a modest place in his theological writings—he does go into the apologetical side of the question. When in controversy he is forced to stress the essential constituents of Christianity, the main thing he emphasizes is not what Christianity teaches but what it does. He sees it first and foremost not as something taught for the benefit of the mind but as a divine force, active in history. It is obviously responsible for the fortitude of the martyrs and the moral transformation known to take place in the souls of Christians; it can be seen at work in the Christian community. It is worth noting that his argument here follows the same lines as St. Augustine's, who in the *City of God* admits that Plato knew nearly every Christian dogma (the statement may well be considered exaggerated), but says that as Christ's grace alone could in fact give men salvation, their mere knowledge only made their burden the heavier.

PART II

ORIGEN AND THE BIBLE

ORIGEN AND THE BIBLE

ITH the study of the part played by the Bible in
Origen's life and thinking, we come to the core of his
writings. His essential idea may be said to be that the
Logos is present under the accidents of the Scriptures as food
for the soul. All his life he was devoted to Scripture and to
Scripture alone—all his life.

We have seen how from his earliest years he was grounded in
Scripture by his father and made to learn passages by heart.
Even at that age, so Eusebius says, he was bent on finding out
the underlying meaning. As a catechist, he spent the greater
part of his nights in studying the Bible. [1] As master of the catechetical school, he laid the foundations of scientific Bible study
and carried the spiritual exegesis of the Scriptures to the highest
pitch. As a preacher at Caesarea he preached on Scripture
every day for years. It might well be claimed that no other life
has been so entirely devoted to Scripture as his.

Scripture was the centre of his life. If he studied philosophy,
it was only because that would help him to a better understanding of God's word and enable him to explain it to his con-
temporaries. But the only master he ever acknowledged was
the Logos speaking through the Scriptures. We have seen, too,
that in his description of the Christian life, he gave the place of
honour to the *didaskalos*, i.e., to the man who explained Scripture. The *didaskalos* was at the centre of the spiritual worship
proper to the New Testament. He was the high priest, whose
function it was to cut up the victim—the Logos—in such a way
as to reveal its inner meaning, and then to share it out on the
spiritual altar, the souls of the faithful. This concept is the
unifying factor in Origen's mental world. He could be said to
be himself the type of the early Christian *didaskalos*, with the
three elements—preaching, speculative thinking and contemplation of the mysteries hidden in Scripture—which the ideal
implies. He united in his own person three functions too often

separated today: he was at once the contemplative, the exegete and the preacher.

Hence it would be quite wrong to attempt to judge his exegesis by a few allegorical interpretations of doubtful validity. Origen was the first of the great exegetes and all his successors, even those who reacted against him, as St. Jerome did, owed him nearly everything. This is true whatever their branch of the subject may have been. We will begin by considering his contribution to the scientific study of the Bible—his writings on textual criticism, biblical philology and the canon of Scripture. The part he played in that field is of first-rate importance. We will then examine his contribution to the typological study of the Bible. There again he will be seen as one of the authorities for Tradition. We will try to find out what he thought about the relationship between the two Testaments, and we shall see how this provided a basis for the distinction between the literal meaning and the typical meaning. Finally, an analysis of his works will reveal the convergence of two streams of interpretation. On the one hand there is the whole of the previous typological tradition as it is found in the Gospels and in the writings of SS. Paul, Justin and Irenaeus. It has various subdivisions, according as it bears on Christ, the Church, the spiritual life or eschatology. On the other hand—and this is typical of the culture of the time—there also is an allegorical method of interpretation current in the schools and found before this time in Philo and Clement. This was the perishable part of the edifice, as is always the way with the elements used to give body to theological and exegetical doctrines during any given period of their development.

I

ORIGEN AND BIBLICAL CRITICISM

THE FIRST thing to do in any study of the Bible is to determine the true text. The need for this was beginning to
be widely felt in Origen's time. In the course of the
Jewish controversy, it was found that the Jews took exception to
some of the texts used by the Christians and questioned whether
they were in Scripture at all. The Christians replied by accus-
ing the Jews of jettisoning certain texts which they found awkward. But none of these disputes could lead to anything until
an attempt was made to grapple with the question of the
authentic text of Scripture by comparing the different versions.
The literal sense of Scripture also needed to be ascertained with
greater accuracy by means of philological and archaeological
research. And it was essential to decide which were the inspired books. Origen was the first to propose solutions of a
general nature—what Eusebius calls ἐξέτασις as opposed to
ἑρμηεία—to any of these questions.[1]

The first question was the textual one. What Origen regarded
as the accepted text was the Septuagint. As it was accepted in
the Church, this text unquestionably was authoritative. Origen
had no thought of making a new translation. But the Septuagint text might have become corrupt; it might be inaccurate
in places. Consequently, it needed comparing both with the
Hebrew text and with other Greek translations, so as to permit
of emendation. Origen undertook the endless labour involved
and gave himself to it for years at Caesarea. Eusebius says he
learned Hebrew for the purpose,[2] which was an unusual thing
for a Greek to do at that time. Even Philo knew very little
Hebrew. "As everyone knows," Jerome says, "he was so
devoted to Scripture that he even learned Hebrew, which at that
time nobody did in his country."[3] His knowledge of the language
was never perfect, but it enabled him to get at the original text.

The second task he set himself was to collect Greek versions of the Scriptures other than the Septuagint. Eusebius says: "He discovered versions made by other translators of the Holy Scriptures besides the Seventy. In addition to the versions in current use, he also found those by Aquila, Symmachus and Theodotion. He took them from the hiding-places where they had long been lying and brought them into the light of day. In the Hexapla, in addition to the four main editions of the Psalms, he gives a fifth and even a sixth version. One of these he says he found in a barrel at Jericho in the time of Antoninus, the son of Severus. He put all these versions into one book, which he divided into *kola*, and he arranged them side by side, together with the Hebrew text. Such was the plan of his edition of the Psalms which has come down to us under the name of the Hexapla."[4]

The passage gives a good idea of the work Origen did. His first step was to seek out as many Greek versions as possible. The Jews had been faithful to the Septuagint until about the beginning of the second century, when they stopped using it, apparently for two reasons. One was that the Christians used it too; the other was the fact that a new Hebrew text had been produced by the rabbis and that the Septuagint was not in agreement with it. Hence the appearance of so many new translations. Aquila and Theodotion are mentioned by Irenaeus. They were both Jewish proselytes living at the beginning of the second century. Aquila's translation was very literal and was influenced by the Palestinian rabbis; Theodotion's was more in the nature of a revision of the Septuagint and did not depart from it to nearly the same extent. To these two versions Origen added the one made by Symmachus. Like Aquila's, this version was made from the Hebrew, but it was not so literal; it aimed more at rendering the meaning. And Origen discovered two more texts in addition to these. His activities in this field amounted to nothing less than a search for all the available manuscripts.

Having done all this and assembled his materials, he composed the Hexapla, i.e., he took the six texts—the Hebrew, the Greek transliteration of the Hebrew, the Septuagint, Symmachus, Aquila and Theodotion—and copied them out or had them copied in six parallel columns. In the case of the Psalms, so Eusebius says, he even produced an Octapla. He explains, in the *Commentary on St. Matthew*, what method he followed in making these compilations. "With the help of God's grace," he says, "I have tried to solve the problem of the variants in the different copies of the Old Testament by checking one version against another. When I was uncertain of the Septuagint reading because the various copies did not tally, I settled the difficulty by consulting the other versions and bringing the passages in question into line with them. When I found a passage that was not in the Hebrew, I marked it with an obelus, as I did not dare to omit it altogether. In other cases, I put an asterisk to show that the passage was not in the Septuagint but was in the Hebrew text and had been added from other Greek versions." [5]

The obelus and the asterisk were the critical signs used by the grammarians at Alexandria in their editions of Homer. Origen was thus taking the bold step of subjecting the text of Scripture to the critical method of the day. The principle behind his method was that of return to the original Hebrew text. But at the same time, the Septuagint was the text approved by the Church. The two points of view had somehow to be reconciled. Origen satisfied the requirements of the second one by reproducing the Septuagint textually, while by juxtaposing the other versions he made it possible for scholars to discuss the value of the various translations. The difficulty was greater where a passage was missing in the Hebrew but found in the Greek, or vice versa; but he got out of it by using the obelus and the asterisk. He saw that what he was doing would seem venturesome. Hence he concludes by saying: "If this method comes as a shock to you, you may accept or reject it as you think fit." [6] But he adds that he has not dared to proceed in the same way with the New Testament.

The Hexapla was the first piece of critical work ever undertaken on the text of the Old Testament. It provided a basis for all subsequent work of the kind. Jerome studied it at Caesarea. [7] The original text, which was kept in the library at Caesarea, was destroyed in the sixth century, and such copies as there were were not complete. Thus, we have only part of the work today. But Origen did what he had set out to do: he provided the one essential instrument for the Jewish controversy. In his letter to

Julius Africanus he says: "As I have tried to take account of all the Jewish editions, we ought not to find ourselves quoting for controversial purposes texts which are not in their copies, and conversely, we should be able to use texts in their copies even if they are not in ours."[8]

But he did not use this critical text for the Jewish controversy alone; it was the text he had before him when he wrote his great commentaries on the Old Testament. Sometimes he discusses alternative renderings, e.g., in the *Commentary on Jeremias*, which, as we have it in Greek, we can be sure is as he originally wrote it. The passage he is referring to is Jer. xv. 10: "I have not lent on usury, neither hath any man lent to me on usury." "There are two readings," he says, "for this text. In most copies the reading is: 'I have helped no man and no man hath helped me'; but in the most accurate ones, those closest to the Hebrew, it is: 'I have not lent on usury, neither hath any man lent to me on usury.' We must of course explain the familiar reading used everywhere in the Church, but that does not mean that the one found in the Hebrew texts should be passed over without a word."[9] The exegesis of both readings then follows. Origen's attitude is quite clear: he recognizes a twofold authority, the authority of Scripture and the authority of Tradition. This, as is well known, is the position the Church has always taken up.[10]

He returns to the same text further on. "What is the meaning," he asks, "of the words: 'Neither hath any man lent to me on usury'? How can that be explained of the Saviour? Well, although I have taken that reading, I must admit that most copies of the Septuagint version do not give it that way. But when I eventually came to examine the other versions as well, I realized that there was a scribe's error in the usual Septuagint text. However, either interpretation could be taken."[11] He is going further in this passage; he is admitting that the Septuagint version is wrong. A similar criticism of the Septuagint text occurs in another passage, where he says: "Our reading of the beginning of the prophecy of Jeremias is: 'The word of God spoken to Jeremias, the son of Chelcias', which is the way the Septuagint puts it, for some reason. In the Hebrew text and the other versions, all of which agree on the point, the reading is: 'The words of Jeremias, the son of Chelcias.'"[12] Swete thinks that in these two cases Origen considered the Septuagint text corrupt and imagined he was restoring the genuine text. But I cannot see on what grounds he bases this hypothesis.

Origen never undertook any critical work on the New Testament. He saw clearly enough that the divergences between Christ's words as reported by one Synoptic and the same words as given by another presented a problem, but he did not feel equal to dealing with it. When he quotes from the Gospels, he often gives the same text in different forms. Von Soden thought it was because he was quoting from memory. That is often the case, but Ernst Hautsch has shown[13] that it was also because he used different manuscripts. In any case, he never tried to use the critical method to reconstruct a better text. He never tackled the problem of New Testament criticism.

The second question he dealt with was the question of the canon. Eusebius quotes the list of Old Testament books he gives at the beginning of the lost *Commentary on the Psalms*.[14] But the books Origen is concerned with there are those "handed down by the Jews",[15] except that he adds the two books of Machabees as well. The list does not, of course, mention the other works recognized at Alexandria as belonging to the canon, viz., Judith, Tobias, Wisdom, Ecclesiasticus, Baruch and the fragments of Esther and Daniel not in the Hebrew text. Origen explained his position with regard to the question in the important Letter to Africanus. Africanus had written to ask if the story of Susanna formed part of the inspired Scriptures. Origen replied that it did. He based his opinion on the fact that the story was read everywhere in the Church.[16] He applies the same reasoning to the book of Tobias.[17] Again, in the homilies on Numbers,[18] he includes Esther, Judith, Tobias and Wisdom among the books suitable for beginners. He thus puts Esther, which belongs to the Jewish canon, on the same footing as the others, which do not.

Harnack questioned this, because of a passage in the *Commentary on the Song of Songs* in which Origen says that no use is to be made of apocryphal writings.[19] But what Origen has in mind here is not the deuterocanonical books but the apocrypha in the Catholic sense of the term, i.e., Jewish works like the *Testaments of the Twelve Patriarchs* or the *Book of Enoch*. He was well acquainted with such writings. We may thus conclude with Fr. Merk that "Origen draws a much sharper distinction between the canonical and non-canonical books than his master, Clement. It can safely be said that no other Father of the Eastern Church will be found to have put the Catholic point of view so firmly and clearly".[20]

There are several passages in which Origen gives his opinion about the canon of the New Testament. The most interesting comes in the *Commentary on St. John*, where, after speaking of St. Paul's Epistles, he says: "Peter left one Epistle which is certainly genuine and perhaps another—its authenticity has been questioned. And what about the man who rested on Jesus' breast? John left a Gospel, of course. . . . He also wrote the Apocalypse . . . He left an Epistle, consisting of a very few lines only. He may also have written two others."[21] But the most noteworthy passage is a little masterpiece of criticism on the Epistle to the Hebrews. It occurs in Origen's homilies on that Epistle. "The style of the work called the Epistle to the Hebrews," he says, "lacks the simplicity characteristic of the Apostle's: St. Paul admits that he is rough in his speech, whereas the Epistle is typically Greek in the artistry of its style. . . . The thought expressed in it, however, is sublime and not at all inferior to the works which are undoubtedly by the Apostle. . . . If I had to give an opinion, I should say that the thought was the Apostle's but that the phrasing and composition came from the person who wrote the Apostle's teaching down. Any Church, then, that regards this as one of Paul's Epistles is to be congratulated; for it can be no accident that the early Christians handed it down under Paul's name. But who actually wrote the letter God alone knows."[22]

II

THE TYPOLOGICAL INTERPRETATION
OF THE BIBLE

ASCERTAINING the correct text was only the first of the steps Origen envisaged. What he regarded as the essential part of the exegete's task was the explanation of the text, ἑρμηνεία. This ἑρμηνεία was of course in the first instance an explanation of the literal meaning, i.e., an explanation of the meaning of the expressions used by the sacred writers. As we shall see, Origen went to rabbis for information of this kind and also made use of philology and archaeology. But the literal explanation of the text was only a preliminary stage in exegesis. Scripture was essentially spiritual, and the exegete's specific function was to peel off the husk of the letter so as to get at the spirit and transmit it to others. The essential thing, as Origen saw it, was to discover the spiritual meaning of the Scriptures. In maintaining this, he was simply echoing what had always been held in the Church. "I will endeavour to show," he writes, "what the accepted methods of interpretation are, and therefore I will follow the rule which has always been used in Jesus Christ's heavenly Church since the time of the Apostles."[1]

However, Origen left his personal stamp on this, as on everything else he touched. The task before us is to try and distinguish between the features in his exegesis which are simply an echo of Tradition and those which reveal external influence. We shall thus have to see what place he held in the stream of the Church's life and in the culture of his time. Otherwise, we cannot hope to see him as he was. Only too often typology has been confused with allegory—historians have spoken as if in Origen's case the two things were the same. I hope to show that he uses both elements in the present instance, as in the others we have examined. Thus, in this

chapter we shall be considering the question of the typological
interpretation of the Old Testament (and, in a sense, of the
New Testament as well), i.e., we shall be studying Origen's
idea of the relationship between the two Testaments. His views
on the point simply represent the tradition we have already
met with in Justin, Irenaeus and Clement. Afterwards, we
shall see which of their characteristics his hermeneutic methods
owe to the culture of his time.

Origen's exegetical theories are stated in all his works without exception, because all that he wrote—the *Contra Celsum*
included—was based on the use of spiritual exegesis. However,
we have the good fortune to possess a systematic statement of
his hermeneutic principles prepared by the man himself: the
fourth book of the *De Principiis* is devoted to Scripture and
scriptural interpretation. The first chapter aims at proving
the divine origin of Scripture. I have already alluded to it.
The second and third deal directly with our subject—How is
Scripture to be read and understood? Why is Scripture obscure
and what is there to account for the impossibilities and ab-
surdities which occur when it is taken literally? We will use
this outline as our starting-point.

To understand the part played by the spiritual interpretation of Scripture in the early days of Christianity, we must
remember that this method of exegesis was directly connected
with the most important of the problems Christians had to face
at the time, viz., the question of the significance of the Old
Testament. Christians found themselves at issue with the Jews
on the one hand, who still held to the literal meaning and kept
the Law of Moses, and the gnostics on the other, who rejected
the Old Testament on the ground that it was the work of the
Demiurge and a part of his creation that had not turned out
properly. The two theories were on common ground in that
they both took the Old Testament in the literal sense only.
Little by little, Christians came to see where they stood themselves and to realise how original their position was. [2] From the
Pseudo-Barnabas to Justin and from Justin to Irenaeus and
Clement, the idea gradually emerged that the difference
between the Testaments was that the one was imperfect and the
other perfect: it implied that the New Testament was an
advance on the Old and not the absolute antithesis of it. For

want of this idea, the secular philosophers of the ancient world had been unable to think out the relationship between the two Testaments. The Old Testament had at one time had a function to fulfil, but that function was to prefigure and pre-pare for the New. Once the New Testament was in force, the Old Testament lapsed as far as its literal meaning was con-cerned but kept its value as a figure.

The question was still an urgent one in Origen's time.[3] It even provided him with a starting-point when he came to explain his views on the spiritual interpretation of Scripture. He first sets out his arguments to prove that the Scriptures are inspired and then, before going on to state his hermeneutical principles, shows where he stands with regard to mistaken methods of interpretation. The passage is of first-rate impor-tance and deserves quoting. Origen summarizes all that had previously been said in the Church about the question and takes it a stage further. "Now that I have said a word or two about the inspiration of God's Scriptures," he writes, "we must take care to ascertain the right way to read and understand them. Many mistakes have been made because so many people have failed to find the right way of dealing with the Holy Scriptures."[4]

He divides the wrong methods of interpretation into three classes. The first of the mistaken interpreters are the Jews, who stick to the letter of the prophecies. They see that Jesus did not literally promise the release of captives (Isa. lxi. 1), rebuild what they take to be the true "City of God", destroy the chariots of Ephraim and the horses of Jerusalem (Zach. ix. 10) or eat milk and honey (Isa. vii. 22). They know it was foretold that the wolf (by which they mean the animal wolf and nothing else) and the lamb should feed together (Isa. lxv. 25), leopard take its ease with kid, calf and lion and sheep be led to pasture together (Isa. xi. 7); and they have not seen it happen. Hence they refuse to believe in the Saviour. "They see that none of the prophecies has been fulfilled in the obvious way through the coming of him whom we believe to be the Christ, and therefore they do not acknowledge him as Lord."[5] Origen states the Jewish position very clearly. The Jews were expecting the prophecies to be fulfilled literally. But Jesus did not fulfil them literally. Therefore Jesus was not the Messiah. The Jews sinned

by being over-literal. As Origen saw it, the fact that the prophecies had not been fulfilled literally was in itself a proof that
they had been meant spiritually.[6]

The second group he turned against were the gnostics. The
heretics (the word "heretic" always means "gnostic" in
Origen), he says, have read the texts: "My anger shall be like
a raging fire" (Deut. xxxii. 22), "I, thy God, am jealous in my
love; be my enemy, and thy children, to the third and fourth
generation, shall make amends" (Exod. xx. 5), "I repent of
having made Saul king of Israel" (1 Kings xv. 10), "I, the
maker of peace, the author of calamity" (Isa. xlv. 7), "Shall
there be evil in a city, which the Lord hath not done?" (Amos
iii. 6), "The evil spirit from God came upon Saul" (1 Kings
xviii. 10), and a great many others of the same kind. "They
did not venture to doubt the divine origin of the Scriptures, but
they decided that they must be the work of the demiurge, who
they thought was the god of the Jews. Hence they concluded
that as the demiurge was an imperfect divinity and not a good
one, the Saviour must have come to proclaim the perfect God,
who, they hold, is not the same as the god who created the
universe."[7]

Here too we have a remarkable statement of the gnostic
position with regard to the Old Testament. Origen was thinking particularly of Marcion, who had gathered together all the
most shocking passages in the Old Testament and then, because
he refused to interpret them spiritually, had concluded that the
two Testaments were incompatible. Here again the mistake
was that the gnostics wanted to keep to the literal sense exclusively. Origen often returns to this controversy with the gnostics
about their exegesis in his other books. The *Commentary on St.
John* appeared as a refutation of the commentary by the gnostic
Heracleon. Several times in the course of it Origen attacks the
gnostic method of interpreting the Old Testament.[8] His
favourite device is to show that the New Testament contains
expressions as unacceptable as anything in the Old if they are
taken literally. The text: "This child is destined to bring about
the fall of many and the rise of many in Israel" (Luke ii. 34) is
a case in point.[9] Similarly, the New Testament attributes
anger and repentance to God and speaks of him as turning his
face away.[10] If Marcion will not use allegory in such cases, he

must either understand the expressions literally of Christ—which is blasphemy[11]—or else consider them spurious.[12] Marcion did consider them spurious; he came to reject a considerable part of the Gospels on the plea that they showed the influence of the compilers' Jewish outlook.

To these two sets of people who both misinterpreted Scripture because they held to the literal sense exclusively, Origen added a third one. This group was to be found in the Church itself, for there were Christians too who refused to interpret Scripture spiritually. The people Origen was really aiming at were the πολλοί, the ἁπλούστεροι. "The simpler members of the Church," he says, "do not imagine that there is another God greater than the Creator, but they do think that God is worse than the cruellest and most unjust of men."[13] They were sure that the God of the Old Testament was the true God, but as they took literally everything the Old Testament said about him, their idea of him was altogether out of keeping with his infinite perfection. They were the people Origen had mainly in view when he formulated his great principle (which, as Fr. Prat says, is unquestionably true) that Scripture cannot say anything about God that is out of keeping with his nature. Therefore, whenever anything of the sort is found in Scripture, it must be interpreted spiritually.[14]

It was with these errors in mind that Origen clarified his own position with regard to the Old Testament. The Law had once served a definite purpose but had now been superseded. The gnostics made the mistake of denying the first part of this proposition; the Jews and the Judaizing party in the Church refused to allow the second. "The house where the Church lived was the part of Scripture comprised in the Law and the Prophets. The King's chamber was there, a room filled with the riches of wisdom and knowledge. There was a cellar, too, where the wine was stored that rejoices men's hearts, the wine, that is, of mystical and moral instruction. When Christ came, he first stayed a while on the other side of the wall. The wall was the Old Testament, and he stayed behind it until he revealed himself to the people. But the time came at last and he began to show himself at the windows. The windows were the Law and the Prophets, the predictions that had been made about him. He began to be visible through them. He began to

show himself to the Church, who was sitting indoors, i.e., she
was engrossed in the letter of the Law. He asked her to come
out and join him. For unless she went out, unless she left the
letter for the spirit, she would never be able to join Christ,
would never become one with her Bridegroom. That was why
he called to her and asked her to leave the things of the flesh
for the things of the spirit and the things she could see for the
things she could not see. That was why he wanted her to leave
the Law for the Gospel. *Surge, veni, proxima mea, formosa mea,
columba mea.*"[15]

The idea of the Law as a preparation for the Gospel comes
out clearly in this passage. The notion that the Law prefigured
the Gospel is not so much to the fore, but Origen brings it out
with some force in another passage by using an image he took
from Melito[16] and comparing the Law to the model a sculptor
makes for a statue. The model shows the lines the statue will
eventually have, but it is destroyed when the statue is finished.
"We who belong to the Church accept Moses, and with good
reason. We read his works because we think that he was a
prophet and that God revealed himself to him. We believe that
he described the mysteries to come, but with symbols and in
figures and allegories, whereas before we ourselves began to
teach men about the mysteries, they had already taken place,
at the time appointed for them. It does not matter whether
you are a Jew or one of us; you cannot maintain that Moses
was a prophet at all unless you take him in this sense. How can
you prove that he was a prophet if you say that his works are
quite ordinary, that they imply no knowledge of the future and
have no mystery hidden in them? The Law, then, and everything in the Law, being inspired, as the Apostle says, until the
time of amendment, is like those people whose job it is to make
statues and cast them in metal. Before they tackle the statue
itself, the one they are going to cast in bronze, silver or gold, they
first make a clay model to show what they are aiming at. The
model is a necessity, but only until the real statue is finished.
The model is made for the sake of the statue, and when the
statue is ready the sculptor has no further use for the model.
Well, it is rather like that with the Law and the Prophets. The
things written in the Law and the Prophets were meant as
types or figures of things to come. But now the Artist himself

has come, the Author of it all, and he has cast the Law aside, because it contained only the shadow of the good things to come [Hebr. x. 1], whereas he brought the things themselves."[17]

The same point of view is found in a passage in the *Commentary on Matthew*. "Lamps are useful as long as people are in the dark; they cease to be a help when the sun rises. The glory on the face of Moses is of use to us, and so, it seems to me, is the glory on the prophets' faces: it is beautiful to look at and it helps us to see how glorious Christ is. We needed to see their glory before we could see his. But their glory paled before the greater glory of Christ. In the same way, there has to be partial knowledge first, and later, when perfect knowledge is acquired, it will be discarded. In spiritual affairs, everyone who has reached the age of childhood and set out on the road to perfection needs a tutor and guardians and trustees until the appointed time comes [cf. Gal. iv.]. Although at this stage he has no more liberty than one of his servants, he will eventually obtain possession of the whole estate. He will cease to be under the care of the tutor, the guardians and the trustees and will be able to enjoy his father's property. That property is like the pearl of great price [Matt. xiii. 46], like the perfection of knowledge. When a man obtains perfect knowledge—knowledge of Christ—he sweeps away his partial knowledge, because by frequenting these lesser forms of gnosis, which are, so to say, surpassed by the gnosis of Christ, he has become capable of receiving Christ's teaching, a thing so much more excellent than his former knowledge. But the majority of people do not see the beauty of the many pearls in the Law and the gnosis (partial though it is) of the prophetical books. They imagine that although they have not thoroughly plumbed and fathomed the depths of these works, they will yet be able to find the one pearl of great cost and contemplate the supremely excellent gnosis, which is the knowledge of Christ. Yet this form of gnosis is so superior to the others that in comparison with it they seem like *stercora*, though they are not *stercora* by nature. . . . Thus all things have their appointed time. There is a time for gathering fine pearls and, when those pearls are gathered, a time for seeking the one pearl of great cost, a time when it will be wise to sally forth and sell everything to buy that pearl.

And anyone who wants to become learned in the words of truth must first be taught the rudiments and gradually master them; he must hold them, too, in high esteem. He will not, of course, remain all the time at this elementary level; he will be like a man who thought highly of the rudiments at first and, now that he has advanced beyond them to perfection, is still grateful to them for their introductory work and their former services. In the same way, when the things that are written in the Law and the prophets are fully understood, they become the rudiments on which perfect understanding of the Gospels and all spiritual knowledge of Christ's words and deeds are based."[18]

The significance of the Law is brought out in this passage to the full; Origen makes no attempt to belittle it in any way. The Law has a glory of its own, is a gnosis of a kind, a gnosis representing a stage man had to pass through, like a child who has to be under a tutor before he becomes his own master. And we must always be grateful for the Law. Yet it would be a mistake to insist on clinging to it now that a greater glory, a superior gnosis, has appeared. The Old Testament was never evil; it was always good. But it has had its time. We must leave it now and take up the Gospels instead. It becomes harmful when people insist on holding on to it, for it represents an order of things that is now over and done with. Origen gets right at the heart of the matter here. What he says about it squares with the profoundest things Irenaeus ever said—his ideas, that is, about the value of the Law as a teacher of divine truth and the fact that it is surpassed by the Gospels—and takes it all a stage further.

Like his predecessors, Origen was fond of seeing in history itself a confirmation of the idea that the Law was a thing of the past. If we go back to the passage from the homily on Leviticus quoted above, we shall find that it continues like this:

For fear you should think that what I have said is difficult to prove, I will ask you to consider it in detail. Jerusalem was at one time a great city, a royal capital, with a famous temple built in God's honour. But then he who is God's real Temple came, he who said of his body: "Destroy this temple" [John ii. 19]; and the mysteries of the Heavenly Jerusalem began to be revealed. The earthly Jerusalem was therefore destroyed when the heavenly one appeared, and as Christ's flesh was God's real temple, not one stone of the temple at Jerusalem was left on another [Mark xiii. 2 etc.]. At one time there was a high priest to purify the people with the blood of bulls and goats, but when the true High Priest came and sanctified those who believed in him with his own blood, the other ceased to exist; there was no room for him anywhere. At one time there was an altar and sacrifice was offered on it, but all that ceased when the true Lamb came and offered himself as a Victim to God, since it had been prescribed for a time only. So, to return to the image used above, it is evident that all these things were like clay models made to suggest the contours of the finished statue; they were all images of the truth to come. That is why divine Providence so arranged it that the city itself and the temple and all those other things should be destroyed. For if they still existed and someone who was still a child or a little one where his faith was concerned saw it, he might be dazzled by the sacrificial rites and the sequence of liturgical formulae and be led astray by the sight of such a variety of forms. But God was watching over our weakness. He wanted his Church to grow, and therefore he did away with all those things, so that when we were faced with the fact of their disappearance, we should not be slow to believe in the truth of what they had preceded and prefigured. [19]

The figure, then, has served its purpose, and its destruction is followed by the coming of the reality which fulfils the figure. There is an admirable passage in which Origen regards Josue ("Jesus" in Greek) as symbolizing this process when he succeeded Moses, Josue being taken as a figure of the Old Testament and Moses as a figure of the New. "We must consider the death of Moses, for if we do not realize in what sense he is dead, we shall not be able to see in what sense Jesus is King. Well, you can see that Jerusalem has been destroyed and the altar put out of use. There is no sacrifice anywhere now, no burnt-offering, no libation; nowhere are there priests or high priests, nowhere levites celebrating the liturgy. You can see that all that has come to an end, and therefore you may say that Moses, God's servant, is dead. You never see people now coming three times a year before the Lord, offering gifts in the Temple, killing the paschal lamb, eating unleavened bread, offering first-fruits or consecrating their first-born to the Lord. You can see that they have stopped all those observances, and so you may say that Moses, God's servant, is dead. But you can also see that the nations are now coming to the faith and that Churches are growing up. Altars are no longer moist with the blood of beasts; they are hallowed by Christ's precious blood. Priests and levites do not now administer the blood of goats and bulls; by the grace of the Holy Spirit they dispense the word of God. In view of this, then, you may say that Jesus has taken over the leadership that Moses had—not Jesus the son of Nun but Jesus the Son of God. You can see that Christ our Paschal Victim has been sacrificed and that we are eating the unleavened bread of purity and honest intent [1 Cor. v. 7]. You can see that the good soil of the Church is yielding a thirtyfold, sixtyfold, hundredfold harvest [Matt. xiii. 8] of widows, virgins and martyrs. You can see the stock of Israel increasing, the race of those who were born not of human stock, nor from nature's will or man's, but from God [John i. 13]. The sons of God were once scattered abroad, but now you can see them gathered together as one. And where God's people once celebrated the sabbath by refraining from their ordinary labours, they now do it by refraining from sin. All this you can see, and therefore you may say that Moses, God's servant, is dead and Jesus, God's Son, holds the power."[20]

This magnificent passage shows that the one economy gave place to the other and yet that there was continuity between them. The novelty of the New Testament and the obsolete character of the Law are clearly brought out, but so too is the resemblance between the spiritual things of the New Law and the carnal ones of the Old. This second idea is what, properly speaking, constitutes the concept of "figure". Here again Origen is summarizing and systematizing the whole body of traditional teaching then existing in the Church. Examples could be quoted from Paul, Barnabas, Justin and Irenaeus for every one of his symbols. It is typology at its most traditional, with its full dogmatic value, typology as an essential part of the Church's deposit. It will be remembered that at the beginning of the *De Principiis*, where he is expounding what the Church believes before he comes to his own personal views, Origen classes the spiritual meaning of Scripture with the objects of faith. "We believe," he says, "that the Scriptures were written by the Spirit of God and that in addition to their literal meaning they have another, which the majority of people are unaware of. The things written in the Scriptures are signs of certain mysteries and images of the things of God. The teaching of the whole Church is the same, viz., that the whole of the Law is spiritual but that what it means in the spiritual sense is not known to everybody: only those who have received such grace from the Holy Ghost as enables them to speak with wisdom and knowledge [1 Cor. xii. 8] know what it is."[21]

Origen develops the theme tellingly in several of his works. We may quote one more example from the homilies on Josue. "Those who observed the Law which foreshadowed the true Law," he writes, "possessed a shadow of divine things, a likeness of the things of God. In the same way, those who shared out the land that Juda inherited were imitating and foreshadowing the distribution that will ultimately be made in heaven. Thus the reality was in heaven, the shadow and image of the reality on earth. As long as the shadow was on earth, there was an earthly Jerusalem, a temple, an altar, a visible liturgy, priests and high priests, towns and villages too in Juda, and everything else that you find described in the book. But at the coming of our Lord Jesus Christ, when truth descended from heaven and was born on earth, and justice looked down from heaven [Ps. lxxxiv. 12], shadows and images saw their last. Jerusalem was destroyed and so was the temple; the altar disappeared. Henceforth neither Mount Garizim nor Jerusalem was the place where God was to be worshipped: his true worshippers were to worship him in spirit and in truth [John iv. 23]. Thus, in the presence of the truth, the type and the shadow came to an end, and when a temple was built in the Virgin's womb by the Holy Ghost and the power of the Most High [Luke i. 35], the stone-built temple was destroyed. If, then, Jews go to Jerusalem and find the earthly city in ruins, they ought not to weep as they do because they are mere children where understanding is concerned. They ought not to lament. Instead of the earthly city, they should seek the

heavenly one. They have only to look up and they will find
the Heavenly Jerusalem, which is the mother of us all [Gal. iv.
26]. Thus by God's goodness their earthly inheritance has
been taken from them to make them seek their inheritance in
heaven."[22]

And so we come to the very heart of the mystery of the
Christian interpretation of history, the meeting-point of symbolism and drama, of progress and the Cross. As Christians see
it, history is symbolical. It is not a succession of heterogeneous
events. It constitutes a plan, every stage of which is at once an
advance on its predecessor and a continuation of it. Only so
does history cease to be dominated by brute fact and become
an intelligible process and a possible object for contemplation
from the religious point of view. Otto says that the great sweep
of history which gave us the prophets produces the feeling that
God was present in it. But there can be no progress in history
without the destruction of what went before. In so far as the
old order has an individual existence of its own it must be
destroyed, if the new order is ever to come into being. Judaism
had to be destroyed before the Church could come into being.
The problem of suffering can be seen emerging even in the Old
Testament, as God began to detach his people from the carnal
economy they had lived under at first. If man was to reach his
full spiritual stature, he would have to make up his mind to
leave his childhood behind him. We have just seen how Origen
explains this with reference to the unwillingness of the Jews to
give up the letter of the Law which had once been their
authorized teacher. His picture of the Jews standing before the
Wailing Wall is a picture of the human race refusing to let go
of its childhood and enter on maturity. Such is the mystery of
growth and the renunciation it entails.

It is the mystery of death and resurrection. And it explains
the significance of Christ's death and resurrection. "Destroy
this temple, and I will raise it up again" (cf. John ii. 19, etc.).
The old Temple had to be destroyed before the new Temple
could make its appearance. In so far as Christ had identified
himself with the old Jewish order of things, he had to die and to
rise again before he could set up the new Temple, his risen
body. From this point of view, Christ's death appears as the
destruction of the old order (the order of the Law, with which

he had deliberately associated himself), because its destruction was a necessary condition of the new order. His death destroyed the figure as such by bringing into being the reality the figure had foreshadowed. The Jews' hostility to Christ also takes on its full significance when it is considered in this light: it expresses the refusal of the figure to accept destruction. Origen puts it in exceptionally forcible terms. "The figure," he says, "wants to go on existing, and so it tries to prevent the truth from appearing."[23] It thus becomes perfectly clear what the enmity the Jews felt towards Christ really meant: it was the visible embodiment of the refusal of the figure to accept its own dissolution.

Origen saw very clearly that the transition from the old order to the new and the unity of the two Testaments had this novel, dramatic side to it. "Jesus had to go to Jerusalem and die the sort of death that would bear out his own words: 'He that shall lose his life for my sake shall find it' [Matt. xvi. 25, etc.]. He had to suffer a great deal there before he could offer the first-fruits of the dead in that Jerusalem which is above [Gal. iv. 26], and despoil and destroy the earthly Jerusalem and the worship that went on there. Until Christ rose from the dead, the first-fruit of all those who had fallen asleep [1 Cor. xv. 20], and until those who had been moulded into the pattern of his death [Phil. iii. 11] and resurrection rose with him, men looked for the city of God, the Temple, the means of purification and the rest, on earth. But when the Resurrection took place, this was no longer the case: all these things were now to be found in heaven. To bring them into being, Jesus had to go to the earthly Jerusalem and suffer a great deal from the elders, the chief priests and the scribes, functionaries prescribed by the Law [cf. Mark viii. 31]. He had to do this if he was to be glorified by presbyters receiving his blessings in heaven and by priests of God functioning under the one High Priest. He had to do it if he was to receive glory from the scribes of the people, not those whose business is to write with pen and ink but those who have to do with the writing made in men's hearts by the Spirit of God. He had to die in the earthly Jerusalem if he was to rise and rule on Mount Sion, in the heavenly Jerusalem which is the city of the living God [Heb. xii. 22]. He had to deliver the dead from the Evil One and his sons, in whom is falsehood,

war and all that is contrary to Christ; he had to free them from
the unclean spirit who passes himself off as the Holy Spirit.
And having set them free, he had to rise from the dead if he
was to secure for them the gift of Baptism in spirit, soul and
body, in the name of the Father and of the Son and of the
Holy Ghost, the three Persons who are the three days eternally
present together to those who through them have become children of the light."²⁴ Thus, the killing of Christ in the earthly
Jerusalem by the leading men of the earthly city is represented
as the essential condition for the building of the Heavenly
Jerusalem and the glorification of Christ by its leaders and
scribes. The transition ($\delta\iota\acute{a}\beta\alpha\sigma\iota\varsigma$ = Pasch, Passover) from the
earthly city to the heavenly, from Israel to the Church, from
the letter to the spirit, is seen to hinge on the drama of the
Passion.

This is the point at which the historical problem of the New
Testament as the successor of the Law touches the problem of
the spiritual interpretation of the Old Testament. The attitude
of the Jews who opposed Christ is not just something that
appeared at a given point in the past. Refusal to accept the
abolition of the Law has been the Jewish attitude ever since
and it always will be, just as it is and always will be the attitude
of those who cling to the literal sense of the Old Testament.
They too hold on to a figure which can no longer serve its
original purpose. Thus, refusal to accept the spiritual sense is
equivalent to a refusal of history, is an anachronism. For
Christ is at once the "new man" who succeeds the "old man"
and the "spiritual Adam" who succeeds the "natural Adam"
(cf. 1 Cor. xv. 44 et seq.). It will be seen that Origen's position
with regard to Judaism is very like his attitude to the pagan
cults. The charge he brings against them too is that they cling
to an unchanging past and refuse the new event which is
Christ. Or rather, the pagan cults can be said to represent this
refusal twice over, since they refuse Judaism as well, and
Judaism too was an event. They are thus doubly antiquated.
Yet they may once have had some justification. Origen says
the cult of the sun may have represented the first of the divine
economies, the economy of the cosmic covenant and natural
religion. But this economy ceased to fulfil its purpose on the
appearance of Judaism, which was a new manifestation to

mankind of God's eternal youth. Thus it is clear that the criterion for judging the historical question is first and foremost a chronological one. God's plan is carried out in successive stages, and any religion that represents an earlier stage, any religion that is anachronistic, is *ipso facto* false.

The theology of history comes in a third time, with a deeper connotation, in connection with the theology of the angels. As we shall see, in Origen's view, human history appears in the last resort as the projection, *umbra et exemplar*, of the history enacted in heaven. We shall come to the ultimate principles, the ἀρχαί, of the theology of history, when we deal with that question, but it is important to point out here and now that the question occupying us at the moment is one of the leading themes in Origen's works, especially as this side of the matter has been entirely overlooked by those who have written about him up to the present. The thing that prevents him from being a mere philosopher is that in his view Christianity is essentially history. Of course, he always maintained that truth was unchangeable; no one more so, because no one held more firmly than he that spiritually-minded men had in all ages been in possession of the *mysteria*. But if truth is always the same, if θεολογία is unchangeable, οἰκονομία, i.e., "human affairs", is, as he sees it, a matter of history. And both human affairs and history itself unfold at two levels. In heaven, to use Berdaieff's terminology, history is made by the aeons; and when this history is projected on to the earth, we have the history of mankind. This is an entirely new view of things, a *Weltanschauung* quite unlike any other. It is neither pure immobility nor pure becoming but a process taking place on two corresponding planes at once. Such is the Christian idea of history. Origen took it from Platonism. But it was Platonism with the eternal ideas changed into angels, replaced by historical persons, i.e., Platonism entirely transformed by the two essential categories of Christian thought, the subjective (the value of the person) and the historical.

The fact that the people who would hear of no interpretation of Scripture but the literal one were taking up exactly the same attitude as the Jews who had persecuted Christ is brought out in a noteworthy passage in the *Commentary on Matthew*. Origen begins by taking the theme of the Passion as the transition

from the physical Israel to the spiritual Church. I will
quote it in full.

Until Jesus was handed over to the chief priests and the
scribes at Jerusalem, until he was condemned to death, held
up to ridicule, beaten with rods and nailed to the cross,
Jerusalem still remained standing and the holy place, as it
was called, was not destroyed. But once his betrayers had
dared to do all that to him, they were taken prisoners themselves. The high priests ceased to be high priests, and there
were no more after them. The scribes who had condemned
him to death were afflicted with hardness of heart and
spiritual blindness; they could no longer see what the
Scriptures meant. As they had given Jesus up to his enemy,
Death, they were given up to Death themselves. The object
of all this was to take their protective function away from
them and give it to those of the Gentiles who had been saved,
together with the faithful "remnant", the object of God's
special choice. If the Lord had not left them a seed, they
would have been like Sodom.

The ancient liturgy contained images and shadows of
things in heaven, but the things in heaven were also the cause
of its abrogation. And when the real High Priest came, the
figurative one ceased to exist, and when the real sacrifices
for sin were offered the symbolical ones were abolished. It
was the same, it seems to me, when Jesus came riding to the
true Jerusalem, mounted on his own body, and the daughter
of Sion saw him and was exceedingly glad, and the daughter
of the Jerusalem that is above shouted for joy. The shadow-
Jerusalem then lost what substance it had. The temple built
of lifeless stones fell in ruins because there was now another
built of living stones [cf. 1 Pet. ii. 5]. The earthly altar
crumbled because the seat of the oracles was now the altar
in heaven and Jesus himself had celebrated its dedication
with the true liturgy.

If, then, in one sense the city is all mankind, Jesus is still
being sent to his death at Jerusalem (I apply the name to
those whose hopes are centred on a place on this earth) even
today. The Jews, who claim to be the only true worshippers
of God, are like the princes, the priests and the scribes,

boasting of their ability to explain the Holy Scriptures. Not a day passes but they hand him over to the pagans, when they ridicule him and his teaching in front of them. They crucify him when they anathematize him and try to hush up what he taught. But his power is greater than theirs. After a little while he rises from the dead, and to those who are capable of seeing him he shows himself alive. . . . The true Light shone out with amazing brilliance but they could not see it: their ill-will blinded them and they did not recognize God's mysteries. Thus, a very strange thing happened, both to the Jews and to the Gentiles. The Jews saw that all the prophets were lamps, but when the Sun of Justice rose they did not recognize him. Hence, when they thought they had a lamp, it was taken from them. But the Gentile nations, "the people that walked in darkness", did see the light. It was no small light they saw, unlike the lights that Israel had seen (for the prophets were all small lights). No, "the people that walked in darkness have seen a great light" [Isa. ix. 2]. They saw the Lord and Saviour Jesus Christ himself, the measure of whose greatness it is that he "reacheth . . . from end to end mightily, and ordereth" the Churches "sweetly" [Wisd. viii. 1].[25]

Thus, all who want to keep to the small lamp of the prophetic writings, i.e., those who want to keep to the literal meaning, are like the Jews. "Anyone wanting to take Scripture literally had better class himself with the Jews rather than with the Christians. But anyone who wants to be a Christian and a disciple of Paul must listen to what Paul says. Paul says that the Law is something spiritual [Rom. vii. 14]."[26] And in another passage Origen says, with regard to the leaven of the Pharisees: "We may appropriately apply this phrase to those who live like Christians but want to live like Jews as well. There are some who will not admit that the Law is spiritual and that it contains only a shadow of the good things to come [cf. Heb. x. 1]. They do not try to find out what future blessings the various details of the Law are shadows of. They have no vision and so do not avoid the leaven of the Pharisees."[27] This was the attitude of those who rejected the spiritual interpretation of Scripture even though they belonged to the

Church, and who attacked Origen for not being of their opinion. "There are even some of our own religion who would like me to follow the literal meaning and interpret what the lawgiver says without any *stropha verbi* or cloud of allegory, to use the sarcastic expressions they use themselves. If I did as they wish, then although I am a member of the Church, living by my faith in Christ and set in the midst of the Church, I should be forced to sacrifice calves and lambs and offer myrrh with incense and oil, on the ground that God's commandments ordered me to."[28] It was in virtue of the same carnal outlook that the Jews persecuted the prophets, put Christ to death and were still persecuting the defenders of the spiritual method of interpretation.[29] But Origen did not allow himself to be worn down by these attacks. "When I take to explaining the words these men used long ago and look for a spiritual meaning in them, when I try to lift the veil that hides the Law, I am doing what I can to bore a well. Yet at once the friends of the letter take up the slanderous cry against me. They attack me and say that there can be no truth that does not rest on the earth. But for our part, as we are servants of Isaac, we must prefer wells of running water and springs. We must keep far away from these men with their untruths. We will leave them the earth, since they love it so."[30]

On the other hand, those who do not cling to the letter, the external expression of the figure, but turn to Christ, the fulfilment of the figure, find that the Law itself becomes clear and spiritual. "In the Law of Moses, the light was hidden and covered with a veil. When Jesus came, it shone out, because the veil was then removed and the blessings which had been only foreshadowed in the letter were suddenly revealed."[31] Scripture is the field where the treasure mentioned by Christ is hidden. "The treasure hidden in the field is the various meanings devised by that wisdom which is hidden in the mystery, meanings masked by the things that strike our sight. . . . The things of heaven and the Kingdom of Heaven are as it were pictured in the Scriptures."[32] This hidden meaning is the spiritual thing in Scripture. It had been known hitherto only to the spiritually advanced, but when Christ came he made it plain to everybody. "The Gospel, the New Testament, frees us from the old order, the order of the letter, and thus, in the light cast by the gnosis, shows up the splendour of the new order, the order of the Spirit [cf. Rom. vii. 6]. This order properly belongs to the New Testament but it is found hidden in the other Scriptures too."[33] At the Transfiguration, the garments Jesus was wearing became white like snow from the brilliance of his divinity. And with that same light he also whitened the corn-fields of the Scriptures on the harvest-day, the day of his coming down to earth.

But for that to happen to us too, Jesus must explain the Law to us himself. So Origen says when he comments on Josue's reading of the Law to the Jews (Josue = Jesus) and links it up with the explanation of the Law that Jesus gave his Disciples at Emmaus. The foreshortening is a stroke of genius—but then, genius in typology is only the perception of affinities in Scripture, just as poetic genius is the perception of affinities in the natural world. This, then, is Origen's explanation of the passage:

When we hear the books of Moses read, by the Lord's grace the veil of the letter is lifted and we begin to understand that the Law is something spiritual—e.g., when the Law says that Abraham had two sons, one by a slave and the other by a free woman, I understand by the two sons two covenants and two peoples. Well, if we are capable of interpreting the Law like that and realizing that it is something spiritual, as St. Paul says, the reason is, so it seems to me, that the person reading the Law to us is the Lord Jesus himself. He it is who reads it for all the people to hear and orders us not to follow the letter, which inflicts death, but to understand the spirit, which is what brings life [cf. 2 Cor. iii. 6]. Thus, Jesus reads us the Law when he reveals to us the secrets of the Law. We do not despise the Law of Moses because we belong to the Catholic Church; we still accept it, provided that Jesus reads it to us. If Jesus reads it to us we can take it in its proper sense; when he reads it, we grasp its spiritual meaning. The Disciples who said: "Were not our hearts burning within us as he spoke to us on the road, and when he made the Scriptures plain to us?" [Luke xxiv. 32] had understood the spiritual meaning of the Law. You will agree, I think, that it was because Jesus had explained

it to them when he read it all to them and made plain to
them what had been written about him, from Moses to the
prophets.[34]

The understanding of the Scriptures was a grace given by
Christ. Only those who had the Spirit of Jesus could understand their spiritual meaning. Here again, Origen inherited a
body of traditional doctrine taught everywhere in the Church.
The gnosis, the spiritual knowledge of Scripture, was a
charisma. The exegete had to be a highly spiritual man. Such
had been the teaching of his predecessors, St. Paul, the Pseudo-
Barnabas, Clement of Rome and Justin.[35] Justin in particular
thought that great grace from God was needed for understanding the Scriptures.[36] Clement of Alexandria regarded the
gnosis, the operation that probes the mysteries of Scripture, as
something bound up with spiritual perfection: only the τέλειος
could discern the spiritual significance of things, because he
was entirely spiritual himself. In this respect again Origen
appears as the perfect *didaskalos*.

Consider Gregory the Wonderworker's testimony again.
"He used to interpret and explain all obscurities and difficulties
as they occurred—and there are many of them in the Holy
Scriptures, whether it is that God decided to conceal certain
things by that means, or whether we only find obscure what is
not so in itself. Of all men now living, I have never known or
heard of one who had meditated as he had on the pure and
luminous words and had become so expert at fathoming their
meaning and teaching them to others. I do not think he could
have done that unless he had had the Spirit of God in him, for
the same grace is needed for understanding the prophecies as
for making them. No one can understand the prophets unless
the Spirit who inspired the prophets himself gives him understanding of his words. Scripture says that he who shuts alone
can open [Isa. xxii. 22]. The divine Logos opens what he had
shut up when he enables us to understand the mysteries. Origen
possessed the sovereign gift, which he got from God, of being
the interpreter of God's words to men. He had the power to
listen to God and understand what he said, and then to explain
it to men that they too might understand."[37]

This testimony is corroborated by all that Origen ever wrote.

In the homilies, for example, he is always asking his hearers to pray that the Holy Spirit may enlighten him. "I will say a few words on this question, if through your prayers the Lord grants me the grace to understand it (and if we are any of us worthy to be told the Lord's meaning)."[38] And again: "If ever I needed God's help—and we always do need the Holy Spirit if we are to understand the Scriptures—now is the time for him to help me and to show me the meaning of his words."[39] The idea is expressed in particular by the image of the lifting of the veil. "No one can find it easy to discover all the allegories contained in this story [the story of Abimelech and Sara]. All the same, we must pray that the veil covering our hearts as they strive to turn to the Lord may be removed. The Lord is the Spirit. We must pray the Lord to lift the veil of the letter himself and let the brightness of the Spirit shine out."[40]

Here are two more passages from the homilies. "Every time Moses is read to us, we should pray to the Father of the Word that the words of the psalm: 'Open thou my eyes: and I will consider the wondrous things of thy law' [Ps. cxviii. 18] may apply in our case too. Unless he opens our eyes himself, how can we see what great mysteries were wrought in the patriarchs, mysteries variously signified by the images of night, marriage and birth?"[41] We are like blind men, whose eyes need unsealing. "We too must take care, for we are often beside the wells of running water—God's Scriptures—and yet we fail to recognize them for what they are . . . We must be always weeping and begging the Lord to open our eyes. The blind men sitting by the road side at Jericho [Matt. xx. 30] would not have had their eyes opened unless they had shouted after the Lord. And yet, why am I talking about the opening of our eyes as if it were something still to come? Our eyes have already been opened. Jesus came to open the eyes of the blind, and the veil that covered the Law has already been lifted."[42] The theme of the healing of the eyes recurs in other contexts. "Our Lord laid his hands physically on a blind man's eyes and gave him back his sight; he also stretched out his hands spiritually over the eyes of the Law. Those eyes had been blinded by the carnal interpretation of the scribes, but the Lord restored their sight, for those to whom he meant to make the Scriptures plain were to see and understand the Law spiritually."[43]

The same teaching is found in the commentaries. Thus, in connection with the parable of the unfaithful servant, Origen first gives the most evident meaning and then goes on to say: "Obviously, anyone enquiring more thoroughly into it would have a great deal to add. To my mind, the explanation and interpretation of such things exceeds human capacities. The words were Christ's, and it takes Christ's Spirit to make us understand them as Christ meant them. 'Who can know a man's thoughts, except the man's own spirit that is within him? So no one else can know God's thoughts, but the Spirit of God' [I Cor. ii. 11]. In the same way, apart from God, no one but Christ's Spirit knows what Christ said in the parables. And no one can contemplate the truths hidden in this passage unless he shares in the life of that Spirit."[44] But the most sublime passage is in the *Commentary on St. John.* "We must, therefore, go so far as to say that the Gospels are the firstfruits of Scripture as a whole and John's Gospel the firstfruits of the Gospels. No one can understand this Gospel unless he has rested against the breast of Jesus [John xiii. 23] and taken Mary for his mother [John xix. 27]. . . . What an understanding we need, then, if we are to grasp as we ought the word hidden in the earthen vessels [2 Cor. iv. 7] of the letter."[45]

Thus, Christ is the Inner Principle dispensing spiritual understanding of Scripture, i.e., knowledge of the most real part of its content. That is the subjective side of the typological method. But Christ is also the Object of this spiritual understanding, for all Scripture is about him and about him alone. "Everything written in the Law refers to Christ, by means of parable and image" (Num. xii. 8).[46] Or as Pascal puts it: "The only thing in Scripture is charity." That is the justification for the use of the Old Testament by Christians. We may still use the Old Testament, but only on condition that we look for Christ in it, for Christ alone concerns us now. And we may look for Christ in Scripture because he really is to be found there. Origen proves this by showing from history that Christ was prefigured in the Old Testament in the institutions and events of the Law. Thus, the spiritual method of interpretation rests on the fact that the Old Testament has its face turned towards the New. This doctrine, which is one of the fundamental tenets of Christianity, has no meaning unless there are parallels between the two Testaments. The spiritual meaning is only the result of a search for those parallels.

Christ is prefigured in the Old Testament in all his fullness. This brings us to the final question, that of the various kinds of spiritual meaning in Scripture. The first thing to do was to show the fundamental parallelism between the two Testaments. It could be said that essentially there are only two meanings in Scripture, the literal and the Christological. But the Christological meaning can in turn be subdivided into as many sections as there are aspects in Christ himself. Christ may be considered either as a historical Person manifested in the events recorded in the Gospels, or as living a hidden life in the "sacraments" of the Church which is his body, or as appearing at the *parousia* at the end of the world and reigning in glory. Further, these three *adventus* themselves, to use a term of St. Augustine's, have more than one side to them. In the historical Christ we may consider either the external actions of his earthly life or the spiritual content of its mysteries. In the mystical Christ, again, we may consider either the collective aspect, which is the whole Church, or the separate members of that Church, each of whom has to "put on" Christ (Rom. xiii. 14, Gal. iii. 27).

Such, at bottom, was the question of the various meanings of Scripture as it appeared to the early Christians. Origen complicated it when he tried to square it with Philo's idea that there were three meanings in Scripture—the literal, ($\sigma\tilde{\omega}\mu\alpha$) the moral ($\varphi\nu\kappa\acute{\eta}$) and the anagogical ($\pi\nu\epsilon\tilde{\upsilon}\mu\alpha$)—corresponding to the three divisions of the human person. We shall return later to this point, which illustrates one of the ways in which Origen's exegesis was distorted by the culture of his time. At the moment we are concerned with him in so far as he represents the established tradition. The various senses of Scripture which Tradition admitted were all known in the Church before his time. They can be found as early as St. Paul. Different authors stressed different ones, according to their personal bent. Several trends in exegesis can thus be discerned from the very beginning of Christianity, long before the appearance of the schools of Antioch and Alexandria. One of these trends, the ancestry of which goes back to the Gospel according to St. Matthew, consisted of searching the Old Testament mainly for analogies with events in the life of Jesus. Thus, it

was considered that the Massacre of the Innocents was prefigured by the killing of Rachel's sons and the flight into Egypt
by one of Osee's prophecies. The tendency is represented
chiefly by Hippolytus of Rome. It has always been congenial
to exegetes in the West. Justin took up a more Johannine
standpoint and regarded the Old Testament figures principally
as referring to the sacraments of the Church. He thus originated
that form of exegesis which came to occupy so prominent a
place in the traditional catechetical instruction, the form used
for teaching converts about the "mysteries". Irenaeus, on the
other hand, depended on the Jewish tradition, with which he
was connected through Papias and the presbyters. His exegesis
therefore stressed the eschatological element. Clement of
Alexandria's exegesis of the Old Testament mostly pointed to
figures of Christ in his members. That is the most strictly
mystical of all the senses in which Scripture can be taken, and
it was to remain the favourite of the Alexandrian school.

These traditional ways of interpreting Scripture are all
found in Origen. Thus, he begins his commentary on the story
of the Flood by determining the literal meaning of the text,
and he does not question its value as evidence that the Flood
did actually occur in history. [47] "The flood represents the end,
the real end of the world." [48] He bases his interpretation on the
important passage in Matt. xxiv, where Christ himself teaches
that the Flood prefigures the events that will take place at the
end of the world. He is here giving the same exegesis as
Irenaeus. He takes the ark as a figure of the Church and Noe
as a figure of Christ. And he ends with a mystical interpretation
of the Flood. Similarly in the case of Isaac, he takes the Epistle
to the Galatians as authority for regarding his birth as a figure
of the Church and the Epistle to the Hebrews as justification
for the view that his sacrifice was a figure of the Passion.
"Abraham knew that he was prefiguring and representing
things to come. He knew that Christ would be born of his
stock and offer himself as the true Victim for the whole
world." [49] When he comes to deal with the crossing of the Red
Sea, like all his predecessors he regards it, as we have said, as a
figure of Baptism. He also gives it a spiritual meaning.
"'Pasch' means 'passing over'. To celebrate the Pasch without
ceasing is to pass over unceasingly in thought, word and deed

from the things of earth to God, and to hasten on towards the City of God."[50] Lastly, he gives the incident an eschatological meaning.[51]

It will, however, be noticed that he shows a preference for one of these eschatological interpretations as against the others. He seems to have been opposed to that school of exegesis which we said depended on St. Matthew, the one that looked on the external events of the Old Testament as figures of equally external (notice that I do not say historical) events in the New, the school of Hippolytus in particular. The method is rarely found applied in his works, and in one passage on the symbolism of the paschal lamb he distinctly takes up his stand against it. He seems to have had in mind the interpretation given by Hippolytus in his paschal homily. Hippolytus regarded the preparation of the lamb as a detailed prophecy of the events recorded in the historical account of the Passion—the four days that elapsed before the lamb was sacrificed represented the time Christ was kept in confinement by Caiphas before he was taken to Calvary; the fact that the lamb was sacrificed in the evening meant that Christ would suffer in the evening.[52] Origen's answer is that "it would be wrong to think that one historical event is a figure of another or one corporal thing a figure of another corporal thing. No; the corporal is a figure of the spiritual, the historical of the intelligible."[53] It would be a grievous misinterpretation to take this as a condemnation of the kind of exegesis that regarded the Old Testament as a figure of the historical Christ in the sense in which we now understand the word historical. What Origen is directly aiming at is the kind of exegesis that saw the Old Testament as a figure of the anecdotal side (which is what ἱστορία means in Greek) of Christ's life and not of the theological side. But in the sense in which we now use the word historical, the theological side is just as historical as the other.

Origen's own preference was obviously for the form of exegesis that interpreted Scripture with reference to the inner life. This is only another manifestation of that general characteristic of his thinking which we have already come across in connection with his theology of the sacraments. Just as when he deals with public worship he stresses the spirit of it more than the external rites, so here he stresses the significance of

Scriptural texts for the inner life rather than their application to the Church. This is the distinctive mark of the exegesis of the Alexandrian school, the one which was later to distinguish it from the exegesis of the school of Antioch. Both were equally typological. The difference between them was not, as has been said, that one was literal and the other allegorical. The exegesis of both was typological and the one was as Christological as the other; but at Antioch theologians concentrated on the catechetical tradition and laid particular stress on the part of it relating to the sacraments, while the Alexandrians concentrated on what Tradition had to say about the spiritual life and put the stress on the mystical side. Both were equally rooted in Tradition. And just as in the case of public worship Origen's leaning towards the spiritual implies not rejection of external rites but only underestimation of their value, so in this case it implies no denial of the typology of the sacraments. Only, he does not dwell on it; he is always in a hurry to discover any meaning his text may have for the spiritual life, always anxious to find food for the soul.

His commentary on the birth of Jacob provides an excellent illustration of this attitude. He begins by reminding his readers of St. Paul's typological interpretation, but he does not dwell on it. "Even the unbelieving Jews know that one people has taken the place of another, i.e., that the Church has taken the place of the Synagogue, and that the elder is now the servant of the younger. Hence there can be no need, I think, to speak of what is common knowledge and a commonplace to you all."[54] It is evident, then, that if Origen did not develop the line of interpretation that understood Scripture of the Church, it was not because he failed to recognize its existence; far from it. The reason was that there was no point in stressing it, because it was so well known. Which shows, incidentally, how familiar the typological method of interpretation was to the early Christians. What Origen intended to do was to bring out the side of Scripture bearing on the spiritual life and "capable of edifying and instructing".[55] "The Apostle is showing us, you see [by contrasting Agar with Sara] how the 'flesh lusteth against the spirit' [Gal. v. 17] in all circumstances. This people, with its thoughts ever on the flesh, fights against the people of the spirit; and even among us, those whose thoughts are on the flesh oppose the spiritually-minded. You yourself, in fact, are a son of Agar if you live according to the flesh."[56] The external conflict thus becomes internal; the strife of Jew against Gentile is something we all experience within ourselves. But this inner conflict rests on the solid fact of the historical conflict between the two peoples and is a legitimate develop-ment of it. The historical is thus considered here not only in its objective reality but as a constituent of human nature. The point has been brought out in our own day by Fr. Fessard in his study of the Jewish, pagan and Christian outlooks. This bringing of the conflict from the outer sphere to the inner is legitimate only in so far as it claims to be a dialectical descrip-tion of man under Christianity, at a particular point in history, and not an *a priori* deduction from the nature of man. Origen certainly did give a dialectical description of that sort. Hegel, perhaps, did not. Fr. Fessard at least tries to.

The first distinctive feature of Origen's typology is its pre-dominantly spiritual tone, its bearing on the inner life. The reader will be clear about the angle we have been regarding it from up to the present. We are not at the moment concerned with any moral allegorizing Origen may have indulged in after the manner of Philo. That deviation we will speak of later. The aspect of his typology we are considering now is quite traditional and legitimate: it is simply the side of the traditional typology which his spiritual bent led him to develop to a parti-cular extent. When we compare his exegetical use of typology with his predecessors', we see that its second characteristic is that Origen was the first to gather the various forms of typology together and make a methodical digest of them. In that sense, he was unquestionably the originator of the subsequent teaching about the different meanings of Scripture. But I must repeat once more that for the moment we are concerned only with such meanings as were recognized by the accepted schools of typology. The relevant material was scattered about in the works of previous writers and Origen, with his systematic temper, digested it into an orderly code. It was the same with his teaching about the spiritual senses, which also was to be found in a fragmentary state in the earlier writers. One had spoken of God's sweetness, another of the light in him, a third of the sweet scents to be found in Christ. Fr. Rahner has shown

that what Origen did was to bring these disparate elements
together to form what has become the traditional teaching about
the five spiritual senses. In the same way, he formed a single
doctrinal unit out of the main spiritual meanings of Scripture,
differentiated according to the chief aspects discernible in the
Christus totus—meanings relating to Christ himself, to the
Church, to the spiritual life and to eschatology.

I have already given an example of this systematization in
connection with the typology of Noe, where Origen groups
Justin's Christological type of exegesis with the eschatological
type given by Irenaeus and adds a mystical interpretation of his
own. Similarly, the *Commentary on St. John* first shows how the
eating of the paschal lamb is a figure that has been fulfilled in
the Church, both in its sacramental and in its spiritual form.
But it adds that "for the moment, we need not raise our minds
to the third passover, which will be celebrated among myriads
of angels when the perfect and truly blessed exodus takes
place".[57] It is worth noticing, too, that here again Origen is
referring to something in Scripture, for it was Christ himself who
said that the perfect passover would be celebrated in the kingdom of God (Luke xx. 16).

Two examples of this gradation in the various levels of
exegesis are particularly worth noting. In the *Commentary on
the Song of Songs* Origen explains the verse: "For winter is now
past . . . the flowers have appeared in our land . . . the voice of
the turtle is heard."[58] He first applies it to the soul. "The soul
is not made one with God's Word," he says, "until the winter
and the storms—the passions and the vices—have been dis-
pelled and she has ceased to be disturbed and tossed about by
every wind of doctrine [Eph. iv. 14]. When everything like
that has gone from her and the storm of her desires has left her,
the flowers of virtue will blossom in her and she will hear the
voice of the dove. She will hear, that is to say, his words of
wisdom who dispenses the word to the perfect, the wisdom of
the Most High God, hidden in the mysteries. That is what is
meant by the word 'dove'." That is the first meaning, the one
concerned with Christ's words to the soul to whom he has
"shown himself and his teaching, urging her to go out of herself
so as to be rid of her bodily senses and no longer immersed in
the things of the flesh".[59]

"But Christ is also talking to the Church. He is using the cycle of the seasons to represent the entire lifetime of this world. By winter he means the time when the Egyptians were smitten by hailstones and other plagues, the time when Israel itself was brought low because it had resisted the Lord. But now that through Israel's sin salvation has been granted to the Gentiles, Christ calls to the Church and says: 'Rise up and come to me.' The wicked had been overtaken by the winter and we had been kept in ignorance by it, but all that is over now. Any moment now the voice of the dove—God's wisdom, that is—will sound on the earth; any moment now it will say: 'I myself that spoke, behold I am here' [Isa. lii. 6]. Flowers—the peoples that believe, the nascent Churches—are now to be seen on the earth. The vines, we are told, are in flower and are full of fragrance. The youngest of the Churches on the face of the earth may be called vines, for the prophet says: 'The vineyard of the Lord of hosts is the house of Israel' [Isa. v. 7]. And they are said to be in flower when they first come to the faith."[60]

We thus have a mystical meaning for the individual and a meaning for the Church, both of them relating to this life. Origen goes on to provide an eschatological interpretation. "We can take the text in another sense," he says, "and consider it as a prophecy to the Church, inviting her to accept what it was promised she should have. Thus, at the end of time, when the resurrection comes, she will be told: 'Rise up.' And because this injunction denotes her resurrection, she is invited in the words: 'Come, my love, my beautiful one, my dove, the winter is past', to reign as queen. Winter denotes the storms and tempests of this present life, for the life of man is exposed to the passions: they are its storms. But this winter is now over. And in the voice of the dove, which the meek will hear when they come into the kingdom, you may discern the Person of Christ, for he will then teach them face to face instead of through a glass and in a dark manner [1 Cor. xiii. 12] as he did before."[61]

Another excellent example is to be found in the homilies on Josue, in connection with the fall of Jericho. "Jericho collapsed at the sound of the priests' trumpets. I said before that Jericho is a figure of this world, the power and defences of which are destroyed, as we see, by the priests' trumpets. The world's power and defences, the walls it relied on, were the worship of idols, organized by evil spirits through cunning manipulation of oracles and served by augurs, *haruspices* and magi. All this surrounded the world like mighty walls. The son of Nave fore-shadowed the *parousia* of our Lord Jesus Christ. When Christ came, he sent his Apostles out, as Josue had sent out the priests, and like the priests they carried resonant trumpets, which in this case were the magnificent, heaven-sent doctrines they preached. The priests blew their trumpets to bring down the walls of Jericho. But that was not all. What I find so striking is this: the text says that all the people shouted loud when they heard the sound, or according to other manuscripts, exulted with great joy. Joy like that seems to me to imply a disposition to concord and harmony of outlook. When such a disposition occurs in any two or three Christians together and they ask their heavenly Father for something in the Saviour's name, he gives it to them [Matt. xviii. 19]. And, when there is so much of this joy that in all Christian people there is 'but one heart and one soul' [Acts iv. 32], there will be a repetition of the event recorded in the Acts of the Apostles—an earthquake will take place like the one there was when the Apostles, the women and Mary the mother of Jesus were 'persevering with one mind in prayer' [Acts i. 14]. By the time it is over, all earthly things will have been destroyed and fallen to pieces; this world will have been destroyed and brought to an end. Yet remember that to give heart to his soldiers the Lord said to them: 'Take courage, I have overcome the world' [John xvi. 33]. As he is our head, we share in his victory over the world; the defences the men of the world counted on already lie in ruins before us." [62]

That is the Christological meaning. The fall of Jericho, i.e., of idolatry, is compassed by Christ through the mysteries of his life between the Passion and the sending of the Holy Spirit. Origen then goes on to the mystical meaning. "We ought all of us," he says, "to experience this in our own persons. Through faith you have Jesus in you as your Leader. If you are a priest, you should make yourself trumpets from the Holy Scriptures and draw out of them a meaning and message that will entitle them to be called resonant. Sound the trumpets of the psalms and canticles, the mysteries of the Law and the prophets, the teachings of the Apostles. Sound such trumpets as these. Carry the Ark of the Covenant seven times round the town by linking the gospel-precepts with their symbols, the precepts of the Law. Strive to produce in yourself the harmony that jubilation implies: endeavour to make the people—your thoughts and feelings—shout in unison and harmony. If you succeed in doing all this, shout for joy, because the world in you will have been brought low and destroyed."[63]

A whole series of vistas emerges out of this, as will have been seen. The fall of Jericho is the fall of this world and its foundations, the cult of evil spirits. It is brought about by the coming of Christ and the coming of the Holy Spirit—Pentecost is the third of the earthquakes St. Gregory Nazianzen speaks of in his Theological Orations, the first being the one that took place on Sinai (the revelation of the Father) and the second the earthquake on Calvary (the revelation of the Son). Thus, the world fell and time ended when Christ came on earth. However—and this is the first aspect of the matter—the downfall of the world has been secured only *de jure* and now needs to be ratified by each individual on his own account. Jesus must come to every individual soul and the world must crumble for each of us separately at the sound of the priests' trumpets. This corresponds to what was later known as the mystical sense when the theory of the various meanings of Scripture came to be worked out. The previous meaning was the Christological one. And it becomes clear from this example how a spiritual bias can be introduced into typology, given a definite fact to start from. But it remains true that Christ's victory over the world has not yet been fully consummated. Thus, Pentecost is only the forerunner of another earthquake, which will be the last. The world lingers on, but the life has already gone out of it; it is like a building with cracks in it, a building ready to fall. When the final earthquake occurs, it will collapse for good and all.

This latter aspect of the question is brought out by Origen a little further on. "This seems to be correct as a figure of what has already happened," he says. "But," he goes on, "I am particularly struck by the fact that the historical figure represents the devil and his army as already destroyed. If that is so, why is it that we still see the devil and his faction, our adversaries, in possession of such power against God's servants? The Apostle Peter has to caution us about it with particular insistency and bid us remember that 'the devil our adversary goes about like a roaring lion seeking whom he may devour'. Let us see if we can find a fitting explanation of the Holy Spirit's words in this connection. When Christ came the first time he came in humble guise, but we are confident that there will be another *parousia* and that the second time he will come in glory. The first *parousia* in the flesh is called a shadow in that mysterious text of Holy Scripture: 'The breath of our mouth, Christ the Lord: in his shadow we live among the Gentiles.' [cf. Lam. iv. 20]. And when Gabriel brought Mary the good news about Christ's birth he too said to her: 'The Spirit of the Most High shall overshadow thee.' Hence it is evident that a great deal in the first *parousia* is only shadow and that it will be given substance and perfection in the second. And the Apostle Paul says that God has 'raised us up too, enthroned us too above the heavens, in Christ Jesus' [Eph. ii. 6]. Well, we believe that that is true, but all the same we do not as yet see ourselves risen and enthroned in heaven. These things are given us now in outline (*adumbrata*) through faith, because in spirit and in hope we rise above what is dead and earthly and day by day lift up our hearts to the heavenly and eternal. The outline will be filled in at the second *parousia*, and what we now possess in anticipation by faith and hope we shall then grasp bodily in its reality. Thus, with regard to the devil, we must take it that he has already been vanquished and crucified, but only for those who are crucified with Christ. For the faithful in general and for the nations, he will be crucified when what the Apostle says—that just as all have died with Adam, so with Christ all will be brought to life [1 Cor. xv. 22]—takes place. Thus, what is contained in this passage is the mystery of the resurrection to come. . . . Then indeed there will be no devil, because there will be no death.'' [64]

This passage brings us to the final aspect of Origen's theory of typology. Up to the present we have studied his figurative exegesis of the Old Testament only. But a new idea comes out here: the New Testament in turn is seen as a figure of the Kingdom that is to come. It is an idea that we have already met with in Origen's theology of Baptism. We have seen that he regarded Baptism as being at once the fulfilment of Old Testament figures and a figure both of the Baptism that will take

place at the end of the world and also of the Resurrection.
Now we have the same outlook again but with reference to the
New Testament as a whole. Another dimension must thus be
added to Origen's view of history. History is not just the
relationship of the Old Testament to the New; it is also the
relationship of the New Testament to the eternal Gospel, to use
the words of the Apocalypse (xiv. 6), as Origen does in a famous
passage in the *De Principiis*.[65]

He comments on the symbolism of Josue's succeeding Moses
(which we have already met with) and shows that it corresponds to the superseding of the Law by the Second Law or
Deuteronomy. He begins by reminding his readers that Josue
is here the "figure of our Saviour, whose Second Law, i.e., the
precepts of the Gospels, brings everything to its perfection".[66]
But there is more symbolism in it than that. "We must see if
there is not something else nearer to the principal meaning of
the text. Just as Deuteronomy meant the promulgation of a
clearer, plainer code of laws than any previously recorded, so
the thing referred to here will be the Saviour's second *parousia*,
which, being accompanied by the Father's glory, will be much
more brilliant than his first, humble coming was when he took
the nature of a slave [Phil. ii. 7]. Considered as a figure,
Deuteronomy will find its fulfilment in the second *parousia*
when all the saints are living in the Kingdom of Heaven in
accordance with the laws of the eternal Gospel. Just as by his
present coming he has ushered in the reality signified by the
Law (which was only a shadow of the good things to come)
[Hebr. x. 1], so by his second coming, in glory, he will give
perfect substance to the shadow of the final *parousia*. The
prophet says that Christ the Lord is the breath of our mouths
and that we shall live among the nations in his shadow. That
will come about when Christ transfers all the saints to a higher
state, from the temporal Gospel to the eternal, as John shows in
the Apocalypse."

Thus, just as the Old Testament is a shadow of the New, the
New Testament in turn is a shadow of the kingdom to come.
Origen elaborated the theme in another fine passage. The text
he is commenting on is the verse from the Song of Songs about
the apple tree: "I sat down under his shadow, whom I desired"
(Cant. ii. 3). "As the word 'shadow' is used," he says, "for that

under which the Church says she wanted to sit, it will not, I think, be out of place to consider what Holy Scripture says about shadows. By so doing, we shall gain a more adequate idea of what that holy thing the apple tree really is. Jeremias says in his Lamentations: 'Christ the Lord is the breath of our mouths, and we shall live among the nations in his shadow.' In that text you see a prophet inspired by the Holy Spirit telling the Gentiles that Christ's shadow can give them life. It would be surprising if Christ's shadow were not life-giving, considering that at the Incarnation Mary was told: 'The power of the Most High shall overshadow thee.' It will make the passage clearer still if we think of the text where the Apostle says that the Law was the shadow of the good things to come and all worship under the Old Testament a likeness and shadow of the worship offered in heaven. This being so, it is evident that the people sitting in the shadow of the Law are those subjects of the Law who penetrated deeper into the shadow of the True Law. We are outside the shadow they were in, because we are not under the Law: we are under grace. We are not in the shadow the Law cast, but that does not mean that we are not in any shadow at all. We are, and it is a better shadow than the Law's. We live among the nations in the shadow of Christ. It is a great thing to have passed from the Law to the shadow of Christ. For Christ is the Way, Christ is Truth and Life; and when we come under his shadow we have the shade of the Way, are overshadowed by the Truth and live in Life's shadow. And whereas we have only glimpses of knowledge, like a confused reflection in a mirror [1 Cor. xiii. 12], if we follow this way we shall eventually come to see face to face what at first we saw confusedly as a shadow."[67]

It thus becomes clear how the one thing contained in Scripture—the mystery which is Christ—is embedded in it at various depths. The part the exegete has to play is to show where these veins or seams correspond and to grasp the analogies between them. Baudelaire says that the world is a "forest of symbols". Long before him, Origen had spoken of the "vast forest of the Scriptures". He saw the Bible as a world of symbols, which it was his task to explore. So off he went to reconnoitre, trying to get his bearings, putting up signposts and little by little cutting a way through. It was a task at which you would fail if you were presumptuous, but you could also fail through laziness or negligence. He was sometimes frightened by the difficulties. "As we advance in our reading, mysteries pile up before us. . . . Poor in merit and weak in understanding, we have the effrontery to brave a vast sea of mystery."[68] And again: "You see how it is: mystery on mystery everywhere. You see what a weight of mystery presses on us. There are so many mysteries that we cannot hope to explain them."[69] For he knew that "it is absolutely beyond human capacities to explain the Spiritual Law in any detail, the truth, that is, revealed by Jesus Christ. That is a thing possible only to the perfect."[70] But he also knew that he could count on Christ's grace to make good his deficiencies; he knew that with time, things would gradually become clearer, the plan behind the corresponding layers of meaning become evident, the darkness change to light.

THE NON-CHRISTIAN TRADITIONS OF EXEGESIS

I HAVE, I hope, shown in the preceding chapter that in its basic outlines Origen's exegesis depends on the common catechetical tradition of the Church. But that was not the only source he drew upon. In his desire to make use of everything that could possibly help him to a better understanding of Scripture, he also turned to the other schools of interpretation in existence at the time. There is an interesting passage in which he tells us himself what these schools were. "Many people try to interpret the Scriptures," he says, "both members of the Church and people outside the Church—heretics [gnostics], Jews and Samaritans—but they do not all express themselves well."[1] Thus, in addition to the catechetical tradition he was also acquainted with gnostic and Jewish methods of exegesis. Traces of these methods can be found in his works. They can be reduced in the main to three: the rabbinical, Philo's and the gnostic. We will examine each of them in turn. Although, as we shall see, Origen managed to find a great deal of useful material in them, nevertheless it is true that not all of it was "well expressed". This was the channel by which one of the ephemeral elements in his system found its way in—his tendency to "allegorize", a feature typical of the culture of the time. Only too often his use of typology is confused with his use of allegory[2] and his exegesis is rejected *en bloc* in consequence. What I want to do in this chapter is to show that the two things represent quite different sides of his work.

1. THE RABBIS

Origen often alludes explicitly to Jewish traditions. The passages in which he does so were collected by Harnack and have been worked on since by M. Bardy.[3] These allusions may reveal the source of certain features in Origen's system; they also provide information about the Jewish exegesis of the time, because he was personally in touch with rabbis. It is worth noticing that the rabbinical tradition in exegesis predominated even at Alexandria—when Philo taught there he did not lecture to the Jewish community. The exegesis of the rabbis bore first and foremost on the letter; its efforts to solve the problems arising out of the text had gradually produced the traditions contained in the Mishna. Origen alludes to them in the *De Principiis*. After speaking of certain passages which seem to him to be indefensible if taken literally, he goes on to say: "In this connection, the Jews and all who are bigoted about the letter think it a mistake to look for a spiritual meaning even in the case of the griffon (which Scripture says is not to be eaten, as though a legendary creature could be eaten) and the vulture (which no one wants to eat). They invent vain silly fables, based on some tradition or other."[4]

A few examples of the more remarkable of these Jewish traditions will show the sort of thing involved. The gnostic Apelles had rejected Noe's Ark as unhistorical, on the ground that it was "quite impossible for so small a space to contain so many animals and the food they would need for a whole year. . . . The space mentioned could not accommodate even four elephants." In reply to this objection, Origen says: "I will tell him something I learned from my masters and from other sensible men who knew a great deal about Hebrew traditions. They used to say that it was clear from Scripture that Moses had been educated in Egypt and hence, they said, he calculated the number of cubits in the Ark by geometry, an art at which the Egyptians excelled. Well, geometricians have a method of reckoning which they call proportional, and by this method one cubit, in square measure and in cubic, can stand for six cubits and even for three hundred."[5] And in the *Contra Celsum* he explains that the Ark was about forty kilometres long and one kilometre wide. This is a proof of the literal accuracy of the text in the rabbinic tradition, a thing not often found in Origen.

It is well known that the rabbis attached a meaning even to the letters of which the sacred text is composed. Origen had recourse to this method to find out the meaning of the letter T.

"I consulted some Hebrews," he says, "to see if they taught anything about the letter T. This is what I learned from them. One pointed out that T is the last of the twenty-two letters of the Hebrew alphabet. The last letter, he said, was taken to symbolize the perfection of those whose virtue leads them to lament and weep for the sins of the people and have compassion on the erring. The second said that the letter T was a symbol of those who observe the Law, because the Hebrews call their Law the Torah and the first letter of Torah is T. The third was one who believed in Christ. He said that the letter T had been put into the alphabet originally as a figure of the cross, a prophecy of the sign that Christians bear on their foreheads and make before they begin their work and especially before they pray or read the holy Scriptures."[6] The passage shows how some of the forms of exegesis practised by the rabbis were continued by Christian exegetes but transposed into another key. The symbolism of the letter T as a figure of the cross is also found in the Pseudo-Barnabas.[7]

Origen gives other examples of interpretation based on this questionable technique. They are all worth noting, but it will be enough if we quote one of them. Commenting on the passage in Ezechiel where it is said that only Noe, Daniel and Job will be saved (Ezech. xiv. 13 et seq.), he asks the reason for this strange juxtaposition. "I once heard a Jew expounding this passage and saying that these three are mentioned because they had each gone through three periods, one of happiness, one of trouble and one of happiness again. Think of Noe before the Flood, with the world as yet untouched by the waters. Then think of the same Noe when the whole world had suffered shipwreck and he alone was safe in the Ark with his children and the animals. Think of him again after the Flood, leaving the Ark and planting the vine and becoming in a way the founder of a new universe."[8] This type of speculation about Noe seems to have been highly developed in the Judaism of Christ's time. The Book of Enoch contains fragments of an Apocalypse of Noe, in which his name is interpreted as "remnant", because he and his children were the remnant that was to be saved.[9] The etymology is due to the similarity of the name Noe with "nouah", "that which remains". We also find the idea of Noe as the head of a new world in Philo. Noe is at once an end and a beginning, τέλος and ἀρχή. "God considered Noe a fit person to be the end and the beginning of our race, the end of the age before the Flood and the principle of the age that came after."[10] Again, the Clementine Recognitions, the final version of which is contemporary with Origen,[11] say that "when the angels sinned with the daughters of men [according to the traditional Jewish interpretation of Gen. vi. 1] the earth became corrupt. God therefore made the waters of the Flood cover the world and destroy all the people on it. Then, when the world had been cleansed, it was restored spotless to the just man who had been preserved to be the beginning of a new life."[12]

It should be noted that besides his knowledge of rabbinical traditions, Origen also had an extensive acquaintance with the Jewish apocryphal writings.[13] He several times speaks of *libri secretiores*.[14] We find him referring to the Book of Enoch,[15] the Testament of the Twelve Patriarchs[16] and the Assumption of Moses.[17] It was from an apocryphal source that he learned that the woman Pharao gave Joseph for his wife was called Aseneth[18] and that the names of the magicians who resisted Moses were Jamnes and Mambres.[19] I will quote only one passage from these apocryphal works. It comes from a very curious book, known only through Origen, who quotes it twice.[20] The second of his quotations reads: "I who am speaking to you am Jacob and Israel, an angel of God and one of the ruling spirits. Abraham and Isaac were created before anything else was done. I am Jacob and am called Jacob by men, but the name God gave me is Israel, that is to say, the man who sees God, because I am the firstborn of every living being God created. . . . When I was ruling over Syria from Mesopotamia onwards, God's angel Uriel came out and said that I had gone down to earth and pitched my tent among men and had been called by the name of Jacob. He was jealous and he declared war on me. He fought against me, saying that I ought to revere above all names his name and the name of the angel who was above all things. And I told him his name and said what his rank was among the sons of God. 'Are you not Uriel,' I said, 'the eighth after me, and of all the sons of God am I not Israel, the archangel of the Lord's power and the supreme commander of his host? Am I not Israel, the first to do service before the face of God, and have I not received from my God an indestructible name?'"[21]

This quite extraordinary passage shows the sort of thing found in the Apocalypses. The basic idea behind it is this. The writers of apocalyptic literature recognized seven chief angels, and in this case Israel is represented as an angel, because the name Israel has the same ending as the names of angels. Israel here, then, becomes the angel of Israel and hence the first of all the angels, so that Uriel goes down to eighth. Israel existed before all other creatures; he came down to earth and dwelt among men. Both these expressions are used of Christ. It is possible that their use here denotes Christian influence. Notice, too, that this angel is one who does service before God, λειτουργός. The name was later given by the Fathers to one of the choirs of angels. Origen built on this passage, and his theory that God's messengers to men, particularly John the Baptist, had previously been angels is derived from it. We can thus be certain that he was influenced by the apocalyptic speculations of the rabbis in this instance. In a general way, too, his angelology, especially his teaching about the angels of the nations and the fall of the nations before the Flood, owes a great deal to apocalyptic influence.

2. PHILO

The rabbinical tradition in exegesis never had more than a limited influence on Origen, but it was otherwise with Philo's writings. He knew and thought highly of Philo, and in the *Commentary on St. Matthew* he praises him explicitly. "Philo, who has won the respect of the learned by his many volumes on the Law of Moses, writes in his book about the traps set for the best by the good . . ." etc.[22] Here he is singing Philo's praises and making a precise reference to one of his works. Further on in the same commentary he writes of a "man who lived before our time and wrote books called 'Allegories on the Sacred Laws'."[23] Clearly, the allusion is again to Philo. And the fact is the more noteworthy in that Origen does not often mention him explicitly. We may conclude, then, from these two quotations that Origen had first-hand knowledge of Philo's works. The *Contra Celsum* also contains several implicit allusions to him and at least one explicit one in connection with the contrast between the literal and the figurative aspects of the Law—an important point. Origen's debt to him, whether directly through the study of his writings (which we know was the case) or indirectly through Clement of Alexandria, was considerable. Philo's influence was sometimes productive of sound fruit but it also contained the seeds of serious deviation from the truth. We shall see how this obtained at every point where his influence was felt.

The first principle Origen took from Philo was that since Scripture is inspired by God, it can never mean anything that would be unworthy of God or useless to man. As Scripture is God's word, spoken by God for man's instruction, it cannot be allowed that there is anything in it that does not conduce to that end. Consequently, whenever there is anything impossible, absurd or immoral in Scripture, an effort must be made to find another meaning than the literal one. To Origen's way of thinking, these awkward texts are σκάνδαλα, stumbling-blocks which God deliberately allows to exist so as to force us to go beyond the literal meaning, at which we always tend to stop short. "In some cases no useful meaning attaches to the obvious interpretation, in others the Law prescribes impossibilities. This is for the benefit of people with enquiring minds, to make them apply themselves more to the careful scrutiny of the text and so convince themselves that they must in these cases seek a meaning not unworthy of God."[24]

The principle is patient of a perfectly legitimate construction. Fr. Prat[25] makes two important observations about it. The first is that as a principle of exegesis it is unquestionably valid. "The fundamental principle that the corporeal meaning, i.e., the proper meaning, must be abandoned whenever it leads to something impossible, absurd or false is unquestionably true and is subscribed to by all Catholic exegetes." Fr. Prat's second observation is that what Origen calls the literal meaning is not what we understand by the term literal; it is what we call the proper meaning. In Scripture the literal meaning is often figurative. Origen's principle obviously holds good, therefore, for all the cases in which the literal meaning is figurative. It will be open to question only in cases where the literal meaning is the proper meaning. Hence the questionable thing is not

the principle itself but the use that may be made of it. Origen
himself gives examples which enable us to judge of that.

"Could any man of sound judgement suppose that the first,
second and third days [of creation] had an evening and a
morning, when there were as yet no sun or moon or stars?
Could anyone be so unintelligent as to think that God made a
paradise somewhere in the east and planted it with trees, like
a farmer, or that in that paradise he put a tree of life, a tree you
could see and know with your senses, a tree you could derive life
from by eating its fruit with the teeth in your head? When the
Bible says that God used to walk in paradise in the evening or
that Adam hid behind a tree, no one, I think, will question that
these are only fictions, stories of things that never actually
happened, and that figuratively they refer to certain
mysteries."[26] It is the same with the New Testament text
which says that Satan took Jesus up a high mountain from which
he could see all the kingdoms on earth. So much for the
impossible and its symbolical interpretation. No modern
exegete would contest the principle. The instances mentioned
are all, in fact, cases in which the literal sense is figurative.

But it is otherwise with passages where symbolical interpretation provides an easy way out of the difficulties arising
from the proper sense. This is the case, for instance, with commands apparently impossible of fulfilment. Origen gives the
law about not moving about on the sabbath as an example. It
cannot possibly be observed literally; therefore a spiritual
meaning must be sought for it.[27] Similar precepts are found in
the New Testament too. "If we look for similar things in the
New Testament, we shall find them. It would be absurd to
refrain from greeting people you met on a journey [Luke x. 4].
Only the unintelligent think that that is what the Lord meant
the Apostles to do. Similarly, it is not likely that anyone would
ever be in a position to offer his right cheek to someone who
was maltreating him [Luke vi. 29]; because when people administer a slap in the face, unless they happen to be left-handed
they strike the left cheek with the right hand. It is impossible,
too, for you to pluck out your eye if it is an occasion of sin to
you [Matt. v. 29; xviii. 9]."[28] The principle may be applicable
to one or other of these cases, but if so, it is only because the
literal meaning is itself figurative.

And the principle becomes highly questionable when it is used to cover up the scandal caused by some of the stories in the Old Testament—Lot's incest, for example, and other episodes —or to remove the sense of unfittingness aroused by certain insignificant details, such as the fact that Christ entered Jerusalem on an ass. "The Lord is represented as needing an ass and a colt. May he show us a meaning in that consonant with his majesty."[29] It is the same with some of God's commandments: they are not absurd but they are scarcely in harmony with our idea of God. In these cases too Origen considers that the meaning is spiritual. He does not, however, deny their historical reality. "I must not be taken to hold," he says, "that because a given event never happened, there was no historical reality in any case at all, or that because a given law seems absurd or impossible if taken literally no law at all could have been observed literally. I decidedly maintain that in some cases these things were historically true."[30] But even so, the principle must still be rejected *in toto*.

The formula with which he concludes this part of his commentary may seem surprising at first sight but it is really quite clear, or will be to anyone who has followed the trend of his thought. "Everything in Scripture has a spiritual meaning," he says, "but not all of it has a literal meaning."[31] There is a spiritual meaning, however, as he uses the term, for every passage in Scripture where the literal meaning is figurative, i.e., for the parables and the passages intended by the author himself to be interpreted allegorically, such as the Song of Songs and the beginning of Genesis. Because of the difficulties involved in interpreting them, Origen enlarges this category to include many passages where the literal meaning obviously coincides with the proper meaning. At the same time—and this is where his own personal views come in—he also places in this category all passages having the proper meaning as their literal one and in addition possessing a figurative meaning that would not in modern terminology form part of the literal meaning. This obtains whether the literal and proper meaning presents difficulties or not.

This brings us to the second principle underlying Philo's exegetical method, viz., the idea that *everything* in Scripture has a figurative meaning. The notion was foreign to early Christian views on the question. The early Christians held that there were certain definitely typological texts in Scripture but that they were limited in number. Philo, on the contrary, saw an allegorical meaning in every single incident. Origen was influenced by him in this respect: he too held that *every* scriptural text without exception had a spiritual meaning. He states the principle in the *De Principiis*.[32] In the tenth homily on Genesis he says: "*Everything* in Scripture is a mystery."[33] If in some cases the spiritual meaning was not immediately evident the fault lay with the exegete, who was not yet capable of understanding what was meant. "As I try to expound the Scriptures, I realize that the mysteries are too vast for my capacities. But even if we cannot explain it all, we still know that it *is* full of mystery, all of it."[34] And again: "Touching the flesh of the Word means separating his *interiora* one from another and expounding their dark mysteries. If I had a mind capable of doing that, I should be able to get at the heart of everything written in the Law and find a spiritual interpretation for it all. I should be able to shed the light of superior knowledge on the mystery hidden in every word. If I could teach the Church like that and leave the text free from obscurity and ambiguity, then perhaps I could be said to have touched the flesh of the Word."[35]

Everything, then, in Scripture has a spiritual meaning and it is only the weakness of our sight that prevents us from seeing it. Origen's whole ambition was to make the zone of darkness recede as far into the background as possible, but he realized that he was incompetent to do so. The most notable thing he wrote on the question has been preserved by Basil and Gregory of Nazianzus in their collection of extracts from his works, the *Philocalia*. It is a passage from one of the homilies on Jeremias, the thirty-ninth, which is not extant in full. I will quote the whole of it.

If in reading Scripture you balk at some thought which, though good in itself, yet makes you stumble and fall, blame yourself. Do not despair of finding a spiritual meaning in this stumbling-block; the words: "Those who believe will not be disappointed" [Rom. ix. 33] can be applied to you too. First believe and then beneath the apparent scandal you will find something very useful spiritually. We are told that we must not say a single word thoughtlessly and that if we do we shall have to give an account of it at the day of judgement [Matt. xii. 36]. How, then, are we to suppose that the prophets acquitted themselves in that respect? It is not surprising that every word they uttered should produce an effect corresponding to the word itself. To my mind, too, every one of those wonderful letters with which God's words are written produces the effect mentioned in the written word; and it seems to me that there is not an iota or a flourish in the Scriptures which will not produce its effect if people know how to use the virtue inherent in the written word.

He develops the idea with an image which can leave no doubt as to what he means.

Every plant is useful for some particular purpose, some for the health of the body, others for other ends. Yet not everyone knows what a given plant is useful for; the only people who do are those who have acquired special knowledge about plants. Botanists can tell what plant to take, whereabouts on the body to apply it and how to prepare it so as to make it serviceable to those using it. Saints are like spiritual botanists. They gather all the letters they find in the Scriptures, even the iotas; they ascertain the special virtue of each and the use it is good for, and they see that nothing in Scripture is unnecessary. If you want another illustration of the same thing, here is a further comparison. Every limb in our bodies was given a particular function by God, the Creator, but not everyone can tell what this special virtue and use is in every single case. Those who have studied anatomy under a doctor can see what purpose every limb, down to the smallest, was created for by Providence. Think of Scripture, then, as the sum-total of all the plants in existence or as one single body, the perfect body of the Logos. If you are not a botanist expert on the flora of the Scriptures or an anatomist competent to dissect the writings of the prophets, do not for that reason think that there is anything unnecessary in the Scriptures. Blame yourself for not finding the meaning of the text; do not blame the Holy Scriptures. This I say by way of general introduction. It is applicable to the whole of Scripture, and those intending to take up Scripture study will realize from it that they must leave nothing unexamined or unprobed.[36]

Origen's views, then, on this side of the question are quite clear. The Bible is one vast allegory, a tremendous sacrament in which every detail is symbolic. But the symbolism is extremely difficult to probe into. Some of it is clear, some of it obscure. In a notable passage in the *De Principiis*, he compares the mystery of Scripture with the general economy of Providence, in which there is a reason for everything, although we do not see it all at once. "If the uneducated do not at once see the supernatural meaning of the text," he says, "there is nothing surprising in that. It is the same with the effects of Providence. In actual fact, Providence extends to the whole universe, but while some things are quite evidently effects of Providence, in other cases the connection is so obscure as to make men seem justified in doubting whether God really does organize everything so very skilfully and irresistibly by his providence. . . . But if people have once acknowledged the existence of Providence, they do not deny it simply because there are things they do not understand. In the same way, we must not deny that the divine inspiration of Scripture extends to the whole of Scripture, simply because there are passages where we are too short-sighted to see the hidden light of its teaching through the base, worthless letter."[37] Here again there is something true in his theory, viz., the principle that in many of the obscure passages in Scripture the exegete ought to look for a spiritual meaning. But he endangers the principle by declaring that *everything* in Scripture has a figurative meaning. The assertion is the starting-point of all the exaggerations of the medieval allegorizers.

The third sign of Origen's dependence on Philo is to be seen in the way he treats symbolism in certain cases. One thing, however, needs pointing out in this connection, and that is that there is a certain amount of numerical symbolism in the Bible itself, where it often constitutes the literal meaning of the text. The use of the number seven is a case in point. It is clear that

there is a feeling for symbolism in the Bible; it is discernible, for
instance, in the story of creation. Hence, when Origen says
that the "number six seems to denote effort and labour and
the number seven to signify rest",[38] he is proceeding on the
same lines as Scripture itself. But when in connection with the
number fifty, Pentecost and the number one hundred, which he
takes to denote fullness, he says, "The people who were
refreshed by [=resting in, ἀναπαυσομένους] the food that
Jesus gave them had to be in groups of a hundred—which is a
sacred number, dedicated to God because of the monad in it—
or in groups of fifty, a number signifying remission, as you can
see from Pentecost and the mystery of the Jubilee, which took
place every fifty years",[39] he is combining the legitimate symbolism of the Bible with pagan symbolism. It is true that fifty
is a symbol of forgiveness in the Old Testament, both in the
case of the Jubilee and in the case of the annual celebration of
Pentecost. And Origen may very likely be right when he
claims to find the same thing in the New Testament. But when
he takes a hundred as a symbol of perfection, he is inserting
into this genuine symbolism a kind of symbolism based on
external considerations and foreign to the text. The idea that
a hundred is the holy number *par excellence* is in fact embedded
deep in Hellenistic tradition.[40] There are thus two inter-
penetrating systems. The genuinely biblical element mingles
with a stream flowing from the culture of the time. The amal-
gamation first took place in Philo. It is then found in Clement of
Alexandria, who has a whole system of numerical symbolism
based on Pythagoreanism.[41] The core of the problem, then, is
to unravel the tangled skein and separate the main threads of
genuine typology from the temporary accretions derived
from the culture of the time. Only too often people pass
judgment on the whole thing together, without making this
distinction.

More subtlety is required to detect the non-biblical element
in Origen's use of certain images, where he slips from Semitic
symbolism into Hellenistic. It is well known that the Hebrews
often took the sea and the river as figures of the dragon's
dwelling-place and the realm of evil—concrete symbols suggesting the struggle between Christ and Satan. In Philo's
mental world the sea was still an evil element, but it had become

a figure of the "disturbance caused by the passions", and the river had come to represent the instability of human things. The strange thing is that both interpretations are found in Origen side by side. Thus, the sea[42] is the "life of man, a stormy thing everywhere in the world"; but also the "mountain of iniquity, i.e., Satan, is cast into the sea, i.e., into the abyss". It is the same with the river. The river of Babylon is the "river of this world",[43] and again it is the river "where the dragon's lair is".[44] Two different ideas of evil are implied in the two sets of images. Similarly, horses suggest either the passions, as in Plato's myth in the *Phaedrus*,[45] or the powers of evil.

Fourth, it might be said that Origen took from Philo the idea of looking to Scripture for allegories applying to the moral life. This is particularly evident at the beginning of the homilies on Genesis, where the whole of creation is regarded as an allegory of the soul, as the macrocosm of the microcosm. Man and woman are the two parts of the soul. If they are in harmony they have children, i.e., good impulses. The fish, birds and beasts over which man reigns are the acts proceeding from the heart and soul (the birds) and the desires of the body and movements of the flesh (the fish and the beasts).[46] All this is based on Philo.[47] Here again we must see just where the distortion lies. It is quite legitimate to look for a mystical meaning in the Old Testament; the mystical meaning is part of typology. It is a sign of Origen's genius that he was the first to bring it out systematically. But he often used Philo's moral allegories to help him, and consequently he introduced an admixture of artificial cultural elements. He managed to transform this method of applying texts to the moral life into something quite different, and it sometimes helped him to come closer to the mystical meaning. But as soon as it is isolated from the mystical meaning it ceases to be acceptable.

Let us consider some examples of this distortion. Philo had transposed the history of the patriarchs so as to make it into an allegory of the inner life. Abraham became the soul turning from the world of appearances to the world of reality; his first wife, Agar, was made to represent the cultivation of human potentialities;[48] his second wife, Sara, stood for perfect virtue. Isaac was the man who has reached perfection, the possessor of infused grace; he married Rebecca, whose name meant ὑπομονή, *patientia*.[49] The idea that the marriages of the patriarchs have a figurative meaning may seem controvertible, but it is in St. Paul in the case of Sara and Agar and it is found in all the early Fathers. But in the Fathers who reflect the purest typological tradition these marriages appear as figures of the mystery of Christ and the Church. Thus, Justin says: "There was a design behind Jacob's marriages. They were predictions of something else. . . . They were types of mysteries fulfilled in Christ. Lea is your people and the synagogue, Rachel is our Church."[50] Similarly, Irenaeus says: "We have seen that Christ used his patriarchs and prophets to prefigure things to come. Rachel is a figure of the Church for which he suffered."[51] This is in the authentic tradition of the Church. But what we see in Philo is quite different. In him, what had been figures of the Church become allegories of the soul. In reading him we pass from a Christian view of history to a pagan view of the universe; we turn from the αἰών to the κόσμος.

Echoes of both traditions are found in Origen. We have just seen that this is true of the catechetical tradition, but it is true of Philo's methods as well. In the sixth homily on Genesis Origen says: "The name Sara means sovereign and I consider that she represents virtue";[52] while in Philo's *De Abrahamo* you will find: "The Hebrew word 'Sara' means 'woman' and 'virtue'; the Greek for it is 'sovereign', as the power of command ought to belong to virtue."[53] We find two of Philo's symbolical interpretations in the eleventh homily on Numbers: Jacob is taken as a figure of people making progress in the spiritual life and Israel as a figure of the perfect.[54] Other examples could easily be given. The baptism of Jesus on the fifth day of the fourth month symbolizes the union of the four elements of the body with the five senses of the soul.[55] The faces of the four animals in Ezechiel are the three parts of the soul and the ἡγεμονικόν.[56] The five loaves and two fishes in the miracle of the multiplication of the loaves and fishes are the five senses and the two λόγοι.[57] All this belongs to a side of Philo's exegesis which cannot possibly be accepted, although unfortunately it enjoyed a great vogue during the Middle Ages. Under Philo's influence, the door and lintels that were smeared with blood at the Passover were widely compared with the three powers of the soul. The comparison was an encumbrance to paschal symbolism and is the classical example of what his influence could lead to.

The last thing Origen took from Philo was the theory that there are three meanings in Scripture, corresponding to the three parts of the soul and the three degrees of perfection. "The words of Scripture should be printed in the soul in one of three ways. The uneducated should be edified by the letter itself, by what we call the obvious meaning. People at a higher level should find edification for their souls. The perfect should be edified by the spiritual Law, as it contains the shadow of the blessings to come. Man is composed of body, soul and spirit, and the structure of Scripture has been planned by God for man's salvation in the same way."[58] The homilies on Genesis show how this classification was applied in practice. We may take the story of the Flood as an example. "The ark I am trying to describe," Origen says, "was built three-storied. It will be well, then, for us too to add a third explanation to the two foregoing ones and so comply with God's commands. The first explanation was historical, and as it was at the bottom it served as the foundation. The second, the mystical one, which reached to a higher level, was the first floor. I will now try and add a third explanation, if I can, the moral one."[59] The historical explanation accounts for the measurements of the Ark by attributing them to Egyptian geometry. The mystical explanation shows that the Ark is a figure of Christ. "The next things mentioned are the length, breadth and height of the Ark. The numbers given in this connection are not without great mystical significance. But before we talk about the numbers, let us see what is meant by length, breadth and height. Speaking . . . of the mystery of the cross, the Apostle somewhere says: 'That you may be able to comprehend what is the breadth, and length and height and depth'" (Eph. iii. 18).[60] The application of St. Paul's words to the cross is found before this, in Irenaeus and Hippolytus. The Ark, too, was traditionally regarded as a figure of Christ. This, then, is the Christological meaning.

Origen next turns to the third meaning. "I must now try and explain the third meaning, the moral one. If, in spite of the pressure of evil and the exuberance of his vices, a man succeeds in turning away from fleeting, perishable things, he builds the saving Ark in his heart. For length, breadth and height he gives it faith, charity and hope. He has faith in the Trinity throughout the whole length of his life, now and in immortality. His wide charity is grounded on his gentle, loving disposition. He has high hopes because he fixes them on the things of heaven, for although he lives on earth he really has his home in heaven."[61] This shows what the moral meaning is: it applies the mysteries to the life of the individual, whereas the "mystical" meaning shows what the mysteries imply in general and for everybody. I will not dwell on the interpretation itself in this case. As far as its content is concerned, it is perfectly correct—the inner meaning of the story is not just a general exhortation to live a moral life; it really does refer to the mystery of Christ and its relation to the inner life. But in form it is extremely artificial and owes much to Philo's perverse idea that every detail in Scripture has a spiritual meaning. It is not at all likely that that is so in the case of the measurements of the Ark.

But what we are concerned with at the moment is the classification itself. It is entirely derived from ideas on the spiritual life inherited from Philo. It depends, in fact, on Philo's division of the spiritual life into three stages, the first being for beginners (Abraham), the second for those who had made some progress (Jacob) and the third for the perfect (Isaac). Each of the meanings of Scripture corresponds to one of these stages in the spiritual life. We have seen how Origen explains that they also correspond to different ways of expounding Scripture so as to obtain spiritual profit from it. He thought that it was not suitable to give the more mystical teaching to everybody. But although the standpoint is sound where the spiritual life is concerned, it is wrong when applied to exegesis. The fact is that there is no hierarchical subordination in the relationship of the three meanings to one another. You have the literal meaning on the one hand, the spiritual meaning on the other; and the spiritual meaning includes both the collective bearing of the mysteries and their implications for the inner life of the individual. Or, if it is ever legitimate in exegesis to speak of the subordination of meanings one to another, the order will be, first the literal meaning, then the application to the Church (with collective implications or with individual ones), and then

the eschatological meaning. The interplay of the two classifications and the distortion involved in Origen's systematization are very evident here.

Moreover, Origen himself could not keep to this division of
the subject-matter. In the following passage from the homilies
on Leviticus, he comes round to the one mentioned above.
"The visible and the invisible—earth and heaven, soul and
flesh, body and spirit—everywhere correspond; together they
make up the world. Scripture too, we must therefore suppose,
is composed of visible and invisible elements. It has a body we
can see—the letter—a soul that we can grasp and understand,
and a spirit which is an image and shadow of what takes place
in heaven. The body was for those who came before us, the
soul is for us, the spirit for those who will inherit eternal life in
the aeon yet to come. What we ought to do, then, is to pray to
him who gave Scripture its body, soul and spirit and without
bothering about the body concentrate on the soul, because that
is the thing reserved for this age. Then, if we are competent, we
shall understand the mysteries referred to in the text and get at
the spirit of Scripture."[62] Here the body corresponds to the
literal meaning, the soul to the application to the Church
(either to the Church as a whole or to its individual members),
the spirit to the eschatological meaning. Which shows how
artificial these classifications are.

Sometimes one of these points of view prevails, sometimes
the other. When Origen looks at Scripture to see what bearing
it has on the spiritual life, the moral meaning and the mystical
meaning become two stages in the soul's journey through this
world. Thus in one of the homilies on Numbers, the moral
meaning is the information the text gives on ethical matters and
the mystical meaning is the "secret of the mysteries of wisdom
and knowledge which the souls of the saints feed on".[63] At
other times, however, individual considerations drop out of
sight and we are left with successive historical epochs. In one
place in the homily on Psalm xxxvi, for instance,[64] in addition
to the moral meaning Origen claims that there is a mystical
meaning and also one relating to Christ's second coming and
involving prophecy of the future. The classification he tries to
impose on the various meanings is based on ideas foreign to
Scripture and, as all this shows, it breaks down when it is faced

with the diversity of the actual meanings themselves. We are therefore led to reject the division of meanings into three as an artificial proceeding, a piece of mere theory, a thing destined to be a great drag on exegesis in later times. We are justified in confining ourselves to the two contrasting meanings known to Tradition—the literal and the typological, the second having as many subdivisions as there are facets in the *Christus totus*.

3. THE GNOSTICS

Now that we have looked at the Jewish and Judaeo-Hellenistic traditions in exegesis, the only thing we still have to do is to glance at the exegetical theory and practice of the gnostics and see what influence they had on Origen. Frau Miura Stange has shown that although Origen criticized Celsus in the *Contra Celsum*, he really shared his outlook all the same. We shall see in the present instance too that although he criticized Heracleon's *Commentary on St. John* (the first work of its kind) paragraph by paragraph in his own *Commentary on St. John*, he nevertheless depended on Heracleon himself to some extent. There was a considerable body of gnostic exegesis in existence and Origen seems to have owed something to it, in two respects particularly. In the first place, the gnostics made much of the allegorical interpretation of Scripture. The Jews, for obvious reasons, did not. In the second place, Origen was very susceptible to external influence and so, inevitably, was affected by their exegesis. Hence his interpretation of the New Testament was coloured by it and in consequence his exegesis of the Old was as well.

What were the characteristics of gnostic exegesis of the New Testament? The question has been studied by Barth in his book, *Die Interpretation des Neuen Testaments in der valentinianischen Gnosis* (Leipzig, 1911). In the case of the gnostics there was no question of transposing historical events so as to make them signify psychological states, as there had been in Philo's case. What they did was to take the events of the New Testament, the things Jesus did and the framework of his life, as symbols of celestial history, the history of the aeons in the *pleroma*. The earthly life of Jesus was a replica of this on a lesser scale. They argued on the same lines as the Platonist theory of exemplars, except that instead of regarding the sensible world as the reflection of static archetypes or eternal ideas, they fixed their minds on a celestial drama and saw events on earth as a shadow of that. Apart from Heracleon, the sources of our knowledge about gnostic exegesis are Clement of Alexandria's *Eclogae Propheticae* and *Excerpta ex Theodoto*, the quotations given by Irenaeus in his *Adversus Haereses* and Ptolemy's *Letter to Flora*.

Had this school of exegesis any effect on Origen? We may begin our investigation of the question by taking a passage from Heracleon's *Commentary on St. John*. John ii. 12 says that Christ went down to Capharnaum. Heracleon thought that this was the "beginning of a new economy. It was no accident that the word κατέβη was used. Capharnaum stands for the lower parts of the world, i.e., matter, which was what Christ went down into. And as the place was not well-disposed towards him, he is said to have done nothing in it."[65] Origen protests strongly against this interpretation and shows from other passages in the Gospel that Jesus did work miracles at Capharnaum. All the same, when he was commenting on the passage himself a few lines further back he had written: "We must try and see why they did not go into Capharnaum or go up to it. Why did they go down to Capharnaum? Perhaps by the brothers of Jesus we ought to understand the powers that went down with him. For reasons already given, they were not asked to the wedding. Being inferior to those who are here called the Disciples of Christ, they were given help in another way, in less important matters. The people called Capharnaum seem not to have received a long visit from Jesus and those who went down with him; their visitors stayed only a few days, which is not surprising, because the region of the soul open to the lesser kinds of consolation [Capharnaum] cannot receive light from many kinds of teaching."[66]

This is typical of Origen's method of interpretation. Places are figures of spiritual states. Going up and going down correspond to the soul's movements in the spiritual life. The different categories of people represent groups at different stages in the spiritual life. This might be due simply to the application of Christ's visible acts, as recorded in the Gospels, to the spiritual life, a perfectly legitimate proceeding. When Origen represents Christ's miracles of healing as figures of spiritual cures and takes

Mary Magdalen at Jesus' feet as a figure of beginners and John resting on his breast as a figure of the perfect, his "contemplation" is in both instances quite justified and in John's case it is in the spirit of the text itself. But in the present passage something more than that is involved. The brothers of Jesus represent δυνάμεις. Downward movement is a figure of the Incarnation, in which, according to a theory familiar to Origen, the Word was accompanied by his brothers the angels, who came down with him. Consequently, the scene in the Gospels becomes a figure of this descent from heaven. The method is very close to Heracleon's, even though detached from the doctrine of the *pleroma* and applied to the doctrine of the Incarnation.

We may pass over Heracleon's interpretation of the ascent of Jesus to Jerusalem and the expulsion of the merchants from the Temple and after the episode of the Samaritan woman come to Christ's second visit to Capharnaum. "And there was a certain ruler whose son was sick" (John iv. 46). He sees this royal official as a figure of the Demiurge, because his power over his subjects is imperfect. "His reign is short and temporary, and he is called βασιλικός because he is a sort of petty king under the supreme king and set over a petty kingdom." His son, who was at Capharnaum, he sees as one in a lower place, the "intermediate place, near the sea, i.e., bordering on matter".[67] All this is interesting as a statement of the gnosis. The Demiurge is a lesser god. "Middle place" is a gnostic term denoting the place that separates the *pleroma* from matter, which is represented by the sea.

We find Origen saying: "We must see whether the βασιλικός does not represent one of the powers that rule this world, his son the people under his power, the illness an evil disposition contrary to the ruler's will and Capharnaum the place where his subjects lived. My own opinion is that some of the rulers were struck by his power and divinity and took refuge with him and petitioned him on behalf of their subjects. As men may do penance and pass from unbelief to faith, I do not see why we should hesitate to say the same of the powers. It seems to me that on the coming of Jesus something happened to those rulers which changed them for the better, with the result that whole towns and races accepted the truth about Christ more readily

than many men."[68] The prospect here suggested is that the
history of the angels is a counterpart of human history. As we
shall see, it has its importance in Origen's system, but as an
interpretation of the incident of the ruler's son it is singularly
like Heracleon's.

With its view that temporal events are an image of what
takes place in the world of pure spirits, the method represents a
special type of exegesis, different both from the rabbis' and from
Philo's and not connected with the exegesis given by Catholic
writers either, whether they interpreted Scripture of the Church
or with reference to the Last Things. We can only call it
gnostic. It occupies a prominent position in Origen's works,
for in his view it represents the innermost meaning of Scripture.
But of all the forms of exegesis he uses, this is the one we find
most disconcerting today, because it enables him to claim that
the whole of his theological system, including its most dubious
components, can be found in Scripture. It is intermediate
between scriptural exegesis and the working-out of a personal
system. His exegesis ceases to be the Church's at this point and
becomes no more than the discovery of his own ideas in Scripture. He was deservedly condemned by Irenaeus and he incurs
his own condemnation as well, for he finds fault himself with
exegetes who expound their own ideas instead of the Church's.
This form of exegesis is not gnostic in the sense in which
"gnosis" stands for a definite system of philosophy and theology, but it is as far as its method is concerned.[69]

Origen considered it so important that he devoted the main
chapters of Book IV of the *De Principiis* to it, those dealing with
the νόησις of Scripture. He begins by explaining that there
was a race chosen by God from among the other races on earth,
viz., Israel. This race occupied a land, Judaea, which had
Jerusalem for its capital and was surrounded by other towns.
Israel is a figure of another race, a spiritual one; Jerusalem
represents the heavenly Jerusalem, the chief town in the celestial
Judaea.[70] This being so, prophecies about Egypt or the
Egyptians or Babylon ought not to be understood of the
terrestrial Egypt or of any Babylon, Tyre or Sidon on earth.
He alludes to Ezechiel's prophecy about the Prince of Tyre
(Ezech. xxviii. 13) and remarks: "This person who, we are
told, fell from heaven and was Lucifer and rose in the morning

[Isa. xiv. 12] was not a man." He goes on to say: "We may not always be able to understand much except what is on the surface, but there is one thing we ought to realize. Just as there is a Jerusalem and a Judaea in heaven and a race of people evidently living there in Israel, as it is called, so it is possible that there are countries adjacent to that Israel, countries called Egypt, Babylon, Tyre and Sidon, inhabited by souls called Egyptians, Babylonians, Tyrians and Sidonians and each governed by its own ruler. From their conduct it seems as if the places they lived in were eventually captured—which is why we are told that they went down from Judaea, i.e., from the better or higher places, or were dispersed among the nations." [71]

The last lines of this passage suddenly bring us back very close to Heracleon and the *Commentary on St. John*. Up to that point it might have been thought that the outlook was the usual typological one, according to which Jerusalem, the city of the Jews, was a figure of the Heavenly Jerusalem, seen as already present, mystically, in the Church. But the last lines show that it is not so. The history of Israel is a figure not of the Church that is to come but of the angelic world with its wars, captivity, dispersion and fall, typified by the Babylonian captivity. In particular, the key to this part of the explanation is to be found in the word καταβασις, "descent", which shows that this is not the world of history or waiting but one made up of goings up and down between the world of the angels and the world of matter.

The impression grows as we go on. "When men die, as we all must, and leave this world, they are divided into different classes according to their deeds and deserts. Some are considered to deserve the place called hell, others the one called Abraham's bosom, others again other places and dwellings. It may be that there is death in the celestial world too, so to say, and that souls come down from those higher regions into the hell just mentioned. The hell to which the souls of the dead are taken when they leave this world is called 'lower hell' in Scripture, because, it seems to me, of this distinction. The souls, then, that come down to earth are assigned to different places, nations and states of life in accordance with their deserts or the positions they occupied in the celestial world. Thus, it

may sometimes happen that an Israelite comes down among
the Scythians or that a poor Egyptian is taken to Judaea. It
follows that the prophecies relating to the various peoples
should be understood of the souls in heaven and their various
dwelling-places. The stories of things which we are told happened to the race of Israel or at Jerusalem when they were
attacked by one of the other nations should also be thoroughly
gone into, because most of the time it is not at all clear how
these physical events can best be applied to the souls who once
lived and, we must believe, still live in that heaven which we
are told will pass away."[72]

It will be seen how Origen has changed the perspective here.
Instead of regarding the events of Jewish history as prefiguring
the Jerusalem that is to come, he as it were reverses the order
and looks on them as an image of the past history of a higher
world. They are a reflection and result of the past history of
heaven instead of being a figure of the history yet to be enacted
in heaven and a preparation for that history. That shows the
subversive influence of the gnostic outlook both on Origen's
exegesis and on his theology. He applies the gnostic thesis to
several other points too. He maintains that there are "mysteries
hidden beneath the surface of Jewish history—beneath the fact
that in Egypt and Babylon some of the Jews were humbled and
made to serve masters, while others who were prisoners in the
same country were treated as men of rank and position, so
much so that they obtained authority and power and were
appointed governors over whole nations".[73] Thus, the story of
Joseph is a figure of what happened to the angels of the nations.
"There is a good deal hidden in Genesis about the various
nations that are composed of souls." The journey made into
Egypt by the "seventy souls" mentioned in Deut. x. 22 is a
case in point; so too is the "descent of the holy patriarchs to
Egypt, i.e., to the world".[74]

A concrete example—the interpretation of the parables—
will show how gnostic exegesis differed from the traditional
kind. In this connection we find in Origen an echo of traditional interpretations going back to a very early period. He
explicitly mentions tradition, too, in connection with the
parable of the good Samaritan. "One of the older men used
to say when he interpreted the parable that the man who went

down [from Jerusalem to Jericho] was Adam, Jerusalem paradise, Jericho the world, the thieves the powers of the Enemy,
the priest the Law, the levite the prophets, the Samaritan
Christ, the wounds disobedience, the beasts of burden Christ's
body, the inn the Church because it accepts everybody who
wants to come into it, and the Samaritan's promise to return
Christ's second coming."[75]

The interpretation here given by Origen as coming from
"older men" is found in Irenaeus, who, as is well known,
depended to a large extent on the Presbyters, i.e., the circle
dominated by the first Jewish followers of Christ.[76] It is also
found elsewhere in Origen's own works. "There can be no
doubt that the story of the man who fell in with robbers on the
way from Jerusalem to Jericho is a figure of Adam's fall from
paradise and his exile in the world."[77] "Jericho is a symbol of
the world. Adam, i.e., the man who went down from Jerusalem
to Jericho, fell in with robbers."[78] There is evidently an early
tradition behind this, one current in the Church and doubtless
going back to the Disciples and perhaps to Christ himself. Our
Lord explained at least one parable to the Apostles—the
parable of the tares—and the interpretation he gave of it is
singularly like the one put forward by Origen's presbyter. "It
is the Son of Man that sows the good seed. The field is the
world, and the sons of the kingdom are the good seed; the sons
of the wicked one are the tares. The enemy that sowed them is
the devil, and the end of the world is the harvest; it is reaped
by the angels" (Matt. xiii. 37 et seq.).[79]

But side by side with this traditional type of exegesis we find
him interpreting the parables like the gnostics. In one exceptional case, in connection with the workmen in the vineyard,
we have the good fortune to see him giving three different kinds
of interpretation in succession—first the "presbyteral" type,
then the kind favoured by Philo and finally the gnostic sort.
"The first category may perhaps be said to be the one that
began with the creation of the world and Adam: the father of
the family went out on the first morning and engaged Adam
and Eve, as it were, to cultivate his vineyard, which is religion.
The second group is Noe and his covenant. The third is
Abraham's and with him, of course, must be counted the other
patriarchs down to Moses. The fourth is the time of Moses, the

economy of Egypt and the giving of the Law in the desert. The last is the Lord's *parousia*, which will take place about the eleventh hour. There was only one Father, although he went out five times, as the parable says, to see to our affairs and send dauntless workmen into his vineyard, men who could be counted on to deliver his message, which was the truth. And there is only one Christ, and it is he who has always organized everything to do with the covenant with the workmen, although he has shown his condescension to men more than once." [80] This interpretation is presbyteral in type. It no doubt represents the literal meaning of the parable, too.

Next comes a very curious passage in which Origen represents these five interventions on God's part as the five stages of the spiritual life, corresponding to the hierarchy of the spiritual senses. "Touch corresponds to the first covenant, because the woman said to the serpent what God had said to her—'You must not touch that tree'. Smell corresponds to the second, because Noe says that the Lord smelt 'such a smell as pleased him' [Gen. viii. 21]. Taste is denoted by Abraham, who entertained angels at his table and gave them bread baked under the ashes. Hearing corresponds to Moses, for he heard God's voice speaking from heaven. Sight, the noblest of all the senses, relates to Christ's coming, since the Disciples saw him then and he called their eyes blessed [Matt. xiii. 16]." [81] The view of the five senses held by the Greek philosophers and Philo here interferes with the symbolism of the Bible itself and suggests a rather artificial moral interpretation.

The moral type of interpretation (Philo's) is followed by one of the anagogical (and gnostic) kind, which enables Origen to discover in Scripture his own theories about the angelic world and the pre-natal life of the soul. "It was not only to the idle but to those who had been on their feet all day, i.e., all the time before the eleventh hour, that the master said, when he went out at the eleventh hour: 'How is it that you are standing here and have done nothing all day?' [Matt. xx. 7]. You may ask why. Well, I have an idea that there is some deep doctrine about the soul hidden in the statement that they had done nothing all day until the eleventh hour, because, as they said, no one had hired them, although they wanted to cultivate the vineyard. . . . If the soul was created at the same time as the body, how can they have been idle all day [i.e., for the whole of time]? If you dislike the idea, it is for you to explain what this time was and what the last hirings were."[82] Origen then states his own view. He remarks that there were other places besides the vineyard and asks if it was not in these that souls lived before they were sent into their bodies. "Those who said: 'Nobody has hired us' had a good excuse, because they were considered to deserve a full day's pay. Thus, the master hired them and paid them a whole day's wages because they had stood patiently all day, waiting for someone to come and hire them in the evening."[83] They were the first to be paid, then, because they had waited patiently.[84]

But realizing that this sort of exegesis may give scandal, Origen ends with a simpler interpretation, applying the parable to the life of the Church. "I have said all this in explanation of the parable, but there is still another thing that occurs to me. It may be useful to people who are scandalized by the more profound and abstruse explanation. The day may be said to be the whole of a man's life. Those who are hired at dawn by the father of the family are those called from childhood to work for God's kingdom. The workmen engaged at the third hour are those who began to serve God in their youth."[85] Similarly for the other groups. And as what counts is zeal and not time, they all have the same reward. "According to this interpretation, the vineyard is God's Church; the market-place and the places outside the vineyard are the things outside the Church." This exceptionally good example thus shows how various types of exegesis may be found side by side in Origen's works. All idea of reducing his exegetical principles to unity must therefore be abandoned. The only feasible thing is to separate the elements of genuine worth from the alien factors mixed up with them.

PART III

ORIGEN'S SYSTEM

ORIGEN'S SYSTEM

LITTLE work has been done on Origen's teaching about the Bible, and in studying the question we have had to tackle points that had not been thoroughly investigated. It is just the opposite with his theological system. His theology is the part of his work which has received the closest attention; in fact, a criticism that has to be made of most of the books dealing with him—those by De Faye, Koch and Cadiou in particular— is that they deal with nothing else. I have tried to bring out other facets of Origen's personality, to say something of his life as a preacher and catechist and to give some idea of his attitude to the Bible; and presently I shall be examining his spiritual teaching. His theological system represents only one side of his remarkably versatile personality. But it is an extremely important side. Origen is the first of the great theologians, as he is the first to have attempted a coherent interpretation of Christianity as a whole. The *De Principiis* is the first *Summa Theologica*, produced long before John Damascene and Thomas Aquinas wrote theirs.

Origen's system was constructed from the data provided by Revelation and considered in the light of a certain set of problems, those of Middle Platonism. Thus, like any other theologian's work, it contains two elements, one being the mysteries taught by Christianity and the other the particular framework built up by the theologian with his reason. Several writers on Origen have claimed that his system was essentially a philosophical one—Platonist in fact—without a shred of real Christianity in it. Thus, De Faye denies that Origen has a theory of the Redemption; Koch questions whether his idea of salvation is the same as Paul's and thinks it is pure idealism; Molland denies his eschatology. From all this it would appear that his system was a variety of Platonism. But he provides a reply himself to these estimates of his work. The *De Principiis* begins with an account of the content of the "apostolic tradition", to

which he declares that he subscribes without reserve. It is of
great value as a profession of faith. It proclaims belief in one
God, Creator of all things. [1] It says that Christ was born of the
Father before any creature, that he took a body like ours, that
he really died and rose again. It associates the Holy Ghost
with the dignity of the Father and the Son. The profession of
faith also includes the existence of the soul, the Judgment, the
Resurrection, freewill, the existence of good and evil angels,
the creation of the world in time, the inspiration of Scripture
and its interpretation in a spiritual sense. All this constituted a
corpus of truth handed down by Tradition, the deposit of the
Church's faith, and for Origen it was the essential thing.

But these revealed truths needed to have their implications
brought out. And side by side with what was certain, either
because it had been directly revealed or because it had been
defined by the tradition of the Church, there were some questions
which, in Origen's day, were still open. As Scripture had not
spoken plainly about them, theologians could still thrash them
out. Origen mentions a number of them. Some of them may
seem surprising, but they help to show how far dogma had
developed at that time. There was the question whether the
Holy Spirit was begotten or unbegotten and whether the soul
derived its origin from the transmission of the seed or whether
it had some other beginning, and if so, whether this beginning
was γενητός or ἀγένητος. It could not be clearly ascertained from the preaching of the Church, either, what existed
before the world began or what would exist when the world
came to an end; [2] nor was it possible to tell when the angels
were created or what their number was or what condition they
were in. And there was no tradition on the question whether
the sun, the moon and the other living creatures had souls. [3]

Consequently, there was a certain dualism in Origen's attitude. On the one hand he accepted the traditional faith, but on
the other he put forward opinions of his own with a view to
making explicit what he took to be the implications of the
faith. He set out these opinions as an exercise, stressing their
personal character and consequently showing that the reader
was entirely free to accept or reject them. It can be shown
that the questions he dwelt on most were the disputed ones of
the origin of the soul, angelology and eschatology. He suggests

answers to them all, pending the time when the Church should define the dogmatic points at issue. If he had recourse to the philosophy of his time, it was chiefly to find a means subordinate to the superior criterion of God's word by which he might solve these difficult points.

What method, then, should be used in studying his system? It would be possible to expound the system by taking the various Christian dogmas one by one and trying to see what he thought about them. That is what De Faye and Denis have done. But the drawback to that method is that it fails to bring out the thing that gives Origen's speculations their unity. The great merit of Hal Koch's book is that it does bring out the central point in the system, the doctrine of *pronoia* and *paideusis*, or Providence considered as an educative force. This enables us to place Origen with regard to the problems current in his time. As we saw in connection with the philosophical background, the question of Providence was at the centre of speculation on philosophy and religion in the second and third centuries. The great theological works before Origen's time also centred round the idea. It will be enough to mention Justin's teaching about the Logos, Clement's theological views and particularly Irenaeus's conception of Christianity. Thus, Origen's teaching was a continuation of what these doctors had taught, and like them he formulated Christian dogma in relation to the outlook of the time. Where Koch goes wrong is simply in thinking that Origen was therefore nothing more than a philosopher. Origen did not take his idea of Providence from Albinus but he stressed the elements in Christianity that correspond to the philosophers' conception of Providence, just as today when we expound the dogma of the Mystical Body we do not take the dogma itself from Karl Marx but we do bring out the factors in it that correspond to what Karl Marx taught.

However, Providence is not the only central factor in Origen's system. A further doctrine—the doctrine that man has freewill —came to have paramount importance for him, not, in this case, because of the philosophical outlook of the time but in consequence of his struggle with his adversaries the gnostics, whose presence was felt everywhere at this period. This side of the matter is well brought out by René Cadiou in his *Introduction au système d'Origène*. "Liberty," he writes, "became [in Origen's view] the most general of all the laws of the universe."[4] The problem was not simply to reconcile the freedom of the human will with God's foreknowledge, as it would be for philosophers today. Origen went much further than that. The gnostics held that created beings had different natures (φύσεις), spiritual, psychic and material, and that that was why there was a hierarchical order among them. These natures could neither be alienated nor acquired; they were entirely beyond the reach of liberty and represented different creations. Origen's own ideas on the subject were given shape by his efforts to reply to this conception. He often attacked the gnostic idea of φύσεις.[5] And as in gnosticism these φύσεις constituted the world of essences, he was led to attack the idea of diverse essences and necessary natures. In his view, essence was determined by liberty. There is no need to remark on the modernity of such a theory. For him, there were only two things at the outset, God in Trinity and a number of free, spiritual persons, all equal. These free persons were not determined by their natures; they determined their natures themselves by their own free choice. What distinguished them from God was their mutability.

Thus—and it is an indication of the profundity of his system that such a thing should be possible—Origen reduces the whole of his teaching to two propositions: "There is a beneficent Providence" and "Creatures are free". Absolutely everything in his system can be deduced from these two principles. Spiritual persons, being free and mutable, were capable of falling and did actually fall. The universe was a consequence of their fall, an arrangement made in view of the different degrees to which the various creatures had fallen. History shows that God respects the liberty of creatures, i.e., that he never forces anyone but acts by persuasion and that in this way he is gradually bringing the entire spiritual creation back to its original unity and after countless aeons will have restored it completely. When all λογικοί have submitted again to the Λόγος, the Λόγος will offer their submission to the Father.

Such is the plan of the imposing yet simple structure raised by Origen. Platonist elements are discernible in it—the theory, for example, of the pre-existence of the soul in the celestial world—and it will be noticed that Origen also aims at solving such questions as were still open at the time. In addition, he worked into the fabric the fragments of theological synthesis which had already been put together by his predecessors. As we have seen, this had been done in the course of the second century. First came the theology of the Logos. It was the earliest attempt at thinking out the theology of the Trinity, and the Logos was envisaged in it chiefly in relation to the cosmos. Origen's theory of the Logos is far from being thin but it is not at all original as far as its principles are concerned. It is entirely dependent on existing tradition. It derives from the view that sees the history of salvation, whether individual or collective, as a process in which man becomes more and more like the Logos, in whose image he was created. The other traditional theme introduced by Origen into his synthesis was the idea of redemption as a victory over the powers of darkness. The point has been almost entirely overlooked by the commentators. It may prevent them from synthetizing Origen's teaching in the way they would like, but it is of the utmost importance for an understanding of his views all the same. And it is one more legacy from the tradition of the second century—we have seen how prominent a place it occupies in the writings of Justin, Athenagoras and Tatian. It is also bound up with the development of Origen's angelology.

In my account of Origen's system I shall follow the main stages in God's providential plan, and we shall see that the idea of Christianity as sacred history is deeply rooted in the Bible. We will begin, then, by considering the origin of the world in the fall of the spiritual creatures pre-existing with the Logos. We will then see how the Logos intervened in the world by coming down among men and defeating the powers of evil. Lastly we will study the process by which in the course of the successive aeons the whole spiritual creation is being gradually restored to its inheritance. In the course of our investigations we shall see what the various problems were that Origen had to face. But it is essential to realize that he approached them from this pedagogical angle; otherwise there will be less likelihood of grasping his meaning.

The chief work in which his system can be studied is, of course, the *De Principiis*. The book consists of four parts dealing with God and created spirits, the Fall and the world, freedom and restoration, and Scripture. We will follow its main divisions. Next in importance are the first books of the *Commentary on St. John*—particularly for Origen's theories about the Logos —the *Commentary on St. Matthew*, the *Contra Celsum*, the *De Oratione* and the homilies on Jeremias. In his other writings, Origen generally confines himself to the common faith of the Church and alludes to his own theories only in passing. The Commentaries on St. John and St. Matthew are of value chiefly as a check on the Latin text of the *De Principiis*, as Rufinus is always open to the suspicion of having watered his author down when he made his translation. [6]

I

COSMOLOGY

THE WORLD appeared to Origen to include a very great variety of different states and conditions. "Some of the beings in the world," he says, "are called supercelestial, because they live in the dwellings of the blessed and have luminous heavenly bodies. They differ from one another in many ways. As the Apostle himself says, the sun has its own beauty, the moon has hers, the stars have theirs; one star even differs from another in its beauty [1 Cor. xv. 41]. There are other beings called terrestrial. These are men, and they too differ from one another to no slight extent. Some are barbarians, others are Greeks, some are civilized, others are savages. Some are born of low rank and, as they belong to the slave class from birth, are given a slave's education and put under masters, princes or tyrants, while others are educated like free men. Some have good health, others are weak from childhood. In addition, there are the invisible powers who have been entrusted with the task of directing events on earth. They also are different from one another to no small degree. There is no point in raising the question with respect to dumb animals, birds or fishes, since they must all be regarded not as ends in themselves but as relative."[1]

This paragraph from the *De Principiis* gives us the starting-point of Origen's speculations, viz., the empirical realization of the inequality existing in the conditions of created spirits. We may note two points to begin with. First, the only creatures that really exist, in his eyes, are spiritual persons; they alone were created *principaliter*.[2] His universe is a world of free beings. The non-free exists only to a secondary degree. Secondly, we see that the world of created spirits contains three main categories—the inhabitants of the supra-celestial regions, i.e., the stars and planets; the people on earth, i.e., men, in

their various states and conditions; and the powers of good and
evil presiding over human affairs. Origen puts all this forward
γυμναστικῶς—as we have seen, it formed part of the corpus
of questions still under discussion. But it introduces us at the
outset to a view of the cosmos, and that view is the same as the
one held by the Middle Platonists, especially Albinus.

The existence of such variety in the cosmos constitutes a
problem. Everything was made by God; consequently,
nothing in creation can be unjust or fortuitous. [3] But how can
the infinite variations between one creature and another be
regarded as entirely just? It is a thing, Origen says, that cannot
be explained by the human mind or in human words. If we
want to understand it we must ask the help of the Word. If we
pray to the only-begotten Son of God, he will vouchsafe to shed
his grace on our minds. So doing, he will throw light on what
we found obscure, reveal what was concealed and expose what
was hidden from us. That is Origen's way of saying that what
he is going to discuss is one of the great mysteries of theology.
The assertion that this world with all its variety is the work of
one God and that that God is good, he says in effect, comes up
against objections from the gnostics. "When we say that the
world in all its variety was made by God and that that God is
good and just, we usually find that an objection is brought
against us. It is apt to come chiefly from members of the school
of Basilides, Valentinian and Marcion, who hold that souls are
of various natures. Many of these people say: 'How does it
square with God's justice that when he created the world he
should send some of his creatures to live in the heavens, and
besides giving them a better place to live in should confer on
them a higher rank as well? Why should he make some
principalities, some powers, some dominations, give some the
places of honour in the tribunals in heaven and others the
power to shine with all the dazzling brilliance of the stars? In
a word, if the creator God lacked neither the will nor the power
to make a good product, whyever should he establish some
spiritual natures on a higher level and the others on lower
ones when he created them?'" [4]

We may observe in passing that this impatience with institutional hierarchies when they do not correspond to a spiritual
hierarchy based on merit may perhaps reveal one of the reasons

why Origen attaches so little importance to the institutional element in the ecclesiastical hierarchy, which he sees as a reflection of the hierarchy of angels. But however that may be, he observes that the same question of inequality of conditions arises in the human world as well and that it there assumes an even more striking form. "With regard to conditions on earth," he says, "the gnostics also object that some men are favoured by being born in happier circumstances than others. Abraham's son, for example, was born in fulfilment of a divine promise, and the son of Isaac and Rebecca supplanted his brother while they were still in the womb and, we are told, was loved by God even before he was born. In the same way, some men are born Hebrews and so receive instruction in God's Law, and some are born Greeks, members of a highly cultivated race devoted to the pursuit of wisdom. But others belong by birth to negro tribes who feed on human flesh, or to the Scythians, who make parricide their Law, or to the people who live in the Taurus and put strangers to death."[5]

The gnostic conclusion was that "liberty has nothing to do with the diversity in things or the variety in human circumstances: no one can choose for himself the country or station he wants to be born in. The diversity must therefore be due to diversities in the natures of souls themselves. If souls are born into an evil nation, it can only be because they are evil souls; if they are born into a good nation, it must be because they are good souls. Otherwise, what alternative is there but to conclude that these things are determined by chance and fortune?"[6] Thus, if natures and circumstances are not determined by liberty, the determining factor must be either chance or natural diversity in the gnostic sense. But the dilemma is serious, because, Origen says, "if we accept this solution, we cannot go on believing that the world was made by God or that it is ruled by his providence. Consequently, we cannot go on expecting that God will judge individual acts". In other words, there will be an end of Providence and of merit, i.e., Origen's two essential tenets will lose all meaning.[7]

It is easy to see from this how he came to adopt the theory that before the existence of the world, all spirits were equal. The only way he could maintain that there was justice in God and liberty in creatures was to say that all differences in the

circumstances of creatures had their origin in the previous merits
or demerits of those creatures. In the essential passage on the
question he says: "When in the beginning God created what
he meant to create, viz., natures endowed with reason, his only
object in creating was himself, i.e., his own goodness. As he
was himself the cause of all he was going to create, and as there
is no diversity, change or impossibility in him, he created all
his creatures equal and similar to one another." [8]

Thus, the first point in Origen's solution—the idea of spirits
existing before the world—is quite clear. It is not to the fore in
the *De Principiis* as the text now stands, but that is probably
because Rufinus whittled it down. The thesis undoubtedly
forms part of Origen's system: it is attributed to him by his
adversaries [9] and his disciples too tax him with it. Koetschau
mentions a passage in Gregory of Nyssa—"The soul had a
previous existence in a life of its own; there was a sort of nation
of them" [10]—which he thinks is a textual quotation from
Origen. And there are frequent allusions to the doctrine even
in Rufinus's text.

But to return to the *De Principiis*. We have seen that all
spirits were originally equal. But they were also free. "As I
have often shown, creatures capable of reasoning were endowed
with the faculty of free-will." [11] Origen devotes a whole book
of the *De Principiis* (the third one) to the question of free-will.
He establishes the existence of free-will by analysing free activity
and showing that it is a consequence of reason, as man is not
determined by images and can give his consent or not as he
pleases. Thus, there is no justification for blaming external
events. Occasions of sin do not make sin inevitable. Of no one
can it be said that he must of necessity be a sinner, and no one
is past conversion either. Moreover, the value of human acts
depends essentially on liberty, which is what makes them
capable of acquiring merit or the reverse. [12] Liberty is essentially bound up with the dignity of the spirit.

Liberty essentially involves a certain degree of changeable-
ness. "Some were led by their liberty to imitate God, others
not to, and so they either advanced or fell back." [13] Origen
explains in greater detail a little further back what he means
by this. "The rational natures that were made in the beginning," he says, "did not always exist; they came into being

when they were created. By the mere fact that once they did not exist and then a time came when they did, they were of necessity subject to change and movement, because however great the virtue communicated to their substance, it did not belong to them by nature but was given them by God. Thus, they did not derive their essence from themselves but had it as a gift from God. Things given may be also taken away and withdrawn. When such withdrawal occurs, it is because the soul has turned in the wrong direction, away from its goal. The Creator gave the spirits he created the power to move their wills freely: they were to make the good their own and to keep it by an effort of will. But they were lazy and grew weary of the effort they had to make to keep the good; the good was far away and they neglected it. That was what gave rise to its withdrawal. Forsaking the good amounts to settling down in evil. It follows that rational creatures do so settle down to the extent to which they turn away from the good." [14]

The theory of liberty that emerges from this is well worth examination. The created spirit receives its being uninterruptedly from God. Its existence is an endless series of advances towards him. It transcends all other natures because it is God's image. But it is radically different from God because it possesses only by grace the good that is his by nature. It must therefore be thought of as a god involved in an everlasting process of becoming. Its existence is continual growth; it never stops at any stage it reaches but by its own choice remains always ready to receive further graces. It is pure thanksgiving. But if it ceases to be amenable to grace, if it tries to stop at any particular stage, if through weariness or fear of effort it stands still and hardens itself against further gifts, or if instead of looking all the time towards God it attempts to find satisfaction in itself, the nature or φύσις is *ipso facto* determined by this conduct. [15] Thus, the principle of the Fall is the same law that we saw operating in the theology of history when the Jews refused to leave their past behind them. The spirit stands for progress, and by definition evil is the refusal to accept progress.

Progress is so essential to the life of the soul that it will continue even in eternity. Origen here prepares the way for Gregory of Nyssa. "Though Father, Son and Holy Ghost are

always at work in us," he says, "whatever our degree of perfection, it still is all we can do to turn our minds once in a while
to the life of the blessed. We shall have many a battle to fight
before we succeed in reaching that life ourselves, but when we
do, we ought to abide in it for ever and never think we have had
too much of it. The more we become aware of our bliss the
more should our desire for it grow and multiply, and as we lay
hold of Father, Son and Holy Ghost, as we cleave to them, we
should see more and more in them and continually grow in
ardour. If one of those in the highest places happens to
succumb to feelings of satiety he will not, I think, be rejected
straight away or fall without more ado; but he will have to
return gradually and little by little recover the state he lost by
his negligence."[16]

We thus come to the basic principle of Origen's cosmology—
free natures are necessarily mutable, diversity of nature has its
root in diversity of choice. "All spirits neglected the good to a
greater or lesser degree, according to the use they made of their
freedom, and then they were swept away towards the contrary
of the good, which is evil. This seems to be the source from
which the Creator took the principles and causes of variety
and diversity: he varied and diversified the world as he created
it, in accordance with the diversity existing among spirits,
i.e., among rational creatures."[17] All created spirits were
affected, with the one exception, as we shall see, of the soul of
Christ, which was in existence before the world was, like all
other spirits.[18] The Fall thus gave rise to the various kinds of
spiritual natures—the hierarchies of angels, the heavenly
bodies, the various races and conditions among men. This is
one of the mysteries hidden in Scripture.[19]

The following passage makes his meaning clearer. "Before
the aeons existed, all spirits were pure; demons, souls and
angels alike, all served God and did what he commanded them.
The devil was one of them. He had free-will and wanted to set
himself up against God, but God cast him down. All the other
powers fell with him. The biggest sinners became demons, lesser
ones angels, the least archangels. Thus, the portions allotted
depended on the sins of the recipients. Other souls were not
sinful enough to be made demons but were too sinful to be made
angels. These God punished by making the world, binding

them to bodies and putting them into it. Although these
spiritual creatures, then, all had the same nature, God made
some of them demons, some angels and some men. That does
not mean that he is a respecter of persons. No, what he did
was in keeping with their sins. If it were not so, and if the soul
had no previous existence, how is it that we find men blind
from birth, before they could possibly have sinned, and why do
others go blind although they have done nothing wrong?"[20]

In another passage, Origen explains that the final consummation will take place when all creatures have submitted to the
Son. "Ends," he says, "are always like beginnings. All
creatures have the same end and it must be concluded that
they all had the same beginning. Just as the many have only
one end, so a single beginning gave rise to them in all their
diversity and differentiation—gave rise, that is, to the diversity
of creatures in heaven, on earth and below the earth. Through
the goodness of God, the unity of the Holy Spirit and surrender
to Christ, they will all be brought to a single term, which will
be like their beginning. These three groups of beings denote the
entire universe, i.e., all creatures, which, from a single common
beginning, were led in different ways, each according to the
way it behaved, and arranged in various classes according to
their deserts. Goodness did not belong to them by nature, as it
does to God, his Christ and the Holy Spirit. They did not pay
proper attention to themselves and thus, by their own fault,
they fell more or less rapidly and to a more or less considerable
extent. For this reason and because God's judgments are proportionate to the good and bad behaviour of individuals and
to their merits, some will receive the rank of angel in the world
to come, some power or command over others, some a throne
from which to rule over others, some dominion over servants.
Those who have not fallen beyond redemption will be guided
and helped by those just mentioned. Thus, there can be no
doubt that when the world recovers its unity the human race
will consist of men subject to the principalities, powers, thrones
and dominations, and in some instances men will have replaced
these beings altogether. We must realize, too, that some of
those who fell from the unity prevailing at the beginning
abandoned themselves to such unseemly and malicious conduct
that they were not considered worthy to be instructed and

educated by the heavenly powers, as the race of men in the flesh is. These creatures are hostile to those under instruction and they fight against them."[21]

It is clear, then, how Origen accounts for variety in creatures. He divides the whole creation into three main classes, corresponding to St. Paul's classification. First come the *caelestia*, the angels and the stars and planets, whom God associates with himself in his own work. These are the spirits whose fall did not go so far as the others', and they have the task of governing and helping their inferiors. It may be observed that Rufinus misrepresents Origen's position on the question. He makes him say that "some remained true to the principle",[22] whereas the Greek text says nothing of the sort. This enables us to correct *De Principiis* 1, 8, 3, for which we have no Greek text. As we have said, Origen regards the Fall as universal. The second class are those in between, the *terrestria*, the human race, who are helped by the first class and thereby enabled to recover their lost happiness. The third class are the wicked angels. They are incapable of being cured, at any rate in this world, and they try to embarrass men in their upward progress. It will be seen at once how this view of the world harmonizes with the spiritual side of the question. Origen represents the soul as caught up between good and evil spirits. It is all a question of the discernment of spirits. Cosmology and spirituality proceed along exactly the same lines.

Origen considers that the spiritual cosmos is described in Scripture and that the description is one of the great scriptural mysteries. The spiritual creation is represented by the diversity of peoples and tribes. Thus in the *Commentary on St. Matthew* he speaks of "lifting up our minds, now that we have spoken of Israel and the twelve tribes, and considering the twelve degrees found among those races which are composed of souls alone, the most excellent being at the top and the others, in eleven divisions, being in the second grade and all of them above our powers".[23] He takes up the theme again in the homilies on Leviticus, where he says that in his opinion the twelve loaves are a "figure of the entire spiritual creation. It is considered that the main classes into which the spiritual creation is divided are twelve in number. They are represented by the twelve tribes".[24] And there is also symbolical significance in the fact that there is more than one nation. "When Christ says that he has come to the lost sheep of the house of Israel, we must understand his words as referring to a spiritual race called Israel."[25] In the same way, the Egyptians and the Babylonians represent other races.[26] These different races of souls occupy various settlements, which again Origen sees figuratively represented in Scripture. "Just as there is a Jerusalem and a Judaea in heaven . . . so it is possible that there are adjacent countries . . . called Egypt, Babylon and Tyre . . . inhabited by souls called Egyptians, Babylonians and Tyrians and each governed by its own ruler."[27]

These various classes of spirits or souls are not shut up in watertight compartments; they simply represent different degrees of the same downfall. If they take themselves in hand they will pass into the hierarchy next above them, and inversely, they may also fall into the one below. And as free-will and love of God are always the essential principles and can never be dispensed with, a further rise or fall is always possible. After one of the passages quoted above, Origen goes on to say: "It seems to me that by doing good and trying to get out of themselves, some of those now subject to the powers of evil, the dominations and the *cosmocratores* will fairly soon fill up the places left vacant among the human race, either in the space of one world or in the course of several."[28] Rufinus says simply, "will turn to the good". But further on, his translation adds: " It follows in consequence that any creature that is rational by nature may pass from one division to another. Any such creature may come to each and all of these divisions and pass through them all—it will depend on the extent to which, in virtue of his behaviour and his liberty, he increases in faults or makes progress in perfection" (1, 6, 3). We shall frequently have occasion to see how Origen applies this principle, especially with regard to angels sent down to earth to become men, like John the Baptist, and devils who achieve their salvation by becoming first men again and then angels before they return to the unity of the beginnings.

What connection is there between the fall of the λογικά and the corporeal world? The problem is one that every cosmology has to face. As Origen sees it, no creature can have a body by nature, because there is no such thing as nature. His views

seem to be something like this. Originally, no created spirit
had a body; they assumed bodies in consequence of the Fall.
But in his eyes, the Fall is not a mere descent into the sensible,
as it is for Plato and Plotinus. Corporeity is not bad in itself.[29]
There is no condemnation of the body in Origen's system. The
point is of great importance, as it answers the main objection
brought by the Platonists against the Incarnation.[30] His
arguments are all directed against those who condemn the
body and regard it as the principle of evil. Evil is in the will
alone.[31] The body is thus bound up not with evil but with
diversity. "There could be no diversity in the world unless
there were bodies."[32] Also, the body a creature has is strictly
proportionate to the degree to which the creature has fallen.
Being in the body is thus a punishment, but in Origen's view
punishments are also means of recovery. Bodiliness, then, is a
consequence of the Fall. One day it will come to an end and
then there will be an *apocatastasis*, a return to a purely spiritual
state. The resurrection is not therefore denied, but it will be
only a stage on the way back to pure spirit: the glorious body
is an intermediate degree between the terrestrial, animal body
and the state that pure spirits are in.[33] This is distinctly affirmed
in a quotation made by Jerome and included in Koetschau's
edition: "If any rational, incorporeal, invisible creature is
negligent, it will gradually fall to lower levels and there assume
a body. The sort of body it assumes will depend on the place
it falls into. Thus, it will first take an ethereal body, then an
aerial one; as it draws near the earth it will put on a coarser one
still, and in the end it will be harnessed to human flesh."[34]

We may take the case of the heavenly bodies as a concrete
example of the process, since we said nothing about them when
we dealt with the diversity existing among creatures in the
world. Origen begins by reaffirming his principle that "all
rational creatures are of their nature incorporeal".[35] He first
proves from Scripture that the stars and planets are living
beings. We are told that the Lord gave them orders, which he
could not have done had they not been endowed with reason.[36]
He concludes: "The sun, the moon and the other heavenly
bodies are living beings. We men acquired our bodies because
of the sins we had committed, and the lights of the heavens were
given their bodies for the same reason. Thus, some shine more

and others less. Contrariwise, the demons were given aerial bodies because their sins were graver."[37] Though made from the aether, these bodies are still material; hence the spirits chained to them hope to be able one day to discard them. Yet while they wait for the sons of God to be made known, they are content to be subject to frustration (cf. Rom. viii. 19–20).

There is, however, one point which we have not yet touched, and that is the question of the origin of matter. Origen's pronouncements on the subject are confused; or rather, it is difficult to see what he really thought about it, because the chapters in which he deals with it have come down to us only in Rufinus's translation. Rufinus makes him say that the Trinity alone is incorporeal and that it can hardly be admitted that rational creatures can ever be absolutely free from matter. But this seems to contradict his thesis that in a previous existence all rational creatures were pure spirits and that they will ultimately return to that condition. It is more likely that Origen admitted not the creation of matter in time but its eternal existence as *materia prima*. If that is so, it brings us back to Albinus's idea, according to which matter was one of the ἀρχαί. Origen explains that God created a definite number of λογικά and that in the same way he created just as much matter as was necessary for the adornment of the cosmos. "Those are the things that were created at the beginning, i.e., before everything else."[38] The matter in question was "first" matter, matter capable of receiving the forms of every species of body [39] —the coarse, earthly body and also the splendour of the heavenly bodies in which the angels and the sons of the resurrection are clad.[40] It was created not *principaliter* but *per consequentiam*.[41]

II

ANGELOLOGY

W E HAVE seen how the cosmos originated and what there is to account for the variety in it; we have also seen how Origen deals with the problem presented by the gnosis. Matter and the world and the various beings in it are not evil and were not produced by a demiurge. As an order of things they are secondary, not evil. The order they constitute was planned by God, with the fact of sin as its starting-point and the restoration of created spirits to their original integrity as its end. This is plainly stated at the beginning of the second book of the *De Principiis*. Origen there says that diversity was introduced into creation through the diverse ways in which those who fell from the unity of the beginnings behaved. "God so arranged things," he continues, "that no spirit or soul should be forced to act under compulsion, against its will, otherwise than as it was freely inclined. If any had, they would have lost their freedom, as far as one can see, and that would have destroyed their very essence and nature. God arranged that the acts of will the various creatures made should fit together harmoniously and render mutual service. They were all to concur within the framework of a single universe. Some spirits would need help and others would be able to give it them; some would be making progress and others would provide them with temptations and occasions of strife, thanks to which their zeal would obviously receive a sounder testing and they would be more firmly grounded in the state they recovered by their victory, as they had obtained it at such great cost. Thus, although the universe is so planned as to include a diversity of functions, it must not be thought of as dissonant or discordant in its parts. The human body has unity because its various members are all made for specific functions in it and it is bounded by a single soul. In the same way, it seems to me, the whole immense, gigantic world should be regarded as one being, kept alive by God's power and logos as by a single soul."[1]

The idea put forward in this passage—that God so planned the cosmos as to enable his free creatures to recover their original status by interacting with one another in all their diversity—is one we have already met with. We must now examine it in greater detail. We cannot fail to notice, too, that the idea of the cosmos as one vast living being is very like the Stoic view: we are in fact presented with a Stoic cosmos seen from a Platonist angle. The idea of the world after the Fall as a specially planned cosmos often occurs in Origen. "The differences separating one rational creature from another," he says at one point, "did not take their rise from the Creator's will or judgment but from the self-will of the creatures themselves. God thought it just that he should allot his creatures their places according to their merits. He therefore made all individual differences conduce to the unity of the world. There was to be only one world, but he used the various spirits to decorate it with, as if it had been a house that had to be stocked with different kinds of utensils, some of them gold and some silver, others wooden and others made of clay, some for use on formal occasions, others for ordinary purposes."[2] There is only one guiding principle to account for this arrangement of the world—as God has only one end in view, which is to induce all created spirits to return to him of their own free will, he will arrange everything so as to obtain that result. He will give the better creatures, i.e., the angels, a share in his own work: he will use them to help those who are not so good and will ask them to postpone their personal enjoyment of full beatitude until they have helped the others to attain it. Sometimes, too, he will allow the wicked to plunge deeper into evil. He will harden .Pharao's heart. He knows that it would be premature to propose the good to wicked souls as the goal for them to aim at. To use Origen's image, the abscess must be allowed to burst. The process should, in fact, even be accelerated, so as to permit of a cure. If sin came from a desire for change provoked by a surfeit of good, salvation will in certain cases come through a surfeit of evil. There are some spirits who must be allowed to batten on evil, if they want to, until they

weary of it and of their own accord turn again to the good.
Thus, sin will sometimes appear as a step towards salvation,
because the essential thing is that souls should return to
God freely. Like a good doctor, God uses the remedy appropriate to the disease. The measures he takes are justified
by deeper reasoning than ours. When he thinks he can make
nothing of a spirit in this world, he defers its salvation
until some future world, but in the meantime he uses it in
this world as a means of testing the saints.[3] Thus, everything has its part to play in the divinely-planned economy
or cosmos.

We shall see later how this gradual reintegration of the whole
spiritual creation is effected. The points we are concerned with
at the moment are the subordination of functions in the cosmos
and the way God uses some of his creatures to act on others.
We shall thus have to examine the question of the angels and
their mission to govern men and also study the demons and the
permission they have to tempt men. In one chapter in the *De
Principiis*, Origen brings together texts relating to the angels
and then shows how the differences between one angel and
another result from their previous merits.[4] In the following
passage, he shows in greater detail how the functions of the
good angels depend on their merits. "To my mind," he says,
"we ought not to consider it an accident that one angel has
received one office and another another, e.g., that Raphael
has to look after the sick and heal them or Gabriel to watch
over mortals. We must suppose that their offices are the fruit
of their deserts and conclude that they merited them by the
zeal and virtue they displayed before the world was created.
After the creation of the world, particular functions were entrusted to all who belonged to the order of archangels. The
merits of other spirits were such as to secure them inclusion in
the order of angels, there to work under one or other of the
archangels, princes and heads of their order."[5] If Origen's
ideas about the angels depend on his philosophical views, his
study of their functions at any rate links up with Tradition.
The two factors are often found together in his works. In the
present instance, we find him incorporating a very important
section of early Christian theology into his own philosophical
framework.

If angelology does not occupy a very prominent position in the Old Testament, it plays a considerable part in the Gospels. As Kittel points out, the angels attending on Christ from the Annunciation to the Resurrection are a witness to the presence of God in him.[6] They celebrate their liturgy in heaven and pour forth unceasing praise to the Blessed Trinity. They are the true heaven, which is not a material place but the part of the spiritual creation that has already entered into bliss. Their presence in the Gospels, in contrast to their absence from the Old Testament, is one of the things which show that the Incarnation is an epiphany, a manifestation of God's Word. The Gospels also bear witness to the existence of evil spirits. If we look beyond the merely visible, we see that from the Temptation to the Passion Christ's life was a struggle with the Prince of This World and his angels, a struggle that issued, after their apparent victory on Good Friday, in their lasting defeat on Easter morning. The fact of the existence of angels and devils is thus an essential element in Christian dogma.

It was one that theologians had begun to work at before Origen's time. Allowances must be made for the influence of Jewish theology on the question.[7] If the Old Testament does not devote much space to the angels, except in the latest books (Tobias, Daniel), the Jews contemporary with the early Christian era concerned themselves a good deal with them in their speculations on religious matters. This is true first of the Jewish apocalyptic writings, in which we find the idea that there are several classes of angels, the highest being that of the "seven who stand in the presence of the Lord" (Tob. xii. 15). The Book of Enoch also mentions these seven archangels.[8] The various classes of angels below these have various tasks entrusted to them: they preside over the life of nature,[9] they have special duties towards men.[10] Many of the constituents of this theology were incorporated into the New Testament, particularly in the Epistle of Jude (i. 9), the Epistle to the Galatians and St. John's Apocalypse.[11] Secondly, in another sphere, Philo of Alexandria attributes considerable importance to the ἄγγελοι as intermediaries between the Logos and man, and he also uses points taken from the current Hellenistic teaching about the gods, which included a fully developed "demonology".[12] The early Christian writers in turn worked

out a system of angelology. It was based both on the data
provided by Revelation and on Jewish theology. It is to be
found in Justin and Hermas and in Athenagoras in particular.[13]

1. The Angels of the Nations

Origen sees the angels first of all as active not in the creation
of the cosmos—he rejects the Hellenistic theory to that effect—
but in the running of it. He found this idea both in revealed
Christianity and in Jewish theology. It also formed part of the
Greek philosophers' speculations on religious matters. The
Book of Enoch shows angels watching over the sun, the moon
and the stars,[14] while others are in charge of the winds, mists,
dew and rain.[15] The Book of Jubilees speaks of angels of the
spirit of fire[16] and the angel of the waters.[17] Fr. Allo thinks
that the four animals of the Apocalypse are the angels commissioned to govern the world. Athenagoras too holds that
God has entrusted the management of the visible world to
angels. "God," he says, "the Creator and Demiurge of the
world, has divided the angels into various classes through the
intervention of the Word that issues from him, and has arranged
for them to look after the elements, the heavens, the world and
the things in it, and to see that there is harmony in it all."[18]
The same ideas are found in the teaching of the Greek philosophers of Origen's time. Albinus, for example, says: "There are
also other divinities, some for all the elements: there are some
in the aether, some in fire, some in the air and others in water.
These divinities have been given sway over all sublunary things,
all things on earth."[19]

Origen echoes all these ideas. "There are angels in charge
of everything," he says, "of earth, water, air and fire: all the
elements alike. They are also used by the Logos as instruments
to regulate the movements of the animals, the plants, the stars
and even the heavens."[20] It is the idea of the angels of the elements and the angels of the various parts of the cosmos over
again. Elsewhere he mentions the "virtues who preside over
the earth and the seeding of trees, who see to it that springs and
rivers do not run dry, who look after the rains and the winds,
the animals that live on land, those that live in the sea and all
that is born of earth".[21] Celsus is thus not justified in charging

Christians with failing to honour the δαίμονες that preside over the life of nature. "The earth brings forth what are called natural products. Water spurts and flows in springs and running pools. The air stays incorrupt and gives life to those who breathe it. The reason for all this is that everything the earth produces, every spring of water and the air as well is in the charge of an invisible being specially appointed to watch over it. We too say this, only we do not call those invisible beings demons."[22] The only point on which Christians differ from Celsus is that they call these protectors "angels"[23] and also, Origen says later, that though they honour the angels they do not worship them.[24]

These functions with regard to the cosmos are discharged by the lowest class of angels. Origen thought that at a higher level angels presided over human societies and persons and thus shared in God's providential activity in the cosmos and in history as well.[25] The first of these two points constitutes the question of the angels of the nations. It is one that occupied a particularly important place in Origen's mental world. Here again he was echoing an existing tradition. In this case it had begun with the text from the Septuagint: "When the Most High assigned the nations their inheritance, he fixed the limits of the peoples in accordance with the number of the angels of God" (Deut. xxxii. 8). The Hebrew reads: "according to the number of the children of Israel". But the Greek translation, which is really a theological interpretation of the text, gave rise to a whole tradition. The Testament of Nephthalim says that before the dispersal of the peoples, Michael asked each nation to choose an angel. Daniel and Enoch represent Michael as having charge of the people of Israel, but, as we shall see later, there was another tradition, according to which Javé had kept his chosen people for himself. This doctrine, it seems, is behind Enoch's seventy shepherds, who are the angels set over the pagan nations.[26]

Origen followed this tradition and used the Septuagint reading. "As we are talking at the moment about intellectual natures," he says in one place, "we must not omit to mention something that has a bearing on ourselves—for we too, as men, are also rational animals. Scripture says that the Lord's portion (i.e., his people) is Jacob, and Israel his share of the inheritance,

while the angels' share is the rest of the nations; because when
the Most High scattered the sons of Adam and divided the
nations, he fixed their limits according to the number of the
angels of God. We must not through carelessness fail to say that
the various categories mentioned in this text have a special
significance for us."[27] Elsewhere in his writings, Origen maintains that the nations have all been entrusted to the protection
of angels. Thus, he speaks of the "angels to whose care men
are entrusted. They were all painstaking and watchful in
guarding those committed to them, but they needed help if
the nations in their charge were to be guarded properly. It was
to them that the angel came and announced the birth of Jesus
and the coming of the true Shepherd".[28] Origen is here giving
an allegorical interpretation of the appearance of the angels to
the shepherds at Bethlehem. He sees the shepherds as figures
of the angels who act as shepherds of the nations. These angels
were engaged in a painful struggle against the idolatry practised
by the nations in their charge, and the manifestation of Jesus
was an enormous help to them.[29]

These ideas, which were Jewish in origin, came up against
others, put forward by Greek philosophers. They thereby
afforded Origen an opportunity of clarifying his own views on
history. For the last few centuries, paganism had been faced
with a complicated problem. On the one hand, there was an
ever-increasing movement towards monotheism; on the other
hand, the cosmopolitanism of the times brought the traditional
cults of the various nations into touch with one another. The
meeting of the two elements eventually produced an outlook in
which both were amalgamated: the view emerged that there
was one supreme God but that every nation had its own deities
—which were δαίμονες—as well. In this way, polytheism
was reconciled with monotheism. There was also a political
side to the question—just as Roman religion upheld a variety
of local cults within one universal religion, so the Roman
Empire upheld a variety of nations within the *imperium
Romanum*. Thus, the political system as it was at the time seemed
to the Romans a reflection of the celestial world with its hierarchy of deities—seemed, too, to share in the immutability of
that world.[30] The union of the two elements found perfect
expression in Julian the Apostate when he wrote: "Our writers

say that the Demiurge is the father of all men and their common king. He has divided the peoples among various gods,
whose business it is to watch over the different nations and
cities. Each of these gods rules over the portion that has fallen
to him in accordance with his nature. . . . Every nation
reproduces the natural characteristics of the deity ruling it."[31]
National cults expressed the reverence the various nations felt
for their own gods.

It was with this idea as his starting-point that at the end of
the second century Celsus made his attack on the universal
claims of Christianity, which he charged with being revolutionary. "The Jews," he said, "are a separate race and have
laws that were specially made for their country. In continuing
to abide by those laws and observe their own religious practices
—I will not attempt to estimate their value but will simply say
that they came to the Jews from their ancestors—they are only
doing what everybody else does, i.e., following ancestral usages
irrespective of their intrinsic worth. It is obvious that the reason
for this state of things is not just that it came into people's
heads to make one set of laws for one community and another
for another, or that what has been laid down by the group must
be carried out. No; the reason is that as the various parts of
the earth were distributed at the beginning of the world to
various overseers and shared out among them according
to their respective spheres of jurisdiction, it is only natural
that they should always be governed in that way. Religion
is as it should be in a nation when it is practised as
these overseers want it to be. Subverting what has been
law from the very beginning is an impious thing."[32] This
shows how Celsus defended Jewish particularism against
Christian universalism in the name of tradition. M. Bidez says
of Julian: "He links together the idea of the nation and the
idea of conservatism. A man is bound to profess the religion of
his country. The religion of the Jews is national and traditional;
it must therefore be defended against the Christians, who are
revolutionaries. He is opposed to the international tendencies
and the idea of progress that we owe to Christianity."[33]

That was the idea that Origen had to wage war against. He
did it by showing that the dividing of the nations and their
consequent sharing-out among the angels did not represent the

original situation but was a consequence of sin. At the beginning, the human race was one; the scattering of the nations
was a punishment. Consequently, in restoring unity, Christianity was not going against the natural order originally instituted by God. Far from it; it was bringing that order back.
Origen also linked up the sharing of the nations among the
angels with another incident, the episode of the Tower of
Babel and the rupture of the original unity of mankind, the
sign of which had been unity of language. Such, in substance,
was his reply to Celsus. "There is a question I would put to
him," he said, "and to people who think as he does. 'Who
was it,' I would say, 'who at the beginning distributed the
various parts of the earth to their overseers? Unless all these
parts of the earth were given out by a single person, the overseers must have obtained their shares by mere chance. That is
absurd and it eliminates Providence.' Celsus does not seem to
have realized what the reasons for the distribution of lands
were. They are not apparent [they are μυστικά], but the
Greeks have come near to knowing them, for they teach that
some of the beings they call gods quarrelled about Attica. We
for our part say that Moses, the prophet and worshipper of the
true God, mentions this division of the earth into parts in
Deuteronomy [xxxii. 9]. He also refers to it in Genesis, where
he says that the 'earth was of one tongue, and of the same
speech. . . . When they removed from the east, they found a
plain in the land of Senaar, and dwelt in it' [Gen. xi. 1–2]."[34]

The "non-apparent" reasons for the assignment of the
nations to their angels are explained by Origen as follows.
"This is the way we ought to look at it. There was one language
common to all men living on the earth; it was a sacred one, and
they kept it as long as they were united. While their thoughts
were inspired by the light and the eternal radiance of the light,
they never left the Orient; but when they came to have
thoughts at variance with the Orient, they did leave it. They
found a plain in the land of Senaar . . . and they dwelt in it.
Then they needs must assemble materials for building and try
to join to heaven something by nature incapable of being so
joined: they tried to reach the immaterial through the material.
They were therefore handed over to angels, who harried them
in varying degrees, according to the distance they had gone

from the Orient, and they were to remain under them until they had atoned for their folly. The angels gave them each a tongue of their own and led them to whichever part of the world they happened to have deserved—some they took to torrid regions, some to glacial ones where the cold would be their punishment, some to fertile countries, others to wild, uncultivated lands.''[35] The significance of the incident is easily seen. In the language of the Fathers, the Orient is at once Christ, *oriens ex alto*, and paradise, which was planted *ad orientem*. It was Christ who enabled men to live in paradise, and when men withdrew from him, God punished them by putting them under the sway of the angels. Variety of speech and variety of environment were punishments too; they were not part of the eternal order of things.

One point in this passage is not very clear: what does Origen mean when he talks about angels harrying their charges in varying degrees? We have just seen that God had entrusted the nations to the care of good angels. Are these the same good angels, envisaged as holding a commission from God to chastise and correct the nations? Or are they bad angels? Origen was aware of the ambiguity. He alludes to it in his homilies on Numbers. "Some of the peoples and kings named in Scripture," he says, "are unquestionably connected with the bad angels or hostile powers. In the same way, what the Bible says about the piety of the people should be referred to the good angels or beneficent powers."[36] He is thus led to conclude that every nation has two angels attached to it. On the one hand, they all have their own protectors. "It is unthinkable that if all nations have bad angels over them, the same provinces or regions should not also be in the keeping of good angels."[37] On the other hand, the nations also have their bad angels. Are these bad angels the angels commissioned by God to punish the nations, the angels who invented the various national tongues and civilizations? Or is the right solution the one put forward in the Book of Enoch—the idea that after God gave the nations into the keeping of angels, some of the angels turned traitor? Origen does not make it clear. Wherever the truth may lie, the bad angels were certainly the instigators of idolatry, because they tried to persuade men to worship them instead of the one true God.

In one curious passage, Origen represents the occult sciences in which the various nations specialized as being not theirs only but as belonging also to their "princes". "By the wisdom of the princes of this world," he says, "we understand such things as the secret, occult philosophy (to use their own term for it) of the Egyptians, the astrology the Chaldaeans practice, the knowledge of the Most High the Hindus profess to have and the innumerable theories the Greeks hold about the Deity. Thus we read in Scripture that there are 'princes' in every nation. In Daniel, for example, we are told that there is a prince in the Persian state and one in the Greek; and the context makes it clear that they are not men but angelic powers. Similarly, in the prophet Ezechiel, the Prince of Tyre is obviously a spiritual power. These and the other powers of this world have each some special science of their own, and they all teach their respective dogmas and opinions to men."[38] What are the motives of this conduct? Origen thinks that the spirits do not intend to do harm but act in the belief that what they teach is true. The powers of this world are undoubtedly the same as the angels of the nations—"as certain spiritual powers have been set over the nations of the world, they are called princes of this world".[39]

But the power the angels were given after Babel of ruling the nations like princes was withdrawn when Christ came. This applied to the good angels as well as to the bad; it was so whether they had received their mission from God or whether they were just good angels gone astray. In the beginning Christ, the Orient, had ruled mankind as Prince; when the nations were scattered, he had given his princely power to the angels, and when he came down to earth he resumed it again. Hence the connection between Christianity and universalism. But as Origen saw it, it was a particular kind of universalism, religious in character and eschatological in colouring. Christ's coming meant that a new world had appeared, in which all men were mystically one in him. The political order dependent on the existence of a variety of nations—an order which, in Origen's opinion, was not natural—was henceforth over and done with. That explains why Origen took no interest in the political question. It has been pointed out in this connection that he regarded polyarchy as a system going with polytheism and

representative of the fallen pagan world. Monarchy was to
appear at the end of the world and was bound up with monotheism. The unity of mankind could not be attained before the
end of time. As Peterson shows, [40] Eusebius applied the same
idea to the world in time and considered that the political unity
of the world achieved by Constantine and the *pax Romana* had
brought the Kingdom of Heaven down to earth. This was a
case where monotheism became a political problem.

But to come back to the angels of the nations—they reacted
in different ways to Christ's coming and their own consequent
removal from office. The good angels welcomed both changes
wholeheartedly: they had toiled for so long among the pagan
nations and the fruits of their labours were so few. It was to
them that the Angel of the Nativity came and announced that
Christ was born. "These shepherds should be taken as the
angels entrusted with the care of the human race. . . . They all
needed help if the nations in their care were to be governed
properly; and now the angel came to tell them that Jesus had
been born, that the true Shepherd had come. (There was a
shepherd, for instance, for Macedonia, and he needed God's
help for his work—that was why a Macedonian appeared to
Paul.) When Christ came into the world, he fulfilled a need
that all the shepherds felt. His coming was a source of great
joy to them, because of the nations in their keeping. The
angel in charge of the fortunes of Egypt found Christ's presence
on earth a great help in converting the Egyptians to Christianity. . . . Before Christ came, the good angels could do very
little to benefit the people in their care. When the angel of the
Egyptians was helping his people on his own, he secured hardly
a single proselyte to belief in God." [41]

But it was quite different with the bad angels, the "princes of
this world". Origen did not exclude the idea that "conversion"
was possible for the bad angels; he regarded the conversion of
the centurion at Capharnaum as a figure of such an event.
"We may wonder," he says, "whether the royal official does
not represent one of the powers called princes of this world, his
son the nation over which the prince holds special sway—his
share, so to speak, of the inheritance—the son's illness the evil
disposition of the nation, persisting against the prince's will,
and Capharnaum the country where his subjects live. It seems

to me that even among these princes there were some who were
impressed by the power and divinity of Jesus; I think they
went over to him and protested against the conduct of their
subjects. If men can repent and pass from unbelief to faith, why
should we hesitate to say the same of the powers? . . . For my
part, I think that it has sometimes happened. I think that
some of the ἄρχοντες were converted when Christ came, and
that that is why some towns and even whole nations accepted
Christianity more readily than others."[42] The idea found in
this passage, the idea that it is possible for the bad angels to be
converted, is one of Origen's favourite ones.

Nevertheless, conversion was the exception; for the most
part, the "princes of the nations" set their faces against Christ
because he had deprived them of their power. The reader will
remember the passage in which Origen speaks of the princes of
the nations and their various intellectual specialities. He goes
on to say: "They saw our Lord and Saviour promising that he
would come into the world and declaring that his purpose was
to destroy absolutely everything taught by the false gnosis.
Not knowing who it was that was concealed behind all this,
they set traps to catch him—'The kings of the earth stood up,
and the princes met together, against the Lord and against his
Christ'. Paul knew what traps they had set and what they had
plotted against the Son of God when they crucified him
to whom all glory belongs. That was why he said [1
Cor. ii. 6–8] that the wisdom he was making known was not
the wisdom of this world's rulers: none of them could read
the secret of him to whom all glory belongs, or they would
not have crucified him."[43] The point is made still more
explicitly in the following passage: "Those words in the Bible:
'Thy descendants shall receive our enemies' cities as their
inheritance' . . . [LXX: Gen. xxiii. 17] were fulfilled in the
person of Christ. Thus anger seized hold of the angels who held
the peoples under their sway. As the Father had said to Christ:
'Ask thy will of me and thou shalt have the nations for thy
patrimony' [Ps. ii. 8], Christ deprived the angels of the power
and authority they had had over the nations, and so he roused
their wrath. Hence, as Scripture says: 'The kings of the earth
stood up, and the princes met together, against the Lord and
against his Christ.'"[44] The idea of the ousting of the angels is

here very clearly stated. Yet we notice that it is represented as a perfectly natural thing; it is simply the replacing of one order of things by another. The good angels welcome it gladly; it is a defeat only for the bad angels, who refuse to accept it.

In another passage, Origen reveals a further element in his view of the question. "They set themselves against us too," he says; "they prepare trouble and strife for us. Christ's Apostle says: 'It is not against flesh and blood that we enter the lists; we have to do with princedoms and powers, with the *cosmocratores*' [Eph. vi. 12]. Unless we draw strength from our faith and resist them [1 Pet. v. 9], they will make captives of us again. If we allowed that to happen, we should be setting at nought the work that Christ has done for us, not caring that he has nailed the princedoms and powers to the cross [cf. Col. ii. 14]. Now I ask you, was it unjust of Christ to snatch the nations out of his enemies' power and bring them under his own? Of course it was not. Israel had once been his portion, but his enemies had led it into sin, led it far from its God. It was because of its sins that God said to it: 'You see, you are divided because you have sinned' [cf. Nehem. i. 8]. But he also said: 'Though you should be led away to the uttermost parts of the world, I will gather you back again from thence.' Because the princes of this world had encroached upon the Lord's inheritance, the Good Shepherd had to leave the ninety-nine sheep on the mountain-side and go down to the plain to look for the one that was lost [cf. Matt. xviii. 12]."[45] Thus, the true Israel is mankind as it was in the beginning, before the dispersal of the nations, and the carnal Israel is only an image of the true one. The true Israel is the one that Christ came to build up again. But the victory he won over the princes of the nations will not be consummated until the end of time. Until then, there will always be forces at work to divide mankind, and Christians will always have to be in arms against them.

There is a curious passage in which Origen shows that even after Christ had come, the princes of the nations still maintained their claims and deputed their satellites to secure the obedience of their former subjects. It was a view of things that corresponded to the "historical" situation of the times Origen was living in; it fitted the conflict between the various national forms of idolatry and the universal claims of Catholicism. In conditions in which politics and religion were as closely bound up together as they were in the Roman Empire, the two questions of necessity overlapped. By the mere fact that they had broken with the gods of the State, Christians had outlawed themselves and deprived themselves of any share in the social life of their country. Origen's outlook needs to be seen in relation to the problems thus arising, problems that all the early Christians had to face. Today we regard the political question and the religious question as two separate things. But this point of view is something we have acquired as Christianity has developed. In Origen's time, the two questions seemed to be part of the same problem. This explains something that seems strange to us, viz., the alleged connection between the angels of the nations and the temptations with which Christians were beset. The greatest temptation of all was idolatry, i.e., the national cults, which, as Origen saw them, were forms of worship paid to the angels of the nations.

We have taken the more practical side of the question first. The strictly religious side comes out in the following passage. "At the beginning, the earth was divided among the princes, i.e., among the angels [Deut. xxxii. 8–9]. Whereas Moses talks about angels, Daniel explicitly calls them princes: he mentions a prince of the Kingdom of Persia, a prince of the Kingdom of Greece and Michael, 'your prince'. These, then, are the princes of the nations. We each have an adversary [Luke xii. 58] dogging our footsteps, one whose business it is to take us to the prince and say: 'Prince of the Kingdom of Persia' (or whatever his title may be), 'this man was a subject of yours. I have kept him for you just as he was. None of the other princes has managed to entice him away, not even the one who boasted that he had come expressly to detach men from the Persian inheritance' (or the Greek, or whatever it may be) 'and transfer them to God's!' Our Lord the Christ has mastered all these princes. He went into their territories and brought salvation to the captive peoples there and transferred them to himself. You yourself were part of some prince's inheritance, the possession of some evil spirit, until Jesus came and snatched you away and gave you to God, his Father. But we each of us have our adversary, who is bent on bringing us back to his prince, as we are not princes ourselves (an Egyptian, for instance, has the Prince of Egypt for his prince). Take care, then, to free yourself from your adversary and from the prince he is trying to take you to."[46] We shall return to the idea of "guardian devils" later. For the moment, the interest is to see how Origen couples these creatures with the angels of the nations as the principle of idolatry.

There is one point that we have not yet touched, and that is the question of the history of Israel. How did Israel stand in comparison with the pagan nations? The pagan nations had been given into the keeping of angels but, as we have seen, Origen held that Israel's prince was not Michael but Javé in person. How did it come about, in the first place, that only a portion of the original Israel, i.e., only one part of the human race, still had Javé as its Protector? Origen has an explanation to offer. First he notes the fact. "It may be asked," he says, "why Christians and Jews do not worship the angels or the sun, moon and stars—things which the Greeks call visible gods. Well, the Law of Moses shows that God gave those creatures to all the nations on earth, except those he intended to keep for himself as his chosen part."[47] The passage is interesting because it shows that Origen regarded the worship of the heavenly bodies and the worship of the angels—the two were closely connected, in his view—as an economy given by God to the pagans to divert them from evil spirits and idols, and thus as a legitimate, though inferior form of religion. This is admirably brought out by Hal Koch.[48] The idea behind it is one we have met with before, viz., that the worship of nature, in which the real object of adoration is the God behind the sacraments of the visible world, represents the first stage in the religious education of mankind. This was the worship the pagan peoples gave the good angels to whose keeping God had committed them after the scattering of the nations.

But there was one part of the human race that went on worshipping the true God as it had done from the beginning. "The Lord's own portion, the Lord's people were those who kept the original language of the world, who never forsook the Orient but stayed there all the time and kept its language. They alone were not put under a prince who had received authority over his subjects merely to punish them, as the others were."[49] Thus, one part of the human race stayed in the east,

i.e., was true to the religion practised from the beginning, and
never turned away from God. This part constituted the true
Israel. Its language was the one originally spoken by all mankind but now surviving only in this one part of the human race.
Its dwelling-place was likewise its original country. The logic
of Origen's system is once more in evidence, here, with its
insistence that you always get the conditions you deserve. Gone
is the idea that when God chose Israel as his special portion he
was simply exercising his sovereign freedom, the idea that his
choice of a sinful people had nothing behind it but a gratuitous
outpouring of divine love. Instead, the choice God made of
Israel is represented as a reward for loyalty in the midst of
universal apostasy. The spirit of the prophets is stifled by the
spirit of the Pharisees. No doubt Origen had in fact delved into
the traditions current among the rabbis about the antiquity of
the Hebrew tongue and the reasons why God preferred Israel
to the other nations. He returns elsewhere to the idea that
Hebrew was the original language of mankind. "When, in the
section of Genesis we are reading, God says, 'Come ye, let us
... confound their tongue' [Gen. xi. 7], he is no doubt speaking
to the angels. Shall we not, then, conclude, that it was the
angels who were responsible for the different languages and
dialects that men speak? There must have been one who gave
the Babylonians their tongue and one who gave the Greeks
theirs. The originators of the different tongues were no doubt
the princes of the various nations. But the language given to
men in the beginning through Adam remained, so we believe,
in the possession of the Hebrews, was kept by that part of the
human race that never became an angel's apanage, because it
never ceased to be God's."[50]

Yet this same Israel that had remained faithful to God, the
Israel of Abraham and Jacob, did not remain faithful to the
end. It eventually turned to the idols the other nations worshipped. God did not place it directly under the rule of an
angelic power, but he made it subject to nations which were so
ruled. Such is the explanation of the "captivity" of Israel.
"Sins were committed in the Lord's portion, trifling ones at
first and then more grievous ones. God waited a long time;
then remedies were applied and, for their sins, the Israelites
were subjected to the princes of the other nations. In the end

they were scattered throughout the earth."[51] This theological view of history thus takes in both Israel and the pagan nations. It will be seen how closely it all hangs together, since in Origen's philosophy everything has its root in moral freedom. The history of civilization, the differences between one nation and another, the different religions—all these are consequences of the sins of the human race in its early days. The history of Israel shows that that nation was in a special position at first because of its loyalty to God, but afterwards Israel too was to experience dispersal and captivity. In the end, Christ will come and restore unity and bring back liberty, both to Israel and to the other nations. Origen is here making a determined and coherent attempt to give an interpretation of history that will cover both its religious and its political aspects. It is strange that when we want to know his views on the theology of history, we should have to look for them in his angelology.

We may observe in conclusion that however tentative his theory of the angels of the nations may have been, it nevertheless provides material for resolving a point that previous theologians had left ambiguous. Professor Cullman[52] and Fr. Bouyer[53] after him have pointed out that in St. Paul's theology the Redemption appears in two different lights. It is represented, first, as the reign of Christ: as Christ has taken over the government of the world, he has deprived the angels of their previous commission to direct the cosmos and human society. It is also shown as a victory over the angels who were holding mankind captive. Was it the same angels in both cases? If they were bad angels, how can God be thought to have trusted them with the management of the world? If they were good angels, why was their removal a victory for Christ? Origen's theory—that God in his providence had entrusted part of the management of the world to the good angels, that with the sanction of the same providence some of the angels lost their integrity and that the loss brought idolatry in its wake and the perversion of the political order—provides materials for a solution of these difficulties. It is thus seen to have a further interest: besides serving to explain part of the theology of the angels, it throws light as well on the various problems connected with the relations between the State and the City of the Evil One. It was worthy of our attention on all these grounds.

2. THE ANGELS AND CHRIST

If the idea of the angels of the nations led us to grapple with the problem of history, the question of the guardian angels will bring us into another field: it will introduce us to the sacramental life and the spiritual life in general. Here again, Origen is simply taking over a body of traditional teaching. It comes down from a very early date. The Book of Tobias shows the angel Gabriel helping a man entrusted to his care. The exclamation, "It must be his guardian angel", which followed the opening of the door to Peter at John Mark's house (Acts xii. 15) is evidence of belief in individual protection by angels. Christ himself, moreover, had occasion to speak of the children's angels (Matt. xviii. 10). The doctrine appears in the early Fathers of the Church—in the Pseudo-Barnabas and in the Shepherd of Hermas. Origen refers to them.[54] Once again we have to note the existence of a Hellenistic parallel in pagan religious circles.[55] The theory that every man has his own δαίμων appears as early as the time of Plato, who mentions it in connection with Socrates, and it is worked out at length in Plutarch.[56] Origen formulates the doctrine thus: "Every one of the faithful, we are told, however insignificant he may be in the Church, is assisted by an angel, and Christ is our witness that these angels behold the Father's face continually."[57] And again: "Every human soul has an angel who guides it like a brother."[58] In another work, he refers to passages in the Acts.[59]

But this body of traditional teaching underwent considerable development at Origen's hands. First, he related what he had to say about the guardian angels to the Incarnation and represented the two as closely connected in the process by which man's salvation was wrought.[60] Our study of the angels of the nations was focussed on the government of the world, but the question of the guardian angels revolves round the Redemption. When Christ came on earth, the angels flocked to him to share in the work he had come to do. "When the angels saw the Prince of the heavenly host [i.e., Christ] dwelling on earth, they began to walk themselves in the path he had shown them; they followed their Lord and did what

God had wanted them to do when he assigned them as *guardians* to those who believe in him. . . . The angels are there to help you to salvation. They were given to God's Son to be his servants. They said to one another: 'If he has gone down and taken a body, put on mortal flesh, borne the cross and died for men, how can we stay idle here? How can we look to our comfort? We too must go down from heaven, angels, all of us.' Thus it was that when Christ was born, there was a multitude of the heavenly army giving praise and glory to God [Luke xiii. 20]. The whole world is full of angels."[61]

That does not mean that they did nothing at all for the good of souls until Christ came on earth. Origen represents them— and so does St. Paul, for that matter—as being active under the Old Testament as well. "Before Christ came, it was the angels who watched over the young Bride."[62] They even tried to intervene in the affairs of pagans but, as we have seen, their efforts came to nothing, because until the coming of Christ the pagans were in the power of evil spirits, the chosen representatives of the princes who ruled the nations. This brings us to one of the essential features of Origen's teaching about the guardian angels. Just as every nation has a good and a bad angel of its own, so has every individual. "What I say of individual nations should also be understood of individual men in general. Every man has two angels at his side, one virtuous, the other wicked. When good thoughts fill the heart, it is because the good angel is speaking—of that there can be no doubt. When the thoughts are bad, it is the bad angel speaking."[63] Origen often comes back to the idea. "All men," he says in one place, "have two angels with them, a bad one prompting them to evil and a good one prompting them to good."[64] It is, moreover, another of the ideas he had inherited from Tradition. He explicitly bases himself on earlier writers. "The Book of the Shepherd [i.e., Hermas] teaches that every man is accompanied by two angels. It says that if good thoughts rise to the mind, they come from the good angel; if they are the opposite, they are suggested, it says, by the bad angel. And Barnabas says the same in his Epistle."[65]

Thus, a battle is fought over every single man. Christ and his servants the angels are on one side, the princes of this

world and their servants the devils are on the other.[66] Origen's
theory of the angels acquires a very special bias in virtue of this
and takes its place alongside the drama of the Redemption. As
long as men worship idols, their devils are all-powerful. Their
angels can do nothing; they dare not look the Father in the
face. "If I belong to the Church, no matter how insignificant
I may be, my angel is free to look upon the Father's face. If I
am outside the Church, he dare not do so."[67] But as soon as a
man is converted and gives himself to Christ, as soon as he
renounces Satan and his following, Christ hands him over to
his angel. "Yes, you used to be a devil's subject but now you
are an angel's."[68] That is the point where the guardian angel's
mission begins. "Come, angel, take charge of this man. He
has turned from the error he used to believe in, turned from
what the devils taught him. Take him, and like a good doctor
give him comfort and instruction. He is only a baby. Take him
and give him Baptism—a second birth. Ask some of your
companions to help you in your task; and then all of you
together must instruct your charges in the faith, since only
yesterday they were still deep in their errors."[69]

Origen here picks out a point well worth noting with regard
to the angels: their influence bears particularly on the beginnings of things. It is not without reason that the Gospels often
speak of them in connection with children. Just as their business is with children in the natural order, so is it in the order of
grace. They guide the steps of their charges at the beginning
of the spiritual life. "May it not be that the children are those
who have angels, since children are led by fear, while the more
advanced have the Lord of the angels saying to them: 'In
affliction I am at his side' [Ps. xc. 15]? As long as we are
imperfect and must have help if we are to rid ourselves of the
ills that beset us, we each of us need an angel, like Jacob, who
said of his: 'He has rescued us from our troubles' [cf. Gen.
xlviii. 16]. But when we are grown up and the time for tutors
and trustees is past [cf. Gal. iii. 23 et seq., iv. 2. et seq.], we are
ripe for Christ's own guidance."[70] It is a piece of spiritual
teaching that has passed into the common stock of Tradition.
St. Ignatius Loyola observes in his rules for the discernment of
spirits that the influence of the angels is felt in the beginning of
the spiritual life. At another level, a comparison could be made

with the angels' activity in the Old Testament, where it bears on the Bride while she is still young.

The guardian angel's activity begins at Baptism. In another of his works, Origen deals with the presence of the angels at the administration of the sacrament of regeneration. "When the mysteries of the faith were revealed to you," he says, "the heavenly virtues were there and the ministering angels, the whole assembly of the firstborn [Heb. xii. 23]."[71] The angels of Baptism had their place, too, in the tradition of the Church.[72] Thus, Didymus of Alexandria says that when the priests immerse the newly-baptized in the water, angels immerse them in the Holy Ghost. We have already pointed out in this connection that the angels are specially concerned with the sacramental life of the souls in their care and in particular are present at the eucharistic *synaxis*. "What must be said about the angels is this. If the angel of the Lord encamps beside those who fear the Lord [Ps. xxxiii. 8] . . . it would seem that when a number of people duly meet together for the glory of Christ, they will each have their own angel encamped beside them, since they all fear the Lord. Each angel will be with the man he has been commissioned to guard and direct. Thus, when the saints are assembled, there will be two Churches, one of men and one of angels."[73]

After ministering invisibly at Baptism, the angels go on to guide the soul by suggesting good thoughts to it as it sets out on the spiritual life.[74] They prompt it to produce good desires. "We know that the thoughts that issue from our hearts sometimes come from ourselves, while at other times they may be induced by the enemy's forces or be sent by God or the holy angels. This might seem mere imagination, were it not vouched for by the testimony of Scripture."[75] If Origen mentions suggestions coming from the bad angels as well as the suggestions made by the good, the reason is that although we cease to be in the power of our bad angel when we are baptized, the bad angel nevertheless goes on attacking us. "God allows the opposing forces to fight against us, because he wants us to get the better of them."[76] This psychological study of the influence exerted by various spirits on the spiritual life places Origen at the beginning of a whole line of tradition. It is well known to what lengths the Desert Fathers and Evagrius were to carry the scientific study of the different spirits.[77] St. Ignatius, too, takes up the point in the *Spiritual Exercises*. Suggesting good thoughts is not the only helpful thing the angels do; they assist the people under their care in every possible way. Origen represents them as interceding for their charges with God. "When a man prays to God," he says, "the angels gather about him and join him in his prayer. And not only that. Every Christian—even those who are quite insignificant in the Church—has an angel of his own, who looks on our Father's face in heaven [Matt. xviii. 10] and sees the Creator's divinity all the time. These angels pray with us and work with us, as far as they can, to obtain for us the things we ask for."[78]

Conversely, the bad angels too have a part to play. In the *De Principiis*, Origen explains at length that their function is to tempt the just and so put them to the test.[79] In another of his works he says: "God has not deprived the devil of his power over the world, because his collaboration is still necessary for the perfecting of those destined to receive a crown."[80] Their second function is to serve as instruments of God's chastisements (the purpose of which, it should be remembered, is always to promote a cure). They are as essential as the hangman is to the State.[81] "No evil spirit is authorized by divine law to rule over things on earth. But as it is fitting that they should lord it over the wicked and punish them, the Word, who governs the universe, has given them power over those men who submit to the sway of sin instead of to God."[82] Hence they are not entitled to respect, as Celsus maintains.

The angels give all the more care to the discharge of their duties in that their own interests are at stake. "The angels exert themselves in the service of the good because they know that if they manage us properly and bring us to salvation, they can confidently look the Father in the face themselves. It means disgrace for an angel if the man in his keeping sins, while if the man makes progress, however insignificant he may be, the angel gains credit for it. And conversely, every time we sin, our Adversary gloats over it."[83] Origen carries his theory of the angel's responsibility to great lengths. "At the end of time," he says, "when the angels come up for judgment, they will produce the men given into their keeping, the men they have helped and instructed. There will be a trial and God will

decide what caused the many sins in human life. He will see
if they were due to negligence on the part of his spiritual
ministers—for he sent them to help the heirs to salvation—or
whether they came from the laziness of the helped."[84] The
degree of bliss the angels will enjoy will depend on the verdict.
"When their good offices obtain salvation for men, they can
stay watching God face to face, but if through their negligence
a man falls, they know what risk they are running. . . . Whether
the angels look at God's face always, or never, or only sometimes, will depend on the merits of those whose angels they
were."[85] One element in the angels' activities is their collaboration with the Apostles. "The Apostles have the angels to
help them to minister the word and spread the Gospel."[86]
They share in the glory accruing to the Apostles from their
spiritual conquests. "Peter has his angel, and so have Paul and
the other Apostles and the lesser ministers. These angels bring
the harvest to the Lord's threshing-floor as well as the men
they have acted through."[87] Just as the Apostles became the
heads, the *episcopi*, of the communities they founded among the
infidels, so do the angels. That is why there are "angels of the
Churches". "The angels all offer the firstfruits of their
Churches. These are the angels John seems to be speaking to
in the Apocalypse. There are also other angels outside, in
every nation, bringing people to the faith. Think for a moment.
Imagine a city where there are no Christians as yet by birth.
If someone goes there and begins to give instruction and strives
to give people a new outlook and bring them to the faith, he
becomes the prince and bishop of the people he has taught. In
the same way, the holy angels will one day be the princes of
the people they have gathered in in the various nations, the
people whose progress they have secured by their labours and
their ministry."[88]

Two things in this passage deserve attention. The first is that
every Church possesses both a visible bishop and an invisible
angel. "One may venture to say, as it is in line with Scripture,
that there are two bishops to every Church, one visible and the
other invisible. And just as men are praised by the Lord for
working well at the tasks they have been set and are open to
blame if they do them badly, so is it with the angels."[89] Origen
justifies this theory from the Apocalypse. He then goes on to

say: "If the angels have the government of the Churches so much at heart, what need is there to bring in men at all? What have men to fear, provided that they really want to be saved with the angels and to work with them? For my part, I think we shall find that in every Church the same functions are shared by an angel and a man and that they are both perfectly good bishops."[90] What we have here is an application to the ecclesiastical sphere of the parallel between the invisible angels of the nations and the visible ἄρχοντες. The comparison is, moreover, suggested by Origen himself, when he calls the same angel both angel of the nation and angel of the Church. The familiar theme of the responsibility of the angels is also found in the passage: they are again represented as not yet confirmed in the state that will ultimately be theirs for ever. We notice in addition that the spiritual hierarchy of the world to come is formed on the same principle: the nations Christ is to reign over then will be composed of souls, each nation will be subject to its own angelic bishop and Christ will thus be King of Kings and Lord of Lords.[91]

It thus becomes clear that there is a remarkable parallel between the way the human race was originally divided into nations, dependent as this was on the angels, and the way it is now divided into Churches, a thing again dependent on the angels. As Origen saw it, the visible and the historical were images of spiritual things and events to be looked for at the end of time. From this point of view, the distribution of the nations among the angels, as we saw it at the beginning of this chapter, appears as a shadow of the allocation of the spiritual nations— the ones composed of souls—to the angels in the world to come. The two distributions, moreover, depend on the same principle. Which nation a soul should belong to in the world was determined by the merits the soul had acquired before it came into the world; which Church it shall belong to in heaven will be decided by the merit it acquires while it is in the world. "At the beginning of this aeon, when God scattered the sons of Adam, he fixed their limits 'in accordance with the numbers of the angels of God' [LXX. Deut. xxxii. 8]; every nation was put under an angel of its own, except the house of Israel, which was chosen to be the Lord's portion, the Lord's share of the inheritance. It seems to me that it will be the same when this aeon ends and the next one begins; the Most High will again divide the sons of Adam. Then those who cannot be the Lord's portion, because their hearts are not pure enough for them to see him, will look at the holy angels instead and be divided 'in accordance with the number of the angels of God'. But happy the man who is worthy to be the Lord's part even during this earthly life."[92]

Thus, at the end of our study of Origen's angelology, we find ourselves faced once more with the leading idea in his interpretation of history—the idea that between the nations whose temporal fortunes are described in the Old Testament and the spiritual Churches in the new universe set up by Christ there is both a historical relationship and a symbolical one. There is a historical relationship because the gradual unfolding of a plan is discernible and there are two successive economies; there is a symbolical relationship, because the division of the human race into peoples and tribes in the economy of the flesh is a figure of the spiritual division one day to be made in the world of souls. As Origen sees them, these processes of division constitute one of the great mysteries about the Church, one that we shall know in full only when we are gathered to Christ. "When we return to Christ, we shall see more clearly the reasons for the things that happen on earth. . . . We shall know, in particular, what Israel is, what the existence of the different nations means and what the twelve tribes signify."[93] It is a mystery turning on the spiritual interpretation of Scripture and the constitution of the spiritual world or world of souls, both in itself and in the course of its development in history. Origen's angelology affords a glimpse of some of the factors involved.

III

THE FORERUNNER

THE NATURAL link between the theology of the angels and the theology of Christ is provided by the theology of John the Forerunner.[1] The question plays an important part in Origen's system and is closely related to his angelology. It is worth noting that these two features are still characteristic of oriental theology even today. The prominent place occupied by John the Baptist in oriental theology is a matter of common knowledge. Bulgakov, for instance, devotes one of his books to the "Bridegroom's friend" and the angels together. As Origen saw it, John the Baptist represented the visible preparation for the coming of the Word, just as the angels represented the invisible one. The visible preparation was the work of all the men God sent for the purpose in the Old Testament[2] but it culminated in John.[3] There is also a fine passage in which Origen explains that while John is the voice, φωνή, Jesus is the Word, the λόγος.[4] But he chiefly observes—and it is the most striking feature of his teaching on the subject—that John is the forerunner of Jesus in *all* his "parousias".[5] John bore testimony to Jesus before he was born, when he leaped in his mother's womb as Jesus came near. He was the forerunner of Jesus in the public life.[6] He died a little before the Son of Man, "so as to ensure that the way should be prepared for the Lord everywhere, preceding him, as he did, in birth and also going first to those who were waiting for Christ to free them from death".[7]

He continues to fulfil this function in the Church and in the individual soul. "To my mind, the mystery of John is still in operation in the world, even today. Before a man can believe in Christ Jesus, if such is his destiny, John's spirit and John's power must first come into his soul and prepare for the Lord a people fit to receive him [Luke i. 17] and make the rough

246

places of his heart into smooth roads [Luke iii. 5]. It was not only then that the roads were levelled; today too John's spirit precedes the Lord's coming, precedes the *parousia*."[8] John will also usher in Christ's second coming, his coming in glory. "He is that Elias whose coming was prophesied" (Matt. xi. 14).[9]

In all this, John's function appears as parallel to the angels'. But as Origen sees it, the relationship between the two is much more intimate than that. He explains it in the *Commentary on St. John*, when he comments on the verse: "A man appeared, sent from God" (John i. 6). "Anyone trying to see more clearly what 'sent' [ἀπεσταλμένος] means," he says, "will ask where John was sent from and where he was sent to. The answer to the second question is evident: he was sent to Israel, or to those Israelites who consented to listen to him. He lived in the desert of Judea and baptized near the Jordan. Anagogically, that means that he was in the world, 'world' denoting the region round the earth that we men live on. There remains the question as to where he was sent from. If we go into the phrase thoroughly, bearing in mind that Scripture says of Adam— 'God drove him out of that garden of delight, to cultivate the ground' [Gen. iii. 23]—we shall perhaps conclude that John was sent from heaven or paradise or some other place outside these terrestrial regions."[10]

This strange passage is connected with a side of Origen's teaching that we have not yet considered. We have seen that to his mind the boundary between the world of men and the world of the angels was not sharply defined. In normal circumstances, he thought, crossing from one to the other was a thing that depended on merit and demerit. Yet there was one exception to that rule. The King of the Angels, the Logos, became Man because he wanted to bring men salvation, and some of the angels from the higher ranks of the hierarchy were sent into the land of exile to prepare the way for him and see that things should be ready when he came down himself. This was without any previous sin on the angels' part. The κατάβασις of the angels was foreshadowed by the "descent" of the patriarchs to Egypt. "It is reasonable to think that God allowed the patriarchs to go down to Egypt, i.e., to this world, so as to provide enlightenment for the others and instruction for the human race: other souls were to receive light and help from them."[11] The same idea is found elsewhere, too. "Not everyone in captivity," he says in one place, "is there for his sins. The Jews as a whole were abandoned by God because they had sinned; they were driven out of the Holy Land and carried off to Babylon. Yet among the Jewish people were some who were innocent; but all the same, they too were taken captive. Not that they had sinned themselves: it was to enable them to help those who were captives because they had."[12] Origen does not actually say that these envoys were angels and that what they really did was to come down to earth; but that is the underlying thought. And if we cast our minds back to a passage we have already quoted—the one dealing with the workmen engaged at the eleventh hour—now that we have it in its context we shall see it take on its full significance. It will be remembered that Origen shows the workmen standing a long time idle and then, when summoned in their turn, receiving the same wages as those who had been hired earlier. The reason for this was that they had wanted to be sent into the world right from the beginning. They are a figure of the messengers sent by God in the various ages of the world's history.[13] As for the origin of the idea, Origen tells us himself that one of its sources is the Jewish apocalyptic literature.[14]

John the Baptist's case is closely connected with this general theory of the "incarnation" of the angels sent to prepare the way for the incarnation of the Word, a thing quite distinct from what we spoke of in the last chapter, where we saw the angels setting out on another mission without taking visible form. "The general opinion is that the soul is not transmitted by generation; it existed before that and there are various reasons why it should have taken flesh and blood. If this is true, it will not seem strange that the expression 'sent by God' should be used of John. And here is another consideration. It is for you to judge whether it solves the difficulty. In the widest sense, all men are men of God, by the mere fact that they were created by God, yet not all men are called 'men of God'; the title is kept for those specially consecrated to God, like Elias [4 Kings i. 10 et seq.]. In the same way, in the loose sense, all men are sent by God, but strictly speaking, only one coming into this life to serve mankind and minister to its salvation can be said to be 'sent by God'."[15]

He explains that John's case is one of those in which the incarnation of an angel is involved. "As we are talking about John and trying to see the significance of his apostleship [ἀποστολή], it will not be out of place for me to state my own opinion about him. In one of the prophets we read the words: 'Behold, I am sending before thee that angel of mine, who is to prepare thy way for thy coming' [Matt. x. 11, etc.; cf. Mal. iii. 1]. We may well ask whether this is not one of the holy angels sent as a forerunner in our Saviour's service. If Christ, the firstborn of every creature [Col. i. 15], took flesh for love of men, it is not surprising that some of the angels should want to be like him and do as he did; it is not strange that they should delight in taking a body like his to honour his graciousness to them. And the fact that John leaped for joy while he was still in his mother's womb [Luke i. 44] is most striking. It surely proves the existence in him of something more than ordinary human nature."[16] The reference is unquestionably to the incarnation of angels as a preparation for Christ's incarnation, the activities of the λόγοι-ἄγγελοι prefiguring and preparing for what was to be done in its fullness by the Λόγος. Origen's opinion is that "from the beginning, those who have occupied the most eminent positions among men and been markedly superior to others have been angels in human form. This explains the passage in scripture [John i. 6–7] which says that John was one of God's messengers or angels who came in the body to bear witness to the light."[17]

Side by side with the Forerunner's relationship to the angels, the further question of his connection with Elias arises out of certain passages in Scripture, which Origen brings together in the *Commentary on St. John* (6, 11). Was John Elias *redivivus*? Origen debates the question several times in one or another of his works.[18] He sets it out in the *Commentary on St. John* as follows: "It may be said that John did not know that he was Elias. That is perhaps the argument that will be used by those who believe in metempsychosis, as they think that the soul assumes one body after another and remembers nothing about its previous lives. People who think this also argue from the fact that some of the Jews said that Christ was one of the prophets risen again—which they take to mean not that he had risen from the grave but that he had risen by being born anew."[19] In the *Commentary on St. John*, Origen contents himself with a mere mention of this opinion; in the *Commentary on St. Matthew*, he attacks it. "To my mind," he says, "in none of these passages is Elias shown as a soul and nothing more. To maintain the contrary would be to fall into the error of metempsychosis, a doctrine foreign to the Church and not found in Tradition or in the Scriptures."[20] If the theory were true, the soul could go on for ever passing from one body to another and the world would never come to an end—which is a pagan idea.

What, then, is the true explanation of the relationship between Elias and John the Baptist? Origen notes that what the Bible says is that John had the spirit ($\pi\nu\varepsilon\tilde{\upsilon}\mu a$) of Elias and not the soul ($\psi\upsilon\chi\acute{\eta}$) of Elias. "Notice that Gabriel did not say that when John came he had the soul of Elias—which would imply metempsychosis—but that he had the spirit of Elias [Luke i. 17]. Thus, John is called Elias not because he had the soul of Elias but because he had the spirit and power of Elias. There is nothing contrary to the Church's teaching in the supposition that the same spirit was first in Elias and then in John."[21] Origen then raises the question of what the $\pi\nu\varepsilon\tilde{\upsilon}\mu a$ is.[22] He observes that there is a difference between a man's own $\pi\nu\varepsilon\tilde{\upsilon}\mu a$, the spirit which is his personally, and the $\pi\nu\varepsilon\tilde{\upsilon}\mu a$ which may happen simply to be in him. Thus, Elias had a special spirit (i.e., a special grace), but it afterwards rested on Eliseus, and when John was born it passed to him. John had the privilege of being filled with the Holy Spirit while he was still in his mother's womb and of going before Christ in the spirit of Elias.[23]

IV

CHRISTOLOGY

THE IMPORTANCE of the Incarnation and the Redemption to Origen's theological system has been questioned by Hal Koch and De Faye respectively. In Hal Koch's opinion, the Incarnation mattered little to Origen, because the principal part in the history of the universe was played by the Logos.[1] In De Faye's opinion, the Redemption was not of great importance, because Christ's function was essentially to reveal the truth: his death on the cross did not come within the field of thought envisaged.[2] But a study of the sources leads one to modify these views: they give too narrow an idea of Origen's outlook. The part played in history by Christ's humanity is given the greatest prominence in the commentaries on the New Testament, and Christ's contest with the powers of evil—the central idea in the dogma of the Redemption in the second and third centuries—occupies an important place in Origen's work as a whole. What is true in the other view is that these dogmas form part of a wider whole, the theology of the Logos, which is an essential element in Origen's system. We will therefore begin by studying the nature of the Logos, whom Origen regards as being between the Father and the *Logikoi*. It is one of the most difficult of his concepts. After that, we will look at the part played by the Logos in the economy of salvation and consider the problems arising out of the Incarnation and the significance of the concept of Christ's passion as a victory over death.

1. THE FATHER, THE LOGOS, THE *Logikoi*

Up to the present, we have studied the chief products of creation—the creatures of the spiritual world—as they are in themselves. One essential factor in their composition, viz., their relationship to the Logos, we have left aside. That is the question we must tackle now, and a very important question it is. In the course of our investigations, we shall have occasion to say something about Origen's teaching on the Trinity. People have questioned whether he devoted much thought to the Trinity, De Faye in particular. Such a verdict greatly over-simplifies the position. On this question, as on all others, Origen upholds the traditional beliefs. At the beginning of the *De Principiis*, he declares that he accepts the dogma of the three Persons without reservation. That he really does is evident from his reference to the baptismal formula and also from the many passages in which he states his own views on the question. Thus he speaks, for example, of the "three eternally present together".[3] But it is also beyond question that when he tries to explain the Trinity in theological terms, he envisages it in connection with the creatures of the spiritual world. It is thus impossible to discuss his ideas on the Trinity without taking those creatures into consideration; and if we deal with both together, we shall be following the same line that he takes himself in his speculations on the matter. He regards the relationship between the Logos and the Father as parallel to the relationship between the creatures of the spiritual world and the Logos. It is one of the factors in his system where the influence of Middle Platonism is most clearly discernible. As Fr. Lieske says, in spite of his sympathies for Origen, the idea of the "cosmological significance of the Logos constitutes the gravest of threats to the mystery of sonship in the Trinity and is the most clearly-marked consequence of neo-Platonist [I would prefer to say myself: 'Middle Platonist'] influence on his system".[4]

In the many passages where Origen describes the Logos in relation to the Father and the *logikoi*, he represents him as inferior to the Father and superior to the *logikoi*. Thus, in particular, he says in the *Commentary on St. John*: "Some people, though friends of God, are troubled when they pray, because they are afraid of seeming to imply that there are two Gods. Consequently, they hit upon ideas that amount to blasphemy. Some deny that the Son has a personality of his own distinct from the Father's; they say that when they call him Son of God, they do so in name alone. Others deny the Son's divinity and maintain that his personality and essence are different from the Father's, in that they were produced by separation from the Father's. Well, there is a way of banishing the fear responsible for such ideas. When we find people troubled by this fear, we should say to them: 'God [i.e., the Father] is God in his own right. We know that he is because the Lord said in his prayer: 'That they may know thee, the only true God' [John xvii. 3]. God alone can be called ὁ θεός, because he alone is God in his own right. If any other being becomes divine through sharing in his divinity, it can be called θεός, but no more than that. The name θεός belongs to the firstborn of every creature [Col. i. 15] on every possible ground. He is the first of the gods because he dwells with God [John i. 2] and draws the Godhead into himself. He is of higher rank than the other gods who have God for their God (as the Bible says [Ps. xlix. 1]: 'It is the Lord, the God of gods, that speaks'). And he it is who enables the other gods to become gods, since he obtains from God in abundance the means to make them divine and of his own goodness imparts those means to them. God is the true God and the other gods are fashioned after his image; they are like copies of the prototype. But here again, the Logos is the original model of all these copies. The Logos dwells with God and has existed from the beginning, because he is God: that is why he has always dwelt with God. He would not be the archetype unless he dwelt with God, and he would not have been God always unless he had always gazed on the abyss of his Father's being." [5]

This passage brings us right to the heart of the question as Origen sees it. We note, first, the contrast between God with the article—the sole αὐτόθεος, God in his own right—and the other gods, who are θεοί only by participation. This is based on Philo, *De Somniis*, 1, 2, 30. In this sense, God alone is ἀληθινὸς θεός, and consequently he is transcendent with respect to the Son. Origen's aim in maintaining this is to reassure those who, in their anxiety to avoid polytheism, fall into modalism or adoptionism; but he does it at the cost of attributing to the Son the same sort of divinity that all other created spirits who are θεοί possess. However—and this is the second point—though the Son is classed with the θεοί, he transcends them all. He alone of them dwells with the Father.

He is of higher rank than they are. He alone knows the Father in his entirety,[6] he alone does the Father's will in every detail.[7] His divinity is not his in his own right—he has it as a gift from the Father; but once he has it, he is the Source from which all other divinization proceeds. Thus, if he is in a different category from the Father, he is also in a different category from the λογικοί.

The two relationships, then—the Father's to the Son and the Son's to the *logikoi*—are to some extent analogical. "The Lord said: 'My Father, who sent me, is greater than I am' [cf. John xiv. 28, etc.]. He refused to let himself be called good in the strict, true or proper sense of the word [Mark x. 18]; with due submissiveness he referred the attribute to the Father and rebuked the man who would have given too much honour to the Son. Obedience, then, requires us too to say that if the Saviour and the Spirit transcend all creatures not in degree but in kind, they are in turn transcended by the Father as much as, or more than, they themselves transcend all other creatures, even the highest. There is no need to point out what glory we owe the Son because he is above everything: above thrones, dominions, princedoms and powers, above every name that is known, not in this world only but in the world to come [cf. Col. i. 16; Eph. i. 21], above the holy angels and the spirits and souls of the just. And yet, superior though he is to all these exalted creatures in essence, dignity, power, wisdom and divinity (for he is the Logos made Man), he is nothing in comparison with the Father. He is only the image of God's goodness [Wisd. vii. 26]. He is not the radiance of God himself but the radiance of God's splendour and eternal light [Heb. i. 3]; not the fragrance of the Father himself but the fragrance of the Father's power. He is a pure outpouring of the Father's splendour and omnipotence. He is an untarnished mirror, reflecting whatever the Father does, the mirror in which Peter and Paul and others like them see God, for, as he says: 'Whoever has seen me has seen the Father' [John xiv. 9]."[8]

Origen's position can be gathered from this without a shadow of a doubt.[9] If the Son and the Spirit transcend all λογικοί, they are themselves transcended to a still greater extent by the Father. They thus form an intermediate category, which though much nearer to the Father than to the rest of creation, is still separate from him because their essence, power and other attributes are different from his. Origen's theory of the Logos is profound and reaches great heights; many points about it would repay study even now. But all the same, it is obviously tainted with subordinationism. The only point on which he wavered was the question of the proportion between the two sets of differences—those separating the Father from the Son and those separating the Son from creatures. In the passage just quoted, he says that the Father is at a greater distance from the Son than the Son is from the rest of creation. In the *Commentary on St. Matthew*, however, we find the opposite idea. "The Saviour," he there says, "is the image of the invisible God [Col. i. 15], and in the same way, he is the image of God's goodness [Wisd. vii. 26]. Whenever the word 'good' is applied to a lesser being, it has another meaning. Considered in relation to the Father, the Son is the image of the Father's goodness; considered in relation to other beings, he is to them what the Father's goodness is to him. And it can even be said that the analogy between God's goodness and the goodness of the Saviour, who is the image of that goodness, is closer than the analogy between the Saviour and a good man, a good deed or a good tree. The fact that he is the image of God's goodness sets the Saviour higher above lesser beings than the fact of being good sets God above the Saviour."[10]

It is a hierarchical view of things, the Logos being entirely dependent on the Father and the other θεοί depending in turn on the Logos. Origen looks out on to a world of created spirits, whom he sees as surrounding the Logos and sharing in his life. It is the Stoic theory over again—the Logos is everywhere in the cosmos and individual *logoi* are mere sharers in his properties—but with the difference that Origen shifts the world of the *logoi* into a region that was in existence before the cosmos began. "In so far as a man possesses wisdom, he shares in the life of Christ, who is Wisdom."[11] An essential feature of the theory is that the world of the *logikoi* is coeternal with the Logos. This is one of the points where Origen's theology is deeply embedded in his cosmology. Some of his predecessors— Tertullian and Hippolytus, for example—did not regard the *logikoi* as eternal; but then, they did not think that the Logos was eternal either: he came on the scene, according to them, when the cosmos was created. Origen very properly reacted against this idea. To his mind, there never was a time when the Logos did not exist. On that point he could be used in the anti-Arian controversy. But as he did not abandon the relationship between the Logos and the *logikoi*, the consequence was that the *logikoi* too became eternal. This comes out in connection with the question: If the world had its beginning in time, what was God doing before the world began? Origen's answer is: "When God made this world that we see about us, that was not the beginning of his activity. There will be another world after this one, and our belief is that in the same way there were others before this one."[12] More explicitly, another passage (one quoted by Justinian) deduces the co-eternity of the *logikoi* from the divine title of Pantocrator borne by the Logos. "It would be absurd to suppose that God found himself in want of things he ought to have had and that he went and seized them. If there never was a time when he was not all-powerful, there must always have been creatures for him to exercise his omnipotence upon. Thus there must always have been beings under his rule and governance."[13]

The idea that there must have been a world of created spirits from all eternity, because without one God could not have exercised some of his attributes, is another of the points where the characteristic influence of Middle Platonism on Origen's teaching comes out. Albinus too refuses to admit that there was a time when the world did not exist.[14] But the influence goes deeper than that: it is reflected in the very idea that the scheme of things is hierarchical. The ultimate ground for the idea is to be found in the fact that some intermediary appears to be necessary between the world of the first God, who is absolutely transcendent, and the world of creatures, which is the sphere of the many. God is "absolute unity and simplicity".[15] He is above "thought and essence".[16] For that reason, he can have no contact with the world of multiplicity. Yet his very nature requires that the world should exist; its existence is an essential condition for the exercise of his goodness and omnipotence. Hence there must be an intermediary between him and the multiplicity of the world. This intermediary is the Logos, who "comes between the unbegotten and the being of things begotten".[17] It thus becomes evident how closely the generation of the Word is linked with the creation of spiritual beings. And the fact that this creation is regarded as an eternal process—and hence that the generation of the Logos too is considered to be eternal—does not destroy its connection with the cosmos. That is specifically the teaching of Middle Platonism. We have already met with the concept of the δεύτερος θεός in Numenius. Albinus in turn writes that the first God, who cannot be adequately described in words, called the soul of the world from its sleep and turned it towards himself; whereupon, once provided with its constitution, the soul of the world in its turn made rules for everything else in the universe.[18] The resemblance here bears on a detail of the highest importance. In one of the passages quoted above, Origen says of the Son that he would not always have dwelt with God unless he had always gazed on the abyss of his Father's being.[19] Fr. Arnou and Fr. Lieske compare this, and rightly so, with the idea of "creative contemplation" in Plotinus. But it did not come to Origen from the author of the *Enneads*. They both took it from Albinus, who says: "God turned the soul of the world and its intelligence towards himself, as if rousing it from apathy."[20]

The essence of the reasoning used by Origen to justify his idea of the Logos as the intermediary between the first God and the spiritual cosmos is, as we have said, the argument that between absolute unity and the multiplicity of creatures there must be a being who is one and yet shares in that multiplicity.[21] This brings us to a point of first-rate importance to Origen's theory, for in the last resort it is the multiplicity in the Logos that makes his dealings with the *logikoi* possible, since it enables him to adapt himself to their diversity. It explains his activity in the world. The argument will be found set out in the *Commentary on St. John*. "The Father," Origen says, "is purely and simply one, is absolutely simple, whereas there is multiplicity in our Saviour, because he was pre-ordained by God to make atonement for the whole of creation [Rom. iii. 25] and be its firstfruits: he was One, but for this reason he became Many as well. He was thus able to become Light when men needed light [John i. 4]—when their sight had grown dim with the darkness and they needed a light that could shine in the darkness and not be put out by it [John i. 5]. If they had not been in the dark, he would not have become Light. The fact that he is the First-Born of the risen dead [Apoc. i. 5: Col. i. 18] can be considered from the same angle. He would not have died out of love for men unless Adam had fallen, and if he had not died he would not have been the First-Born of the risen dead. And it might well be asked whether he would ever have become a shepherd if men had not lost their reason and become like beasts. One might make a list of the Word's titles and see which of them would have been superfluous if men had never lost their beatitude. He would perhaps just have kept the names Wisdom, Word, Truth and Life. He might not have had the others at all, for it may be that he assumed them only on our account. You are fortunate indeed if you have no need to call the Son of Man Redeemer or Shepherd when you pray to him, happy if you need not ask him as Doctor to heal your sick soul. You are fortunate if you can pray to him as Wisdom, Word, Justice or any of the other things he is to those whose perfection enables them to receive what is best in him."[22]

This passage gives us the main factors in the theory. In the first place, there are various different facets in the Word, various ἐπίνοιαι[23] or θεωρήματα.[24] Some of these ἐπίνοιαι, such as the names Wisdom, Word, Truth and Life, denote the Word as he is eternally in himself; others are bound up with the economy of the Redemption. Consequently, it is evident that there will be degrees of excellence among them: to the sick the Word will appear as Healer, to those who need guidance he will show himself the Shepherd; his self-revelation as Wisdom and Life will be kept for the perfect. In essence, Origen's theology of the Word is simply a catalogue of the different ἐπίνοιαι, the "unfathomable riches of Christ" (Eph. iii. 9). He denotes the first book of the De Principiis to the names of the Word. "The many good things promised by the men with the beautiful feet [Isa. lii. 7; Rom. x. 15]," he says in the Commentary on St. John, "are merely so many names for Jesus. Life is a good thing, and Jesus is life. Light is a good thing—the light in the world, the light that shines on men, the true light— and Jesus is that light. The road that leads to these is also a good thing. Well, the Lord himself shows us that he is both the road and what it leads to when he says: 'I am the way; I am truth and life' [John xiv. 6]. Restoring mankind to life is obviously a good thing. That too is something the Lord Jesus can do, for he said: 'I am the resurrection' [John xi. 25]. Again, the door through which we pass to eternal happiness is a good thing. Well, Christ said, 'I am the door' [John x. 9]. I need not say anything about Wisdom. You know that the Lord made it his own when first he went about his work [Prov. viii. 22] and that the Father took pleasure in it, delighting in the variety it offers the mind; you know that it can be seen only by the eyes of the spirit and that when a man looks steadily at God's beauty it draws him to love the things of heaven. No one doubts that justice, sanctification and redemption are good things. Well, the preachers who said those things were coming were really saying that Jesus was coming."[25]

Origen protests against those who treat the name "Word" as if it were the only name the Son of God possessed, and he takes the opportunity of giving a further catalogue, in the course of which he adds to the previous list the names Good Shepherd, Master, King of the Jews, True Vine, Bread of Life, the First and the Last, Lamb of God, Consoler, Atonement, High Priest, Prophet, Juda and Israel, Christ and Rock.[26] The detailed explanation of these names in the first book contains some excellent observations. Christ is the Light that lights up the spiritual world.[27] He is the Way, which those bent on following must travel along without any luggage, with no spare clothing, without a stick and with their feet bare (Matt. x. 10).[28] He is the Vine, whose wine rejoices man's heart (Ps. ciii. 15), weans him from human pleasures, fills him with God and makes him drunk, not in the ordinary senseless way but divinely.[29] He is the First and the Last "because he became everything to everybody, to bring everybody salvation" (cf. 1 Cor. ix. 22).[30] He is the Lamb of God because he takes away the sin of the world (John i. 29).[31] He is the High Priest of all created spirits.[32] He is Justice because his government of the universe is orderly and measured (cf. Wisd. xi. 21)—he provides all the spiritual assistance creatures need to prepare them for receiving the Father's goodness at the last. He is Israel because he alone sees the Father.

As there are so many sides to his personality, Jesus can manifest himself to men in different ways, according to their capacity for seeing him. "Not all who see Christ receive an equal degree of light from him. The amount of light they receive depends on the amount they are capable of receiving."[33] The Logos is here envisaged in relation both to theology and to the spiritual life. The spiritual life—which is essentially what the life of the *logikoi* is—is a process of feeding on the Logos. But the Logos appears to different classes of souls in different guises, according to their capacities, and reveals his mysteries to them only by degrees. "Although Jesus was in fact one, there were many ways of looking at him; he did not look the same to everyone who saw him. That he could be considered in various ways is quite clear from his own words; he said himself that he was the way, truth, life, bread [John vi. 35 etc.], the door. And to come to the actual seeing—that he did not show himself in the same shape to all who saw him but showed them only what they could take will be clear to you if you consider what he did when he went up the high mountain to be transfigured. He did not take all the Apostles with him; he took only Peter, James and John, because they alone were capable of looking at his glory, seeing Moses and Elias when they appeared in that same glory, listening to their talk together and hearing the voice that came from heaven in the cloud. He went up a mountain on another occasion too. His Disciples came to him there [Matt. v. 1] and he talked to them about the beatitudes, whereas previously, at the foot of the mountain, he had healed everyone who was brought to him [Matt. iv. 24]. I cannot think that he seemed the same to the sick as he did to those who were healthy enough to go up the mountain with him."[34] Those who look at him in a purely natural light think there is no beauty in him, to use Isaias's expression (Isa. liii. 2); but those who study him with the eyes of the soul see him transfigured.[35]

The Word adapts himself to the capacities of the men he is dealing with. There is a whole gamut stretching from the beginner, who has only a natural knowledge of him, i.e., who knows nothing of his godhead, to the soul admitted to a sight of the dark mysteries of his divinity. "Not everyone who saw Christ when he was here in the flesh could see him as he really was. His Disciples could—they could see how great he was, they could see he was divine. That, it seems to me, explains the Saviour's reply to Philip's request: 'Lord, let us see the Father [John xiv. 8]. That is why he said: 'Anyone who has seen me, Philip, has seen the Father' [cf. John xiv. 9]. Pilate too saw Jesus, but the Jesus he saw was not the real one. And Judas the traitor never saw he was the Christ."³⁶ There is adaptation to the needs of the individual soul on the Word's side too. "To children God's Word comes as milk, to the weak as vegetable fare, to those engaged in combat as meat. The extent to which people receive the Word is proportionate to their likeness to him."³⁷ It is a point Origen often explains. In one place, for instance, he says that the Word "appeared to men in so far as they deserved to see him. And though he was what he was, he was seen by everyone as other than he was. It was like what the Bible says about manna [Wisd. xvi. 20–1]. The bread God sent from heaven to the children of Israel had every possible flavour in it and suited every taste; and when anyone took any of it, it yielded to his desires and changed into whatever he wanted. For my own part, I find no difficulty in believing the tradition, whether I interpret it of Jesus in the body, showing himself to men from various angles, or whether I understand it of the nature of the Logos, which is not revealed to everyone in the same way."³⁸

However suggestive this theology of the Logos may be in some respects, the fact that Origen pressed it into the mould of Middle Platonism means that it is distorted on two essential points and that the value of his teaching about the Trinity and about grace is thereby seriously diminished. In the first place, through his idea of the superiority of the Father to the Logos, he falls into the error of subordinationism. He holds that Father and Son are different not just because they are different Persons but because they have different natures. Consequently, the Son merely shares in the Godhead instead of possessing it absolutely. Origen has no hesitation in representing the Son as the Father's image in little. Contrariwise, he does not allow difference enough between the Logos and the *logikoi*. On that point he was influenced by the Stoic idea that the Logos is imminent in all individual *logikoi*. "In so far as a man possesses Wisdom, he shares in the life of Christ, who is Wisdom."³⁹ It is true that because of their sins spirits may, in his opinion, be incapable of living a fully spiritual life unless the Word helps them; they will need his assistance for that. But even so, the spiritual life is still only the development of that participation

in the life of the Logos which is rooted in all spirits by nature.
Hence the difference between them and the Logos can only be
one of degree. And that destroys the essentially gratuitous
character of grace considered as a sharing in the life of a
transcendent Trinity.

2. THE INCARNATION

Origen does not devote much space in his writings to the
Incarnation. There is one short chapter on it in the *De
Principiis* (2, 6). The reason is that there never was a time when
the Word was not acting on the human race. But at any rate—
and this is what De Faye does not realize—the Incarnation
does represent the pre-eminent instance of the Word's intervention in human affairs. Origen begins by reminding his
readers of the Word's remarkable attributes and then shows
what an extraordinary thing it was that he should come down
and live among men. "We have seen so much to admire," he
says, "in the nature of God's Son, but we are struck dumb with
wonder when we reflect that possessing, as he did, this most
sublime of natures, he divested himself of the majesty surrounding him, became Man and lived among men. . . . Of all the
wonderful things about him, this most surpasses the powers of
admiration the human mind possesses. Our minds are too weak
to see why we should have to believe that the Power of God's
majesty, the Father's Word and Wisdom, in whom all created
things, visible and invisible, took their being [Col. i. 16], was
confined within a man who appeared on earth at Judaea, was
born a baby and cried like a baby. My own opinion is that it
even exceeds the capacities of the holy Apostles; in fact, it
would be beyond the abilities of all the powers of heaven to
explain the mystery."[40]

All the same, he does try to find a place for it in his system.
It will be remembered that in his opinion the soul exists from
all eternity. The same will be true, then, of Christ's soul too.
"Freewill produces variety and diversity among souls. This gives
them leanings in different directions, so that some are possessed
by more ardent love of their Creator than others and some are
more lukewarm. Thus the soul of Jesus—which he mentioned
himself when he said that nobody could rob him of it [John x.

18]—was attached to him inseparably and irrevocably in his capacity of Wisdom, Word of God, Truth and true Light, ever since it was assigned to him at the beginning of creation. The whole soul received the whole Word, and continuing in his light and in the radiance he shed became pre-eminently one spirit with him [1 Cor. vi. 17]."[41]

Yet at this point a problem arises. "My contention that Christ had a rational soul will be a difficulty to some people," Origen says, "because I have so often shown that the soul is by nature capable of evil as well as of good. Well, there can be no doubt that Christ's soul was of the same nature as other souls; otherwise, it could not be called a soul at all. Like all souls, Christ's soul had the power to choose good or evil; only it chose to love justice so intensely [Heb. i. 9: Ps. liv. 8] that the boundless love it put into the pursuit joined it to justice irrevocably and made defection an impossibility. Its resolve was so unshakable, its affection so immeasurable, its love so ardent and unquenchable that all possibility of change was taken from it."[42] He takes the comparison of iron heated in the fire as an illustration to drive the point home. "This soul has always been immersed in the Word," he says, "in some such way as that. Hence it can feel nothing, will nothing, do nothing but God." It is noteworthy that the solutions here given by Origen were afterwards applied to other problems. The first is found in connection with the Immaculate Conception. The second was used by Cyril for the Incarnation; but as used by Origen himself, it applies to the eternal relationship between the Word and his soul before the Incarnation.

If Origen lays so little stress on the incarnation of the Word, the reason is to be found in his peculiar attitude to the visible, which he regards as no more than a sacrament of the invisible. That applies to the Saviour's humanity as well: it is simply a means of approach to the Logos, who is the real food of the soul. And in this connection Origen again makes use of an idea we have already met with, the idea that the visible phenomena of Christianity are shadows and prophecies of things yet to come. "It seems to me," he says, "that the prophet Jeremias realized what nature it was that Christ took for our salvation and what his other nature was—the nature of divine Wisdom—when he said: 'Christ the Lord is

the breath of our mouths, and we shall live among the nations
in his shadow' [cf. Lam. iv. 20]. The shadow of the human
body is inseparable from the body itself and it makes exactly
the same movements and gestures as the body. That makes me
think that Jeremias was talking about the activity and working
of Christ's soul, for Christ's soul was inseparable from Christ
himself and acted only under stimulus from his will. For that
reason, it seems to me, Jeremias called it the Lord Christ's
shadow and said that we should live in that shadow among the
nations. The nations do live by the mystery of Christ's incarnation: it is by reproducing that mystery in themselves through
faith that they achieve salvation. The Law observed on earth
is a shadow [Heb. viii. 5]; our whole life is a shadow [Job viii.
9]; Christ's shadow will be over us as we live among the nations.
May it not be that the real things, of which these are the
shadows, will be known when God's glory is revealed and the
saints gaze upon it, as they deserve, not as in a mirror and
confusedly but face to face? [1 Cor. xiii. 12]."[43]

The theology of the Incarnation here merges with exegesis of
the New Testament and the theology of the sacraments. All
three spheres are dominated by Origen's idea of the relationship between the visible and the invisible. He by no means
belittles the visible. He is no more a Docetist in his theology
of the Incarnation than he reduces everything to the spiritual
in his theory of the sacraments. He believed that Christ really
did become incarnate. But just as in his theory of the Eucharist
he lays little stress on the visible eating and makes much of the
invisible feeding on Christ, so here he does not dwell for long
on the historical aspect of Christ, because he is in a hurry to
examine its spiritual significance. The *Commentary on St.
Matthew* says that Christ is like the field (Matt. xiii. 44) where
the hidden treasure was. "A man goes into the field, i.e., he goes
to Christ, who is a field full of things—things we can see and
things we cannot see—and there he finds hidden treasure in the
shape of Wisdom. It is by exploring the field and trying to get
to know Christ that he finds the treasure in him. Having found
it, he hides it, because he thinks there would be danger in
showing to all and sundry the treasure of Wisdom and gnosis
hidden in Christ."[44] Christ, then, is made up of visible and
invisible components. The spiritually-minded man tries to

"reach the Word who became flesh for those who live in the
flesh".[45] Following the same line of thought, Origen draws a
contrast between natural or fleshly knowledge of Christ and
spiritual knowledge of Christ.[46] It will be seen that this is the
same principle as the one governing his exegesis of the New
Testament—the one that leads him to distinguish between the
sensible and the spiritual sides of the Gospels and ask what
good an explanation of the sensible side is if it does not lead to
the spiritual.[47] Thus, his position is the same whether the
question at issue is the material side of worship, the literal
meaning of Scripture or the visible humanity of Christ: he
affirms the reality of all three, but at the same time he regards
them only as starting-points.

As for the invisible essence hidden behind the visible pheno-
menon, the Incarnate Word, there are two different aspects of
that. The historical Christ is a sacrament of the Christ who
presides over the inner life and is present unseen in the Church
and in souls; he is also a sacrament of the glorious Christ who
will be revealed at the end of time. The first of the two is the
one more often found: we are often told that we must go
beyond Christ's humanity and get at his hidden divinity. But
it is the other that figures in the passage just quoted about living
among the nations in Christ's shadow. It might be, Origen
there said, that the thing which cast the shadow would be
known at the time of revelation, when the saints gaze on God
face to face, as they deserve.[48] The passage has a familiar ring.
It was in fact Origen's *leitmotiv* in his explanation of the figurative meaning of Scripture. Here again, then, the theology of
the Incarnation comes into line with exegesis, for it too recognizes a spiritual Gospel, which is the mystery of Christ living
in the Church and in souls, and a divine, eternal Gospel,
which is the mystery to be accomplished at the end of time.
"The prophet said in this connection: 'Christ the Lord is the
breath of our mouths, and we shall live among the nations in
his shadow.' We shall do that when God does us the wonderful
service of bringing all the saints from the temporal Gospel to the
eternal Gospel, as John calls it in the Apocalypse [Apoc. xiv.
6]."[49]

But this is equally true of the sacramental order. In connection with the theology of Baptism we observed, as the reader

will remember, that Origen regarded Baptism as a figure of
the Baptism that is to be conferred at the end of time; and
again, in connection with the Eucharist, we said that he stressed
the spiritual content of the sacrament. We did not suggest that
there was any relationship between the two facts; we regarded
them more as representing two different tendencies. But it will
now be seen that they both fit into a general outlook in which
the sacramental economy too is regarded as having three
different components: the visible rite, the spiritual reality
behind it and the prophecy of events that will take place when
time is over. It so happens that in the case of Baptism the side
Origen stresses most is the eschatological one, whereas in the
case of the Eucharist he dwells chiefly on the spiritual aspect.
But it is none the less true that he regards both sacraments as
possessing both aspects. Baptism is a figure of the ultimate
purification, but, as we have said, Origen also regards it as the
principle of the mysterious dying and rising again with Christ
in one's own soul which constitutes the spiritual life. The
Eucharist, too, has an eschatological bearing: it is a figure of
the third Pasch, the Lamb's eternal feast.

Yet the maintenance of this triple point of view does not
prevent Origen from always stressing the spiritual side more
than the others. The reason is that the ritual side seemed to be
too well-known to need stressing and the eschatological side
was of no immediate use. We thus have the key to the emphasis
we find in his works on the spiritual side: it is from this side of
things that real ὠφέλεια, real advantage and profit for the
soul will be obtained. Here again, Origen's conduct is governed,
in the last resort, by his apostolic zeal, as Fr. de Lubac shows
so clearly. In his controversy with Celsus, the principle of
ὠφέλεια came to seem to him characteristic of the New
Testament; consequently it became his main argument for
purposes of apologetics. Christianity was true because Christ
had in fact set us free and men were in fact transformed by
grace. It is the same principle as the one which seems to
provide the ground for his theological position and his standpoint in exegesis. His activities in these two spheres at
first look as though they tend in opposite directions, but
deeper analysis shows that ὠφέλεια unexpectedly brings them
together.

His theology of the Incarnation affords an illustration of just that point. He does not dwell on the externals of Christ's life, nor does he lay much stress on the eschatological side, the comparison between the two "parousias", a theme to which Justin had given such prominence. What he was out to do was to discover the relevance of the mysteries of Christ's life to the life of the soul. He regarded Christ's whole life as one great sacrament, which continued to operate, invisibly, in the Church. The mysteries of Christ's life were still being enacted in the Church. What Christians had to do, then, was to go behind the external details of the historical Christ's behaviour and try to discern the spiritual activity of the Christ who lives in the soul. We may take as an example the passage in which Origen expounds the straightforward text: "Then he sent the multitude away, and went back into the house. There his disciples came to him and said, Explain to us the parable" [Matt. xiii. 36]. This is his commentary.

When Jesus was with the crowd, he was not in his house— the crowd was outside the house. Leaving his house and going out to the people who could not go in to him was an act of love. When he had spoken to them long enough in parables, he sent them away and went back into the house. There his Disciples came to him—they did not stay outside with the people he had sent away. The fact is that everybody who listens to Jesus with more than ordinary attention first follows him, then asks where he lives and obtains permission to visit him, then goes to see him, stays looking at him and remains with him for the day at least. Some may perhaps stay longer [cf. John. i. 35–40]. If we are not content with hearing Jesus like the crowd he sends away, if we want to go to his house and receive something better than the mass of men, we must go close up to him. Then, when he comes, we shall go into his house, as the Disciples did, and when we are inside we shall be in a fit state to hear him explain the parable.[50]

Origen also explains his method. "People who want to gain a clearer idea," he says, "of what the house of Jesus stands for, should pick out everything in the Gospels that deals with that house and the things done and said in it. The passages so collected will convince any attentive reader that the text of the Gospels is not meant to be taken in the obvious sense alone, as some people think. For pedagogical reasons, it is so constructed that the simple will think it simple; but people who want to go deeper will find, if they have the ability, that wisdom really worthy of God's word is hidden in it."[51] It is a pity that we cannot quote in full as an illustration of this doctrine the incomparable meditations on the Samaritan woman and the coming of Jesus to Jerusalem, in the *Commentary on St. John*. The tone of those few pages is quite unexpected. It is so like the one that all spiritual masters were henceforth to take when they meditated on the Gospel mysteries for the nourishment of their own souls and other people's. Thus, what Origen was here introducing was the practice of studying the Gospels for the purposes of the spiritual life. But, once again, that does not at all mean that he denied the historical reality of Christ's humanity. It means that he saw Christ's humanity as a sacrament of Christ's life in the Church as well. In so doing, the great commentator on St. John was only continuing the line of thought that the author of the "spiritual" Gospel had been inspired to take himself.

Let us take a few examples. Further on, he comments on the text: "He prevailed upon his disciples to take ship and cross to the other side" (Matt. xiv. 22). He embroiders the text like this: "The crowds could not cross to the other side, because they were not Jews in the spiritual sense, i.e., they were not 'people who cross over'. It was left for the Disciples of Jesus to cross over to the other side, to pass beyond the bodily and the visible and hasten on to the invisible and the eternal."[52] Similarly, in connection with the Jews who tried to lay hands on Jesus, he says: "There are different ways, you know, of trying to lay hands on Jesus. There was the way the high priests tried to seize him and the way the Bride did in the Song of Songs. Because she longed for him, the Bride got up and went through the alley-ways and streets until she found him, and then she said: 'I held him and I will not let him go' [Cant. iii. 1–4]."[53] Which means that Jesus eludes the soul that would lay hold of him by its own power and reveals himself to those who stay open to the influence of his grace. "If you too would lay your hands on Jesus and hold him in your arms and become fit to leave your prison, strive with all your might to have the Holy Spirit for your guide, as Simeon had, and, like him, to come to God's temple [Luke ii. 26–8]." [54]

3. THE REDEMPTION

Origen's teaching about the Redemption has perhaps given rise to a greater volume of adverse criticism from the moderns than any other theory of his. De Faye says: "Nothing could be more incoherent and contradictory than his teaching about the Redemption." [55] On the one hand, we find him echoing the tradition handed down by previous writers—St. Paul and the apologists—to whom the essence of the Redemption had seemed to lie in Christ's victory over the powers of evil who had been holding mankind in captivity. It is an extremely important factor in Christian tradition. On that point, then, Origen is obviously a strong supporter of the traditional belief. On the other hand, he regards the world as the scene of an educative process carried on by the Logos, who as Master and Healer was gradually inducing all free creatures to return to the good. De Faye and Koch think this a purely philosophical outlook and consider that it runs counter to the other. We must begin by observing that the idea of a divine process of education did not come to Origen from a philosophical source; he got it from the Bible and the Church. It corresponds to one aspect of Christian dogma. The Christian view is that the world is the scene at once of history and of drama. Any theological system which excluded one or the other of these would be incomplete. That the two aspects should never quite coincide is only to be expected: it is characteristic of mysteries that the formulae we invent to express them can never exhaust their essence. That is equally true of the Eucharist, the Redemption, the Trinity and the Church.

We must therefore add a further statement—that the idea of the Redemption as something pedagogical came to Origen from Tradition and the Bible. Koch is thus wrong in regarding it as due simply to the influence of philosophy. His mistake arises from his Protestant outlook, which makes him think of salvation as justification or pardon coming from without [56] and not as the rebirth of liberty. But this latter concept provides a means of reconciling both the aspects found in Origen's theory. On the one hand, Christ's death had to set our freedom free from the tyranny of sin that was weighing upon it, as Augustine was later to show with such force. But freedom, though recovered, still had to turn freely to God, and thus the idea that there is an educative side to the Redemption remains valid. That is not where Origen is wrong. His mistakes lie in some of the details of his educative theory—he is wrong in applying it to all spirits without exception, devils included; wrong in supposing that the process of education continues in successive worlds; wrong about the ultimate universality of forgiveness, because he bases it on a philosophical theory (the theory that evil cannot be eternal), whereas he ought to have stayed, as we all have to, on the threshold of the mystery. That is the way the question ought to be stated. Since its two aspects emerge one after the other, we will examine each in turn and show in both cases what comes from Tradition and what belongs to Origen's own system, as we did with his other tenets.

I shall keep the title "doctrine of the Redemption" for the first part of the programme. The viewpoint here is that mankind was under the yoke of the powers of evil until Christ came on earth. The powers in question are the whole of that company of bad angels we spoke of when we discussed Origen's angelology, and particularly the wicked angels who had been ruling over the nations. Christ's life is considered to have been a struggle with these opposing powers from the beginning.[57] The δύναμις in him—he himself is the μεγάλη δύναμις—weakened the opposing powers right from the time of the Incarnation. "When Jesus was born, a multitude of the heavenly army praised God and said: 'Glory be to God on high.' (Luke says so and I believe him.) That weakened the powers, exposed their charlatanism and thwarted their machinations. They were defeated by the angels who had come down to this terrestrial region for the birth of Jesus; they were defeated, too, by the power of Jesus and the divinity that was in him. Consequently, when the magi tried to achieve their usual results from spells and incantations, they did so in vain. They looked for the reason, which their instinct told them would prove to be anything but trifling. Then they saw a sign from

God in the sky and they tried to find out what that meant.
Eventually they realized that the man heralded by this star of
Balaam's . . . had entered on this life. Realizing, too, that he
was more powerful than all the devils that used to appear to
them and do their bidding, they determined to worship him."[58]
But until the Resurrection takes place, the evil spirits will still
be able to exercise their powers. Thus, when Peter said to
Jesus: "No such thing shall befall thee" (Matt. xvi. 22), Jesus
replied: "Back, Satan", because the words had been suggested
to Peter by one of the spirits who had not yet been vanquished
on the cross or put to open shame with those mentioned in the
text: "Despoiling the principalities and powers, he hath exposed them confidently in open shew, triumphing over them"
(Col. ii. 15) through the cross.[59]

What finally ousted the powers of evil was Christ's passion
and resurrection. The text just quoted is the *leitmotiv* in this
case, as the text "In his shadow" was in the case of history.
"The cross of our Lord Jesus Christ can be regarded," Origen
says, "from two points of view. It was obvious to the eye that
the Son of God was crucified; what was not obvious to the eye
was that the devil too was nailed to the cross, with his princedoms and his powers. You will see that this is so if I quote
Paul's testimony. 'Despoiling the principalities and powers,'
Paul says, 'he hath exposed them confidently in open shew,
triumphing over them through the cross' [cf. Col. ii. 15].
There are thus two ways of regarding Christ's cross. The
Apostle Peter mentions one of them when he says [1 Peter ii.
21] that the crucified Christ left us an example. The other way
is to consider the cross as the trophy won by Christ's victory
over the devil, who was the means at once of crucifying him
and of bringing him glory."[60] In another homily, Origen
represents the two effects of Christ's achievement on the cross
as the despoiling of the powers of evil and the opening of
paradise. "When he said to the man who had just confessed his
belief in him: 'This day thou shalt be with me in paradise'
[Luke xxiii. 43], he opened the gates of paradise to him
and thereby gave to all who believe in Christ the entry into
paradise which he had denied to Adam when Adam sinned.
No one but Christ could have turned aside the sword of
fire [Gen. iii. 24] set to guard the tree of life and the gates

of paradise; no one could have stripped the possessions from those princedoms and powers and rulers of this world whom the Apostle speaks of; no one could have driven them into the desert of hell but he who said: 'I have overcome the world' [John xvi. 33]."[61]

Origen explains the meaning of the Passion in other books too. He shows "how for love of us the Father gave up his Son to the powers of evil and they in turn gave him up to men, to be put to death. Death, his enemy, was to hold him in his power, as he holds all who die with Adam [cf. 1 Cor. xv. 22]. Death was in the devil's power—not the ordinary kind of death, the morally neutral kind that all composed of soul and body die of; not that kind, but the death that is hostile and inimical to him who said: 'I am life' [John xiv. 6]. The Father did not spare even his own Son [Rom. viii. 32], because he wanted to look down from heaven and laugh at the devils for taking him and handing him over to men. The Lord was to make them a laughing-stock, too, for unwittingly causing the overthrow of their own power when they accepted the Son at the Father's hands and then found that on the third day he rose from the dead, destroying his enemy, Death, and fitting us closely into the pattern of his death and resurrection" (cf. Rom. vi. 5).[62]

It will be seen that what emerges from this is the essence of St. Paul's teaching on the Redemption, which Origen very ably lays bare. The devil and death are one and the same thing, one and the same evil power. This evil power thought it had triumphed over Christ, its enemy, but its apparent victory was in reality a defeat, for by dying himself and rising from the dead, Christ destroyed death's power and thus outwitted the devil. The outwitting of the devil was much stressed by the Fathers. The doctrine has also been much criticized, because its underlying meaning has not been perceived. It is only an echo of the ironical question: "Where then, death, is thy victory?" (1 Cor. xv. 55), flung out by St. Paul after Death had been fooled. "When he gave his life as a ransom for the lives of many [Matt. xx. 28], who was it he gave it to? He did not give it to God. Did he, then, give it to the devil? Yes, the devil it was who had us in his power, until he accepted the soul of Jesus as a ransom for us and thus allowed himself to be outwitted, as he thought he could lord it over that soul and did not see that he would never be able to keep a hold on it by his own efforts. Death thought it could lord it over him but it cannot do so now [Rom. vi. 9], because he is 'free among the dead'' [Ps. lxxxvii. 6] and his power is greater than death's; so much so that if any of those in death's power want to follow him, they can follow him—over them, too, death can no longer prevail."[63]

All the same, the victory Christ won on the cross will first have to be applied to the individual soul, and the powers of evil must be ousted afresh in each individual case. "All who are crucified with Christ despoil the principalities and powers and expose them in open shew, triumphing over them through the cross [cf. Col. ii. 15]; or rather, all that is done in them by Christ."[64] The martyr especially is regarded as continuing what Christ achieved when he mastered death and the devil and gave the human race its freedom. He "despoils the principalities and powers with Christ and triumphs with him, because he shares in his sufferings and in the victories springing from them."[65] That is what crushes the devil's power.[66] It shows, too, how profitable martyrdom is, shows what its ὠφέλεια is. The evil spirits are well aware of the blessings martyrdom brings to Christians; they dread it so much that they strive to slow down persecution.[67]

It may be observed in this connection that Origen's theology of the Redemption is in keeping with what one would expect from a Christian living in the age of the martyrs. Consequently, it reflects the outlook of the Christian community in those early times, with its awareness of the struggle going on against the powers of evil entrenched in idolatry. The Origen we see here is Origen the ordinary Christian. As a matter of fact, a considerable part of his theology could be said to fit into the same context. As he was both martyr and doctor, his theology may be considered to share in the charismata of both. That is perhaps what gives it its special individuality. It cannot be reduced to either of them alone; they both flow in it together. A whole sphere of his thought has its character determined by his experience of the Christian life. And it is that experience that colours his theology of the Redemption.

One splendid passage in which the whole mystery of the

Redemption is set out in this light calls for quotation. "What are we to say," Origen asks, "of the Lamb of God? He was sacrificed to take away the sins of the world [John i. 29]. With his own blood he cancelled the deed which excluded us; he swept it out of the way, by nailing it to the cross, so as to leave no trace at all of the sins we had committed; and despoiling the principalities and powers, he exposed them confidently in open shew, triumphing over them through the cross [cf. Col. ii. 14–15]. Consequently, though we find tribulation in the world, we learn to take courage, knowing that courage is justified by the fact that the world has been mastered [cf. John xvi. 33], since obviously the world must do its Master's bidding. Thus, all the nations serve him, now that he has set them free from their former rulers, because by his passion he has delivered the poor from the mighty [Ps. lxxi. 11–12]. Because by humbling himself he has humbled the Oppressor [ibid. 4], the Saviour is regarded as a kind of sun, shining age after age upon the shining Church, symbolically called the moon [ibid., 6]. When he made his victorious progress, with his load of spoils and his risen body, some of the powers asked who this was coming from Edom, coming on the road from Bosra, with garments dyed with blood [cf. Isa. xliii. 1–3]. But those in front of him in the procession said to the keepers of the gates of heaven: 'Swing back the doors, captains of the guard; swing back, immemorial gates, to let the King enter in triumph' [Ps. xxiii. 7]. The keepers, however, seeing that his right hand seemed covered with blood and his whole person eloquent of his prowess, persisted in their questioning. 'Why are thy garments stained with red?' they asked. 'Why dost thou go clad like the men who tread out the wine-press?' [Isa. lxiii. 2]. . . . Having captured his spoil and mounted up on high, he came down again and brought various charismata with him [Eph. iv. 8 et seq.]. He also brought the tongues of fire that were divided among the Apostles; he brought the holy angels, too, to help and aid them with all they had to do. In all this, he was not so much obeying his own desires as doing his Father's will, since his Father had given him up to the powers of evil for the benefit of the wicked. Christ gave his services to the whole world—it was through him that God reconciled the world with himself [2 Cor. v. 18–19]—but he bestowed his blessings one after another, in accordance with a plan previously laid down. He did not receive the footstool right at the beginning—did not, that is, receive his enemies as a stool to put his feet on. The Father said to our Lord: 'Sit here at my right hand while I make thy enemies a footstool under thy feet' [Ps. cix. 1]. And sit there he did until his last enemy, Death, had been mastered."[68]

V

ESCHATOLOGY

WHEN WE studied Origen's teaching about the Incarnation and the Redemption, we were moving all the time within the sphere of universally-received tradition, even if Origen had brought into it ideas belonging more to his own personal system. But when we come to the Last Things, we find ourselves in the same sort of country as we did when we studied the beginnings of things: eschatology corresponds to "archaeology". Scripture has little information to give about it. We shall thus be faced once more with Origen's personal system in its most characteristic form. We said at the beginning that that system had two main axes: Providence and liberty. We saw how those factors shaped his cosmology—as it was the will of Providence that all λογικοί should possess the good to the same degree, any difference of status among them would have to be accounted for by the use they had made of their freedom. A similar principle governs his eschatology. Sin is the withdrawal of the will from the good. Therefore the question—the only question—is to know how free creatures are to return to the good. Origen applies the principle in the most radical way possible and makes everything that came into existence in consequence of the Fall a means of education. This is true of the visible world, which was created for that specific purpose; it is true of the differences in creatures' circumstances, which are meant to help other creatures; it is true of the Logos made man and it applies to the Church, which is a *schola animarum*. It might be said that being a *didaskalos* himself, Origen regarded his God as a *Didaskalos* too, as a Master in charge of the education of children, and looked on God's universe as a vast *didaskaleion* in which every single thing contributed to the education of the free human beings at school there.

It is with the aid of this principle in particular that he outlines his solution of the problem which is at the heart of all
philosophical systems, the problem of evil. On the one hand,
he rejects the gnostic theory, which makes evil an alien substance, not created by God; on the other, he excludes the Stoic
idea that evil is only apparent. In his opinion, evil is certainly
real, but it can be conducive to good and it will eventually cease
to exist. Hence the existence of evil is consistent with the goodness of God. When God created the world, he knew that evil
would one day come into it, because where there are creatures
endowed with freedom it is inevitable. If he did not prevent it,
the reasons were, first, that he has a sovereign respect for the
freedom of the will and, second, that he knew it would help the
execution of his plan. As always, Origen means this quite
literally. There is no evil except in men's wills. The sinner's
ill-will may have consequences both for the sinner himself and
for other people. This corresponds to the two sides of evil: in so
far as evil acts against its author, it is sin; in so far as its acts on
others, it is suffering. But both may lead to good. Sin is allowed
to exist so that if men want to see what it is like, they may
wallow in it, and then, finding how bitter it tastes, grow weary
of it and of their own accord go back to the good. Experience
of evil thus appears as the essential preliminary to the recovery
of the good by creatures possessing freewill. It teaches such
creatures the one thing they need to learn—humility. Or, in
other words, it shows them they are contingent. Suffering, too,
will be a means of education, to the extent to which it becomes
a punishment. Punishment is thus regarded by Origen as
something educational: all suffering teaches a lesson. If the
idea is extended to future lives as well as to this one, all providential activity in the world is reduced to this one educational
activity, which, after an infinite lapse of time, will inevitably
lead to the conversion of all creatures endowed with freedom.
Even Death will give in in the end; even Death will be
converted.

Let us first consider the medicinal character of punishment.
"God is good and merciful. If enforcing penalties against
sinners were not useful for their conversion, he would never
requite sins with punishment. He is like a good father who
corrects his son to teach him a lesson or like a master who has

the great foresight to put on a severe face and administer correction to his pupil, for fear the child should go to the bad through realizing that he is loved. . . . All the bitter-seeming things God sends turn out to be educative or medicinal. God is a Healer and a Father, a kind and not a cruel Master. . . . He took vengeance on men . . . at the time of the Flood, when he destroyed Sodom and Gomorrah and when he brought ruin to . . . the six hundred thousand Israelites. But do not imagine that it was only by way of punishment for sin and nothing more; do not suppose that after they had suffered death and torments, further torments still were to take hold of them. They were punished in their lifetime so that there should be no need to punish them afterwards."[1]

Origen replies in the same way to the gnostics, who were shocked by the passages in Scripture where God is said to deal out punishment. How could such conduct be reconciled with his goodness? The gnostics used the difficulty as an argument for the existence of two Gods, each the enemy of the other. Origen shows that punishment actually proceeds from God's goodness. "None of that is understood by the people who slander the God of the Law and cast their accusations at him regardless of the fact that he was slow even to reprove men. You will ask how any of it can be expressive of God's goodness. Well, to my mind, the words 'I will kill' and 'I will strike' denote goodness just as much as 'I will make to live' and 'I will heal' [Deut. xxxii. 39]. God sometimes causes suffering—but the doctor too, you know, often does. And when God makes men suffer, it is as a means of restoring them to health. Thus, when he strikes men, what impels him to do it is his goodness. What I am going to say may seem paradoxical, but I am going to say it, all the same. What Scripture calls God's rage works with salvation in view when it administers correction, because it is a good God's rage; and what it calls his anger is educative because, again, it comes from a God who is good. A great deal could be said about God's goodness if people could take it in without harming themselves. Not unreasonably, God hides all that from those who fear him, because he does not want them to presume on that abundant kindness of his that bears with men and waits for them [Rom. ii. 4]; for if they did, they would be laying up still greater store of anger for themselves."[2]

That states the question to perfection: it shows where Origen stands with regard to the gnostics, his everlasting enemies; it justifies punishment on medicinal grounds. Let us look at the first point first. In one of the homilies on Jeremias, Origen shows that bodily pain is good in itself. "It is possible for parts of a body to wither," he says, "and become lifeless. If they do, they will probably be able to bear pains which the parts with more life in them could not stand."[3] The idea is then transferred to the soul. "Suppose a soul were like a body with limbs so numb that it could not feel anything when it was struck, even if the blow were as hard as it could possibly be. Such a soul would become paralysed without realizing it, whereas another would be aware of what was happening. Obviously, a man who does not feel the impact of a thing that ought to cause him pain is more seriously ill than one who is aware that something unpleasant is being inflicted on him and hopes he will suffer from it; for ability to suffer is a sign of life."[4] Thus moral sufferings, the reproaches that come from the conscience and serve as *flagella Dei*, are good in themselves. It is much better that the sinner should be in torment than that his mind should be at ease. "I wish to God I could feel a fire scorching my heart and burning my bones [cf. Jer. xx. 9] the minute I committed any sin or said anything I deserved to be blamed for."[5]

If God did not punish sinners, there would be no conversions. "'How,' the heretics ask, 'can a God who says *I will not spare* and *I will not have mercy* be a good God?' I will give you an example to show how it is possible—if a judge shows mercy to a murderer, the man will go back to his crimes. The same thing can often be seen in the Church too. Someone sins and then goes and asks for communion. If he is allowed to have what he asks for, the forgiveness granted him only does him harm: once the penalties are waived, the road to sin lies open again. If, on the other hand, the judge carefully thinks the matter over and concludes that if he pardons the man it will turn out badly for the community, then clearly he will excommunicate him to save the community. He will not be acting out of weakness or cruelty; he will be promoting both the sinner's welfare and the community's."[6] The doctor too may sacrifice a limb to save the rest of the body. And thus a further reason for punishment emerges. "God provides for the

community as well as for the individual." What is evil where
the individual is concerned may be necessary for the well-being
of the whole. That seems to Origen to be the arrangement the
economy of divine Providence works by. God may sometimes
have to sacrifice an individual's good to the good of a wider
group, but he will come back to the individual's good later.

The passage quoted above also touches on another aspect of
the question, one that brings us right to the heart of Origen's
view of it—the idea that God could not reveal his goodness too
soon, because men would probably have presumed upon it.
That enables him to solve the great question arising out of the
Old Testament, the question as to why God is there represented
as a stern master. Origen's theory is an extremely bold one
and is in line with the viewpoint we have already met with in
Maximus of Tyre. It is the idea that God's conduct depends
on his care for men's education. If God had shown too much
kindness to men when they were still like children, they would
have taken his goodness for granted. (A similar idea is found in
Irenaeus.) God therefore had to look stern. Was he really
stern? No; he was only pretending. The sternness in the Old
Testament is thus there for pedagogical reasons. What follows,
then, is this. God is pure love and he calls men to the life of
love. But that was a secret and could not be revealed until the
proper time. Men had first to be brought up in fear. Thus,
the whole of the punitive side of the Old Testament was a sort
of pretence—it was necessary but it did not express the reality
of the situation; it was like the letter of the Law. Hidden behind
it was the mystery of God's love, the mystery of his desire that
all men should be saved; but this mystery was not to be
revealed before the time was ripe. That is the ultimate reason
for the "anthropomorphisms" in the Old Testament.

Let us take one or two examples. "When divine Providence
intervenes in human affairs, It uses human ways of speaking
and thinking. If we have to talk to a two-year-old, we use the
sort of language that children can understand, for they cannot
possibly understand what we say to them unless we put aside
our grown-up dignity and condescend to their way of speaking.
We must suppose that God does the same when he deals with
mankind and that he did so particularly when mankind was
still in its childhood. You know how we grown-up persons even

use one word for another when we talk to children: if we have
to mention bread, we refer to it by the word they use for bread;
if we mention water, we use their word for water. We do not
use the words we do when we talk to people of our own age.
But that does not mean that there is something wrong with us.
No one who heard us talking like that to children would say:
'That old man is mad.' Well, that is how God talked to the
human race when it was in its childhood."[7] Hence, when
Scripture says that God was "sorry" or "angry", the expressions are not to be taken literally. "You must not think that
these words denote passions in God. They refer to God's scheme
for the conversion and correction of his children. If we behave
sternly to children, it is not because we feel like that towards
them; it is done deliberately. If we give a child kind looks and
let him see the love we bear him, instead of changing our
demeanour to some extent so as to correct his ways, we become
responsible for his downfall, we make him worse. That is the
sense in which God is said to get angry with men. He is not
really angry; he wants their conversion."[8] It will be seen that
the expressions in question are not just metaphors to denote
other things; the point is that the other things do not exist at
all. Origen's God is pure love and his anger a mere appearance
of anger, not the translation of his holiness and the demands it
makes into human terms.[9]

The question is thus one of deceit. Origen is not frightened
by the idea. "How," he asks, "can the prophet say: 'Thou
hast deceived me, O Lord, and I am deceived' [Jer. xx. 7]?
He said it when he had discovered the deceit, and he implied
that it was by deceit that he had been taught the rudiments
and given his first lessons. He could not have learned the rudiments or gained knowledge enough of the truth to realize that
he had been deceived, had it not been for that preliminary
deceit. An example bearing on the subject will be enough to
show you what I mean. When we talk to children, we behave
like children ourselves. We do not talk to them as we talk to
grown persons; we treat them as children, who need teaching.
We deceive children: we frighten them to make them docile.
We frighten them with the sort of lies that are effective at that
age, in the hope that our lies will instil fear enough into them
to make them attend school regularly and do what children

must if they are to make due progress. God looks on us all as
children, and we all need the sort of education children receive.
Hence, out of pity for us, God deceives us. He does not let us
become aware of the deception until the proper time, because
he wants us to learn from these fictions of his; he does not want
us to get our schooling from reality, as though we had out-
grown our childhood."[10]

As we have seen, the theory that lying can be of value for
educational purposes is also found in Maximus of Tyre. But
Origen shows that he was influenced by rabbinical traditions as
well. This is not without importance, as the point in question
is regarded by Koch as the one where Hellenistic influence is
most clearly discernible in Origen's teaching. "I will draw
upon a Jewish tradition on the question," Origen says; "one
that I had from a Jew who had forsaken the traditions he used
to live by and come instead to know and believe in Christ.
The tradition goes like this. God, it says, is not a tyrant but a
king. He governs without doing violence to anyone—he uses
persuasion. His desire is that those who belong to him should
submit to his providence of their own accord and thus obtain
their good not by necessity but by freewill. . . . As he is the God
of the whole universe, he could have made us in such a way
that we should of necessity be kind and temperate. It might
seem to us that that would have been to the good, but God did
not want it so. Thus, the things we have to do are not laid
down for us by necessity; God prescribes that what we do we
should do freely. He tries to find a means of making us do his
will willingly."[11] It is strange to find that a theory so typical
of Origen as this had in fact been worked out before his time.

Let us take one last example of these deceits—a remarkable
one: the case of apologetics. As Origen sees it, the method to use
in apologetics is to put forward Christian ideas without saying
straight away that they are Christian. He explains that
"Jeremias passed off God's words as his own to get them
accepted. We too do the same when it seems advantageous.
We sometimes borrow expressions from the pagans so as to
bring them to the faith. We may notice that they are hostile
to Christianity and contemptuous of the very name and
impatient if it is even mentioned. In that case, if we want to
use a word and it happens to be a Christian one, we see no

point in representing it as such. We explain the force of the term, but not until we see that the person we are talking to wants a more detailed explanation do we admit that this word which he has thought fit to commend is a Christian one."[12]

The question of the medicinal significance of punishment arose out of those texts in the Bible in which God is represented as inflicting punishment on men. But there are other passages in Scripture where God seems not to be punishing men but inciting them to sin. The question is studied at length in the *De Principiis* (3, 1, 6–12). Origen there assembles several of the texts attacked by the gnostics, particularly the one about the hardening of Pharao's heart. He first shows that the gnostic argument is worthless, because if Pharao had been evil by nature, there would have been no need for God to harden his heart. He then gives his own solution. "If God hardens some and is merciful to others," he says, "the reason is the same in both cases. When he hardens people, it is not that he wants them to become hard. No; he is patient and kind to everybody. He hardens the hearts of those who abuse his patience and kindness and only scorn and flout him when he postpones the punishment of their crimes; but those who take advantage of his patience and kindness to repent obtain his mercy."[13] That is the general principle. Now for its application to the particular case of sin. "Why did you spare us when we sinned? Why did you not call us back to you? Why did you leave us alone and let things get worse? . . . If God leaves people alone and takes no notice of them, it is because he considers them incapable of correction. Those who give him proof of instability show that they are not yet ready to receive temptation. They are therefore said to be forsaken by God, i.e., they receive no teaching [from punishment] because they are not yet ready to be taught; their οἰκονομία and their healing are evidently put off to some other time. They cannot tell what to ask God for unless they first reach the point of wanting him to give them something—which they will if they first admit to themselves what they are, realize what they need and understand who it is they can and must ask for it. Unless you realize that you are ill, you do not ask for a doctor. Or at any rate, you are not grateful to the doctor when you recover your health unless you know beforehand how dangerous your illness was. In the same way, a man cannot be cleansed and absolved unless he first sees the depravity and evil in his sins and confesses them with his own lips. Otherwise, he might not realize that what he now possesses was given him by grace; he might take God's generosity for his own excellence. If he did, that would obviously bring arrogance back into his soul and lead him to fall again. That was what happened to the devil: he thought he owed his primacy to himself and not to God, and so what Christ said would happen—'Everyone that exalts himself shall be humbled' [Luke xiv. 11; xviii. 14]—did happen."[14]

Yet the state of abandonment in which God leaves sinners is not without its own justification. "His patience is to their advantage, because the soul is immortal and therefore, even if it is not cured at once, it is not debarred from salvation for ever: salvation is only put off to a more suitable time. It is, perhaps, only fitting that the worse the infection of sin, the longer salvation should take to acquire. Sometimes a doctor could close up a wound in a quite short space of time, but he prefers not to restore health at once, because he is aiming at a more stable state of health than that. He thinks it better to delay the cure of an abscess and let the noisome humours discharge gradually, rather than to hurry over it and cover up the seat of infection to obtain a merely superficial cure; because once the outlets are stopped up, the humours will spread through the body and endanger the patient's life. It is the same with God. He knows the secrets of men's hearts, he foresees the future, his patience is without bounds. He allows things to happen which come to men as apparent misfortunes and bring to light the passions and vices inside them. It is a means of cleansing and curing men when they have been so grossly careless as to let the roots of sin grow within them."[15]

This very profound doctrine plays a leading part in oriental theology. There is no sin but pride, i.e., man's claim to be self-sufficing and his refusal to admit that he depends entirely on God, his refusal to accept the fact that he is a creature. In the light of that, the pedagogical bearing of sin becomes evident at once. The aim is that men should become aware of their radical insufficiency. If God forgives their sins too readily, they will not realize what his forgiveness is worth to them. And it is not a question of forgiveness: men have also to be induced to realize their dependence on God. To that end, they need to experience their own helplessness. From that point of view, it may be good for a man to plunge into sin until he becomes aware of his insufficiency and therefore turns to God of his own freewill. Until that happens, religious experience will be useless, because it will not be felt to fulfil a need. This, then, explains the part played by sin, the fact that God may let a man plunge into sin and the fact that sinning may last so long. [16]

We now come to the final questions raised by this eschatological theory. "The soul must experience a surfeit of sin; it will not be restored to its former state until it has committed many offences. The reason is that God arranges things for the soul's benefit, not for the span of this life only, confined as it is within the space of sixty years or a little more, but for an eternity of time—he is eternal and immortal himself and the souls he governs are immortal too. Because the soul is immortal, it is not debarred from receiving medicine and a physician's attention from God by the shortness of this life." [17] This brings us to the last and not the least important factor in Origen's system—his theory of educative punishment is not restricted to this life; it embraces punishment in the life to come as well. *All* punishment is educative. If Scripture does not say so, that is because it is adapting itself to the mentality of children, who need to be frightened. The theory presupposes that there will be other worlds after this one, so that souls who have not returned to God in this world will be able to do so in another. That implies that there will be as many worlds as are necessary to enable all created spirits to return of their own freewill to their Creator. In this way, the theory that God's love intends the good to triumph in the end and the theory of human freedom, according to which the subordination of man to God must be freely accepted by every human creature, can both be maintained intact. God's infinite patience and forbearance will in the end wear down the resistance of the faithless soul. It is the familiar biblical theme of the Covenant and the God unswervingly faithful to his promise, who eventually makes the nation he has chosen as his Bride grow weary of her infidelities; it is this theme, only extended now to the whole of the spiritual world.

In Origen's opinion, this is the mystery which is denoted by the Jubilee, i.e., by the week of weeks, the fiftieth or pentecostal year (Lev. xxv. 8, 10). One week stands for the lifetime of a world, the week of weeks symbolizes the series of worlds in the course of which the rehabilitation of the soul is effected. "We must see whether what is said about feasts and assemblies prescribed for certain days, months, seasons or years ought not to be applied to the aeons. If what is contained in the Law is a shadow of blessings still to come [Heb. x. 1], the many sabbaths mentioned in the Law must be shadows of many other days, and there must be new moons occurring at intervals of time determined by the conjunction of some other moon with some other sun. . . . And then, over and above the feast of the seventh year, there is the feast called the Jubilee. No one can form a clear idea of that feast or understand how the rules for it are applied unless he sees why God instituted the system of aeons which his inscrutable judgments and undiscoverable ways [Rom. xi. 33] have led him to establish. Here is my own guess about it. I think that a number of aeons have formed a sort of year and that the present aeon is its consummation [cf. Heb. ix. 26]. There will be other aeons after this one, the series being inaugurated by the next aeon. And in the aeons still to come, God in his goodness will display the riches of his grace [Eph. i. 7; ii. 7]. Thus those who commit blasphemy, the greatest sin of all, will be possessed by their sin throughout the present aeon, but after that, in the next aeon, they may be treated in some other way."[18]

It is quite clear what Origen means. He is alluding to Christ's assertion that the sin against the Holy Ghost will never be forgiven, either in this world or in the world to come (Matt. xii. 32; Mark iii. 29). The aeon, i.e., the lifetime of a world, represents a day in the sum-total of time, which consists of seven times seven years of aeons (cf. Lev. xxv. 8). The present aeon is one of these units. It is said to be a consummation because it is the last aeon in one of the years in one of the groups of seven. The next aeon will be another such unit and will usher in another year. Consequently, if the sinner does not achieve salvation in that aeon, he may in one of the succeeding ones—for there will be as many aeons as the superabundant goodness of God requires as instruments in that long quest of his, that ceaseless effort he makes to win men's love. It will be noticed that of this long series of aeons, the one in the course of which Christ became incarnate has an importance all of its own. Its unique importance is no more undermined by the immensity of Origen's chain of aeons than the unique importance of the earth as the scene of Christ's incarnation was undermined by the discovery of immensity in the stellar spheres.

Will a limit ever be set to the process by which the conversion of the entire world of created spirits is being accomplished? It will be remembered that at the beginning we saw how Origen's system depended on two principles, God's love and man's freewill.[19] Now that we have come to the end, we again find ourselves faced with the same principles. There are passages where Origen seems to say that as created spirits never lose their freedom and as freedom always involves a certain amount of change, they may go on falling and rising and falling again for ever. That is the chief point criticized in his system by Gregory of Nyssa, who remarks on its affinities with the Platonist theory of metempsychosis. It must be admitted that some passages do seem to teach this doctrine.[20] But on the other hand, sin made its appearance not in eternity but in time. And that seems to be one of its essential characteristics—only the good is eternal. The principle that everything which had a beginning must also have an end is one of those referred to by Origen in the *Commentary on St. John*.[21] But sin is the aversion of the will from God. It would seem, therefore, that in the end God's patient love will succeed in making all his creatures weary of their unfaithfulness. The most stubborn will eventually give in and consent to love him, and at last even his enemy death will be overcome. But in Origen's opinion there will be no victory unless there is free submission. The only thing that can give God glory is that all created spirits should freely acknowledge his excellence and love him for it.[22] The end of the creature is the glory of God and his own perfection; and as God has the whole of time at his disposal, he pursues that end throughout all the aeons in the Pentecost of years. The time will come when God is all in all (1 Cor. xv. 28); all creatures with freewill will have returned to him and his rule will be universal. The whole creation will be restored to its original integrity.[23] Origen calls this the *apocatastasis*.[24] When once it has been achieved, the Father will take the now perfect creation and hand it over to the Son, because the Son

will have finished the work he was sent to do from the beginning
of the world.[25]

Such is the major chord on which this great theological
symphony ends. In eschatology, as in "archaeology", there
was not much traditional teaching to set Origen his limits.
Consequently, he made freer use of doctrines reflecting his own
philosophical views. And again, as in "archaeology", the too
personal parts of the edifice were later rejected by Tradition.
The point that appears questionable in the present instance is
the philosophical principle that evil must eventually disappear
altogether. If that is the case, universal salvation becomes a
matter of purely physical necessity, and the long duration of
the process in no way diminishes the necessity. But that makes
nonsense of the tragic part of man's lot, the terrible power he
has, through freewill, of refusing his God. For that matter,
Origen himself saw the difficulty; as he thought so highly of
liberty, he could hardly fail to. He admitted that a creature
with freewill could always refuse to give itself to God. But the
inference he drew from that fact was that it was possible for
such creatures to go on falling and rising and falling again for
ever. And that is contrary to another element in Christian
dogma, viz., the doctrine that the choice made in this life is
decisive in character. The weak point in Origen's theory is
thus his idea that there is more than one existence. A spirit will
go through many incarnations and in none of its existences will
it remember anything of the previous ones. This comes from
the Platonist theory of metempsychosis, which set its mark
indelibly on Origen's arguments and distorted them. The final
point on which his views are at variance with Tradition is the
idea that the soul will return to the purely spiritual state it was
in before it came down into the body. This point in particular
was condemned by the Fifth General Council in its first canon
under the name of *apocatastasis*. "If anyone teaches the
mythical doctrine of the pre-existence of the soul and the
apocatastasis that follows from it, let him be anathema."

But it should be observed that what the Church rejected in
Origen's theory was not the doctrine of *apocatastasis* itself—
i.e., the doctrine that at the end of time everything will be
re-established in Christ (Eph. i. 10), though how it will be
done remains a mystery; it was not that doctrine but the

Platonist distortion of it. That, according to St. Barsanuphius, is what St. Gregory of Nyssa was so clear-sighted as to discern. "Clearly he does talk about an *apocatastasis*," Barsanuphius says, "but it is not the one that they [i.e., Origen and others] preach, i.e., not one by which men will be restored after their punishment to what they were at first, viz., pure spirits."[26] Gregory of Nyssa did in fact formally condemn the idea of the *apocatastasis* as it was distorted by Origen. He defines it with great precision. "I have heard people maintain that the life of the soul did not begin when the soul was joined to the body; there were souls alive, they say, and grouped in nations in a world of their own before that. . . . Yielding to a sort of inclination towards evil, they lose their wings and come to have bodies. They afterwards return by the same stages and are restored to the heavenly regions. . . . There is thus a kind of cycle, perpetually passing through the same stages; the soul never settles in any one state for ever. People who teach that are simply jumbling things up together and producing a mixture of the tenable and the untenable." That shows what it was that Gregory rejected—the return of the soul to the purely spiritual state it was in originally, the idea of successive lives and the theory of permanent instability. He did not in any way reject the doctrine of the re-establishment of all things in Christ. But how is this re-establishment to be reconciled with freedom? That is precisely the mystery which man's gaze cannot fathom. Origen saw clearly enough, then, that there were two things involved—God's love and man's freedom. But his attempts to reconcile them led him to put forward two theses, one of which—the *metaphysical* necessity of the ultimate elimination of evil—safeguards God's love but destroys man's freedom, while the other—the perpetual instability of the free— safeguards man's freedom but destroys God's love. Gregory of Nyssa was humbler in the face of the mystery of the *apocatastasis*; he was content with admiring it as the supreme work of a love that would do no violence to freewill. To him it stood for the certitude that in Christ salvation had been acquired for man's "nature" without any possibility of loss, but that the individual still had the power of dissociating himself from it by his own free choice.[27]

PART IV

ORIGEN'S THEOLOGY OF THE SPIRITUAL LIFE

ORIGEN'S THEOLOGY OF THE SPIRITUAL LIFE

ORIGEN occupies a conspicuous position in the history of exegesis and was the most eminent theologian in the early Church. The part he played in working out the theology of the spiritual life is historically no less important. This side of him was for long neglected by students, but it has recently been made the subject of a considerable number of monographs.[1] This is a consequence of the interest now taken in the study of spirituality: the subject has shown how important Origen is. Gregory of Nyssa[2] and Evagrius Ponticus, the two great theorists who wrote on mystical theology in the fourth century, were both disciples of his, and if Gregory went further than Origen in stressing the part played in the mystical union by love without light, he still was closely dependent on him. The line of thought started by Origen was carried on in the spirituality of the east by the Pseudo-Dionysius, who was a disciple of Gregory of Nyssa. Maximus the Confessor depends on him, either directly or through Evagrius and the Pseudo-Dionysius, as Fr. von Balthasar has shown.[3] In addition, his spiritual teaching was transmitted to the west through Evagrius Ponticus, who handed it on to Cassian.[4] The influence Cassian exerted on Western monachism from his monastery at Marseilles is a matter of common knowledge. And although it is not always possible to say whether the influence was direct, it is nevertheless to Origen that we must ascribe at least the remote beginnings of St. John of the Cross's spirituality of the desert, St. Bernard's analogy between mysticism and marriage, St. Bonaventure's devotion to the humanity of Christ and Tauler's devotion to the eternal Word.

So extensive an influence would be inexplicable if Origen himself had not lived the spiritual life to an eminent degree. What exactly, then, was the part he played? He was not the first of the great mystics; there had been others before him. St. Ignatius of Antioch and St. Irenaeus had been far advanced in

the spiritual life; so too had the martyrs, visited as they were
by the Lord in the midst of their torments. There is evidence
of deep spiritual experience in these men, but you do not find
them giving a systematic account of their experience. The
introduction of systematic description was mainly the work of
Origen. On that point there is general agreement. In order to
achieve this result, Origen made use of some of the concepts
found in the Platonist mystical writings in circulation at the
time, just as Clement of Alexandria had done before him.
That is the side of the question which is usually stressed. But
it is not the only side. If it were, his influence would be hard
to account for.

If his theology of the spiritual life struck a chord in the hearts
of so many Christians, the reason is that it was first and foremost a product of the Bible. In Origen's opinion there was no
book to equal Scripture. All dogmatic theology was contained
in it, all mystical theology was too—the one coming to light
when Scripture was interpreted of the Church, the other when
it was applied to the individual. Thus, from that point of view,
the whole of Scripture had a bearing on the life of the soul and
its relations with Christ. As we have seen, Philo too thought
that the spiritual meaning of Scripture was the chief one. It
was not the same in Origen's case: he realized that there was a
dogmatic meaning as well. Yet he did think that the spiritual
meaning was just as essential as the dogmatic. The man who
regarded things in a purely natural light—the Israelite—did not
look beyond the surface of Scripture; but the spiritually-
minded man, the man with a taste for spiritual things, had the
veil removed from his eyes by the Holy Spirit and then,
beneath the letter of Scripture, he could find food for his soul.
This idea that Scripture speaks in symbolical terms of the
spiritual life was to play a very prominent part in the mystical
writings of later ages. It struck root in Tradition when Origen
took it up. He describes the main stages in the soul's journey to
God in function of it.

The first stage is that in which a man returns to himself or
is converted. A concept much to the fore in the theology of the
spiritual life, the idea of the image, comes up in this connection.
It originated in the meeting of two great doctrines, the biblical one that man was created κατ' εἰκόνα τοῦ θεοῦ and the

Platonist one that man's perfection depends on his likeness to God. Fr. Festugière has given an illuminating account of the way in which the two themes converged.[5] The concept is first found in Philo.[6] It next occurs in Theophilus of Antioch and Clement of Alexandria. Origen develops it to the full. It gives the theology of the spiritual life a dogmatic basis. God created man in his own image. Man's real being is therefore his inner being, his spiritual being, which in a sense partakes of the nature of God. But man is also involved in the life of the senses, which is foreign to his essence. He loses God's image in so far as he moulds himself to the pattern of the animal life. The spiritual life will therefore consist of the process by which he returns to his true nature—his efforts first to realize what he is and then to try and recover his real nature by destroying the power of his corrupt animal life. To the extent to which he succeeds, he will recover the image of God that once was in him and in it will see God.

We meet with this theme in the homilies on Genesis:[7] "The man who was made in God's image is the inner man, the incorporeal, incorruptible, immortal one." To be more precise, man was made not just in God's image but in the image of the Logos. "What was the image of God that man was modelled on? It could only have been our Saviour. He is the firstborn of every creature [Col. i. 15]. He said of himself: 'To see me is to see him who sent me' [John xii. 45]: 'Whoever has seen me has seen the Father' [John xiv. 9]. If you see a picture of someone, you see the person the picture represents. Thus, when we see the Word of God, who is God's picture, we see God himself." Man lost his likeness to God when he sinned. "Sin made him like the devil, because he went against his nature and looked at the devil's image. When our Saviour saw that man, who had been modelled on him, had shaken off his likeness to him and acquired a resemblance to the devil, he was filled with pity and made himself like man and came down to man." Ever since then, it has been possible for men to recover their likeness to the Word if they will but consent to turn to him. "All who come to him and strive to be like him are inwardly renewed, day by day, according to the progress they make, in the image of him who made them."[8]

Thus, the spiritual life begins when the soul realizes the

dignity that belongs to it as God's image and understands that
the real world is the world inside it. Here again a biblical
theme—"If thou knowest not thyself, O fairest among women,
go forth and follow after the steps of the flocks" (Cant. i. 7)
—converges with a Platonist one—γνῶθι σεαυτόν. Origen
links the two quite explicitly.[9] Applying the text: "If thou
knowest not thyself, O fairest among women" to the soul, he
says: "And perhaps you may not know, either, why you are
beautiful, may not realize that because you were made in
God's image there is great beauty in you by nature. If you are
not aware of this and if you do not know what you were
originally, then my orders to you are that you should go out
after the flocks" (whose way of life you share, as you live like
an animal yourself). We have seen that the idea of the image is
found in Philo; so too is the application of the maxim "know
thyself" to the spiritual life. After Origen, it occurs in Gregory
of Nyssa,[10] Ambrose[11] and William of St. Thierry.[12] After
that, the idea of the image is found in mystical theology chiefly
in the school of William of St. Thierry and St. Bernard. St.
Bernard was also influenced by Gregory of Nyssa, whom he
knew through William of St. Thierry's translation, as Dom
Déchanet has so ably shown. We next meet with it in the
Rhineland, in Tauler's mystical teaching. It is one of the
leading themes in the theology of the spiritual life.

In the form it takes in Origen it possesses the same sort of
ambiguity as the one mentioned in connection with his theology
of grace. The Platonists held that when the soul entered into
itself, it discovered its true essence, which was divine.[13] Origen
never quite managed to rid his mind of that belief. It was not
until the fourth century that the radical transcendence of the
Trinity was strongly emphasized and the image of God in the
soul was seen to be a product of grace and not a natural
property, a personal gift from God and not the soul's own true
nature, which it could recover by ridding itself of all foreign
elements. In Origen, the soul's kinship with the divine is still
represented as a natural property.

The second stage in the spiritual life is reached when the
soul embarks on its passage through the period of purgation.
This stage, with its trials and its occasional flashes of light, is
figuratively represented by the exodus. Here again Origen's

spiritual teaching stands at the confluence of two streams of thought. On the one hand, the traditional view held by all Christians was that the departure of the Israelites from Egypt and the crossing of the Red Sea typified man's deliverance from the tyranny of the devil and his release by Baptism. On the other hand, although we do not find Philo systematically fitting the account of the exodus to the stages of the soul's return to God, as was the case with the lives of the patriarchs, he does at least take certain details of the story, such as the darkness on Mount Sinai, and interpret them of the spiritual life. By uniting these two streams, Origen evolved a whole theory about the route followed in the mystical life from the departure from Egypt to the arrival in the Promised Land. Two things need pointing out in this connection. In the first place, the symbolism does not refer to the sacraments: crossing the Red Sea does not stand for entering the catechumenate, crossing the Jordan does not mean being baptized. In this case, it is Baptism that is the crossing of the Red Sea and the beginning of the soul's journey through the mystical life. Secondly, on Origen's map of the soul's route, the term is not the summit of Mount Sinai but the Promised Land. Sinai does not come in at all. Yet it had played an important part in Philo's theory and in Clement's too, and with Gregory of Nyssa it became important once again. The fact is that Origen's theology of the spiritual life takes no account of the part played by darkness in the life of the soul; it deals only with light. That, perhaps, is where its limitations lie. It is a speculative theory of the way the mind is illumined by the gnosis rather than a description of mystical experience, an account of the way the presence of the hidden God is felt in the darkness by the soul as it reaches out and touches him. It is important to get this point clear.

Origen deals with the theme of the soul's journey in his homilies on Exodus and Numbers. The most important of these is the twenty-seventh homily on Numbers, which gives a summary enumeration of all the stages the soul has to pass through. "The children of Israel were in Egypt, toiling with straw and clay in Pharao's service, until the Lord sent them his Word, through Moses, to lead them out of Egypt. We too were in Egypt—we were in the darkness of ignorance and error,

working for the devil and sunk in the lusts of the flesh—but the
Lord was sorry to see us in that sad plight and he sent us his
Word to set us free.''[14] This gives us the starting-point—the
soul sunk in sin. With the Bible, Origen regards the soul in
that condition as being under the tyranny of the devil; with
Plato he thinks of it as sunk in the mire.[15] The spiritual
journey begins with the advances made by the Word, the
Deliverer. The soul's response is her conversion: she sets out
after him as the Hebrews in Egypt did after the pillar of cloud,
which was a figure of the Word or of the Holy Ghost. Origen
then goes on to describe the successive stages in the journey,
the various places where the soul stops and rests. "When we
have made the decision and left Egypt, our first resting-place is
the one where we stop worshipping idols and honouring evil
spirits, the one where we come to believe that Christ was born
of the Virgin Mary and the Holy Spirit and that he came into
this world in the flesh."[16] The basis of the spiritual life is
faith. The point is of the utmost importance and it shows at the
outset that the kind of asceticism Origen has in mind is not at
all what Plato envisaged. The liturgical equivalent of this
initial step is the abjuration of Satan, i.e., of idolatry, and the
acceptance of Christ which precede the ceremony of Baptism.
This is the first step. "After that, we must strive to go further
and pass through the various grades of faith and virtue one
after another."[17]

The great event in the three days' journey from Egypt to the
Red Sea was the pursuit of the Israelites by Pharao and the
Egyptians. Origen comments on it in another of his works.
"The Egyptians pursue you," he says, "and try to bring you
back into their service. By Egyptians I mean the rulers of this
world and the evil spirits you used to serve."[18] Such are the
temptations that begin to attack the soul when once she has
set out on the road to perfection and strive to make her change
her purpose and return to the world. But if she perseveres, the
Egyptians will be swallowed up in the Red Sea and the soul
will "go from one to another of those resting-places of which,
we are told, there are so many in our Father's house [John xiv.
2]. In each one she will acquire a fresh degree of light and little
by little will become used to the sight of the true Light, who
enlightens every soul born into the world [John i. 9]. She will

gradually learn to endure the brightness of his wonderful majesty."[19] What is happening is that the soul is beginning to cross the desert. In the course of the crossing, she is "trained in the keeping of the Lord's commandments and her faith is tested by temptation. . . . What are called resting-places are the stages of her progress through the various temptations against virtue and faith. The words: 'They shall go from virtue to virtue' [Ps. lxxxiii. 8] apply to them. Such souls will indeed go from virtue to virtue until they come to the highest degree of virtue and cross God's river and receive the inheritance promised them."[20]

This trek across the desert corresponds to the gradual stripping-away of the merely natural life which takes place when the soul awakes to the importance of the spiritual life. Origen begins by pointing out that the people were led by Moses and Aaron. That means that if the soul is to make progress, she will need both action, which is what Moses stands for, and contemplation, which is what is signified by Aaron. "When we leave Egypt, we must have some knowledge of the Law and the faith and we must also bear fruit in the shape of works pleasing to God [cf. Col. i. 10]."[21] That, too, comes from Philo. The stripping-process will begin with renunciation of sin, which is prefigured by the vengeance God took on the gods of Egypt. The next halt is called Ramesses (Exod. xii. 37), which according to Origen, means "violent disturbance". "The first progress the soul makes is that she withdraws from the bustle of earthly things and realizes that like a traveller, she must live in tents: she must be free and unattached and so in a position to face her enemies."[22] After the struggle against sin comes the struggle against the passions, πάθη, and the acquisition of ἀπάθεια, spiritual freedom, which comes with the practice of detachment and makes recollection possible. The vocabulary here is Hellenistic, Stoic in fact, but diverted into a Christian context.

Two more stages follow. The special characteristic of the first is the practice of penance to a moderate extent, for "excess and lack of measure in abstinence are dangerous to beginners". The second is called Beelsephon (Exod. xiv. 2), which is translated as *ascensio speculae* and means that the soul is beginning to get a dim idea of the good things in store for her and to see

that she is making progress. The idea of the *specula* is found in
Plotinus as well and it plays a prominent part in Gregory of
Nyssa's theology, where it signifies that earthly things recede
into the background as God's good gifts come closer to the
soul. In the next stage, Mara (Exod. xv. 23), spiritual trials
are to the fore: the spiritual life is distasteful to nature, which
hankers after the flesh-pots of Egypt. But the soul begins to
receive spiritual consolation. This is signified by the springs of
water and the palm-trees at Elim (Exod. xv. 27). "You could
not have reached the palm-groves unless you had passed through
the harsh region of temptation; you could not have come to the
fresh water of the springs without first going through rough,
unpleasant country. Not that this is the end; this is not the
height of perfection. But as God is the soul's guide in this
journey, he has arranged *refrigeria* for her in the midst of her
exertions, oases where she can repair her strength and so be
able to return with greater fervour to the labours still awaiting
her."²³

The soul then comes to the desert of Sin (Exod. xvi. 1). The
word means both "vision" and "temptation". And there are
in fact, Origen says, "visions which are also temptations, for
sometimes the wicked angel 'transformeth himself into an
angel of light' [2 Cor. xi. 14]".²⁴ It is the time when illusion
comes into the spiritual life. Origen analyses it with great
insight. "That is why one must be on the alert and try to
identify accurately the class to which the vision belongs. The
soul that has reached the point where she begins to identify the
class to which her visions belong will prove that she is really
spiritual when she is able to classify them all. It is for this
reason, too, that the gift of the discerning of spirits [1 Cor. xii.
10] is included with the other spiritual gifts among the gifts of
the Holy Ghost."²⁵ The doctrine of the discerning of spirits is
worked out at length in the *De Principiis*. It is one of the chief
elements Origen studied in the spiritual life. The Fathers
of the Desert inherited the doctrine from him. It came
to play a considerable part in the spiritual teaching of
Evagrius. It has a prominent place assigned to it in the *Life
of St. Antony*.

The next stages are taken as relating to the soul's recovery of
health and the destruction of concupiscence. Now that she is

cured and her strength restored, she begins to enter the specifically mystical region. It will be noticed that Sinai is passed
over without mention. The soul arrives at Aseroth, which
means "perfect courts" or "blessedness". "Everyone travelling by this road, whoever he may be, should carefully consider
the order the various stages come in. First you kill the impulses
of corrupt nature and bury them; then you come to the spacious
courts, you come to a state of blessedness—for the soul is
blessed when she is no longer a prey to the desires of corrupt
nature. From Aseroth she goes to Rathma, which means
'perfect vision'. The significance of that must be that the soul
grows so strong when she ceases to be disturbed by natural
desires that she is granted perfect vision, perfect understanding
of things, fuller and deeper knowledge of the reasons why the
Word became incarnate and planned things the way he did."[26]
That brings us to the gnosis, the object of which is the knowledge of the things of God. In another of his works, Origen
defines it as consisting of the "knowledge of divine things and
human things and their causes".[27] It bears particularly on
created spirits and their various dwelling-places.[28] It also bears
on the origin of man and on his end and present lot. Knowledge
of the things of God detaches the soul from the fleeting things
of earth and admits her to the intelligible world. This is the
operation which is carried out at the next resting-place. The
gnosis is essentially a kind of knowledge that transforms the
soul and brings her into the heart of the things she knows by
means of it.

Yet the fact that the soul has reached these heights does not
mean that she escapes temptation. "Temptations are given her
to guard her and keep her safe."[29] Several of the resting-places
stand for these temptations. They try the soul's patience. At
the same time, now that she has so many virtues to serve her as
armour, she must of necessity go out and fight with the princedoms, dominions and *cosmocratores*. The battle will take place
in the realm of the spirit, but it will also be a matter of doing
the work of preaching and teaching. In Origen's view, the
end which the man leading a spiritual life must aim at is not
mere contemplation. If God fills him with his own light and
strength, it is to enable him to undertake the hard battles of
the apostolate for his sake. Völker is right in dwelling on this

side of the question.[30] "He has made us ministers of the New Testament," Origen says, quoting St. Paul (2 Cor. iii. 6). The battle against the powers of evil is also a means of sharing in the Redemption, whether it be fought by martyrs or by ascetics.

All that now remains is for the soul to pass through the final stages of the contemplative life. "From there we come to Thara, the Greek for which is ἔκστασις, a word used when the mind is so astonished at something as to be stunned by it. Ἔκστασις, then, occurs when in knowing things great and wonderful the mind is suspended in astonishment."[31] These few lines have given rise to quite a controversy. Völker regards them as a declaration on Origen's part that he had experienced ecstasy himself. He compares the passage, which unfortunately survives only in the Latin translation by Rufinus, with another passage, in which Origen talks about "withdrawing from the things of men, being possessed by God and getting drunk, not in the usual senseless way but divinely."[32] H. C. Puech discusses this interpretation at length in his article on Völker's book.[33] He shows that according to Philo,[34] ἔκστασις may mean either excessive astonishment at unexpected events or the annexation of the mind by the divine πνεῦμα and the expulsion of the νοῦς ἴδιος. The second of these meanings is the one that eventually came to be denoted by the term "ecstasy" in the technical sense. But in the *Commentary on St. John*, the word is obviously used by Origen in the first sense. And the passage where it occurs speaks of passing from the things of men to the things of God and not of that "withdrawal from the self" which is the essence of ecstasy. Fr. Rahner,[35] Fr. Viller[36] and Fr. Hausherr[37] are of the same opinion and do not consider that there is any allusion at all in Origen to ecstasy properly so-called.

These observations seem justified. It is undeniable that at the beginning of the third century ecstatic phenomena of a doubtful nature were regarded with distrust, because of the excesses committed by the Montanists. It is also undeniable that the trend of Origen's mystical theology is more towards intellectual contemplation than towards the experimental awareness of the presence of God and the transformation of the soul by love, such as Gregory of Nyssa was afterwards to describe them. He was always the *didaskalos*, and as his mystical theory was in keeping with this fact, he considered that the highest point attainable in mysticism was the contemplation of the mysteries of Christianity. It was left for Gregory of Nyssa to lay the foundations of mystical theology properly so-called by describing how the soul goes out into the dark and there experiences God's presence, not with the aid of concepts, which she leaves behind her, but by love. Origen stays in the sphere of the gnosis, whereas Gregory goes beyond it. Or at any rate, Origen's description of the mystical life stops short at the gnosis.

Such is Origen's spiritual interpretation of the exodus. It contains a wealth of admirable teaching on the spiritual life. The central theme is the idea of the desert—the journey through the night of the senses, with the taste for the things of God growing as the taste for feeding on the things of earth is mortified. Origen describes the stages of this journey. But there was another thing, to his mind, even more characteristic of the spiritual life. This was an idea he bequeathed to Gregory of Nyssa, the idea that the spiritual life is an affair of continual progress. Thus, the second theme is the one centring round the tabernacle, the desert tent, which is never more than a provisional dwelling-place. "Here we have no abiding city." "If you want to know the difference between houses and tents, this is the distinction. A house has fixed foundations, is made to last and stands on a particular site. Tents are where people live when they are travelling and have not reached their journey's end. . . . Those who devote themselves to the pursuit of knowledge and wisdom have no end to their labours. How could there be an end, a limit, where the wisdom of God is concerned? The nearer a man comes to that wisdom, the deeper he finds it to be, and the more he probes into its depths, the more he sees that he will never be able to understand it or express it in words. Travellers, then, on the road to God's wisdom have no houses, because they have not reached their goal. They have tents, which they carry with them on their perpetual journeys, their never-ending travels; and the further they go, the more the road before them opens out, until it stretches to infinity. Everyone who has made any progress in knowledge or had any experience of it knows that when the soul attains to clear sight or knowledge of spiritual mysteries, she uses it like a tent and stays in it. When another of her

discoveries comes up for inspection and she proceeds to consider this other thing, she picks up her tent and goes with it to
a higher spot and, leaving her senses at peace, dwells there in
spirit. Thus, she finds fresh spiritual experiences accessible to
her in consequence of her previous ones. So it is that pressing
forward the whole time, she seems to be always on the road and
under canvas.''³⁸ The last words of the passage introduce what
was to be the central theme in Gregory of Nyssa's mystical
theology—the idea of *epectasis*. The essence of the spiritual life
is that non-proprietary attitude towards things which makes
the soul refuse to rest in what she has already acquired and
keeps her in a state of readiness to receive further gifts. It will
be noticed that this brings us back to Origen's idea of the
created spirit as a being perpetually advancing towards the
good. On this point, his theology of the spiritual life is the
practical application of his anthropology.

We now come to the zenith of the spiritual life, the perfect
union foreshadowed by the Song of Songs. We possess two
homilies by Origen on this book and also a commentary. It is
the commentary which is important for his teaching on the
spiritual life. Origen's was not the first commentary on the
Song of Songs. There had been one by Hippolytus of Rome,
but it had treated of the union of the Word with the Church.
Origen was the first to regard the Song of Songs as celebrating
the union of the soul with the Word. Or rather, he saw it as
both these things together: the Word's marriage was at once a
union with the whole Church and a union with the individual
soul. The *Commentary on the Song of Songs* is the most important
of Origen's works, as far as getting to know his ideas on the
spiritual life is concerned. It is also the one that had the
greatest influence on other writers; through Gregory of Nyssa
and St. Bernard, it introduced a new method of symbolizing
the mystical life.

In it, Origen works out a theory about the three stages of the
spiritual life. He took the idea from Philo and Philo in turn
had taken it from the Greek philosophers. It was destined to
have a very far-reaching influence. Origen begins by reminding his readers that the Greeks reduced the abstract sciences
(as distinct from the elementary curriculum) to the three
subjects of ethics, physics and "theory". He calls them by the

names of morals, physics and contemplation. He then goes on to say that "to distinguish between these three sciences, Solomon treated of them in three separate books, each in keeping with the degree of knowledge it was concerned with. First, in the book of Proverbs, he taught morals and set out the rules for living a good life. Then he put the whole of physics into Ecclesiastes. The aim of physics is to bring out the causes of things and show what things really are, and thus to make it clear that men should forsake all this emptiness and hasten on to what is lasting and eternal. It teaches that everything we see is frail and fleeting. When anyone in pursuit of Wisdom comes to realize that, he will have nothing but scorn and disdain for those things. He will, so to say, renounce the whole world and turn to those invisible, eternal things the Song of Songs teaches us about in figurative terms, with images taken from love-making. Thus, when the soul has been purified morally and has attained some proficiency in searching into the things of nature, she is fit to pass on to the things that form the object of contemplation and mysticism; her love is pure and spiritual and will raise her to the contemplation of the Godhead."[39]

The passage is of the greatest importance for the history of the theology of the spiritual life. What it amounts to is, in fact, an account of the three ways, the purgative, the illuminative and the unitive. We may take special note of what Origen says about the second of these, as it is particularly interesting. The essential operation of the illuminative way is the formation of a true estimate of things: the soul must come to realize the nothingness of temporal things and learn to understand that the spiritual world alone is real. What she has to do, then, is to rid herself of her illusions about the world and get a firm grasp of reality. Once this conviction is securely established in her, the way is open for her to enter on the contemplation of the things of God. We may also take particular note of the parallelism between the three ways and the three sapiential books. Basing himself on Philo, Origen also links the three ways with the three patriarchs, Abraham, Isaac and Jacob. Abraham represents obedience to the commandments, Isaac is natural philosophy, and Jacob, because of his name Israel,[40] stands for contemplation. In Philo, Jacob had represented the soul on the way to

perfection and Isaac was the soul that had already reached
perfection. The three classes are symbolized in Numbers by
the Israelites, the levites and the priests (this again comes from
Philo) and in the Song of Songs by the concubines, the brides-
maids and the Bride. They correspond to beginners, those busy
acquiring perfection, and the perfect.[41]

The Song of Songs corresponds to the third way. The subject
of the poem is spiritual love. Origen reminds his readers in
passing that Plato too speaks of spiritual love in the *Symposium*.[42]
There are two kinds of love. "There is a kind of love that is
physical; the poets also call it desire. There is a spiritual kind
of love as well, engendered in spirit by the inner man when he
loves. To put it more plainly, anyone who still has the image
of the earthly in the outer man goes where earthly desire and
eros lead him. But one who has the image of the heavenly in
the inner man will go where the desire and love of the things
of heaven take him. The soul is actuated by this love when
she sees how beautiful God's Word is and loves his splendour:
he shoots an arrow at her and wounds her with his love."[43]
"Children cannot know what the passion of love is. If you are
a child where the inner life is concerned, you cannot understand these things."[44] The Hebrews showed their wisdom
when they refused to allow everyone indiscriminately to read
the book.

The subject of the Song of Songs is the soul whose "one desire
is to be made one with God's Word: to go to her heavenly
Bridegroom's room—to the mysteries, that is, of his wisdom
and knowledge—on her wedding-night."[45] If she is to do that,
she must receive the light she needs from the Word himself, as
her natural resources, her reason and freewill, are not equal to
the task. "The Bridegroom's kiss [Cant. i. 1] is the working of
God in the mind, the operation by means of which, with a
word of affection, he shows the mind the light and makes
plain what had been obscure and unknown to it before; provided, at any rate, that the mind deserves to have God working
in it. . . . Every time we turn over in our minds some question
about dogma and find out the answer without help from a
master, the Word, we may conclude, has kissed us."[46] This
shows unmistakably how the unitive way differs from the earlier
ones. In the earlier ones, God acts on the soul through masters

outside her; in this case there is a master inside the soul, teaching her from within.

Thus, the mystical life appears as a kind of experimental knowledge of the things of God. Origen gives expression to this belief in the doctrine of the spiritual senses, a theory of the utmost importance and one that he was the first to propound. It is hinted at in Scripture, e.g., in the "How gracious the Lord is! Taste and prove it" of Psalm xxxiii. 9. The chief texts relating to it are grouped together at the beginning of Ziegler's *Dulcedo Dei*. Where Origen showed his originality was in interpreting these texts in conjunction with one another and evolving a coherent doctrine out of them. His method has been studied by Fr. Rahner.[47] The spiritual senses are aspects of the life of grace which, as it grows, enables the soul to taste, touch and contemplate the things of God. Fr. Stolz[48] regards them as a restoration of the unsullied sense-activity exercised by man in paradise. In my *Platonisme et théologie mystique*, I argue against this thesis and show that nothing more is involved than a set of metaphors denoting spiritual experience.

Origen expounds the doctrine in the *Contra Celsum*. "If you examine the question more closely," he writes, "you will see that there is, as Scripture says, a common sense for perceiving the divine. Only the blessed will be able to discover it: 'You will discover a sense that can perceive the divine,' the Bible says [cf. Prov. ii. 5]." It is a sense that comprises several subordinate species. There is a sense of sight for seeing non-corporeal things, as is obvious in the case of the cherubim and seraphim; a sense of hearing capable of catching voices that make no sound in the air; a sense of taste with which to taste the living bread that came down from heaven to give life to the world [John vi. 51 et seq.]; a delicate sense of smell—which is what led Paul to say that he was the "good odour of Christ" (2 Cor. ii. 15); a sense of touch such as John used when he handled the "Word of life" (1 John i. 1). We have senses of two different kinds in us, as Solomon knew: one set is mortal, corruptible and human, the other immortal, spiritual and divine.[49] The idea is developed in the *Commentary on the Song of Songs*. The soul is attracted by the fragrance of the Word's perfumes and is drawn along after him. "What will she do when God's Word comes to occupy her hearing, sight, touch and taste as well? . . . If the eye can see his glory, glory such as belongs to the Father's only-begotten Son [John i. 14], it will not want to look at anything else. If the ears can hear the saving, lifegiving Word, they will want nothing but that to listen to. The Word is life. When a man's hands have touched him, he will never again touch anything that can corrupt or perish. And when his taste has tasted the good Word of God [Heb. vi. 5], tasted life, tasted his flesh, the bread that comes down from heaven, he will be unable after that to bear the taste of anything else. In comparison with the satisfaction that that flavour gives him, all else will seem unappetizing. . . . If a man becomes fit to be with Christ, he will taste the Lord and see how pleasant he is." The pleasure he obtains through his sense of taste will not be his only joy; all his senses will delight in the Word who is life. "I urge my readers, therefore, to mortify their bodily senses and instead of giving admittance to the impressions that come from them, to use the 'inward man's' senses [Rom. vii. 22], the senses that perceive the divine, and to try and understand this by means of them. That is what Solomon was referring to when he said [cf. Prov. ii. 5]: 'You will discover a sense that can perceive the divine'." [50]

That gives us all the factors comprised in the doctrine of the spiritual senses. The spiritual senses are put into operation in the soul by the Word. They are the unfolding of the inner life. They correspond to various spiritual experiences, all concerned with the Word present in the soul. They are thus bound up with the perfection of the spiritual life. "Those who reach the summit of perfection and the height of bliss will find their delight in God's Word." They are bound up with the mortifying of the life of the body: as the outward man declines, the inward man grows strong. In the end, they bewitch the soul and tear her away from herself. Those who taste the things of God find that the things of the body lose their appeal. [51]

From the spiritual point of view, the doctrine was one of the most fruitful of any Origen taught. Gregory of Nyssa worked out its implications at length. [52] His special contribution consisted of grading the different senses in accordance with their bearing on the successive stages of the mystic's ascent to God. He lays considerable stress on the incompatibility of the bodily senses with the spiritual. The spiritual life seems uninviting at first, because the bodily senses are frustrated and the spiritual ones are not yet at work. But if the soul consents to cross this desert, the taste for God will gradually grow in her. St. Augustine owes to the doctrine what is perhaps the finest chapter in his *Confessions*.[53] St. Bernard makes much of it. Fr. Rahner has shown the use St. Bonaventure makes of it. And the part played by the spiritual sense of touch in St. Teresa's writings is a matter of common knowledge.[54]

CONCLUSION

F RANÇOIS MAURIAC once said of Pascal: "Every kind of greatness met in one man, and that man was a Christian". Now that we have finished our study of Origen, we can say the same of him too. He is of that rare class of men whose genius is equalled only by their sanctity. Pascal belongs at once to the history of thought and science and to the history of the spiritual life. So does Origen. That explains how it is possible for philosophers like De Faye to claim him as one of themselves and for men like Völker, whose interest is in spirituality, to regard him as a master of the spiritual life. Both schools are right. But they both go wrong when they try to reduce him to the particular facet of his personality they are struck by themselves. What I have tried to do in this book (and it is one of the things that made me choose the form I did) has been to show what different kinds of greatness Origen possessed and to avoid reducing them all to a single species. In the course of our investigations, Origen has come before us in several guises, one after another—as an active Christian, as a learned exegete, as a philosophical genius, as a great master of the spiritual life. We may have been inclined to think that every new side of him we discovered was the main one. That is the way of it with really great men: they are equally good at all the possible ways of being great.

The first thing to do, then, was to assemble within the covers of a single book a certain amount of material bearing on the different aspects of Origen's teaching. The task was facilitated by the works of previous writers who had studied one or other of these aspects in detail—there was Koch's book, for instance, on Origen's philosophy and Völker's on his mystical teaching. But certain reaches of his thought, and not the least important of them, had hitherto been overlooked. The first of the things that had been left in the shade was the significance of his teaching as a source of information about the life of the Christian community. Origen spent his whole life in teaching and preaching, during one of the most intensely dramatic periods ever known in the history of the Church. He was a "church-man" in the fullest sense of the term. It may even be said that that was the most important and essential thing about him. Nothing could be further from the truth than to picture him as a philosopher and nothing more, a mere reasoner whose membership of the Church had no effect on his innermost life. But that is practically what De Faye does do. It was thus essential to restore the proper perspective and show how Origen was part and parcel of the Christian community of his time. I have laid still more stress on the part he played as an exegete: a third of the book is devoted to that point. All his writings are really commentaries on the Bible. The extent of the prejudice against patristic exegesis can be gauged from the fact that so little importance has been attached to this side of his work. But far from being negligible, it actually appears to be the most considerable part of his achievement. He created the critical study of the Old Testament text and, more important still, worked out the theology of the relationship between the Old Testament and the New. In so doing, he was handing on the tradition everywhere received in the Church. The perish-able elements in his theology of the Bible, the things he derived from the culture of his time—the allegorical methods of inter-pretation he borrowed from Philo and the gnostics—in no way lessen the value of his work as a whole. He is first and foremost an expositor of God's word, an inspired interpreter of Scripture. All the rest, whether dogmatic theology, theology of the spiri-tual life or apologetics, rests on that.

Of the various aspects, then, of Origen's writings, some had been studied separately, others had been passed over altogether. To produce a complete picture of his genius, it was essential to bring them all together in one book. That is what I have tried to do. Anyone wishing to go more deeply into any particular question discussed by Origen can always consult one or other of the monographs mentioned in the course of the book, as they deal with individual points more fully than is possible in a work so general in scope as this. Völker's book and Fr. Lieske's are still indispensable to any serious study of Origen's mystical theology; a single chapter was all I could

spare for the subject here. I have only hinted at the importance
of Origen's theology of the Trinity. When H. C. Puech's book
appears, it will show how complex the question really is. Thus,
different features have been shown up, one after another, by
the work done on Origen in recent years. What remained to be
done was to have the features fitted together and a face made
out of them, so that the man himself who had possessed all
these gifts in his own person should appear before us as he was.
I have tried to perform that operation and have refused to
simplify a personality whose predominant characteristic was
diversity.

The refusal to simplify I have carried over into the study of
individual problems as well. It became evident that in no field
of thought were Origen's views amenable to systematization;
the only thing to do was to admit that his mind could follow
several lines of thought at the same time without bringing them
into harmony with one another. Incidentally, that explains
how previously different people came to give such different
accounts of him: it was because they had devoted their attention to one or another of these lines of thought exclusively.
That is still the case with his exegesis. People are continually
talking about his love of allegory and comparing it with
Clement's. How far is that true? I think I have shown—it is
in fact one of the conclusions that emerge most plainly from the
book—that Origen had the greatest respect for the traditional
typology; he followed the rest of the Church in seeing figures
of the mysteries of Christ's life in certain texts of the Old
Testament. His works thus contain a whole theology of history,
which shows him to great advantage as an exponent of biblical
theology. I have devoted a long chapter to that point. But side
by side with the traditional attitude, the influence of rabbinical
and gnostic methods of exegesis is discernible and Philo's
influence is particularly noticeable. All that has nothing to do
with typology. The confusion that often arises between the two
things is most regrettable and quite destroys the value of the
majority of books written on the question. It would seem that
a certain amount of sifting needs to be done in this field before
patristic exegesis can be studied with any degree of success. I
have given some of the criteria necessary for such an undertaking.

The same can be said of Origen's theology. The school of De Faye and Koch regard it as a piece of systematization based on Platonist principles. But in several fields, Origen is also an authority for the tradition of the Church. The fact is that some of his doctrines are purely and simply an echo of the common teaching of the Church, while others depend on the philosophical system he had forged for himself. One comes to see that where the traditional teaching of the Church was already clearly defined, he simply echoes it. This is particularly striking in the case of the theology of the Redemption, which, like everybody else, he considered as a victory over the powers of evil; it is also very noticeable where the theology of Baptism and martyrdom is concerned. These doctrines had their roots too deep in the life of the Christian community for Origen to cast them off. But side by side with this attitude, we find a philosophical theory about the origins and end of the history of salvation. As Tradition had no clear teaching to offer, as yet, on those points, Origen took two facts he could be sure of —God's love and man's freewill—and tried to use them as the starting-point for an explanation of his own. The coherent, lucid system he worked out in consequence, with its doctrines of the previous existence of the soul and the *apocatastasis* to come, is what people are thinking of, often enough, when they talk about his "theology". Actually, it is only part of his theology, the part in which he *suggested* a possible explanation where there was no traditional teaching for him to follow. It can thus be said that the two things which make the real theologian are both found in him: on the one hand he attempts to systematize, and on the other he is determined not to distort revealed truth by forcing it into the framework of the system, and therefore he accepts a certain incoherence.

Must we then abandon the hope of finding a vantage-point that will enable us to see something of the unity in this many-sided personality and these complex writings? There is such a vantage-point, but we must not look for it in the speculative order. Origen was a man who had met with Christ. This religious experience, this familiarity with the risen Christ, determined the cast of his whole life. It has been pointed out that when he speaks of Christ, thinker though he essentially is, he puts such affection into his words, that the mind goes for a parallel to saints like Bernard, Francis and Ignatius. He was first and foremost a witness to Christ by the way he lived. And it was because Christ was the supreme interest of his life that he made him the centre of his writings. If we examine what he wrote, we find that what gives it its unity is Christ; it is all of it Christocentric. The Christian community, as Origen saw it, was the mystical body; its head was Christ. The purpose of exegesis was to reveal Christ, "present everywhere" in the Old Testament beneath the veil of the letter. Dogmatic theology was the study of the Incarnation, the means the Word took to restore created spirits, who shared in his life, to full union with himself. Mystical theology centred round the Incarnate Word; its sole purpose was to enable the soul to become like him and be transformed into him. There can thus be little point in asking whether every part of the system is logically coherent. The source of unity lies deeper than that, in Origen's intimate knowledge and eager love of the Lord Jesus.

NOTES

INTRODUCTION

1. *Giovanni Cassiano ed Evagrio Pontico*, Rome, 1936.
2. In his *Kosmische Liturgie*, Freiburg im Breisgau, 1941.
3. *De Res.*, 1, 29 and 20.
4. *Panarion*, 64, 4.
5. *Hist. Eccl.*, 6, 32, 3.
6. *Ad Heraclium*, P.G., 14, 1292-4.
7. *Hom. in Gen.*, 4, 1.
8. *De Princ.*, preface, 2.
9. Paris, 1935.
10. Vol. i, cols. 1084 et seq.
11. "Die Hiera des Evagrius", *Zeit. Kath. Theol.*, 1939, pp. 86 et seq., 181 et seq.
12. Jan. 1946, pp. 84 et seq.
13. *Journ. Theol. Stud.*, 1945, pp. 192 et seq.
14. The first edition of Origen's *opera omnia* with the Greek text was De la Rue's, 4 vols., Paris, 1733-59. This was reproduced, with some additional matter, by Migne in P.G. 12-17. Since then, a considerable part of the new edition in the Berlin Corpus has appeared, viz. vols. 1-2, *Contra Celsum, De Oratione, Exhortatio Ad Martyrium* (Koetschau); vol. 3, Homilies on Jeremias (Klostermann); vol. 4, *Commentary on St. John* (Preuschen); vol. 5, *De Principiis* (Koetschau); vols. 6, 7, 8, Homilies on the Old Testament (Baehrens); vol. 9, Homilies on St. Luke (Rauer); vols. 10 and 11, *Commentary on St. Matthew* (Klostermann). Lommatzch's edition, Berlin, 1831-48 (25 vols.), may also be mentioned. A few French translations have recently appeared—Bardy, *De la prière, Exhortation au martyre* (Gabalda, 1932); De Lubac-Doutreleau, *Homélies sur la Genèse* (*Sources chrétiennes*, 1945); De Lubac-Fortier, *Homélies sur L'Exode* (1947).
15. P.G., 17, cols. 633 et seq.
16. *Rech. sc. rel.*, 1936-7.

PART I

CHAPTER I

1. H.E., 6, 2, 1.
2. H.E., 6, 33, 4.
3. Ibid.

4. P.G., 10, 1049–1105.
5. *Texte u. Untersuchungen*, 42, pts. 3 and 4, Leipzig, 1918–19.
6. Berlin Corpus, 9, p. 109.
7. H.E., 6, 2, 7–11.
8. H.E., 6, 2, 2.
9. H.E., 6, 2, 11.
10. H.E., 6, 1, 1.
11. H.E., 6, 2, 4–6.
12. H.E., 6, 39, 5.
13. See *Cels.*, 1, 2, 4; 2, 47; 8, 44; *Comm. Jo.*, 6, 54 (Preuschen, p. 163).
14. H.E., 6, 2, 12.
15. Ibid.
16. H.E., 6, 2, 15.
17. H.E., 6, 2, 14.
18. *Comm. Jo.*, 5, 8.
19. *Hom. Jos.*, 7, 6 (Baehrens, p. 334, 11–15).
20. H.E., 6, 3, 1–8.
21. *Origène*, i, p. 10.
22. *Jeunesse d'Origène*, p. 31.
23. "Aux origines de l'Ecole d'Alexandrie, Vivre et Penser", *Revue biblique*, 2nd series, pp. 85 et seq.
24. Ch. 12 (ed. Botte, p. 43).
25. Bardy, p. 87.
26. *Cels.*, 3, 15.
27. *Hom. Lev.*, 6, 2.
28. Bardy, p. 87.
29. H.E., 6, 3, 9.
30. H.E., 6, 8, 6.
31. H.E., 6, 3, 3–7.
32. Cf. H.E., 6, 3, 9.
33. Ibid.
34. See H.I. Marrou, *Saint Augustin et la fin de la culture antique*, pp. 169 et seq.
35. H.E., 6, 3, 8–12.
36. *Or. Paneg.*, 11 (P.G., 10, 1081c).
37. H.E., 6, 15.
38. Bardy, "Origines", p. 94.
39. Eus., H.E., 6, 9, 12–13.
40. H.E., 6, 18.
41. In his *Saint Augustin et la fin de la culture antique*.
42. *Hom. in Ps. xxxvi*, 3, 6.
43. *Hom. Num.*, 18, 3.
44. Op. cit., 20, 3.
45. *Hom. Gen.*, 11, 2.
46. *Hom. Lev.*, 5, 8.
47. *Hom. Gen.*, 11, 2.
48. *Ep. Greg.*, 1.
49. *Or. Paneg.*, 6 (P.G., 10, 1072a, b).

50. O.P., 7 (P.G., 10, 1077a).
51. O.P., 8 (P.G., 10, 1077b, c).
52. O.P., 13 (P.G., 10, 1088a).
53. O.P., 14 (P.G., 10, 1089b).
54. O.P., 14 (P.G., 10, 1092c).
55. O.P., 15 (P.G., 10, 1093b).
56. O.P., 15, (P.G., 10, 1093c).
57. O.P., 15, (P.G., 10, 1096a).
58. O.P., Loc. cit.
59. H.E., 6, 19, 1.
60. H.E., 6, 19, 15.
61. H.E., 6, 21, 3.
62. *Relig. orientales*, 4th ed., p. 105.
63. H.E., 6, 23, 1.
64. Loc. cit.
65. *Jeunesse d'Origène*, p. 99.
66. H.E., 6, 27.
67. Op. cit., 6, 30.
68. This has now appeared under the title of *Entretiens d'Origène avec Héraclide* . . ., (Cairo, 1949). (Tr.)
69. H.E., 6, 36, 1.
70. "Un prédicateur populaire au IIIᵉ siècle", *Rev. prat. Sap.*, 1927, pp. 513 et seq., 679 et seq.
71. *Sources chrétiennes*, 1945.
72. Preface (P.G., 17, 545b); cf. *Hom. Ex.*, 7, 5.
73. *Hom. Gen.*, 10, 3.
74. Op. cit., 2, 3.
75. *Hom. Ezech.*, 1, 11 (P.G., 13, 677a).
76. *Hom. Num.*, 20, 4.
77. *Hom. Ezech.*, 5, 4 (P.G., 13, 707a).
78. Eus., H.E., 6, 39, 5.

CHAPTER II

1. *Texte und Untersuchungen*, 42, pts. 3 and 4, Leipzig, 1918–19.
2. *Hom. Num.*, 5, 1.
3. *De Or.*, 32.
4. "La symbolique des rites baptismaux", *Dieu vivant*, i, p. 20.
5. *Adv. Valent.*, 3.
6. *Strom.*, 7, 7, 43.
7. *Dial.*, 121, 2.
8. *Hom. Lev.*, 9, 10.
9. S. E. Assemani, *Acta SS. Mart. Orient. et Occident.*, Rome, 1748, ii, pp. 52 et seq.
10. *De Or.*, 31.
11. Loc. cit.
12. *De Or.*, 23 (P.L., 1, 1191a).

13. Vagaggini, *Maria nelle opere di Origene*, Rome, 1942, p. 89.
14. *De Or.*, 31, 4.
15. Loc. cit.
16. *Hom. Jos.*, 9, 4 (Baehrens, p. 350).
17. *Hom. Luc.*, 23 (Rauer, p. 157).
18. Op. cit., 32; see also *Hom. Isa.*, 5, 2.
19. *De Or.*, 12, 2.
20. Loc. cit.; see also *Comm. Ser. Matt.*, 60.
21. *Cels.*, 8, 17–18; see also 3, 34; 6, 14; 7, 65.
22. Op. cit., 8, 19.
23. *Enn.*, 1, 6, 9.
24. *Cels.*, 8, 21.
25. Op. cit., 8, 22.
26. "Art und Sinn der ältesten christlicher Osterfeier", *Jahrbuch für liturgische Wissenschaft*, 1938, 14, pp. 1 et seq.
27. *Cels.*, 8, 22. On the symbolism of feasts, see also *Hom. Num.*, 33, 2; *Hom. Lev.*, 9, 5.
28. *Hom. Gen.*, 10, 3.
29. P. Boyancé, *Le culte des Muses chez les philosophes grecs*, p. 163. Heinemann, *Philos griechische und jüdische Bildung*, p. 108, thinks that the Cynics were the originators of the idea.
30. *Cels.*, 8, 23.
31. *Comm. Jo.*, 13, 18 (Preuschen, p. 242).
32. *Cels.*, 4, 26.
33. Op. cit., 3, 30.
34. *Hom. Ez.*, 5, 4.
35. *Cels.*, 1, 46.
36. Op. cit., 1, 24.
37. Op. cit., 7, 8.
38. *Hom. Jer.*, 4, 3.
39. *Hom. Gen.*, 10, 1.
40. *Hom. Ex.*, 12, 2.
41. Op. cit., 13, 3.
42. *Hom. Ezech.*, 13, 3.
43. *Hom. Jos.*, 10, 1.
44. *Comm. Matt.*, 15, 26.
45. *Hom. Jer.*, 12, 8.
46. *Hom. Gen.*, 5, 3.
47. *Hom. Lev.*, 11, 7.
48. *Hom. Psalm.* 37, 1, 6.
49. *Comm. Ser. Matt.*, 12 (P.G., 13, 1616b).
50. *Comm. Matt.*, 16, 8.
51. *Hom. Lev.*, 14, 3.
52. *Comm. Matt.*, 15, 15.
53. Ibid., 16, 22.
54. Ibid., 14, 22.
55. *Hom. Lev.*, 6, 6.
56. *Comm. Matt.*, 14, 22.

57. "He regarded the teaching office as belonging to the bishops and presbyters. In theory, the various degrees of the gnosis coincided with the degrees of the hierarchy" (Van den Eynde, *Les normes de l'enseignement chrétien dans la littérature patristique des trois premiers siècles*, p. 233).

58. *Hom. Lev.*, 1, 4.

59. The same spiritualization is found in *Hom. Lev.*, 9, 1: "'The Lord spoke to Moses, giving him a message for . . . Aaron: He must never present himself without due preparation in the sanctuary' [Lev. xvi. 2]. . . . That applies to all of us. . . . It is a warning to us that we ought to learn the proper way to approach God's altar. The altar is what we offer our prayers on. . . . You have been given the priesthood, you know: the whole of God's Church has, the whole nation of the faithful. Peter, remember, calls the faithful a chosen race, a royal priesthood [1 Pet. ii. 9]. You have the priesthood, then, because you are a priestly race. You ought therefore to offer God the sacrifice of praise, the sacrifice of prayer, the sacrifice of mercy, the sacrifice of purity, the sacrifice of holiness."

60. *Hom. Jos.*, 9, 9.

61. *Hom. Lev.*, 5, 3.

62. *Hom. Num.*, 4, 3.

63. Loc. cit.

64. *Hom. Lev.*, 12, 7.

65. *Hom. Num.*, 2, 1.

66. *Les normes de l'enseignement chrétien aux trois premiers siècles*, p. 233.

67. *Hom. Lev.*, 6, 3.

68. *Hom. Num.*, 9, 1.

69. "Mysterion", p. 46.

70. Op. cit., p. 50.

CHAPTER III

1. *Hom. Num.*, 5; cf. *Comm. Rom.*, 5, 8.

2. On the question of Baptism, there is an essay by Fr. Hugo Rahner entitled, "Taufe und geistliches Leben bei Origenes", *Zeitsch. für Aszese und Mystik*, 1932, pp. 205–23.

3. *Cels.*, 3, 55.

4. Op. cit., 3, 51.

5. *Rech. théol. anc. et med.*, 1933, v., p. 129.

6. *R.S.R.*, 1934, p. 129.

7. p. 14.

8. *Hom. Luc.*, 22 (Rauer, p. 146).

9. Op. cit., 21 (p. 140). See also *Hom. Ezech.*, 6, 7.

10. *Hom. Lev.*, 6, 2.

11. *Hom. Luc.*, 21.

12. Loc. cit.

13. *Comm. Rom.*, 5, 8.

14. *Comm. Jo.*, 6, 17 (Preuschen, p. 142).

15. *Comm. Rom.*, 5, 8.

16. *Hom. Exod.*, 5, 2 (Baehrens, p. 186).

17. Op. cit., 5, 1 (p. 182).

18. Op. cit., 5, 5 (p. 190).

19. *Comm. Rom.* 4, 9 (P.G., 14, 997c). See also *Comm. Jo.*, 20, 37 (Preuschen, p. 377).

20. *Comm. Rom.*, 8, 5 (P.G., 14, 1168).

21. *Fragm. Gen.* (P.G., 12, 100).

22. *Hom. Lev.*, 9, 9 (Baehrens, p. 436).

23. *Hom. Gen.*, 10, 5.

24. *Comm. Jo.*, 6, 47.

25. Loc. cit.

26. *Ecl. Proph.*, 5, 6 (ed. Stählin, p. 138).

27. *Hom. Jos.*, 4, 1.

28. *Hom. Num.*, 3, 1.

29. "Mysterion", pp. 56–7.

30. *R.S.R.*, 1945.

31. *Comm. Matt.*, 15, 23.

32. In *Le fleuve de feu.*

33. Battifol, *L'Eucharistie*, p. 270.

34. "Mysterion", p. 545.

35. *Hom. Num.*, 5, 1.

36. *Cels.*, 8, 33.

37. Op. cit., 8, 57.

38. *Hom. Rom.*, 10, 33. See also *Comm. Cant.*, 1 (Baehrens, p. 92).

39. *Hom. Ex.*, 13, 3.

40. *Hom. Ps.*, 37, (2), 6 (P.G., 12, 1386). See also *Hom. Lev.*, 13, 5.

41. *Comm. Matt.*, 11, 14.

42. *Hom. Num.*, 16, 9 (Baehrens, p. 152).

43. *Comm. Jo.*, 6, 32 (Preuschen, p. 468).

44. *Hom. Ex.*, 13, 3.

45. *Hom. Lev.*, 7, 5 (Preuschen, p. 387).

46. *Hom. Num.*, 16, 9.

47. *Comm. Ser. Matt.*, 85 (P.G., 13, 1734).

48. *Rev. Sc. Phil. Théol.*, Nov. 1935 to April 1936.

49. Op. cit., April 1936, p. 328.

50. *Pronoia und Paideusis*, p. 82.

51. *Die Sündervergebung bei Origenes*, 1912.

52. See Galtier, *L'Eglise et la rémission des péchés aux premiers siècles*, pp. 184–213.

53. *Hom. Lev.*, 2, 4 (Baehrens, p. 279).

54. *De Or.*, 28.

55. Op. cit., ante.

56. *Hom Lev.*, 11, 2 (Baehrens, p. 451).

57. *Hom. Jos.*, 7, 6.

58. *Hom. Lev.*, 15, 2.

59. *Hom. Num.*, 10, 1.

60. Loc. cit.

61. *Comm. Matt.*, 12, 14.

62. "Mysterion", p. 50.

CHAPTER IV

1. *Hom. Lev.*, 10, 2.
2. *Or. Paneg.*, 14 (P.G., 10, 1093a).
3. On this question, see the passages collected by Harnack in *Der Kirchengeschichtliche Ertrag*, i, 39 et seq.
4. See Caster, *Lucien et la pensée religieuse de son temps*, pp. 123 et seq.: "La Providence".
5. In *Pronoia und Paideusis*.
6. Eus., H.E., 6, 19, 5.
7. Loc. cit.
8. Origen is no doubt referring to Ammonius when he mentions a "master of the philosophical sciences", whose lectures he had attended (Eus., H.E., 6, 19, 13).
9. *De Vit. Plot.*, ch. 3, s. 18, 19.
10. *Bibl.*, 214 (P.G., 103, 701a).
11. P.G., 40, 567b, 593b.
12. *Jeunesse d'Origène*, p. 190.
13. *De Vit. Plot.*, ch. 14, s. 72 et seq.
14. *Jeunesse d'Origène*, pp. 204 et seq.
15. "Le thème néo-platonicien de la contemplation créatrice chez Origène et saint Augustin", *Gregorianum*, 1932, p. 271.
16. Eus., H.E., 6, 19, 8.
17. *Mélanges Bidez*, ii, p. 745.
18. Cambridge, 1937.
19. Rennes, 1945.
20. *Lucien*, p. 55.
21. *Cels.*, 2, 13.
22. Op. cit., 1, 43; 7, 3; 8, 15.
23. "Origène et l'aristotélisme", *Mélanges Glotz*, i, p. 75.
24. *Dial.*, 2, 3.
25. Caster, p. 60.
26. Gregory the Wonderworker, *Orat. Paneg.*, 13 (P.G., 10, 1088b).
27. *Cels.*, 7, 54.
28. See Otto, *Preister und Tempel*, ii., p. 216.
29. *Cels.*, 6, 41.
30. Caster, pp. 42–3.
31. p. 40.
32. p. 45.
33. Op. cit., p. 41.
34. *Lucullus*, 69.
35. *Origène*, ii, pp. 98–140.
36. Op. cit., p. 99.
37. *Cels.*, 5, 57.
38. See the index to Koetschau's edition, p. 437.
39. Lebreton, *Les origines du dogme de la Trinité*, i, pp. 230 et seq.
40. *De Defectu Oraculorum*. See Soury, *La démonologie de Plutarque*.

41. Soury, p. 49. Cf. Boyancé, "Les deux démons personnels dans l'antiquité grecque et latine", *Rev. Phil.*, 1935, pp. 189–202.

42. *Mélanges Bidez*, ii, pp. 746–78.

43. Stuttgart, 1940, Supplement, vii, pp. 664–78.

44. *De Nat. Hom.*, 2, 29.

45. *De Vita Plot.*, ch. 21, s. 123.

46. *Cels.*, 1, 15; 4, 51.

47. *Strom.*, 1, 22, 150 He also knew of Christ: "In the first book of his treatise *On the Good*, Numenius the Pythagorean, the best interpreter of Plato by far . . . mentions an anecdote about Jesus, though without expressly naming him, and gives it a spiritual interpretation" (*Cels.* 4, 51).

48. *Cels.*, 5, 57.

49. *Epist.*, 2, 312e.

50. *Laws*, 10, 896e.

51. *Rep.*, 509b.

52. *Mélanges Bidez*, ii, p. 767.

53. *Enn.*, 2, 9, 13.

54. *Cels.*, 1, 15.

55. Op. cit., 5, 57.

56. See also op. cit., 5, 38.

57. *Comm. Tim.*, 93.

58. *Cels.*, 5, 7.

59. *Praep. Ev.*, 11, 22.

60. *Pronoia und Paideusis*, p. 276.

61. *Origène*, ii, p. 154.

62. *De Princ.*, 4, 2, 8.

63. *Cels.*, 8, 70.

64. Op. cit., 4, 19.

65. P.G., 12, 1533.

66. *Cels.*, 6, 55.

67. Koch, pp. 268–74.

68. *De Anima*, 28–29.

69. *Epitome*, 7, 1.

70. Exactly the same expression is used by Albinus: "We must discuss the principles ($\pi\epsilon\rho\grave{\iota}$ $\tau\hat{\omega}\nu$ $\dot{\alpha}\rho\chi\hat{\omega}\nu$) . . . of theology" (op. cit., 8, 1).

71. Op. cit., 10, 3.

72. Ibid., 10, 7.

73. Ibid., 10, 5, 6.

74. Ibid., 10, 3.

75. Ibid., 10, 16.

76. *Cels.*, 7, 43.

77. Op. cit., 7, 42.

78. Ibid., 5, 9.

79. *De Princ.*, 2, 1–3; *Comm. Jo.*, 6, 30.

80. *Cels.*, 5, 4, 7.

81. Op. cit., 7, 3.

CHAPTER V

1. De Faye has two chapters on Celsus (i, 10; ii, 13); there is an excellent chapter by Fr. de Labriolle in his *Réaction paienne*, and Frau Miura-Stange has written on *Celsus und Origenes*.
2. *Cels.*, 3, 59.
3. Op. cit., 1, 9.
4. Ibid., 1, 62.
5. Ibid., 2, 59.
6. Ibid., 3, 44.
7. Ibid., 1, 27.
8. Ibid., 3, 44.
9. Ibid., 3, 49.
10. Ibid., 6, 13–14.
11. Ibid., 3, 62.
12. Ibid., 6, 2.
13. Ibid., 1, 9.
14. Ibid., 3, 9.
15. Ibid., 2, 77.
16. Ibid., 1, 9.
17. It is the same with regard to the pagan oracles. In their case too, Origen asks what the effect is on the spiritual life (ibid., 7, 6).
18. Ibid., 7, 54.
19. Ibid., 1, 43.
20. Ibid. 3, 14.
21. Ibid., 6, 66.
22. Ibid., 7, 36.
23. Ibid., 6, 3.
24. Ibid., 7, 42.
25. Ibid., 7, 45.
26. *Rep.*, 6, 509b.
27. *Cels.*, 7, 38.
28. Op. cit., 7, 39.
29. Ibid., 7, 42.
30. Ibid., 7, 44.
31. Ibid., 7, 58.
32. Ibid., 1, 48.
33. Ibid., 4, 21.
34. Ibid., 3, 26.
35. Ibid., 2, 55.
36. Ibid., 7, 58.
37. Ibid., 4, 37.
38. Ibid., 4, 39.
39. Ibid., 4, 40.
40. Ibid., 1, 65.
41. Ibid., 1, 67.
42. Ibid., 4, 23.

43. Ibid., 4, 74.
44. Ibid., 4, 88.
45. Ibid., 4, 78.
46. Ibid., 4, 99.
47. Ibid., 4, 74.
48. Ibid., 4, 75.
49. Ibid., 4, 79.
50. Ibid., 8, 2.
51. Ibid., 5, 6.
52. Ibid., 8, 35.
53. Ibid., 8, 58.
54. Ibid., 8, 33 (P.G., 11-8, 28).
55. Ibid., 3, 26.
56. Ibid., 8, 45.
57. Ibid., 8, 55.
58. Ibid., 8, 68.
59. Ibid., 1, 1.
60. Loc. cit.
61. Ibid., 8, 75.
62. Loc. cit.
63. Ibid., 5, 25.
64. Ibid., 5, 27.
65. Ibid., 5, 28.
66. Ibid., 5, 37.
67. Ibid., 4, 69.
68. Ibid., 4, 65.
69. Ibid., 4, 7.
70. Ibid., 5, 37.
71. Ibid., 4, 7.
72. Ibid., 4, 8.
73. *Comm. Jo.*, 13, 46.
74. *De Princ.*, 4, 2, 8 (Koetschau, pp. 320-1 .
75. See also *Cels.*, 2, 2; 3, 42.
76. *Comm. Cant.*, 1, 1 (P.G., 12, 84–5).
77. *Comm. Jo.*, 13, 48 (Preuschen, pp. 274–5).
78. Op. cit., 1, 7.
79. Ibid., 2, 34.
80. Ibid., 6, 3.
81. Ibid., 6, 4.
82. Ibid., 6, 3.
83. *The Conception of the Gospel in the Alexandrians' Theology*, Oslo, 1938, p. 109.
84. *Comm. Jo.*, 6, 5.
85. Op. cit., 13, 48.
86. *Hom. Jos.*, 3, 2.
87. Loc. cit.
88. *Comm. Jo.*, 19, 5 (Preuschen, p. 303, 29).
89. Loc. cit. (Preuschen, p. 304, 1).

PART II

1. Eus., H.E., 3, 8.

CHAPTER I

1. H. E., 6, 15. See Merk, "Origenes und der Kanon der Alten Testaments", *Biblica*, 1925, p. 200; Bardy, "Les traditions juives dans l'œuvre d'Origène", *Revue biblique*, 1925, p. 217; Zöllig, *Die Inspirationslehre des Origenes*, 1902; H. B. Swete, *An Introduction to the Old Testament in Greek*, Cambridge, 1902, pp. 59–85; E. Hautsch, *Die Evangelienzitate des Origenes*, Leipzig, 1909.
2. H.E., 6, 1.
3. *De Vir. Illustr.*, 54.
4. H.E., 6, 16, 1–4.
5. *Comm. Matt.*, 15, 14.
6. Loc. cit.
7. *Comm. Ps.*, 5.
8. *Ep. Afric.*, 5.
9. *Comm. Jer.*, 14, 3 (Klostermann, p. 107, 28).
10. Pope Pius XII's encyclical, however, stresses the prime importance of the original text.
11. *Comm. Jer.*, 15, 5.
12. Op. cit., 19, 5.
13. *Die Evangelienzitate des Origenes*, p. 4.
14. H.E., 6, 25, 2.
15. Op. cit., 6, 25, 1.
16. *Ep. Afric.*, 2 (P.G., 11, 80).
17. Op. cit., 13.
18. *Hom. Num.*, 27, 1.
19. *Comm. Cant.*, prologue; Baehrens, p. 88.
20. *Biblica*, 1925, p. 205.
21. H.E., 6, 25, 8–10.
22. Op. cit., 6, 25, 12.

CHAPTER II

1. *De Princ.*, 4, 2, 2 (Koetschau, p. 308, 14).
2. Pierre Lestringant, "L'unité de la révélation biblique", *Je Sers*, 1942.
3. Einar Molland, *The Conception of the Gospel in the Alexandrians' Theology*, Oslo, 1938, pp. 25–174.
4. *De Princ.*, 4, 2, 1 (Koetschau, pp. 305–6).
5. Op. cit. (Koetschau, pp. 306–7).
6. *Cels.*, 7, 18. It is worth noting that the Jews still use the same argument today. In *Dieu vivant*, no. 7, p. 83, Edmond Fleg wrote: "Jesus declared that the messianic kingdom had come, but did he fulfill what had been

prophesied of it? Have swords been melted down into ploughshares? (Isa. ii. 4). Does the wolf feed beside the lamb?" After an interval of eighteen centuries, the position is still the same. And the only way I could reply was to say with Origen: "This may be a proof that they are not to be taken literally" (p. 87). Origen's arguments have lost none of their force.

7. *De Princ.*, 4, 2, 1 (Koetschau pp. 307–8).

8. e.g., *Comm. Jo.*, 1, 13 (Preuschen, p. 18, 24); 6, 6 (p. 113, 17); 2, 34 (p. 91, 10).

9. *Hom. Luc.*, 16 (Rauer, p. 109, 2).

10. *Comm. Matt.*, 17, 18.

11. Op. cit., 15, 3 (Klostermann, p. 357, 7).

12. Ibid. (p. 365, 30).

13. *De Princ.*, 4, 2, 1 (Koetschau, p. 308).

14. Prat, *Origène*, p. 179.

15. *Comm. Cant.*, 3 (Baehrens, p. 220).

16. *Homily on the Passion*, ed. Campbell Bonner, pp. 29–30.

17. *Hom. Lev.*, 10, 1.

18. *Comm. Matt.*, 10, 9–10.

19. *Hom. Lev.*, 10, 1. The question of the significance to be attached to the ending of Jewish institutions is also dealt with in *Cels.*, 4, 22 and 7, 8; *Comm. Matt.*, 11, 11 and 14, 19 and 12, 4; *Hom. Gen.*, 6, 3. Origen says in particular that if a new covenant is to be made with God, the existing one, i.e., the Law, must first be abrogated (*Hom. Gen.*, 6, 3; *Hom. Jos.*, 1, 3). Also, it had been prophesied that Judaism would come to an end, and the prophecy had been fulfilled more obviously than most (*De Princ.*, 4, 1 and 3–4 (Koetschau, pp. 296–7)). See also *Hom. Num.*, 23, 1.

20. *Hom. Jos.*, 2, 1.

21. *De Princ.*, 1, preface, 8 (Koetschau, p. 14, 6-13).

22. *Hom. Jos.*, 17, 1 (Baehrens, pp. 401–2).

23. *Comm. Jo.*, 28, 12 (Preuschen, p. 404, 3).

24. *Comm. Matt.*, 12, 10.

25. Op. cit., 16, 3.

26. *Hom. Gen.*, 6, 1.

27. *Comm. Matt.*, 12, 5.

28. *Hom. Lev.*, 1, 1.

29. Op. cit., 14, 4; 15, 2.

30. *Hom. Gen.*, 13, 3.

31. *De Princ.*, 4, 6 (Koetschau, p. 302, 8-10).

32. *Comm. Matt.*, 10, 5.

33. *Comm. Jo.*, 1, 6 (Preuschen, p. 11, 20-25).

34. *Hom. Jos.*, 9, 8.

35. See Van den Eynde, *Normes*, pp. 82 et seq.

36. *Dial.*, 92, 1.

37. *Or. Paneg.*, 16 (P.G., 10, 1093).

38. *Hom. Ez.*, 4, 3.

39. Op. cit., 11, 2.

40. *Hom. Gen.*, 6, 1.

41. Op. cit., 12, 1.
42. Ibid., 7, 6.
43. Ibid., 15, 7; see also *Comm. Matt.*, 16, 11.
44. *Comm. Matt.*, 14, 6.
45. *Comm. Jo.*, 1, 4 (Preuschen, p. 9).
46. Op. cit., 13, 26 (p. 251, 6).
47. *Hom. Gen.*, 2, 3.
48. Op. cit., 2, 4.
49. Ibid., 8, 1 (Baehrens, pp. 78, 25).
50. *Cels.*, 8, 22.
51. *Hom. Num.*, 26, 4.
52. P.G., 18, 740.
53. *Comm. Jo.*, 10, 18 (Preuschen, p. 189).
54. *Hom. Gen.*, 12, 3 (Baehrens, pp. 108, 28).
55. Loc. cit.
56. Op. cit., 7, 2.
57. *Comm. Jo.*, 10, 18 (Preuschen, p. 189).
58. *Comm. Cant.*, 4 (Baehrens, p. 224).
59. Ibid., p. 223.
60. Ibid., pp. 226-7.
61. Ibid., p. 228.
62. *Hom. Jos.*, 7, 1.
63. Op. cit., 7, 2.
64. Ibid., 8, 4.
65. See also *Comm. Jo.*, 1, 7 (Preuschen, p. 12, 12).
66. *De Princ.*, 4, 3, 12–13.
67. *Comm. Cant.*, 3 (Baehrens, pp. 181–2). See also 4, 187b, 192c; *Comm. Jo.*, 2, 6; *Hom. Num.*, 17, 12 (P.G, 11, 798b).
68. *Hom. Gen.*, 9, 7.
69. Op. cit., 10, 5.
70. *Comm. Jo.*, 6, 51 (Preuschen, p. 160).

CHAPTER III

1. *Sel. Pss.* (Lommatzch, 13, p. 82).
2. As Fr. de Lubac very properly observes, it is only recently that these two terms have been used as opposites. It is, however, convenient to use them in that sense. The main thing, after all, is to make the distinction between the two things quite clear—which Fr. de Lubac does not, perhaps, altogether succeed in doing (*Rech. Sc. Relig.*, 1947, pp. 180 et seq.).
3. Harnack, *Der Kirchengeschichtliche Ertrag der exegetischen Arbeiten des Origenes*; Bardy, "Les traditions juives dans l'œuvre d'Origène", *Rev. Bibl.*, 1925, pp. 194 et seq.
4. *De Princ.*, 4, 3, 2. For another allusion to Jewish traditions, see *Comm. Jo.*, 19, 15.
5. *Hom. Gen.*, 2, 2.

6. *Sel. Ez.*, 8 (P.G., 13, 800d).
7. 9, 8.
8. *Hom. Ez.*, 4, 8.
9. 106, 18.
10. *De Abrahamo*, 46.
11. See Cadiou, "Origène et les homélies clémentines", *R.S.R.*, 1930, p. 506.
12. *Clem. Recog.*, 8, 12. On the continuation of this line of speculation in Christian tradition, see "Déluge, baptême, jugement", *Dieu vivant*, 8, pp. 10 et seq.
13. See J. Ruwet, "Les apocryphes dans l'œuvre d'Origène", *Biblica*, 1944, pp. 143 et seq., 311 et seq.
14. Harnack, *Der Ertrag*, ii, pp. 42–3.
15. *Comm. Jo.*, 6, 42; *Hom. Num.*, 28, 2.
16. *Hom. Jos.*, 15, 6.
17. Op. cit., 2, 1.
18. *Sel. Gen.* (P.G., 12, 136a).
19. *Comm. Ser. Matt.*, 117.
20. *Comm. Gen.*, 3; *Comm. Jo.*, 2, 31.
21. *Comm. Jo.*, 2, 31.
22. *Comm. Matt.*, 15, 3.
23. Op. cit., 17, 17.
24. *De Princ.*, 4, 2, 9.
25. *Origène, le théologien et l'exégète*, p. xix.
26. *De Princ.*, 4, 3, 1.
27. Op. cit., 4, 3, 2.
28. Ibid., 4, 3, 3.
29. *Comm. Matt.*, 16, 14.
30. *De Princ.*, 4, 3, 3.
31. Op. cit., 4, 3, 5.
32. Ibid., 5, 3, 5.
33. *Hom. Gen.*, 10, 1.
34. *Hom. Lev.*, 4, 8.
35. Loc. cit.
36. *Hom. Jer.*, 39 (Klostermann, pp. 196–7).
37. *De Princ.*, 4, 1, 7.
38. *Comm. Matt.*, 14, 5.
39. Op. cit., 11, 3.
40. See Ovid, *Fasti*, 3, 125.
41. See Delattre, "Un fragment d'arithmologie dans Clément d'Alexandrie", *Etudes sur la littérature pythagoricienne*, pp. 231 et seq.
42. *Comm. Matt.*, 10, 12.
43. *Hom. Ez.*, 1, 5.
44. Op. cit., 13, 4.
45. *Hom. Jos.*, 15, 3.
46. *Hom. Gen.*, 1, 17.
47. *Leg. All.*, 2, 4, 11.
48. *De Congressu*, 4.

49. Op. cit., 7.
50. *Dial.*, 134, 2.
51. *Adv. Haer.* (P.G., 7, 1045b).
52. *Hom. Gen.*, 6, 1; see also 14, 3.
53. *De Abrahamo*, 99.
54. *Hom. Num.*, 11, 2. See also *Hom. Gen.*, 14, 3.
55. *Hom. Ez.*, 1, 4.
56. Op. cit., 2, 16.
57. *Comm. Matt.*, 11, 1.
58. *De Princ.*, 4, 2, 4.
59. *Hom. Gen.*, 2, 6.
60. Op. cit., 2, 5.
61. Op. cit., 2, 6.
62. *Hom. Lev.*, 1; cf. 5, 5.
63. *Hom. Num.*, 9, 7.
64. P.G., 12, 1319.
65. *Comm. Jo.*, 10, 11.
66. Op. cit., 10, 9.
67. Op. cit., 13, 60.
68. *Comm. Jo.*, 13, 59.
69. This charge was brought against Origen in his own lifetime. He several times defends himself against it (*Hom. Ez.*, 2, 3).
70. *De Princ.*, 4, 3, 8.
71. Op. cit., 4, 3, 9.
72. Op. cit., 4, 3, 10.
73. Loc. cit.
74. Op. cit., 4, 3, 11.
75. *Hom. Luc.*, 34.
76. *Adv. Haer.*, 3, 17, 3.
77. *Hom. Jos.*, 6, 4.
78. *Comm. Matt.*, 16, 9.
79. Origen also says: "Most of the explanations Jesus gave of the parables the evangelists never wrote down" (*Comm. Matt.*, 14, 12). This may be an oral tradition.
80. *Comm. Matt.*, 15, 32.
81. Op. cit., 15, 33.
82. Ibid., 15, 35.
83. Loc. cit.
84. When he interprets the parable of the Good Samaritan, Origen first gives an explanation of the presbyteral type and then modifies it in accordance with his own views: he turns the innkeeper into an angel (*Hom. Luc.*, 32).
85. *Comm. Matt.*, 15, 37.

Part III

1. *De Princ.*, preface, 4.
2. Ibid., 7.
3. Ibid., 10.
4. p. 39.
5. *Comm. Matt.*, 10, 11 (P.G., 13, 860b); *Comm. Jo.*, 2, 23; 20, 17; 38, 21.
6. De Faye, *Origène*, iii; Denis, *La Philosophie d'Origène*; Hal Koch, *Pronoia und Paideusis*; Cadiou, *Introduction au système d'Origène*; H. C. Puech, *La théologie trinitaire d'Origène* (unpublished lectures); David Amand, *Fatalisme et liberté dans l'antiquité grecque*, pp. 275–325. Oscar Cullmann has a book in preparation on Origen's theology.

CHAPTER I

1. *De Princ.*, 2, 9, 3.
2. Op. cit., 1, 1, 2, 2.
3. Ibid., 2, 9, 4.
4. Ibid., 2, 9, 5.
5. Loc. cit.
6. Loc. cit.
7. See also *De Princ.*, 1, 8, 2.
8. Op. cit., 2, 9, 6.
9. Justinian, *Ep. ad Mennam* (Mansi, 9, 513b, c).
10. *De Hom. Op.*, 28; *De Princ.*, 1, 8, 4; see also *De Anim. et Res.* (P.G., 46, 112c).
11. *De Princ.*, 2, 9, 6.
12. Op. cit., 3, 1, 2–5.
13. Ibid., 2, 9, 6.
14. Ibid., 2, 9, 3.
15. Origen calls such spirits souls or ψυχάς because they have "cooled" (ψυχρούς) (*De Princ.*, 2, 8, 3).
16. *De Princ.*, 1, 3, 8.
17. Op. cit., 2, 9, 2. Cf. *Comm. Matt.*, 12, 41; *De Princ.*, 2, 2, 1.
18. *De Princ.*, 1, 8, 3.
19. *Hom. Gen.*, 15, 5; *Cels.*, 5, 29.
20. *De Princ.*, 1, 8, 1.
21. Op. cit., 1, 6, 2; cf. 1, 8, 4.
22. Ibid., 1, 6, 2.
23. *Comm. Matt.*, 15, 24.
24. *Hom. Lev.*, 13, 4.
25. *De Princ.*, 4, 3, 8.
26. Op. cit., 4, 3, 9.
27. Loc. cit. Cf. *Hom. Jer.*, 21, 2; *Hom. Ez.*, 2, 14; 12, 2; *Hom. Gen.*, 15, 5; *Hom. Jos.*, 23, 4.
28. *De Princ.*, 1, 6, 3; cf. 4, 3, 10.

29. *Cels.*, 3, 42.
30. Op. cit., 4, 14–15.
31. Ibid., 4, 65.
32. *De Princ.*, 2, 1, 4.
33. See Koch, p. 37.
34. *De Princ.*, 1, 4, 1.
35. Op. cit., 1, 7, 1.
36. Loc. cit.
37. Op. cit., 1, 7, 4.
38. Ibid., 2, 9, 1.
39. Ibid., 2, 1, 4.
40. Ibid., 2, 2, 2.
41. Loc. cit.

CHAPTER II

1. *De Princ.*, 2, 1, 2.
2. Op. cit., 2, 9, 6.
3. *Hom. Num.*, 13, 7.
4. *De Princ.*, 1, 5, 3.
5. Op. cit., 1, 8, 1.
6. *Theolog. Wörterbuch*, art. "ἄγγελος", p. 84.
7. Frey, "L'angélologie juive au temps de Jésus-Christ", *Rev. Sc. Phil. Théol.*, 1911, p. 75.
8. 20, 1–4.
9. Enoch, 60, 12.
10. Jub., 4, 23.
11. See M. Dibelius, *Die Geisterwelt im Glauben der Paulus*, 1909.
12. Cumont, "Les anges du paganisme", *Rev. Hist. Rel.*, 1915, p. 157.
13. See Andres, *Die Engellehre der griechischen Apologeten des III Jahr.*, 1914.
14. 43, 2.
15. Enoch, 60, 21.
16. 14, 18.
17. Op. cit., 16, 5.
18. *Apol.*, 10.
19. *Ep.*, 15, 7.
20. *Hom. Jer.*, 10, 6.
21. *Hom. Jos.*, 22, 3.
22. *Cels.*, 8, 31 (Koetschau, pp. 246–7).
23. Op. cit., 5, 4 and 12.
24. See also *Hom. Num.*, 9, 11; *Hom. Ez.*, 4, 2.
25. In Origen's view, the allocation of functions depends, of course, on the merit acquired by the angels in their previous lives (*De Princ.*, 1, 8, 1; *Hom. Jos.*, 23, 3).
26. Enoch, 89. Oscar Cullmann thinks that the doctrine also finds expression in St. Paul's ἄρχοντες and ἐξουσίαι (*Christus und die Zeit*, pp. 169–86).
27. *De Princ.*, 1, 5, 2; see also 4, 3, 11.

28. *Hom. Luc.*, 13.

29. See also *Hom. Jer.*, 5, 2; *Comm. Jo.*, 13, 50 (Koetschau, p. 278, 29–32); *Comm. Cant.*, 3 (Baehrens, p. 258, 32); *Hom. Ez.*, 13, 1 (Baehrens, pp. 440–2); *Comm. Matt.*, 11, 16 (Klostermann, p. 60, 23); 17, 23 (p. 647, 26).

30. On all this see Erik Peterson, *Der Monotheismus als politisches Problem*, Leipzig, 1935, pp. 50–81.

31. *Contra Gal.*, 115d.

32. *Cels.*, 5, 25.

33. *Vie de Julien*, pp. 308–9.

34. *Cels.*, 5, 30.

35. Loc. cit.

36. *Hom. Num.*, 11, 4.

37. *Hom. Luc.*, 13.

38. *De Princ.*, 3, 3, 2.

39. *Cels.*, 8, 75.

40. *Monotheismus als politisches Problem*, p. 71.

41. *Hom. Luc.*, 13; see *Comm. Jo.*, 12, 50.

42. *Comm. Jo.*, 13, 59 (Koetschau, pp. 290–1).

43. *De Princ.*, 3, 3, 2.

44. *Hom. Gen.*, 9, 3.

45. Loc. cit.

46. *Hom. Luc.*, 35 (Rauer, pp. 209–11).

47. *Cels.*, 5, 10.

48. *Pronoia und Paideusis*, p. 50.

49. *Cels.*, 5, 3, 1.

50. *Hom. Num.*, 11, 4.

51. *Cels.*, 5, 31.

52. *Christus und die Zeit*, pp. 177 et seq.

53. "Le problème du mal dans le christianisme antique", *Dieu vivant*, 6, p. 28.

54. *De Princ.*, 3, 2, 4.

55. Origen himself brings the two streams of tradition to his readers' notice in *Cels.*, 8, 34 and often refers to the doctrine elsewhere.

56. Soury, *La démonologie de Plutarque*, 1942, pp. 131 et seq.

57. *De Princ.*, 2, 10, 7.

58. *Comm. Matt.*, 13, 5 (Klostermann, p. 191, 1–3).

59. *Hom. Num.*, 11, 4.

60. *Cels.*, 8, 34. See J. Barbel, *Christos Angelos*, 1941, p. 103.

61. *Hom. Ez.*, 1, 7.

62. *Comm. Cant.*, 2 (Baehrens, p. 158).

63. *Hom. Luc.*, 12.

64. Op. cit., 35.

65. *De Princ.*, 3, 2, 4.

66. See Dom E. Bettencourt, *Doctrina Ascetica Origenis, Seu Quid Docuerit de Ratione Animae Humanae cum Daemonibus*, 1946, pp. 12 et seq.

67. *Hom. Luc.*, 35.

68. *Hom. Ez.*, 1, 7.

69. Loc. cit.

70. *Comm. Matt.*, 12, 26.

71. *Hom. Jos.*, 9, 4 (P.G., 12, 874).

72. P. Lundberg, *La typologie baptismale dans l'ancienne Eglise*, 1942, pp. 44–5, mentions several ancient liturgical texts in which the angel of Baptism appears.

73. *De Or.*, 31, 4 (P.G., 11, 553). Origen does not forget that in consequence, when he addresses the Church, he is speaking "to men and at the same time to angels" (*Hom. Luc.*, 23 (Rauer, p. 156)).

74. *Comm. Matt.*, 13, 26.

75. *De Princ.*, 3, 2, 4.

76. *Hom. Jos.*, 15, 5.

77. Athanasius's Life of St. Antony contains a whole treatise on the discernment of spirits (chs. 21–44).

78. *De Or.*, 11, 5.

79. *De Princ.*, 2, 3, 2.

80. *Hom. Num.*, 13, 7.

81. *Cels.*, 7, 70.

82. Op. cit., 8, 33.

83. *Hom. Luc.*, 35.

84. *Hom. Num.*, 11, 4.

85. *Hom. Luc.*, 35 (Rauer, p. 208).

86. *Hom. Num.*, 11, 4.

87. Loc. cit.

88. Loc. cit.

89. *Hom. Luc.*, 13 (Rauer, p. 91).

90. Loc. cit. (Rauer, p. 92). See also 35 (p. 208).

91. *Hom. Num.*, 11, 4.

92. *Hom. Num.*, 11, 5.

93. *De Princ.*, 2, 2, 5.

CHAPTER III

1. Origen's teaching about our Lady might also be discussed at this point. He is in agreement with Tradition on the question but does not work out the traditional teaching in detail, as he does in the case of John the Baptist. See C. Vagaggini, *Maria nelle opere di Origene*, Rome, 1942.

2. *De Princ.*, 2, 6, 1.

3. *Comm. Jo.*, 1, 13.

4. Op. cit., 2, 32.

5. Ibid., 2, 37 (Preuschen, p. 96, 11).

6. *Hom. Luc.*, 6.

7. *Comm. Jo.*, 2, 37.

8. *Hom. Luc.*, 4, 29.

9. *Comm. Jo.*, 2, 37.

10. Op. cit., 2, 29.

11. *De Princ.*, 4, 3, 12.

12. *Hom. Ez.*, 1, 1.
13. *Comm. Matt.*, 15, 35.
14. *Comm. Jo.*, 2, 31.
15. Op. cit., 2, 30.
16. Ibid., 2, 31.
17. Loc. cit.
18. *Comm. Jo.*, 6, 7; *Comm. Matt.*, 10, 20; 12, 9; 13, 1; *Hom. Luc.*, 4.
19. *Comm. Jo.*, 6, 7.
20. *Comm. Matt.*, 13, 1.
21. Op. cit., 13, 2.
22. See G. Verbeke, *L'évolution de la doctrine du Pneuma du Stoicisme à saint Augustin,* Paris, 1945, pp. 450–69.
23. *Comm. Matt.*, 13, 2; see *Comm. Luc.*, 4, 29.

CHAPTER IV

1. *Pronoia und Paideusis*, p. 63.
2. *Origène*, p. 230.
3. *Comm. Matt.*, 12, 20.
4. *Die Theologie der Logosmystik des Origenes*, p. 186.
5. *Comm. Jo.*, 2, 2.
6. Op. cit., 32, 28.
7. Ibid., 10, 35.
8. Ibid., 13, 25. See also *Cels.*, 8, 13; 5, 58.
9. The most thorough-going enquiry yet made into the question is the one undertaken by H. C. Puech in a series of lectures at the Ecole des Hautes Etudes, 1943–7.
10. *Comm. Matt.*, 15, 10.
11. *Comm. Jo.*, 1, 34; see 6, 38; *Hom. Jer.*, 14, 10.
12. *De Princ.*, 3, 5, 3.
13. Op. cit., 1, 2, 10.
14. *Epitome*, 14, 3.
15. *Comm. Jo.*, 1, 20.
16. *Cels.*, 7, 38.
17. Op. cit., 3, 34.
18. *Epitome*, 10, 4.
19. *Comm. Jo.*, 2, 2.
20. Op. cit., 14, 3.
21. *Comm. Jo.*, 1, 20.
22. Op. cit., 1, 23.
23. *Cels.*, 2, 64.
24. *Comm. Jo.*, 2, 8.
25. Op. cit., 1, 9; cf. *Hom. Jer.*, 8, 2.
26. *Comm. Jo.*, 1, 22–3.
27. Op. cit., 1, 25.
28. Cf. ibid., 6, 19.
29. Ibid., 1, 30.

30. Ibid., 1, 31.
31. Ibid., 1, 32.
32. Ibid., 1, 35.
33. *Hom. Gen.*, 1, 8.
34. *Cels.*, 2, 63; see also 4, 16, 18.
35. Op. cit., 6, 77.
36. *Hom. Luc.*, 3. See *Cels.*, 6, 77; *Comm. Matt.*, 12, 36.
37. *De Or.*, 27.
38. *Comm. Ser. Matt.*, 100. See also *Hom. Ex.*, 7, 6; *Cels.*, 4, 18.
39. *Comm. Jo.*, 1, 34.
40. *De Princ.*, 2, 6, 2. See *Comm. Jo.*, 1, 12.
41. *Comm. Jo.*, 1, 32; 20, 12, 19.
42. *De Princ.*, 2, 6, 6.
43. Ibid.
44. *Comm. Matt.*, 10, 6.
45. Op. cit., 12, 4.
46. *Hom. Lev.*, 4, 6.
47. *Comm. Jo.*, 1, 8.
48. *De Princ.*, 2, 6, 6.
49. Op. cit., 4, 3, 13.
50. *Comm. Matt.*, 10, 1.
51. Loc. cit.
52. Op. cit., 11, 5.
53. Op. cit., 17, 13.
54. *Hom. Luc.*, 15 (Rauer, p. 103).
55. *Origène*, iii, p. 210.
56. *Pronoia und Paideusis*, p. 19.
57. *Hom. Luc.*, 30–1; *Cels.*, 6, 45.
58. *Cels.*, 1, 60; see 8, 39.
59. *Comm. Matt.*, 12, 40.
60. *Hom. Jos.*, 8, 3.
61. *Hom. Lev.*, 9, 5. See *Hom. Num.*, 16, 3; 17, 6; 18, 4; *Comm. Matt.*, 12, 18; *Comm. Jo.*, 1, 28; 6, 55; *Comm. Cant.*, 3 (Baehrens, p. 222).
62. *Comm. Matt.*, 13, 9.
63. Op. cit., 16, 8; see *Comm. Jo.*, 6, 53.
64. *Comm. Matt.*, 12, 25.
65. *Ex. Mart.*, 41.
66. *Comm. Jo.*, 6, 54.
67. *Cels.*, 8, 44.
68. *Comm. Jo.*, 6, 56–7. Logically, this would be the place to study Origen's ecclesiology, after his Christology and before his eschatology. But we have already examined this side of his teaching in connection with his idea of the Christian community (Book I, Ch. II). There is an excellent chapter on the subject in Gustave Bardy's book, *La théologie de l'Eglise de saint Irénée au Concile de Nicée*, pp. 128–65. What M. Bardy stresses is that as Origen sees it, the mystery lies essentially in the fact that the Church is Christ's body and that it lives the mysteries of his life over again. See especially *Hom. Lev.*, 7, 2 (Baehrens, pp. 376–8).

CHAPTER V

1. *Hom. Ez.*, 12. See *De Princ.*, 2, 10, 6.
2. *Comm. Matt.*, 15, 11.
3. *Hom. Jer.*, 6, 2.
4. Loc. cit.
5. *Hom. Jer.*, 19, 8.
6. Op. cit., 12, 5.
7. Op. cit., 18, 6.
8. Loc. cit.
9. See *Hom. Ez.*, 1, 2; *Hom. Num.*, 16, 3.
10. *Hom. Jer.*, 18, 15; see *De Princ.*, 3, 1, 2.
11. *Hom. Jer.*, 19, 2.
12. Op. cit., 19, 5. See also *Hom. Jer.*, 4, 1-4; *Comm. Matt.*, 17, 31.
13. *De Princ.*, 3, 1, 10.
14. Op. cit., 3, 1, 12; see 3, 1, 17.
15. Ibid., 3, 1, 13; see *De Or.*, 28, 13.
16. See *De Princ.*, 3, 1, 17.
17. Op. cit., 3, 1, 13.
18. *De Or.*, 27; *Comm. Matt.*, 11, 3; 14, 3; 12, 36.
19. *De Princ.*, 1, 8, 3 and 3, 5, 6.
20. *Comm. Matt.*, 13, 12; *De Princ.*, 3, 1, 23.
21. *Comm. Jo.*, 1, 16 (Preuschen, p. 20).
22. *De Princ.*, 1, 2, 11.
23. Op. cit., 3, 6, 3.
24. Ibid., 2, 10, 8.
25. Ibid., 3, 5, 6; Koetschau, p. 277.
26. P.G., 86, 900a.
27. "L'apocatastase chez saint Grégoire de Nysse", R.S.R., 1940, pp. 328 et seq.

PART IV

1. The study of Origen's theology of the spiritual life really began with Walter Völker's book, *Das Volkommenheitsideal des Origenes*, Tübingen, 1931, which regards him as a great mystic and describes the stages of the soul's journey to God as it is mapped out in his works. F. Bornemann had previously studied his influence on the beginnings of monasticism in his *In Inuestiganda Monachatus Origene Quibus de Causis Ratio Habenda Sit Origenis*, Göttingen, 1885. Fr. Jules Lebreton had also written on "Les degrés de la connaissance religieuse" in R.S.R., 1922, p. 265. Völker's book was reviewed by H. C. Puech in an important article, "Un livre récent sur la mystique d'Origène", in the *Rev. Hist. Phil. Rel.*, 1933, pp. 508 et seq. Puech questioned what Völker had said about ecstasy in Origen but otherwise was basically in agreement with him. The chief work written in consequence of Völker's book was Fr. Aloysius Lieske's *Die Logosmystik bei*

Origenes, which accused Völker of failing to see that Origen's mystical theology was rooted in dogma and the Church. Those were the main attempts to examine the question. In the way of general studies, M. Bardy's article, "La spiritualité d'Origène", *Vie Spir.*, 1932, [80] – [106], and Nicole Duval's "La vie spirituelle d'après Origène", *Cahiers de Neuilly*, 8, pp. 39 et seq., deserve special mention. Fr. Viller, also, studies Origen's theology of the spiritual life in his book, *La spiritualité des premiers siècles chrétiens*, Paris, 1930, pp. 45 et seq. It has been translated into German and issued with additional matter and a bibliography (Viller-Rahner: *Aszese und Mystik in der Väterzeit*, Freiburg im Breisgrau, 1939, pp. 72 et seq.). A certain number of important monographs on particular points should also be noted—K. Rahner, "La doctrine des sens spirituels chez Origène", *Rev. Asc. Myst.*, 1932, pp. 113 et seq.; Karl Rahner, "Coeur de Jésus chez Origène", *Rev. Asc. Myst.*, 1934, pp. 171 et seq.; Hugo Rahner, "Taufe und geistliches Leben bei Origenes", *Z.A.M.*, 1932, pp. 105, et seq.; Hugo Rahner, "Die Gottesgeburt", ibid., 1935, pp. 351 et seq.; H. Lewy, *Sobria Ebrietas*, Giessen, 1929, p. 119; J. Ziegler, *Dulcedo Dei*, Münster, 1937, pp. 185 et seq.; I. Hausherr, "L'origine de la doctrine occidentale des huit péchés capitaux", *Or. Christ. An.*, xxx, 3, p. 164; "Les grands courants de la spiritualité orientale", *Or. Christ. Per.*, 1935; pp. 114 et seq.; "Penthos: La doctrine de la componction dans l'Orient chrétien", *Or. Christ. An.*, 132, pp. 28 et seq.; Seston, "Remarques sur l'influence d'Origène sur les origines du monachisme", *Rev. Hist. Rel.*, Sept., 1933, pp. 197 et seq.; Dom E. Bettencourt, *Doctrina Ascetica Origenis*, Rome, 1947.

2. See my *Platonisme et théologie mystique. Essai sur la doctrine spirituelle de saint Grégoire de Nysse*, Paris, 1943.

3. H. Urs von Balthasar, *Kosmische Liturgie*, Freiburg im Breisgau, 1941.

4. D. Marsili, *Giovanni Cassiano e Evagrio Pontico*, Rome, 1936.

5. "Divinisation du chrétien", *Vie Spir.*, 1939, May, pp. 97 et seq.

6. Willms, Εἰκών, Münster, 1935.

7. *Hom. Gen.*, 1, 13. See also *Hom. Gen.*, 13, 3; *Hom. Lev.*, 4, 3; 4, 7.

8. *Hom. Gen.*, 1, 15.

9. *Comm. Cant.*, 2, 8 (P.G., 12, 123b).

10. *In Cant.* (P.G., 44, 806).

11. *Hom. Hex.*, 6, 6, 39.

12. *Epistola ad Fratres de Monte Dei*, 180.

13. Plotinus, *Enn.*, 1, 6, 5.

14. *Hom. Num.*, 27, 1.

15. *Phaed.*, 69c.

16. *Hom. Num.*, 27, 3.

17. Ibid.

18. *Hom. Ex.*, 5, 5.

19. *Hom. Num.*, 27, 5.

20. Loc. cit.

21. Op. cit., 27, 6. See also *Comm. Jo.*, 1, 91; 6, 103; 28, 37; *Hom. Num.*, 22, 1.

22. *Hom. Num.*, 27, 9.

23. Op. cit., 27, 11.

24. Loc. cit.
25. Loc. cit.
26. Op. cit., 27, 12.
27. *Comm. Matt.*, 12, 5.
28. *De Princ.*, 2, 11, 15.
29. *Hom. Num.*, 27, 12.
30. *Volkommenheitsideal*, pp. 68 et seq.
31. *Hom. Num.*, 27, 12.
32. *Comm. Jo.*, 1, 30.
33. pp. 529–33.
34. *Quis Rerum Divinarum Heres?*, 249–56.
35. R.A.M., 1932, p. 135.
36. Op. cit., 1930, p. 255.
37. *Or. Christ. Per.*, 1936, p. 129.
38. *Hom. Num.*, 17, 5.
39. *Comm. Cant.*, 78.
40. "Israël" is often interpreted by the fathers as meaning "one who sees God". See, e.g., *De Princ.*, 4, 12 (Tr.).
41. See K. Rahner, R.A.M., 1932, pp. 125 et seq.
42. Prologue (Baehrens, p. 63).
43. *Comm. Cant.*, 67.
44. Op. cit., 62.
45. Ibid., 91.
46. Ibid., 92.
47. "Les débuts d'une doctrine des cinq sens spirituels chez Origène", R.A.M., 1932, pp. 113 et seq.
48. *Théologie de la mystique*, p. 231.
49. *Cels.*, 1, 48.
50. *Comm. Cant.*, 1 (Baehrens, pp. 103 et seq.).
51. See also *De Princ.*, 1, 1, 7 and 9; *Cels.*, 1, 48; 7, 34; *Hom. Lev.*, 31, 7; *Hom. Ez.*, 11, 1; *Comm. Cant.*, 2, Baehrens, p. 167).
52. See *Platonisme et théologie mystique*, pp. 235 et seq.
53. 10, 27.
54. Now that we have come to the end of our study of Origen's spiritual teaching, we see that it is related to his theory that all *logikoi* share in the life of the Logos (see above, ch. 4, s. 1, where the idea is expounded in full). Spiritual progress is the soul's recovery of her likeness to the Word who dwells within her and enables her to become one with him by seeing and loving him. This is very well brought out by Fr. Lieske in his book, *Die Theologie der Logosmystik bei Origenes*, pp. 120 et seq. But it is also true that Origen's mystical teaching is not a merely speculative thing; it is a consequence of deep spiritual experience. Völker was right in stressing that side of the question. Origen's experience has an independent value of its own and gives him considerable importance in the spiritual sphere properly so-called.

APPENDIX

This translation is made from the 1948 French edition. I have, however, taken advantage of the reviews the book has received to make corrections on some points of detail; and in this connection I am particularly indebted to Mr. Henry Chadwick's review in the *Journal of Theological Studies* (July–October 1949, pp. 219–21). I have revised the passages which deal with Origen's statements touching on private Penance. There have since appeared a remarkable series of articles by Fr. Karl Rahner, which establish the sacramental nature of public Penance as far as Origen is concerned, together with the absence of private Penance (R.S.R., 1950, pp. 47–97, 252–86, 422–56).

Mr. Hanson's book *Origen's Doctrine of Tradition* (S.P.C.K., 1954) discusses the themes of my own book in several places. However, I have not found myself convinced by his arguments on the questions of the unity of the two Origens (p. 6) or Origen's attitude with regard to the rule of faith (p. 111), or concerning the canon of the Scriptures (p. 144), or on Origen's position with regard to secular philosophy (p. 153). His book is, nevertheless, full of interest and, in particular, shows clearly the difference of attitude between Origen and Clement of Alexandria on the subject of the traditions deriving from the primitive Church. He is, however, wrong when he identifies these traditions, whose sole claim to authority lies in their primitive status, with tradition in the sense of a living transmission of the faith by way of the hierarchy.

Controversy continues as to whether Origen is a biblical theologian or a neo-Platonic philosopher. Fr. De Lubac has emphasised the biblical foundation of his thought in his *Histoire et Esprit* (Aubier, 1950), while H. Jonas, on the contrary (in his "Die Origenistiche Speculation und die Mystik", *Theologische Zeitschrift*, 1949, p. 24 et seq.) makes him out to be a gnostic thinker who should be placed somewhere between Valentine and Plotinus. This merely serves to confirm me in my view that he is both these things—which is also the position taken up by Vagaggini ("La Natura della Sintesi Origeniana", *La Scuola Cattolica*, May–June, 1954, pp. 169–201).

INDEX

AEONS, 286
Albinus, 95–8, 219, 256–7
Alexandria, school of, 9–10
Allegorizing, 188–91
Altar, 34, 46–7
Amand, Dom D., 85
Ammonius Saccas, 76–7
Angels, 32–4, 214–16, 217, 220 et
    seq., 247 et seq., 270 et seq.
  of the nations, 224–37
  guardian, 238–45
Antiochus of Ascalon, 86
Apatheia, 299
Apocatastasis, 287–9
Apocrypha, Jewish, 177, 248
Aristotelianism, 80
Ark, Noe's, 176, 188
Arnou, R., 257

BALTHASAR, Hans Urs von, xiv, 50,
    59, 72
Baptism, 52 et seq.
  of fire, 59
Bardy, G., xii, xvi, 9 et seq.
Bettencourt, Dom E., xvii
Bodies, heavenly, 98, 113, 210–18,
    235
Bréhier, E., 84–6

CADIOU, R., xiv, xvi, 23, 76 et seq.,
    205, 328 n.11
Casel, Dom O., 37
Caster, M., 80
Catechesis, 10–12, 52–4
Celsus, 98 et seq.
Chairemon, 83
Charismata, 41
Christ, soul of, 262
Church, 8, 40, 274
Cicero, 86, 112
Clement of Alexandria, 73, 185
Clergy, 44
Condescension, divine, 280

Consolation, 300
Contemplation, creative, 257
Cornutus, 79–80
Cross, the, 271
Cullmann, O., 237, 331 n.26
Cumont, F., 21
Cynicism, 81

DARKNESS in spiritual life, 297
Deceit, 94, 281
Degrees, of spiritual life, 48, 189,
    304 et seq.
  of divinity in Trinity, 252
Demons, 56, 88, 113–14, 242, 270
Descent of patriarchs, 196, 247
Desert, 303
Discernment of spirits, 241–2

EAST, 28–30, 228, 235
Easter, 37
Edsman, C. E., 61
Education of men, divine, 277 et
    seq.
Efficacy of Christianity, 103, 127,
    266, 273
Elias, 249–50
Enoch, 176–7, 225
Epectasis, 304
Epictetus, 103
Eros, 306
Eschatology, 59–61, 170
Eternity of world, 255 et seq.
Eucharist, 61 et seq., 264
Eusebius of Caesarea, 3 et seq.
Evagrius, 293
Evil, 277 et seq.
Exodus, 55, 296 et seq.
Eynde, D. van den, 46

FAITH, 298
Fall, always possible for spirits, 287
Faye, E. de, xvi, 269
Festugière, A. J., 295

Figures, 146 et seq.
Foreshadowing of future, 149, 169 et seq., 263
Freewill, 203-19, 237, 285-8

GALTIER, 320 n.52
Gnosis, 45 et seq., 300
Gnosticism, 142, 191 et seq., 206, 210, 278
Gregory of Nyssa, xii, 289, 293, 304
Guéraud, xiv

HARDENING OF HEART, 283
Harnack, A. von, 4
Heracleon, 191 et seq.
History, theology of, 113-19, 146 et seq., 226, 237
House of Jesus, 267

IDOLATRY, 34, 113, 226
Illusions, 300
Image of God, 294-6
Israel, 177, 244, 259

JERICHO, 167-9, 197
Jewish exegesis, 141, 171
John the Baptist, 246-50
Jordan, River, 57-8
Josue, 48, 147
Jubilee, 285-7
Julia Mamea, 20-2

KISS in Christian ritual, 6, 62-3
Knowledge of God, human, 97, 104-9
Koch, H., xvi, 68, 74, 269

LANGUAGES, origin of, 228
Law, 144 et seq.
Learning, secular, 14-18, 100 et seq.
Lieske, A., xvii, 252, 257, 338 n.54
Logos, 5, 65-7, 207, 251 et seq.
Lot-Borodine, 67
Love for men, God's, 280-5
Lubac, H. de, 315 n.14, 327 n.2

MARROU, H. I., 15
Martyrdom, 6-7, 41, 273
Matter, 98, 215 et seq.
Maximus of Tyre, 92-4, 280-2
Melito, 144
Merit, 210, 244, 265

Metempsychosis, 249-50, 288
Middle Platonism, 85 et seq.
Moses, 147
Mystagogy, 28 et seq.
Mysteries, pagan, 22
Christian, 48-9
of Christ's life, 267-9

NAMES of Christ, 258-9
Natures, 206
Neo-Platonism, 76 et seq.
Nock, 54
Noe, 176
Numbers, symbolism of, 184
Numenius, 79, 90-2

ORIENT, v. East

PARABLES, 196-9
Penance, 68 et seq.
Pentecost, 37, 185
Person, human, 111
Peterson, E., 29, 332 n.20
Philo, 178 et seq., 294
Philosophy, 12, 17, 73 et seq.
Philostrates, 83
Plato, 75, 106, 306
Plotinus, 36, 77, 337 n.13
Plutarch, 87-9
Pneuma, 250
Porphyry, 20, 76
Prayer, 28 et seq.
Preaching, 24-5
Pre-existence, 206, 209 et seq., 248
Priesthood, 45 et seq.
Princes of this world, 231
Progress, spiritual, 212-13, 303
Providence, 112, 205 et seq.
Puech, H. C., ix, xvii, 89, 302, 312, 334 n.9, 336 n.1.
Punishment, 277 et seq.
Pythagoreanism, 83

RACES, spiritual, 194-6, 216, 244
Rahner, H., 59
Rahner, K., 307
Revelation, progressive, 117 et seq.
Rufinus, xi-xii
Ruwet, J., 328 n.13

SACRAMENTS, 52 et seq., 264
Scepticism, 81
Scherer, J., 23

Scripture, 5, 18-19, 24-5
    meanings of, 156 et seq., 186, 264
Senses, spiritual, 307
Shorthand, 22
Sin, 283 et seq.
Song of Songs, 166, 304 et seq.
Soul of world, 97
Stoicism, 82
Stolz, Dom A., 307

T (letter), 176
Temple, 35, 146, 150
Temptations, 298-302

Transfiguration, 260
Trinity, 124-7, 250 et seq.
Typology, 139-73

UNIVERSAL CLAIMS of Christianity,
    227

VARIETY in world, 209-11, 214
Völker, W., xvi-xvii, 336 n.1

WITT, R. E., 79
Worship, Christian, 34 et seq.